ARTUR SCHNABEL

Artur Schnabel

ARTUR SCHNABEL

A Biography

By

CESAR SAERCHINGER

WITH A TRIBUTE BY CLIFFORD CURZON

17 pages of half-tone illustrations

GREENWOOD PRESS, PUBLISHERS
WESTPORT, CONNECTICUT

Library of Congress Cataloging in Publication Data

Saerchinger, César, 1889–
    Artur Schnabel, a biography.

    Reprint of the ed. published by Dodd, Mead,
New York.
    Discography: p.
    1. Schnabel, Artur, 1882–1951.
ML417.S36S3   1973   786.1'092'4 [B]   73–7101
ISBN 0–8371–6910–0

Reprinted in 1973 by Greenwood Press,
a division of Williamhouse-Regency Inc.

Library of Congress Catalogue Card Number 73-7101

ISBN 0-8371-6910-0

Printed in the United States of America

To Therese Behr Schnabel
IN FRIENDSHIP AND ADMIRATION

Artur Schnabel

A TRIBUTE BY CLIFFORD CURZON

(A B.B.C. broadcast of December 6th, 1951)

'YOU will never be a pianist. You are a musician.' These were the words of the great piano teacher Leschetizky, to the small boy, Artur Schnabel. However, great teachers are rarely great prophets where their own pupils are concerned, and Schnabel became, as we know, not only a great musician but also one of the world's greatest pianists.

In later years, Schnabel took special delight in repeating Leschetizky's prophecy as a paradox, because he himself could never make any distinction between pianist and musician, even for his pupils. And, in his own case, the musician and the pianist were completely fused—though the pianist remained always the servant of the musician.

However we may interpret early prophecies, Leschetizky had recognized that here was an infant prodigy who was also a true musician. Schnabel, in his own later teaching, did occasionally take very young pupils; though his teaching touched on so many fields of culture that only the student who had already reached a fair degree of maturity could hope to understand all that he had to give.

Schnabel's superb control at the piano may sometimes have made him appear remote and uncompromising. But his constant striving towards what he termed 'a greater and greater isolation with the music' could not help but produce a certain distance between him and his hearers. He himself once compared the concert pianist to a chef. 'The chef,' he said, 'is expected to cook as well as he can, but he need not necessarily love the eaters!' He thought the public artist's task was threefold: to perform, to re-create and to criticize simultaneously, and his own playing was a perfect example of this threefold achievement.

Another characteristic of Schnabel's public appearances was the relatively small number of composers included in his repertoire. But within these self-imposed limits, his repertoire was comprehensive;

it covered practically all the works of the composers he did play.
His choice of composers, however, implied no lack of appreciation
of the others. It was simply that he considered the music of Mozart,
Beethoven and Schubert—to him the three greatest composers—his
greatest challenge. In his book, characteristically called *Music and
the Line of Most Resistance*, he has said: 'I felt it an honour to accept
the limitation which kept me in the upper region where, no matter
what height one has attained, the summits continually seem to rise
and rise.' Schnabel recognized his own power to give most where
his feelings were deepest and it was part of his genius that he lost no
time or energy on music that did not draw forth his best qualities as
interpreter. But he was not unconscious of the reaction of many
concertgoers to his programmes. He used to say, 'The difference
between my programmes and those of other pianists is that mine are
boring not only in the first half but also in the second!'

Schnabel's peculiar excellence as a teacher was due to many
qualities, first of all to his superbly analytical mind. He maintained
that the rôle of a teacher is to open doors, and not to push the pupil
through. I have known him even to advise a young student not to
come for lessons for a time, in order that he should learn 'to make
his own mistakes and not his teacher's'. For Schnabel considered
spiritual independence to be 'the core of human art production, and
art unthinkable without it'.

He was opposed to the idea of any particular method in teaching;
and, in any case, in regard to methods of technique, he never accepted
pupils who had not already learned considerably more than the mere
elements of piano playing. He could be as witty on the subject of
methods as on most other subjects. A young music-teacher once
said to him: 'Mr. Schnabel, to which of the two schools of piano
playing do you adhere, the one in which you play in time, or the
one in which you play as you feel?' And his immediate reply was
'Why not feel in time?' He always said he had learned to play the
piano three times: firstly from his early teachers, secondly from his
pupils, and lastly from his gramophone records. In fact, one thing
that made lessons with him so stimulating was his conviction that
teaching music was the best means of learning it.

Once a pupil was accepted for lessons, there was no limit to his
patience. I remember one occasion when the whole class was ready
to explode with indignation at the behaviour of an opinionated and
argumentative pupil. After the lesson, when we were all marvelling
at Schnabel's calmness in the face of much time-wasting, he said,

'But it was my duty to remove his wrong ideas as patiently as I could.' Such a remark was typical of his optimistic and charitable belief that any pupil who even conceived the idea of trying, was apt to have some ability.

Schnabel had little sympathy with a literary approach to music, and when he did use word-imagery in his teaching, he did so sparingly but with peculiar aptness. He coined phrases not only to describe the music, as teachers have always done, but, more important, he used words in which the rhythm was identical with the musical phrase. Altogether his gift for language made him use words in memorable ways; he once told me that the first rhapsodical passage for solo piano in the slow movement of Brahms' B-flat concerto should be 'streaming, not dreaming'. Another time, he asked me to savour a particular harmony 'like a rare wine on the tongue'. We were asked to trill 'with the evenness of a bumble-bee', or, 'slowly, and passionately, like a nightingale'. (He himself had a dozen different trills at his command.) In a lyrical passage, the melody would be likened to a human figure in the surrounding landscape of the accompaniment. This suggested the necessary plasticity or sense of another dimension. Again, he would make more sweeping analogies, this time to contrast composers: 'Mozart is a garden; Schubert is a forest—in sunlight and shadow; Beethoven is a mountain range.'

His love of paradox appeared in almost every other sentence. He would say: 'When you play solos, play more chamber music'—meaning, 'Give each inner voice a life of its own.' Or he would say: 'Fast music and slow music are the same'—in other words, fast music was only slow music played at a quicker tempo, and should not be so fast as to be musically unintelligible. Another favourite phrase was 'Don't start with a stop'—emphasizing the fact that music must flow from the very first note of the phrase. In fact, a sense of movement, of going somewhere musically, was what he most often insisted upon, and he frequently used the words 'immer weiter' ('always forward'). Schnabel's love of word-play was not always confined to music, and a childlike sense of fun, little suspected by his audiences, gave rise to many original puns. Once, after a visit to a new dentist, he told me, 'I paid fifty shillings for these shifty fillings.'

To return to Schnabel's use of language in teaching: he recognized that all verbal means were only secondary; he always insisted that music should be 'approached, received, and presented solely as music'. (For instance, he was particularly averse to what he called the 'Dresden china conception of Mozart'.) As a general admonition, he often repeated the phrase, 'Get more pleasure out of your playing.' He felt, while many could express sorrow in music, few could attempt the more difficult task of expressing joy.

Technique, in the usual sense of pianistic facility, which in any case he preferred to call 'training', was not a branch of teaching Schnabel was ever much interested in. But he could, on occasion, demonstrate a short cut to the mastery of a difficult passage that made nonsense of one's long days of practice.

Ordinary technical shortcomings in his pupils he never tolerated. For instance, a pupil with an indifferent trill was promptly told that 'thousands of people all over the world can trill perfectly, and yet you expect to make your way as a pianist without it'. Not until all such basic elements of piano playing had been mastered—and indeed, forgotten—did the question of real technique (in his sense) arise; technique as the complete equipment for projecting one's inner vision of the music, phrase by phrase, including gradation and beauty of tone, balance of voices, and rhythmic proportion in the spacing of the actual notes. On this level, the technique required for each composer is a different one; and not only for each composer, but also for each work—or even phrase—of that composer. And it can only be determined by the particular music in hand.

Schnabel's views on technique embraced also the question of posture. His own characteristic poise at the piano illustrated his theory that physical stillness was essential for command of the keyboard. He thought the body should be relaxed right to the base of the spine, which should touch the back of the chair whilst playing. He disliked all superfluous movement, and advocated a loose, hanging arm and equally loose wrist, with the fingers always in touch with the keys. Only the tip of the finger, the transmitter, had always to be steely firmness. This relaxed muscular condition was essential, because, without it, one could not make the correct arm, hand and finger movements (he coined the words 'arming' and 'handing' as parallels to 'fingering'); and according to Schnabel, the right movements would automatically produce the right phrasing.

Once he had assumed this position of physical ease and command, he would sit back and say (as usual by means of a paradox), ' Play nothing before you hear it'—or, 'First hear, then play.' He knew that only certainty of conception could produce clarity of presentation.

Schnabel never advised starting to study a work by practising the difficult parts. In fact, he disliked the word 'practice'; he preferred to use the word 'work', and this was no mere quibbling over terms. 'Work' (to him) meant endless experimenting with a phrase as music, in order first to discover the easiest way to play without 'practice'. This exhaustive experimenting with a phrase was not only to gain technical ease, but also to reveal the musical meaning—a method of approach which is the antithesis of those performers who rely on indulging their own personal feeling on the spur of the moment. Schnabel used to refer to this latter method as 'hand to mouth expression'. But all of his own detailed analysis was simply the putting of his musical house in order, so as to leave the way open for those moments of spontaneous revelation which may come to any artist in performance—and which came to him more often than to most.

On the subject of editions, Schnabel had as definite ideas as on other matters. He liked pupils to bring the *Urtext* when possible, for he felt that only in the original, unadulterated text could one hope to discover the composer's intentions. He *was* interested in serious editions by other pianists—and, after all, he himself produced an exhaustive edition of Beethoven's Sonatas; but he expected all such editions to be consulted only for comparison, after a considerable amount of independent thought and study. He disapproved strongly of using any edition as a crutch, for unsolved problems in the music itself worried him less than the facile solutions of these problems by editors—solutions which often only obscure the composer's intention.

And it is noticeable, in his own elaborately annotated edition of Beethoven, that he never leaves the student in doubt as to which marks are the composer's and which the editor's suggestions.

The complete assimilation of the text was, however, only a phase of study to be passed through, leaving the pianist free to relive—to re-create the emotional and mental processes of the composer; but as such re-creating is largely an act of imagination, it follows that one's interpretation will differ at different periods of one's development. In fact, Schnabel used to say that this was one of the enduring charms of the pianist's life. After a not very convincing performance by a student, he often said, 'Don't worry! I played it like that for twenty years myself.' And only a year or so before his death, when he was playing a Beethoven concerto under the same conductor with whom he had played it fifteen years earlier, the conductor referred to some changes in Schnabel's interpretation. And Schnabel replied, 'I should hope so; I am fifteen years older.'

Tradition in playing, so venerated in the nineteenth century, found little sympathy with Schnabel; his own approach to the music was too direct.   One of his forceful overstatements was that tradition in piano playing was largely 'a collection of bad habits'.   He held a similar view of that overworked term 'personality', which, he said he suspected, referred only too often to 'conspicuous and recurrent mannerisms'.   And yet the very impersonality of his own attitude to performance was so individual as to make his playing strongly personal.

It is not easy to organize the many unforgettable details of Schnabel's teaching that spring to mind.   He really taught one how to teach oneself—to stand on one's own feet; for he never imposed his own interpretation of the music.   Some of his criticisms seemed, after a lesson, so self-evident that one wondered at not having thought of them oneself.

His physical gifts were no less unusual than his mental.   His hand was perfectly shaped for the piano, neither very large nor very small —contrary to most great pianists.   It was a hand that was both sensitive and muscular.   The importance he attached to fingering is exemplified throughout his edition of the Beethoven Sonatas.   By good fingering he never meant the most convenient—this was a distinction he thought many pianists failed to make.   His choice of fingering was conditioned entirely by the phrasing and never by undue regard for the comfortable position of the hand over the keys. In fact, he tended to finger phrases in all keys as though they were in the key of C major, ignoring any sense of discomfort that this might cause on the black keys; and he usually let the fingers run out with the end of the passage.

His unique rhythm was justly famous; it was as effective in the simple folk music and dance forms of his native Austria as it was in more complex musical structures.   He emphasized that rhythm was a matter of proportion and not of accent—in other words, rhythm was mainly concerned with the spacing of notes in time rather than with dynamic accentuation.   It was the fundamental rhythm or pulse that he first sought in a composition and only afterwards did he think in terms of harmony, and finally, of melody.   Bar lines were anathema to him; they led to mechanical accents which could only disturb the flow of the music.   On the other hand, he felt one could never give sufficient attention to the up-beats and their rhythmic and melodic importance.   He waged constant war against the almost universal habit of hurrying the ends of bars; he realized that attention to the ends of bars mitigated the tendency to accentuate the first beats.

He phrased with infinite patience, but he would also, when he thought the occasion demanded it, take bold technical risks. He pedalled with courage, and he always held the much-discussed long pedals that Beethoven marked in his music, arguing that it was not the pedalling that needed to be altered on the modern piano, but the quality of the tone we produced.

★   ★   ★

We can never again visit this great artist in his lofty, book-lined music-room in Berlin, and listen to his classes whilst sitting under the portrait of his teacher, Leschetizky, with its inscription: 'In remembrance of many happy—and difficult—hours'; nor can we, on brilliant, Italian mornings, climb the two hundred steps to the *dépendance* of the hotel on Lake Como where Schnabel went into voluntary exile at the beginning of the German holocaust; nor can we again seek him out after his second move into exile (he afterwards became a citizen of the United States of America) in his little study overlooking New York's Central Park, with its pictures by Paul Klee, the neo-primitive 'Grandma' Moses, and its portrait of Einstein. But for those of us who enjoyed his friendship and guidance, these places will ever conjure up lasting memories of great and enriching musical experiences.

CONTENTS

ILLUSTRATIONS

ILLUSTRATIONS IN THE TEXT

Foreword

ASKED about the merits of musical biographies, Artur Schnabel once remarked that 'it is a sort of tribute to a great man to know the facts of his career'. Obviously he did not think very highly of the educational value of this type of literature. Music, to him, was an experience—intangible, inexplicable, mysterious—resulting from a predisposition of nature rather than an effort of the will. No amount of information about a musician, he thought, would bring us nearer to the music he produced or performed.

During his lifetime, Schnabel discouraged all attempts to publicize his work or his way of life. Never thinking of himself in terms of greatness, he certainly would have disapproved of any plan to write a book about him after his death; indeed, he kept virtually no journalistic comment on his work, and such letters and documents as remain were preserved without his knowledge. The record of his life is therefore not as complete as one would wish. A full estimate of his stature as a creative artist will in any case not be possible until a later day.

But there are today many hundreds of people who admired him as an artist and revered him as a man of unique character and integrity; there are many thousands more for whom he opened the door to a deeper comprehension and love of the great masterworks of music. Many of these will want to know 'the facts of his career', and may come to accept them as a 'tribute to a great man'.

In telling these facts I have been as objective as my natural predilection for the subject permitted me to be. I have refrained from dramatizing the incidents of what was, after all, the normal development of an exceptionally gifted human being. But since Schnabel's life ran its course during one of the most eventful and tragic periods in the history of Europe, I considered it necessary to give some attention to the background of social change and political upheaval which inevitably influenced his career and in the end cast its shadow on one of the most serene and affirmative spirits of our time.

To what extent the outward phenomena of the time influence the inner life of a fundamentally creative person is always debatable. In Schnabel's case the transition from the horse-and-carriage days of his youth to the jet transportation of his sixties left the man inwardly unchanged, a living protest against what he considered the deteriorating forces of the mass-production age. His compositions—the permanent product of his life—proclaim him to be a 'modernist', a musical thinker far ahead of his time. Yet he himself would deny that they were essentially different from the works of the classic and romantic composers of the past. 'The means of transportation have changed,' he would say, 'but the passengers remain the same.'

Artur Schnabel, who grew in stature, in accomplishment and in his powers of communication with every year of his life, remained basically the same man, upholding the same principles, fighting the same battles with the same means, his eyes fixed on the ever-distant but luminous vision, the same goal of beauty and truth. It was this that gave his personality the monolithic unity which made it proof against the wiles of fashion and the lure of success.

In setting down this account of Schnabel's life, I have followed, with due caution, the transcript of Schnabel's own reminiscences of his youth, with which he entertained his audiences at the University of Chicago in 1945, supplemented by the testimony of his sisters and other members of his family; but for the record of his adult years I have drawn mainly on the recollections of Mme. Therese Schnabel, his chosen companion throughout a half-century of partnership in life and art. I am also indebted to Mme. Schnabel for placing at my disposal many of Schnabel's letters to her, and such documentary material as programmes, personal records and whatever was left of the press reviews of Schnabel's appearances on three continents.

To supplement this material I have searched the files of pertinent newspapers and musical journals in Vienna, Berlin and London, and especially the press cuttings and other material in the Music Division of the New York Public Library.

In addition to my own memories of Schnabel during an acquaintance of thirty years, I have had the benefit of the personal reminiscences of his surviving boyhood friends, including Messrs. Franz Hutter, Ernst Possony, Bruno Eisner, Mrs. Kate Wykert and Mrs. Ernst Cassirer; some of his fellow students at Leschetizky's in Vienna (notably Miss Katharine Goodson, Mr. Mark Hambourg, Mr. Heinrich Gebhardt and Miss Ella M. Richards); a few of his companions and colleagues of the early Berlin days, including Prof. Eugen Spiro, Dr. Werner Wolff, Mr. Gregor Piatigorsky, Dr. Fritz Stiedry and Prof. Heinz Tiessen; and many of his pupils, particularly those of the earliest years—Messrs. Edward Ballantine and Henry

Jolles, Mr. Lee Pattison, Mrs. Mary Boxall Boyd and Miss Elisabeth Martienssen—and those of a somewhat later period, including Miss Marguerite Macintyre, Messrs. Clifford Curzon and John Hunt.

I also wish to thank Messrs. Werner Grewe, Hans-Erich Riebensahm, James Loder and Claude Frank, and Mesdames Maria Donska and Martha Baird Rockefeller for revealing sidelights on Schnabel's teaching, and others too numerous to mention for anecdotal material.

I am indebted to Sir Robert and Lady Mayer and Mrs. Emmie Tillett for interesting details concerning Schnabel's several sojourns in London, and to Mr. Walter Legge for information concerning Schnabel's recording sessions for H.M.V.; also to Mr. and Mrs. Joseph Brinkman, Prof. Roger Sessions, Mr. Joseph Szigeti, Mrs. Arthur Schwarz and many others for the period of Schnabel's residence in the United States. I am especially grateful to Prof. John U. Nef of the University of Chicago for a large number of valuable letters from Schnabel during these later years; to the late Mrs. R. A. Butler (née Courtauld) for Schnabel's correspondence with Mrs. Courtauld and the records of the London Concert Club; to Mrs. Artur Bodanzky for the records of the New York Friends of Music and to Mr. Ira A. Hirschmann for those of the New Friends of Music of New York; also to Messrs. Stefan Schnabel, J. Christopher Herold and Mrs. Poldi Zeitlin for their kind co-operation.

Finally I extend my thanks to Mr. Ernst Křenek and Prof. Roger Sessions for their help in analysing some of Schnabel's compositions and for their valuable essays contributed to the Supplement of this work; also to Dr. Bernardo Cohn (of Buenos Aires) for compiling the Schnabel discography.

CÉSAR SAERCHINGER

Bedford, New York

PART ONE

BOYHOOD AND ADOLESCENCE

1. Beginnings

ARTUR SCHNABEL was born on April 17th, 1882, at Lipnik, a rural suburb of Bielitz-Biala, in Austrian Silesia, the son of Austrian parents of Jewish faith. The Peace Treaties of 1919 have now made the region Polish. During Schnabel's youth it was Germanic, politically, ethnically and for the main part linguistically, and had been so for generations. It also had a strong Protestant tradition, dating back to the time of the Reformation and the wars of religion. Less than two hundred miles north-east of Vienna, the thriving provincial centre of Bielitz lay firmly within the economic and cultural orbit of the Austrian capital, many of whose citizens frequented its pleasant environs, in the foothills of the Beskid mountains, as a holiday resort.

In later years Schnabel remembered Bielitz as a clean and prosperous-looking town, and its twin—Biala, on the other side of the River Biala —as a poor and rather dirty one. Inhabited by a typically provincial German middle-class population, with a sprinkling of moderately prosperous Jews, Bielitz had considerable pretensions to culture. It took pride in its municipal theatre, its churches and public buildings, clustered together in a handsome business and residential quarter, with a still distant background of smoke-stacks—symbol of the inevitable encroachments of the industrial age.

Biala, connected with Bielitz by a single bridge over the usually dry and stony river bed, was the home of the poorer classes, still largely agricultural workers and belonging to a branch of the Slavic race known as Slomsakians, whom the Germans called *Wasserpolacken* ('diluted Poles', in Schnabel's facetious translation). It was definitely a poor region, and the neighbouring village of Lipnik was, if anything, still poorer. As Schnabel remembered his birthplace, it had a main street and little else. Its architectural pride was the residence of the leading local distiller, whose son, Sigmund Fraenkel, became Artur's boyhood friend and, like himself, a musician.

Schnabel's antecedents were as varied as his environment at birth. His father, Isidor Schnabel, was the son of a wine merchant in Austrian Poland, who came to Bielitz to learn the textile business, the chief and growing industry of the town. The mother's parents (named Labin)

3

had emigrated from Rumania to settle in Bielitz, where her father and his in-laws operated a small wool mill. Here Isidor met Ernestine Labin, having entered the family business as a clerk. Both were young —Isidor a tall, handsome, blond youth of twenty, Ernestine a small, dark, winsome girl of seventeen. Both were younger children in large families, Isidor one of six and Ernestine one of seven. They married and moved into a tiny flat on Lipnik's main street and in due course had three children, of whom Artur was the youngest. Of his two sisters, Clara was six years, and Frieda one year older than he.

Isidor Schnabel has been unanimously described by friends and acquaintances as a quiet, thoughtful, kindly man of studious habits, who spent most of his spare time reading the scriptures in the original Hebrew. Essentially he was a religious man though not orthodox in observance. There is no indication that he had any enthusiasm for business. He was unaggressive and—in his son's words—'even afraid of money'. He eventually became a partner in the family business, but with so many other relatives in it his share could not have been great. Ernestine, the mother, is reputed to have been sprightly, energetic and socially ambitious, with a hankering for elegance and finery and a great fondness for parties.

According to Schnabel's own account, his parents were 'poor people'—a very flexible term which has been variously interpreted. Certainly they were people 'in a small way', belonging to that Jewish middle-class which though primarily engaged in trading also formed an increasingly important part of the learned professions—the intelligentzia of Central Europe—during the nineteenth and early twentieth centuries. It was a notably energetic and striving group, with high cultural aspirations and an astonishing degree of artistic endowment, especially in the field of music. A remarkable crop of outstanding instrumentalists, conductors and teachers has sprung from this fertile human soil, and even more astonishing is the quantity of prodigies raised by families devoid of musical or artistic antecedents.

Schnabel's own parents were what he called in his purposely choice German *amusisch*, i.e. unrelated to art. As a matter of fact his mother was by no means unmusical, and she certainly was ambitious for her children. In all probability it was she who gave the decisive impulse for the family's move to Vienna, which according to some accounts occurred when Artur was two, while in his own reminiscences he placed it much later. The confusion probably arose from the fact that throughout his childhood the Schnabels maintained close ties with the home town, the family and its business, returning there periodically, and at one time with the intention of staying. Many summers were spent in the nearby resort of Zigeunerwald, a favourite summer rendezvous for Viennese families, close to the West Beskid range. Bielitz, after all, was only an overnight trip from Vienna, on a spur of the railway line to Cracow. In after-life Schnabel retained vivid memories of this background to his youthful years.

The primary purpose of the Schnabels' move to Vienna was to have Isidor act as the representative of the family firm for the marketing of its woollen cloth, but it is most probable that Ernestine had more exalted things in mind.

The family's first Viennese abode was a small flat on the Grosse Schiffgasse in a rather poor section of the Leopoldstadt, the quarter which Schnabel used to describe as a 'voluntary ghetto', because it was still inhabited by a large proportion of Vienna's Jewish population. As a matter of fact the quarter had once held a real ghetto, with grim memories of the distant past. The Schnabels' accommodations were definitely cramped, but they were soon exchanged for others—in the Herminengasse, quite near the Danube Canal. Here the young Schnabels must have been taken for airings along the water, interestingly crowded with tugs and barges conveying the city's produce and freight. In other respects the neighbourhood was rather sordid, consisting of endless rows of lower middle-class tenements, interspersed here and there with more picturesque gabled houses reminiscent of an earlier time.

*   *   *

When Artur was four the family acquired a piano, in order that his elder sister Clara, then ten, might begin her musical education. Clara was considered the beauty of the family, and seemed destined for a stage career. In any case piano playing was an indispensable social equipment for aspiring young ladies, and a young Bielitz woman named Minka Patzau was engaged to take her in hand. Almost from the start little Artur evinced great curiosity in the proceedings and soon began to imitate his sister at the keyboard. Without lessons, without encouragement of any kind, he soon played by ear the exercises and pieces which Clara had laboriously learned— to the utter amazement of the methodical teacher who, according to Schnabel himself, thought that a boy who could do that must have talent and began teaching him. It appears, however, that the boy didn't take very readily to Miss Patzau's ministrations, saying that he didn't like her looks, but continued playing all the same.

His musical gifts revealed themselves in other ways as well. From
early childhood he had been extremely sensitive to sounds—the ringing
of bells, music in the street, and later the playing of a piano in the
flat below. When he first heard this the boy was observed to fling
himself to the floor, press his ear to the boards and listen in childish
ecstasy. One of his favourite games was to turn his back to the keyboard and guess the notes as his sister struck them. Thus it was
discovered that he had inherited his mother's gift of absolute pitch.
Observing that the pieces Clara played utilized only the piano's
middle range, he kept urging her to use *all* the keys, because they were
'all beautiful'. His own childish improvisations rambled all over the
keyboard, from the bass to the highest treble.

One day, hearing church bells tolling, he cried, 'Listen, a child has
died', and proceeded to improvise a dirge to accompany the bells.
He also improvised a piece entitled 'Funeral March of a Frog', which
was followed by others based on some children's tales he was given
to read. Ernst Possony, a neighbour's son considerably older than
Artur, later recalled a children's party given by his own parents, at
which the young man with great vigour and earnestness performed
his first composition, solemnly announced as 'Emperor Rudolph's
Ride to the Grave' (based on an illustrated history book). This boyhood acquaintance, who lived on the same floor of the Herminengasse
house, has described Artur as 'a charming, chubby and affectionate
child, loved by everybody, though somewhat "peculiar" (i.e., uninhibited) in his reactions to the common phenomena of childhood'.
From all accounts, he was perfectly natural, good-natured and not
in the least embarrassed in the presence of adults. When Mr. Possony
saw him again in middle-age he was startled to find that his
friend of early memory had retained the same childlike countenance,
easily recognizable despite the passage of time.

Although he was what is called a 'good boy', Artur was not above
childish pranks such as tormenting his sisters and tinkering with the
mechanism of the piano. His peak accomplishment in this respect
came some years later, when he and his sister Frieda proceeded, in the
parents' absence, to take the interior of a newly acquired grand piano
apart so thoroughly that only an expensive repair job could put it
right again.

★   ★   ★

By the time Artur was six, it was clear to the Schnabels and their
friends that they had a prodigy on their hands. On Minka Patzau's
advice he was taken to the Vienna Conservatory to play for Professor

Hans Schmitt,[1] whom Artur remembered in after years as 'a dignified, bearded gentleman and the author of fifty thousand daily exercises' designed to produce the perfect virtuoso. Actually Professor Schmitt, then fifty-three, and head of the Conservatory's senior piano class, was widely reputed to be a first-class musician and pedagogue. Evidently a man of keen perspicacity, he immediately accepted the diminutive youngster as a private pupil, though he was much too young for admission to the Conservatory. Henceforth the little fellow was regularly conducted to the professor's house for lessons, usually by one of his sisters. A régime of practice hours was set up, and everything else was subordinated to the purpose of making him a pianist. Instead of sending him to school, it was decided to engage a tutor, whom Artur remembered as 'an old man with a white beard, and not very tidy'. He taught the boy some Hebrew, perhaps out of deference to the father, but of this Artur remembered almost nothing in later life. After a time the white-bearded sage was replaced by a young university student named Müller who followed a more general curriculum and seems to have understood how to hold the boy's interest. Also he realized that music was, after all, the chief concern.

The family's great problem was how to provide the wherewithal. It does not seem that Isidor Schnabel's agency brought in enough to keep the family in Vienna and provide for the children's education. He was a highly respected and gentlemanly character, but hardly adapted to the aggressive commercialism of the big city. He would have preferred the easy provincial pace of Bielitz, and his former, more sedentary occupation. Therefore the task of finding ways and means fell to the ambitious Ernestine, who held out for staying in Vienna. One can imagine the anxious little woman running from Peter to Paul for advice and help. She obtained both through Albert Gutmann, the music dealer and *deus ex machina* of musical Vienna. Herr Gutmann not only sold music and pianos but also managed artists, arranged concerts and exerted a potent influence in important quarters of the musical world. It was through Gutmann's help that a number of experts as well as leading financial supporters of music heard Artur and unanimously declared that he 'had the equipment to

---

[1] Hans Schmitt, a native of Bohemia, taught advanced pupils at the Vienna Conservatory for twenty-five years. He composed 300 *Études* for young pupils, also 120 *Little Pieces*, and edited Clementi's *Gradus ad Parnassum*, also a progressive repertoire for young pianists. He wrote a treatise on the use of the pedal—a subject in which Artur Schnabel later made an important contribution in his playing and teaching.

become a professional musician'. This modest phraseology is
Schnabel's own. More likely the prospective backers decided that
he was a prodigy. In any case, from that moment he considered
himself a professional musician 'by the decision of my parents and my
patrons'. Who the patrons were he did not know until many years
later: a group of three wealthy families provided a monthly stipend
without ever expecting to see the prodigy, much less to receive his
thanks.[1] All Artur knew was that his mother—and later himself—
collected the money at the office of their 'charity department', and
this continued until his sixteenth year. Thus Ernestine Schnabel won
her struggle to remain in Vienna—for a time at least.

Artur's lessons with Professor Schmitt went on for two years.
Just what he learned in that time we do not know. When asked
about it later he said he had no recollection of it, adding: 'It obviously
was not inspiring—perhaps I was not yet awake'. Nevertheless it is
most likely that Schmitt laid the foundation of the technical skill and
facility which became second nature before Artur reached maturity.
Also it probably set up in him the aversion to exercises and mere
technique which he retained throughout his life. However, Schmitt
must have taught him more than just Études, since at the age of nine
the boy was able to play Mozart's D minor concerto—'a work still
considered to be chiefly suited for children', as he remarked wryly in
after years. This feat was performed at a private concert arranged by
the excellent Herr Gutmann for invited guests in the large music-room
of his establishment. The event, of which there is no printed record,
fulfilled its purpose in that it confirmed and prolonged the subsidy
which assured Artur's musical career.

*   *   *

Schnabel was always anxious to absolve his parents from any
intention of exploiting him as a *Wunderkind*. His father, noted for
his retiring disposition, hated the thought that one of his children
might become a sensation or even a source of profit. However, the
mother, 'though not greedy, was quite ambitious' according to
Schnabel's own words. Certainly the temptation to exhibit her
talented offspring lay close at hand. Prodigies were becoming fashionable, and there were two other children of Artur's age in Vienna at
this time making their bid for world fame, both of whom came from

---

[1] For the sake of the record his chief benefactors were Baron Königswarter,
Baron Gutmann (not to be confused with the music dealer) and Herr Cahn-
Speyer.

similar social environments. Both received a great deal of publicity, and both had played at the Imperial Court, which Artur did not— much to his mother's disappointment. So-called friends would aggravate the situation by teasing him: 'Did you read that Poldi Spielmann has played for the Kaiser again?' Or: 'Did you see Ilona Eibenschütz's Polka in Gutmann's shop window? She has dedicated it to the Archduke X. . . .' According to Mama Schnabel, Artur retorted, 'What does the Kaiser know about music?' The adult Schnabel discounted this by saying, 'My mother had much imagination'.

In any case, *she* was the motoric factor in the family, and she certainly basked in the local fame which her son had already acquired. It was she who most wanted to see him become a great artist. It was she who saw to it that he practised and fulfilled his assignments, not always an easy task. His sisters have given vivid accounts of the weekly 'scenes'—usually on Fridays—caused by Artur's indolence. He himself confessed to a congenital laziness against which he struggled all through his early life. But this natural sluggishness seems to have been purely physical, if not emotional. Mentally he was always active and alert, even while physically inert. Always fond of verbal tricks, he later coined the word 'alertia' for his own peculiar tendency to 'creative laziness'.

In general he was given to daydreaming, reading or just contemplating, when not busy with musical exploring. There is no record of an eager pursuit of book-learning, though his tutor seems to have had no complaints. However, he was very quick in grasping the essentials of a problem or the general contents of a story. Equipped with a remarkable memory he avoided the drudgery of learning things by rote. He grew up in the knowledge of being different from other boys and girls. He spent very little time on games and the usual juvenile pastimes; in fact he had few companions of his own age. According to his own account he had no playmates, and he did not associate with people his own age until he was a grown-up himself. There were to be notable exceptions to this, as we shall see, but it is probably true that his astonishing precocity was due in some degree to his almost exclusive association with adults.

On the other hand there is little evidence of parental influence on his intellectual development. The father's constant preoccupation with scriptural reading seems to have precluded more worldly and timely interests: there is no record of a convivial family life, of excursions, or visits to zoos, circuses and museums, likely to stimulate interest in natural history, literature or art and least of all a taste for

sports. Father Schnabel's only pastime seems to have been a quiet
game of taroc. Artur always spoke of him simply as 'kind', without
reference to any cultural interest or accomplishment.

His tutor, Herr Müller, instructed him in the usual curriculum of
the Volksschule (council school) to the age of ten in order to comply
with the law. A subsequent attempt to send him to a Gymnasium
(classical high school) in order to avoid a charge of truancy ended in
failure four or five months later. The boy seems to have been unable
or unwilling to concentrate and submit to the rigid school discipline.
His class instructor, a Professor Soffer, approved his withdrawal and
even taught him privately for a time, but eventually the more congenial Herr Müller returned. Despite Artur's slackness he seems to
have been ahead of the average child of his age and, though small in
size, he was treated as an equal by people much older than himself.

★   ★   ★

About the time of Artur's debut in Gutmann's showrooms, the
Schnabel family moved into somewhat better accommodation on the
Obere Donaustrasse (No. 87), which directly faces the Danube Canal.
The house, which is still standing, must have been quite new at the
time, being built in the somewhat pretentious style of the period—a
rather large structure with an ornamental stucco façade, having front
and rear buildings separated by a court. Presumably the family's
situation had improved as the result of Artur's subsidy. In place of
the old Pokorny piano, there was now a Bösendorfer 'grand', furnished
gratis by the famous house which then supplied the Imperial Family,
and whose instruments were played in Austria by most of the famous
artists of the time. The two girls were going to the common school.
Clara, aged fourteen, continued her music lessons with a view to
becoming a singer. The apartment, though larger than the old one,
still had only three rooms and a kitchen, to house the entire family
including a servant, Cäcilie (called 'Cilly' for short). Artur, its most
precious member, slept on a plush sofa in the dining-room.

Schnabel at the age of eleven

Photographs exchanged as sweet-
hearts by Artur and Therese, Berlin,
February 1900

2. *Apprenticeship*

WHEN Artur was nine he seems to have exhausted the educational possibilities offered by the formidable Professor Schmitt. He had acquired a remarkable dexterity for his age, and an astonishing ability to play at sight. At this time it was suggested to his mother that he ought to be taken to the great Professor Leschetizky, then the most celebrated piano teacher in Vienna and, for that matter, in the world. This might have seemed a presumptuous undertaking to anyone but a very proud mother, but Frau Schnabel secured an appointment, and presently the great man received her and little Artur at his famous villa in the 'Währinger Cottage' section (an upper-class garden suburb) of Vienna. With this event a new and decisive period began in Schnabel's development as a 'professional musician'.

At the age of sixty-one Theodor Leschetizky was at the pinnacle of his fame as a pedagogue; a vigorous, strong-minded man and a formidable personality, worshipped by his pupils, yet feared because of his exacting demands and occasionally choleric temper. He had won European fame as a pianist and composer, and world renown as the teacher of Ignace Paderewski. He himself had studied with the great pianist Czerny who in turn was a pupil of Beethoven, thus establishing an authentic apostolic succession from the highest of the high. For a quarter of a century he had been a professor at the Imperial Conservatory of St. Petersburg, and for over twenty years he had taught in Vienna, where his position in musical life was hardly less important than that of his famous contemporaries Brahms, Bruckner and Johann Strauss. He was, in short, a figure calculated to strike terror in the heart of any applicant, and especially in that of a mere child.

Recording his impressions of the visit, Artur remembered that the great man was two hours late; also that—like all the old men in his life, including his father—he wore a beard, though 'not yet quite white'. Mother and son waited in a small room of the two-winged, square-towered brick mansion in the Carl Ludwigstrasse,[1] whose plushy mid-Victorian interior struck the boy as 'rather more inspiring'

[1] Now changed to Weimarerstrasse.

than the austere simplicity of Professor Schmitt's abode. At last they were summoned into the master's own music-room, where Artur played him a part of his repertoire. Next, the Professor opened a brand-new piano score of the recently published *Cavalleria Rusticana*, and asked the boy to play it, evidently to test his ability in sight-reading. When he had heard enough to satisfy him, Artur was promptly accepted as the youngest pupil of the class. No financial conditions were proposed or made: it seemed a matter of course that this kind of talent had a free pass to Parnassus. Indeed, none of Schnabel's instructors ever asked or received any fee for teaching him. At first, however, the lessons were with Madame Essipoff, Leschetizky's wife and assistant, and a virtuosa in her own right. During the earlier years the new pupil was 'heard' by the master only from time to time.

Annette Essipoff, a handsome Russian woman of forty, was very kind to the boy, and very painstaking about his technical development. She tried to make him hold his hands level while lifting his fingers like hammers in order to develop their muscles. She would place a silver *Gulden* on the back of one of his hands and if he succeeded in playing a Czerny study through without dropping it, would give him the coin as a present. This 'static technique', of course, was the very antithesis of what was to be his way of playing later on, but in retrospect he admitted that it might have been excusable as a temporary expedient for very young beginners. In any case he appreciated Madame Essipoff's generosity each time he won the *Gulden*. As with his first teacher, the emphasis seems to have been on technical exercises and études. Only this time they were by Czerny, instead of Schmitt. Unfortunately the happy time with the genial Madame did not last very long, for in the following year (1892) she was divorced from Leschetizky and returned to her native St. Petersburg, where she taught in the Imperial Conservatory for the rest of her professional life, and where Serge Prokofief and Alexander Borowsky were among her best-known pupils. She had been married to Leschetizky for twelve years, as his second wife.

By the time Madame Essipoff left, Artur was of course also studying the classics, including the earlier Beethoven sonatas. Indeed, it seems that he had already explored them by himself, regardless of his teachers. After Madame Essipoff his most constant preparatory teacher was Madame Malwine Brée, a Viennese, who like Artur came from Austrian Silesia and like him had been a child prodigy. At the age of sixteen she was married to Dr. Moritz Brée, who took her to

Weimar to study with Franz Liszt. For one reason or another she did not make a successful concert career, but she certainly was highly reputed as a teacher.

Madame Brée, like Madame Essipoff, was principally occupied with technique and later wrote a book on Leschetizky's method which had a wide circulation.[1] But she also supervised Artur's learning of a sort of repertoire—a rather mixed bag of classical, romantic and neo-romantic pieces (including Rubinstein and Leschetizky) which the little fellow dutifully performed. Yet he seems not to have been an easy pupil to manage. An American contemporary considerably older than Artur recalled how Madame Brée complained bitterly to Leschetizky that the eleven-year-old Artur 'would not do a thing she told him to do'. However, even at this early age he was considered eligible for playing to the 'class', or bi-weekly assembly of all the students.

'Three times Madame Brée brought Beethoven's *Sonata Pathétique* to the class for him to play,' reports Miss Ella Richards, a co-student, 'but Leschetizky would not let him finish it—much to our indignation. I can still see that child, so small he could scarcely reach the pedals, completely absorbed in the music. I can still remember the dignity and authority with which he played the majestic introduction to the first movement.' But evidently Artur's eagerness to express himself sometimes exceeded his physical powers, and occasionally he made slips caused by the smallness of his hands, and nothing enraged Leschetizky more than inaccuracies. 'We used to wonder why he tried to regiment that little genius. He taught him exactly as he taught the rest of us.'[2]

Many stories are told by fellow-pupils of the pathetic little youngster who had to undergo humiliating tongue-lashings by the irascible master. Once, because he left out a few notes in a Beethoven sonata, he was told that he was a thief, since stealing from Beethoven was as reprehensible as taking money out of someone's pockets. Artur took it silently, sat immovable on his chair against the wall, his feet dangling and tears running down his face. Another time he

---

[1] *Grundlage der Methode Leschetizkys* (1902), translated as *The Groundwork of the Leschetizky Method* (1902). Schnabel rejected this and other so-called Leschetizky textbooks by saying that Leschetizky never created or followed a 'method'. However, it must be added that four editions of Mme. Brée's book appeared during Leschetizky's lifetime, and to the author's knowledge he never protested or repudiated it in public.

[2] Ella Richards, of St. Paul, Minnesota, American pianist and teacher, who studied with Leschetizky as a young girl.

was told that if he couldn't do better he would have to become a
Dienstmann (porter) instead of a pianist.

Following Leschetizky's example Madame Brée was a stickler for
note-perfect accuracy, and probably she was rather hard with her
little pupil. But there is no evidence of resentment in a letter Artur
wrote her a little later, signed 'your grateful pupil', to which we shall
return in another connexion. For one reason or another, however,
the adult Schnabel never mentioned Madame Brée as one of his
teachers. Speaking of his preparatory teachers in general he liked to
say, half-jokingly, that he 'soon unlearned what they taught me'.

Be that as it may, it seems likely that the child's phenomenal
musical comprehension and his avidity to express the essence of a work
outran his patience in the effort to master it. There were times when
he would play a piece almost perfectly the first time—with the perception of a mature artist—and then disappoint the teacher by not
attaining the degree of finish that is expected to come after many
hours of practice. Even at this early age he was apt to be bored by
mere technical problems, being interested in musical rather than
mechanical solutions. All his life he revolted against the persistent
'practice that makes perfection'. Even as a child he always strove to
know more and more music rather than learn to play a few pieces
better and better. Unless the music itself compelled him to work, he
would pass on to more tempting fare. Already he was acquiring a
general knowledge of piano literature rather than a mere repertoire.
But no matter who was teaching him, there is no doubt whatever that
he was making rapid progress in the mastery of essentials and that the
real difficulty between him and his teachers arose from the fact that
he was already intent on going his own way.

It was not long—though it is difficult to fix the date—before he
studied with Leschetizky alone, and by that time he was definitely
learning music rather than technique. 'In all my years of study,'
Schnabel once said, 'Leschetizky never spoke of technique. He simply
helped pianists the way a good mountain guide helps the climber who
does not always know where to take the next step: he unfailingly
leads him toward the goal.' On the other hand we may judge what
Leschetizky must have thought of his youngest pupil from the fact
that frequently, when other pupils encountered difficulties in trying to
master a piece or a passage, he would call on Artur to demonstrate to
the class how it should sound. Time and again he would advise a
pupil to 'look through this piece with Schnabel'—a practice which
established young Artur, while still a pupil, as a teacher of people

much older than himself. And thus he earned—for the first time in his life—some welcome cash.

We know, moreover, that throughout his years of study Artur was invariably asked to perform in the famous 'classes' on alternate Wednesday evenings, when all the students, as many as seventy or eighty, were present. What happened to most other pupils on more or less rare occasions—to be thus singled out for exhibition—was the rule with Schnabel throughout his seven years' scholarship. At these famous assemblies Leschetizky would occasionally interrupt and criticize the players, and with Artur he seems to have been especially strict and even severe. But even at this early age the tiny pupil was permitted to bring works of his own choice to play to the class. One day he brought Brahms' piano pieces, opus 119, which were then hot off the press. For some reason Leschetizky became angry, thinking that Artur had maliciously chosen pieces which he, the Professor, did not know—or did not like. In a burst of fury the master sat down at the piano and played a parody of the first piece, cheapening and vulgarizing it, and holding it up to the ridicule of the class. Artur was deeply hurt, Brahms being his newly acquired hero. To make matters worse, Leschetizky 'fired' him from the class. Not until three months later, after someone convinced the master of the absurdity of ascribing malice to his youngest pupil, was Artur permitted to come back into the fold. After this Leschetizky actually encouraged him to play Brahms, and though still strict, he never was hard with him again.

*   *   *

Taken together, these incidents may help to explain a rather cryptic admonition of Leschetizky's which Schnabel first resented and then cherished for the rest of his life. 'Artur,' he said, 'you will never be a pianist. *You* are a musician.' Schnabel's interpretation of it (which may have been gratuitous) was that Leschetizky despaired of making him the kind of pianist then fashionable: the man to whom technique—sheer mastery of the keyboard—is the end and aim of pianism. After all, Leschetizky was famous as the maker of virtuosi, and he was still interested in producing the type of artist who had the widest public appeal; yet he understood this youngster's deviation from the accepted norm, and eventually encouraged him in it.

Schnabel only gradually became aware of the distinction. His admiration for his master was unequivocal; he revered and adored him, to use his own words. 'Leschetizky,' he said much later, 'belonged to the virtuoso world of the second half of the nineteenth century, but this virtuosity was genuine and creative—not mechanical. His great quality was his vitality. I think he conceived of music, not as an exclusive sphere of personal experience, but as something which has to be presented, shown to others, performed. He saw music as a public function, so to speak. For him the musician as a person was the giver, and he who listened the taker. When he stated that I was primarily a musician—he meant that I was a type that *takes from music*. Or, as one might express it, a person dedicated to music as the primary source.'

If this is a true interpretation it is supported by the rather curious but prophetic advice Leschetizky gave to young Schnabel when he told him to explore the then almost completely neglected piano works of Schubert. 'Schubert,' he said, 'has written fifteen sonatas for piano, which almost nobody knows. They are absolutely forgotten. No one ever plays them. *You* might like them.' It certainly indicates a remarkable understanding to have chosen this eleven-year-old boy for what turned out to be a major work of resurrection. On the other hand, Schnabel was one of a mere handful of Leschetizky's pupils (among the 1,800 he taught in the course of fifty years) who were not told to learn the *Hungarian Rhapsodies* of Liszt! 'He didn't always like me,' said Schnabel, 'but he absolutely respected what he believed to be my musical disposition.'

Many years later, in answer to a question, Schnabel found it difficult to estimate all he had learned from Leschetizky. Contrary to the general belief that his great teacher had some sort of technical secret or royal road to the solution of all problems, Schnabel said that Leschetizky's teaching was much more than a method. 'It was a current which activated or released all the latent vitality in the student's nature. It was addressed to the imagination, to taste, and to personal responsibility. It was not a blueprint or a short cut to success. It did not give the student a prescription, but a task. What he aimed at was truthfulness of expression, and he would not tolerate any violation or deviation from what he felt to be true. Altogether his devotion, seriousness and artistic integrity seemed incompatible with the virtuoso type which he was supposed to represent.'

Above all, he had an inspiring personality, as a man, an artist and a teacher who lifted the student to his highest potentialities. Whatever their differences of opinion in questions of æsthetics, Leschetizky and Schnabel were destined to remain friends for life. Schnabel loved his old master always and respected him for his high principles and his absolute loyalty to his art. 'Not once,' he wrote, 'did Leschetizky mention success or money in my hearing, as long as I knew him.'

★   ★   ★

Shortly after Artur had started to study under Leschetizky's guidance someone suggested to his mother that he ought also to have instruction in musical composition. There were at least three great composers living in Vienna at that time. Feeling that nothing was too good for her boy, Mama Schnabel bethought herself of old Anton Bruckner, then 'a man of sixty-seven, whose eighth symphony, dedicated to the Emperor Franz Josef, was about to be performed by the Vienna Philharmonic under Hans Richter. Some eight years before, when Bruckner was a professor at the Conservatory, Fritz Kreisler had been a member of his class, and it is possible that Dr. Kreisler, the violinist's father and the Schnabels' neighbourhood physician, may have mentioned his name to the family. In any case Ernestine took her little boy by the hand, and walked across the Stephanie Bridge to the Hessgasse to find the great man.

They climbed up a flight of stairs and knocked at the door of Bruckner's flat. Presently they heard the shuffle of slippers slowly approaching, and finally the door opened—just wide enough to disclose a dusty hallway piled high with music and laurel wreaths. Through this narrow opening the huge, bald, heavy-jowled head of Bruckner appeared, inquiring, 'What do you want?' 'I want you to give theory lessons to my son,' said Frau Schnabel briefly and to the point. 'I don't teach children,' growled Bruckner with a savage glance at little Artur, and closed the door. 'That,' said Schnabel when he related this unforgettable episode, 'was the sum of my personal relations with Bruckner.'

After this, Leschetizky recommended another and rather less famous but bearded composer, who in slippers and dressing-gown began to teach Artur the elements of musical theory. But he turned out to be 'dry, pedantic and uninspiring'. The young pupil evidently showed some resistance, for the experiment came to an end after a few months. Finally, Artur was taken to Eusebius Mandyczewski, a musical scholar who was to play a decisive rôle in his life. Mandyczewski, then only thirty-five, was already one of the most important musicologists of his time. He was not only a first-class musician and theorist, but a warm-hearted human being whose genuine love of music was likely to kindle the latent enthusiasm of an impressionable boy.

Dr. Mandyczewski held the post of archivist to the historic Society of the Friends of Music, whose library and museum were the repository of priceless manuscripts and other musical treasures. This voluntary, unofficial institution also controlled the Vienna Conservatory, one of the world's most illustrious schools of music, and sponsored the famous series of orchestral concerts known as the *Gesellschaftskonzerte*. Its massive building housed, as it still does, two of the most beautiful concert halls in Europe. Mandyczewski was the custodian of its library and archives. Here, during the 1890's (when young Schnabel was his pupil) he was engaged in preparing a monumental forty-volume edition of the Collected Works of Franz Schubert based on the original manuscripts, for publication. Associated with him in this task was his great and intimate friend Johannes Brahms, for whom he also acted as amanuensis during a considerable part of his life.

Mandyczewski (this 'wonderful man' as Artur called him) lived very simply in the quiet seclusion of a single room in the Beatrixgasse (*III. Bezirk*)—a mile or more from the Schnabels' flat in the Obere Donaustrasse. Artur, quite capable at ten of finding his way through the maze of streets of the inner city, would arrive at eight in the morning, the only time that Mandyczewski could spare for teaching him. Regularly at 9.15 he began his official and editorial duties in the archives of the Musikverein. Invariably he would invite his little pupil to accompany him on this walk along the Heumarkt and across the Schwarzenbergplatz to his office in the Bösendorfergasse, talking all the way; and there would turn him loose to browse among the musical and historical documents as long as he liked. Manuscripts and first editions lay about unprotected. Slightly awe-struck at first, the boy would linger in complete solitude in this musical shrine, poring over scores and, as it were, imbibing music at its source. This experience remained one of the indelible memories of his youth. It was the first great impetus toward that life-long process of exploration which gave him an almost universal knowledge of the great masterworks of music, and which led to the revival of a great body of piano literature that had been neglected during the second half of the nineteenth century. It also helped to develop his independent judgment of musical values, which eventually determined the uniquely high programme standard associated with his name.

3. *Alone in Vienna*

'I HAVE no very definite memories of my first ten years, except for places and smells. They must have been strong.' Thus Artur Schnabel in his reminiscences, or 'improvisations on themes of his life'. If this is true, then his recollections and comments on the place of his birth, on the neighbouring 'dirty' town of Biala and the 'clean' town of Bielitz are either based on hearsay or on rationalizations dating from later visits—after he had grown to an early adolescence in Vienna. His first impressions of that city must have been, rather, a gradual realization of what a great city was in comparison with the provincial place from which he had come. Nevertheless, it is interesting to know what he thought of it, even though it grew upon him slowly instead of bursting upon his consciousness all at once.

Vienna in the Gay Nineties was at the height of its effulgence as the capital of a great empire and the chief trading centre of central Europe, drawing on the products and handicrafts of its Hungarian, Bohemian, Polish and Italian crown lands and possessions, as well as the Balkan states and the Near East. Indeed, the influence of these almost exotic cultures was so vivid that, as the saying was, 'the Balkans began at the Landstrasse', i.e. in the very suburbs of Vienna. It was a colourful city in which many nationalities and customs mingled, brilliant with the military pomp and social glitter of the Imperial Court at the twilight hour of a long period of peace. These were the last years of the so-called *Ringstrassenzeit,* the time in which the great wide circular boulevards that had taken the place of the old fortifications served as the background for fashionable promenades, parades and popular festivities to the accompaniment of the music of Joseph Lanner and Johann Strauss. These were the great days of the *Prater* and its noisy amusements, and of the ubiquitous Vienna cafés at which burghers, bohemians and intelligentzia spent incredible amounts of leisure time.

Curiously enough, we discover very little of this atmosphere in Schnabel's recollections, perhaps because he was too young to take an interest in this kind of public activity, but also because he lived a life of his own, with his limited and very special companionships, his private preoccupations and diversions, all more or less centred about one thing—music. What he later remembered about the Vienna of his childhood was not so much its advantages as its drawbacks; he liked to recount not so much what it had but what it lacked—with a certain nostalgic feeling for earlier, simpler and 'better' times. Vienna was still in the gaslight era, and even gas—in the home—was very rare. There was no central heating and almost no electricity. Telephones were virtually non-existent, so were baths, typewriters, illustrated newspapers and thousands of things now considered indispensable.

Urban locomotion was by horse-drawn vehicles. Such things as films, gramophones, radio, etc., were decades in the future. Mass production had only just begun. Little Artur was shown the first machine-made shoes—imported from America—in a shop window as a great curiosity, and soon he also learned about factory-baked bread. He was amazed at the sight of the first department store. The age of technology had just dawned—but very dimly—in Vienna.

Years later, when asked whether he thought that people were happier without all the commodities and gadgets of modern life, he was not sure, but it is certain that even in his youth he was not greatly impressed by modern improvements. 'It may well be,' he said, 'that the more one is inclined—or persuaded—to possess, consume or enjoy material things, the less one is able to give in the personal exchange of heart, mind and soul.' This was, of course, his opinion in retrospect, and so was his criticism of the social aspects of the generation into which he was born. He seems to have become conscious of the rigid stratification of Viennese society at a very early age—partly from observation and partly as the result of his almost exclusive association with adults. Vienna, in this eleventh hour of its function as 'the Ballroom of Europe', had four principal social groups. The first comprised the aristocracy, still centred about the Court. The second included the Church, the army and the higher civil service, or bureaucracy. Then came the *bourgeoisie*; and finally the 'lower classes', which he found to be 'pretty rough' in contrast with their superiors, who excelled in elegance and charm.

The aristocrats performed all the functions about the Court, the social prima donna of Vienna. They also held the highest civic positions, which required little work. Not to do work, in the ordinary sense of the word, was a part of *noblesse oblige*. This Schnabel considered an important fact; for the less time was spent in working, the more was left for the tasks of *noblesse*, which were based on quality and refinement. Incidentally, every high government job in

the Austro-Hungarian monarchy was filled not by one but by four
people—a German-Austrian, a Czech, a Hungarian and a Pole—so
as not to offend any of the principal nationalities of the realm. This
in itself was well calculated to assure a minimum of work, if not of
intrigue, for each. There was also a lower aristocracy—a titled
group without centuries-old pedigrees—which was composed of men
and descendants of men who had earned their rank with outstanding
achievements in the army or government. Merchants and bankers,
artists, scientists and educators were sometimes also rewarded in this
way. The *bourgeoisie* included the politicians and the large body of
lower civil servants who formed the bulwark of the 'white-collar
supremacy', as well as the business and professional classes. Below
them were the working people of all sorts, including the wine-
growers who formed the peasantry of the country about Vienna.
Very good and plentiful wine was grown in the immediate vicinity
of the city.

In the wine-cellars and (in spring and summer) the wine-gardens
nearly all the social classes met and mixed, and if sufficiently animated
by young wine they fraternized 'for a few hours of drowned
inequality'. Women and song were never missing: this was the
intoxicating ensemble which led to freedom from care.

How early in life Schnabel became conscious of these social
phenomena it is hard to tell. He was, of course, extraordinarily
precocious, and very soon sensed that all was not well beneath the
glittering surface. A slightly perfumed scent of decay was in the air
and the upper classes had a glimmering suspicion that they were
'doomed'. They were having their last fling—an escape into a
refined and luxurious defeatism. 'Life in this atmosphere was not
always pleasant,' he said; 'I was not always happy there.'

*   *   *

About a year after Artur had been accepted by Leschetizky, an
important change took place in the Schnabel family. For some time
Isidor had been dissatisfied with the life in Vienna. His business
there had not come up to expectations: he had established a clientele
for the products of the Rabinowitz's woollens, but there seemed to
him no compelling reason for his presence in Vienna, particularly
now that Artur's education was provided for. Besides, he must have
disliked the family's partial dependence on the patrons of his young
son. In 1892 he spent some time in Bielitz and—probably as the
result of a decision reached while there—he turned the agency over

to an old-established Vienna firm. In the following year the entire
family, without Artur, returned to Bielitz. Isidor remained with the
firm, the family was established in a commodious flat in the Bahnhof-
strasse, and the two girls continued their education in a local convent
school. As for Artur, arrangements were made for him to board
with friends in Vienna. He would visit the family during the summer
months and for the rest he was considered competent (at eleven) to
take care of himself.

This domestic upheaval was certainly not due to a sudden or
arbitrary decision, and Frau Schnabel was perhaps not easily persuaded
to part from her favourite child. One may well imagine a protracted tug-of-war between the parents before the move was accomplished. In the long run it proved to be beneficial for the family as
well as for Artur, who came to love the countryside in the moun-
tainous environs of his native place. He seems, moreover, to have
been quite satisfied with the arrangements which left him in Vienna
as an independent though diminutive man-about-town.

His first lodging was with the Nelkens, a highly respected and
cultured family living in the Leopoldstadt. There were two children
—a son who later became a journalist and a daughter who married
the noted psychoanalyst Wilhelm Stekel. Artur, as usual, had a tutor—
this time a very learned but 'rather untidy' one, according to his
recollections. To him, life at the Nelkens was 'boring', and after a
while he moved in with another family—the Husserls, who were
very lively indeed. Frau Husserl, a widow with four sons and a
little daughter, was a relative of Leschetizky's preparatory teacher,
Malwine Brée, and lived in the Mariannengasse (*IX. Bezirk*), a good
deal nearer to the Professor himself. Here Artur enjoyed himself
hugely. Three of the sons were students at the University, and the
liveliness of the place was mainly due to their activities. Their chief
home occupations were fencing with sabres and the rapid consumption of large mugs of beer—both considered very noble and indispensable accomplishments at German universities. Artur watched
this, his 'introduction to academic life', with wide-eyed wonder, but
determined then and there to remain unacademic. Nevertheless,
one of the sons, a future physician, became his tutor in Latin and the
humanities, while another tried to help him in mathematics—his
weakest subject. In idle moments he proposed marriage to the pretty
little daughter of the house.

*   *   *

Shortly after the family's return to Bielitz, an extraordinary event occurred of which Schnabel makes no mention in his reminiscences. The only evidence is the letter he wrote to his teacher Malwine Brée in September, 1893, from his native town. In it he reports on what must have been his first public recital anywhere, in Bielitz's largest hall, holding 1,000 people. This bit of juvenile correspondence seems to show that Ernestine Schnabel, while determined not to 'exploit' the little prodigy, was nevertheless quite willing to let the public know what he could do.

'I had such strong applause,' writes the eleven-year-old, quite in the vein of an old trouper, 'that I cannot think I deserved it. I hope that the reviews, which I shall send to a Viennese paper, will also turn out to be favourable. The public even demands a second concert, but not now—perhaps in the autumn. I could not wish for a better success anywhere.' The letter was enclosed in one from his mother, in which she confirms the intention to give a second concert later on, 'when we hope for a material success, since for this one the time was too short and the expenses too great'. It is a pity that the programme of this, Artur's real debut, cannot be found, nor can the reactions of the Press.

The second concert evidently did not take place—and for a very good reason. According to verbal but plausible evidence, Leschetizky was furious when he heard of what he considered a premature appearance, and threatened to stop the boy's lessons. Ambition had evidently got the better of Mother Ernestine, not to mention the young man himself. On the other hand, it must have enormously increased his self-confidence and feeling of independence at the moment when he was starting life on his own in Vienna.

He was described about this time as 'an unusually small boy of twelve, with a remarkably firm little body surmounted by a rather large, round but shapely head'. On special occasions he wore a blue velvet suit with short trousers, and his society manners 'had the perfect polish of the born courtier'. One of these occasions was his first visit to the Bondys, a wealthy and cultivated family living in Mödling, then a rather select suburb of Vienna. Herr Bondy was the head of Austria's first cable works, an enlightened industrialist who favoured and supported the fine arts. Someone—perhaps the energetic Herr Gutmann again—had suggested that the Bondys, who had three young children of diverse ages, might be helpful in furthering Artur's career. All the members of this cultured family became his friends from the moment they saw him. One of the daughters

has left us the following impression of his first visit to the Bondys'
house, for the purpose of giving them a sample of his art:[1]

'With his big intelligent grey eyes he looked around the room till he
spotted the two parents. He bowed, first to Mother, then to Father, and
kissed Mother's hand. Then he turned to us children. Standing before me,
he raised his hand to his heart and repeated the bow, this time accompanied
by a charmingly comical smile. Then he marched up to the two boys and
slyly pinched their arms—a gesture to which they responded in kind. Three
minutes later the *Wunderkind* was just a jolly little boy, delighted with the
discovery that he could deal with these "rich people's children" on his own
terms. . . . My father asked him to play, just as he would ask a favour
from a grown-up. The boy, used to being exhibited, went resolutely to the
piano, twirled the seat of the stool very deliberately till it had reached the
precisely correct height, and began. What he played I don't recall. What
I do remember exactly is the change that took place in me—a feeling that
this little boy was not like the rest of us. A moment ago we could still chat
with him and parry his witty remarks without embarrassment. Now I felt
that we, the others, had to protect this child, to admire and love him, and
never measure him according to our standards, judgments and prejudices.
The mission which had been entrusted to him was the concern of all of us.

'Those who never heard Artur Schnabel until the latter part of his career
will hardly believe that the playing of the twelve-year-old child had all the
essential characteristics which distinguished the mature artist. . . . Since it
was true beyond all doubt, it confirmed my conviction that the true artist is
not the result of slow development, but a complete, divinely created person
who discovers himself by degrees.'

That very summer Artur spent a holiday with the Bondy family
in their country house, and delighted the older and younger children
with his sparkling wit, his funny stories and his amusing pranks.
However, all attempts to discipline him or to enforce his obligatory
practice period were fruitless. Even a locked door was of no avail,
since Artur found another way of joining his young friends in the
garden, namely through the window and via a chair which they
surreptitiously placed beneath it.

Another life-long friendship began during the following summer,
which Artur spent with his own family in the environs of Bielitz.
A friend introduced him to the Hutters, a Viennese family spending the summer at Zigeunerwald. At the friend's urging he sat
down to play one Schumann piece after another. Then, in order to
show 'what this child can do', the friend placed before him a volume
of pieces which he had never seen before. After looking at the first

---

[1] Recollections of Mrs. Ernst Cassirer, née Bondy, widow of the distinguished
German philosopher.

few pages very intently the boy returned to the piano and played what he had just read from memory—without a hitch. When the listeners voiced their astonishment Artur said in his Viennese dialect, *'Ach, das ist gar nix, Sie müssen mal hören, wie ich das Stück mit der Zunge schnalzen kann.'* (Oh, this is nothing, just listen how I can click that piece with my tongue.) He then showed his opinion of the opus by reproducing its melody and rhythm as announced—apparently one of his favourite tricks.

Later Artur became a welcome visitor at the Hutters' house in Vienna, where Franz Hutter, the son, became one of his few boyhood friends near his own age. Franz was radically different from Artur; he was a clever and sophisticated youngster, who was later to become a successful editor and publisher of fashion magazines, first in Berlin, then London and finally New York. Franz Hutter was destined to become his boon companion in his bachelor years, and later still a helpful adviser in matters of business.

Certainly Artur was exceedingly fortunate in his youthful friendships. As time went on he became acquainted with more and more people who recognized his talents and were able to give him substantial encouragement. They were usually a 'very special type of people' as he described them, having the same general characteristics as those who were naturally attracted to him in later life. For the most part they were moderately well off, always cultured, generally concerned with matters of the intellect and able to appreciate the spiritual values in life as the source of happiness. 'But,' he remarked, 'their names were hardly ever mentioned in the newspapers.' In his boyhood days in Vienna these grown-ups treated him not only as a friend and equal but as a member of their families. They invited him to adult dinner-parties—sometimes to the chagrin of their own children who being of school age had to go to bed. Once or twice this resulted in violent outbursts of juvenile jealousy which Artur countered with a show of cool dignity.

At twelve and thirteen his social life resembled that of an eligible young bachelor. When not studying, teaching his co-pupils or otherwise practising his profession, he engaged almost exclusively in adult pastimes. Indeed, his real 'playmates' were the young pianists in Leschetizky's class who with a single exception were far older than he. His only male competitor among them was Mark Hambourg, a stocky and rather aggressive lad of fifteen. Young Mark was a typical *Wunderkind*. He was a protégé of Paderewski and the favourite of Hans Richter, the eminent conductor of the Vienna

Opera and the Philharmonic concerts. He had the ideal equipment for a virtuoso and was already famous for his bravura passages and his powerful tone. Artur remarked maliciously that if Leschetizky's remark ('You'll never be a pianist, you're a musician') was true about himself, the reverse might be equally true of Mark. There was bound to be jealousy between the two youngsters, and more than once they came to blows over boastful remarks by the one, or ironically sympathetic inquiries ('Did you have a good lesson today?') from the other. In later years they became more tolerant of each other and even spoke kindly about each other's abilities. But their ideas and ideals were worlds apart.

From all accounts of these formative years one gathers that Artur, left alone in the great city to board with strangers, to pursue his own education and seek his own diversions, was neither lonely nor homesick. At the threshold of adolescence he had the interests, the capacities and the airs of a young journeyman of the arts. It was not long before he travelled in the company of the Great.

4. *Prodigy on the Loose*

THE two channels through which he came into contact with the great world were Professor Leschetizky's class and Dr. Mandyczewski's circle of friends. At the bi-weekly gatherings in the Professor's villa he met all the older pupils such as Ossip Gabrilowitch, Ignaz Friedman, Katharine Goodson and others who were shortly to attain world renown. These brilliant elder colleagues gave their friendship to the 'baby' of the class, and their affection grew to mutual admiration in after years. Through these co-students Artur was introduced in the homes of prominent music lovers and amateurs, some of whom became his life-long friends.

At Leschetizky's Artur was also presented to the greatest international musical celebrity of the time—Anton Rubinstein himself. He was an impressive impersonation of the traditional nineteenth-century virtuoso, with his long flowing locks, deep-set fiery eyes and high cheekbones, dressed in a long coat and a trailing bow-tie around his neck. Artur remembered him as a kind and rather theatrical old gentleman who was 'very sweet' to him, and who took him on his knee while playing whist at Herr Gutmann's or Leschetizky's house, calling him 'my youngest kibitzer'. Artur also heard Rubinstein play his own compositions (then considered on a par with the works of the greatest contemporaries), an 'impressive but not overwhelming' experience. Whether Artur was made to play for him is not clear, but Rubinstein is said to have remarked as he looked at the boy: 'If you don't become great, I shouldn't be Rubinstein'—or words to that effect.

Another great and picturesque figure whom Artur remembered meeting at this time was Mark Twain, then about sixty and world-famous as the author of *Tom Sawyer* and *Huckleberry Finn*. Here was another white-haired gentleman—unforgettably striking in appearance, a great personality and the father of two charming young ladies, both members of the Leschetizky class. (Clara Clemens, the elder, later married Artur's friend Ossip Gabrilowitch.) Artur remembered many tea-parties in the Clemens' rooms in the Hotel Metropole, his first introduction to international society.

Through Eusebius Mandyczewski, whom we may regard as his

musical, as distinct from pianistic mentor, he was introduced to the circle of Johannes Brahms, that is to say those families whose chief pride was their intimacy with the great composer, then the most eminent musical personality of Vienna. Brahms, although born and raised in North Germany, had made Vienna his home from his thirty-sixth year, and lived there almost without interruption from 1869 to his death in 1897. He had conducted the famous concerts of the Gesellschaft der Musikfreunde for four years, and continued to make his bachelor home in the immediate vicinity of its headquarters for the rest of his life. Mandyczewski, twenty-four years his junior, remained his close friend for life and acted as a buffer between him and the outside world. Little Artur first came into contact with the Brahms circle at the house of Frau von Hornbostel, a formerly well-known singer and the guiding spirit of a private ladies' choir which regularly rehearsed in her home. Mandyczewski was its conductor and he asked Artur, then ten or eleven, to act as accompanist. This he did, to the evident satisfaction of all concerned, sometimes teaming up in four-hand accompaniments with the slightly older son of the house.[1] It is probable that Artur's acquaintance with Brahms' *Liebeslieder* waltzes (for four voices and piano four hands), which he helped to perform in public so many times in later years, dates from this time. Brahms himself attended these evenings occasionally.

But this was only the beginning. Schnabel recalled that he was often in Brahms' house in the Karlsgasse. Most likely Dr. Mandyczewski, whenever he had to confer with Brahms, stopped there on his way to his office, and took his pupil along. Artur was impressed by the smallness of the two rooms Brahms occupied and the modesty of the furnishings.

At this time the great composer was a frequent guest at the house of Hugo Conrat, who wrote the German texts of Brahms' *Zigeunerlieder* (Op. 103 and 112).[2] Conrat was a prosperous merchant and a passionate devotee of the arts. His house, in the fashionable Walfischgasse (close to the Opera House) was, on Sunday afternoons during the winter, given over to convivial gatherings for the performance of chamber music by professionals or amateurs, including

[1] Erich von Hornbostel, later a well-known physiologist, who died prematurely in New York.

[2] Hugo Conrat's attention was called to the Hungarian originals of these gipsy verses by a house guest, Fräulein Witzl, who was born in Hungary. She made a rough translation of them, and Conrat fashioned these into the texts which Brahms then set to music. (*Cf.* letter of Frau Marie Brüll to Frau J. Kalbeck, in Max Kalbeck's *Life of Johannes Brahms*.)

the host himself. It was a time for leisure and pleasure, where one might play or listen, or just sit. Artur was invited, not only as a potential musician but as a presumptive companion to the three young daughters of the house. He frequently took part in the ensembles while Brahms was there. Usually the old gentleman sat in the library at the far end of a long suite of rooms, reading. He might have heard little Artur play, but never gave a hint that he did. As for Artur, he enjoyed himself hugely and later said that his life-long love of chamber music was rooted in this early encounter with it at the Conrats' house. Only once did Artur hear Brahms play, namely the piano part of his own G minor piano quartet, opus 25, which became one of Schnabel's favourites and which he often played with the 'Bohemians' and other famous ensembles in Europe and America. When Brahms played it in Vienna Artur had never heard it before. 'It was the great music that shook me,' he said later, 'but also the creative vitality and wonderful carelessness with which he played.'

His biggest moments with Brahms, however, came on the glorious Sundays of the spring and autumn, when the great man, with Mandyczewski and a few other friends (usually musicians), would set forth on excursions into the Wienerwald, the wooded hills which surround Vienna. The group would meet on the Ringstrasse in front of the Opera at eight in the morning, take a horse-drawn tram to the suburbs and then continue on foot. Usually the goal was one of the modest and cosy inns where good food and local wines were served in liberal quantity, to be consumed either indoors or more often in the vine-covered yard or terrace—the kind of place traditionally connected with the Schubert period but still patronized by the nature-loving people of Vienna. When Artur was twelve or thirteen he was occasionally invited to come along. Thus he enjoyed, at the most impressionable age, the beauties of nature in the company of unconstrained and easy-going elders, including the greatest living master of absolute or, in Schnabel's own phrase, 'self-contained' music.

Naturally, this fortuitous association with Brahms was later built up and featured by interviewers as a sort of mystical laying-on of hands. Schnabel vigorously discounted these stories. Whenever he was asked what Brahms said to him on these occasions he replied: 'Two things: he always asked if I were hungry, and later, whether I had had enough to eat. After all, what *should* he say to a child?'

Nevertheless, it is unlikely that so wide-awake a youngster, filled as he was with music, could have refrained from listening to 'shop talk' in such company. It is certain that his keen interest in Brahms' music dates from this time, and perhaps also his love of verbal witticism.   Brahms' reputation for austerity was, according to Schnabel, greatly exaggerated, and one of Mandyczewski's functions as his famulus was to supply him with funny stories, grotesque misprints, and plays on words.[1]

There is no doubt that Schnabel's predilection for Brahms' music —long before it was generally accepted—derives from his early acquaintance with the master, however slight.   It was on his own initiative that he tackled Brahms' late piano pieces as a boy and brought them to Leschetizky's class with the aforementioned dire results.   He continued to play them, however, throughout most of his career, and the two concertos became his 'specialities' at a time when they were still considered novelties.   Later in life his enthusiasm for some of this music diminished—not because he thought less of it but because he considered Beethoven, Schubert and Mozart a more important task.   During his early days it made him, of course, a Brahmsian (if not a 'Brahmin') when this meant—almost as a matter of course—an anti-Wagnerian in the hotly partisan atmosphere of Vienna.   Much later, in answer to questions, he explained his attitude to the two great rival contemporaries thus:

'Brahms wrote only self-contained music, and none that is associated with visible action.   He was therefore the hero of the more exclusive group, the more refined and individualized.   Wagner provided the sensation needed by those who desired escape—or simplicity.   But Brahms and Wagner had much more in common than most musicians have.   Today they appear to me as musical brothers.   I think Wagner to be the greater genius.   He tried to solve new problems, express grandiose visions.   Yet Brahms' untheatrical and less pretentious work is closer to me.   What they have in common is romantic pessimism, romantic sensuousness and sentimentality.'

*   *   *

Beside the Conrats' house there was in Vienna another musical household where kindred souls foregathered—in a less reverential and perhaps gayer atmosphere, yet equally partisan when it came to Brahms versus Wagner.   This was the home of the Löwenberg family, which in Schnabel's youth became the rendezvous of musicians and music-lovers, predominantly of the younger generation, with a strong representation of the Leschetizky class.   Among the habitués, besides

---

[1] Every year a Leipzig publisher issued, by subscription, two volumes of flaws of speech, misprints and similar amusing items, to which Mandyczewski subscribed.

Artur, were Ossip Gabrilowitch, Richard Buhlig, Gottfried Galston, Douglas Boxall, a young Englishman, Bertha Jahn, Heinrich Gebhard and Ethel Newcomb, an American pianist who later wrote a popular book on Leschetizky.

The Löwenbergs kept open house on Sunday afternoons—from four-thirty to midnight. The family consisted of Frau Löwenberg, an elderly widow, quiet but wide awake, and two daughters—one an intellectual spinster known as 'Tante Irene', the other the wife of Dr. Kolmer, a member of the Austrian parliament. Together they were the embodiment of Viennese *Gemütlichkeit* and warm-heartedness. Their hospitality has been described as 'incredible'. After the traditional *Jause* (the Viennese equivalent of afternoon tea) the young musical guests would try out their pieces before the family and other friends on the two magnificent Bechstein grands (probably Artur's first acquaintance with these instruments—later his favourite make). Then, following a sumptuous supper, there would be entertainment, fun and frolic without restraint. Besides the Leschetizky pupils there would be other musicians, including Leone Sinigaglia, the young Italian composer, Eduard Kremser, a popular conductor, and similar kindred spirits.

Artur, though the youngest, was from all accounts the life of the party. He was up to any kind of fun—when in the mood. A favourite form of musical joke was the on-the-spot improvisation of an operatic skit. He would quickly outline a plot, and Gebhard would assign the parts. There would be the conventional lover and the inevitable tragic heroine, also the hated rival, the irate father and the usual minor characters. Arias, duets and trios were projected, and a Wagnerian *leitmotiv* given to each character. Then Artur would improvise an overture on the piano, delegate Gebhard to play the accompaniments for the singers, who enacted a sequence of scenes—inventing both words and music based on the *leitmotifs*. The whole was 'frantically' conducted by Artur. Most of it was in a caricatured Wagnerian idiom, alternating with ear-splitting foretastes of *Zukunftsmusik*. The company revelled in this orgy, especially the hosts, who were notorious 'Brahmins' in the feud then raging between the rival camps.

★ ★ ★

The friends of the genial circle often went to concerts given by the famous artists of the period, particularly their favourites—Eugene d'Albert, Teresa Carreño, and their 'own' Ossip Gabrilowitch; also the lieder singer Camilla Landy and a gifted young violinist named

Rosa Hochmann, who was later to strike fire in Artur's heart. They
listened to the Philharmonic concerts then conducted by Hans Richter,
and the Gesellschaftskonzerte, in which Brahms himself conducted his
Academic Festival Overture in 1894 to celebrate the Society's jubilee.
Occasionally they would visit the Imperial Opera to hear Mozart,
Weber or even Wagner operas, though Artur definitely disliked
Wagner at this time.

A visit to the Opera—that is, to the unreserved seats in the 'gods'
—normally required an expenditure of some eight hours. The
young enthusiasts would begin to queue up at three in the afternoon
and stand until seven, when the doors opened. Then followed a wild
rush up four flights of stairs, and a scramble for the best seats. These
queuing hours were social events at which the young hopefuls would
meet and exchange their opinions. Here Artur first met, among
other future colleagues, Arnold Schönberg, who frequently raced
him up the stairs. One didn't see very well from the gallery, but one
heard all the better, and Artur enjoyed these performances as he
rarely enjoyed any later in life.

There were other diversions besides concerts and operas and
parties. There was the theatre, though Artur seems to have had
remarkably little interest in the drama at this time. He did go to
see the great Eleonora Duse act, and he managed to be present at
the Vienna debut of the daringly French *diseuse* Yvette Guilbert—
a type of entertainment then strictly forbidden to minors. This was
the time when children were still isolated from adult amusements
and shielded from the 'unpleasant' facts of life. They were subject
to the stern discipline of school with its hated homework, but left
to their own resources for recreation, play and mischief. There were
as yet no children's performances and 'educational' amusements. The
hygienic and social virtues of sports were still largely ignored, and
even the bicycle was only a new-fangled invention used by the
adventurous few.

How, then, did little Artur, alone in the big city, spend his time?
He himself often wondered in after-life. He had no school—only a
few irregular hours' tutoring with the two roisterous students. He
had one or two weekly lessons with Leschetizky, the perambulating
lectures of Mandyczewski, and a few lessons with Malwine Brée.
His daily stint at the piano, besides his lessons, was three hours—much
less than is demanded of incipient pianists today. What did he do
with the rest of his time?

True, the lessons with Leschetizky consumed a lot of time—

often as much as six hours, partly because the Professor was always late—two hours or more. The lesson itself was at least two hours long, and the trip to the Leschetizky villa and return took another two hours—on foot, of course, for Artur didn't like the trams, and always loved walking. Besides, it was cheaper. He walked everywhere: all over the sprawling city, enjoying the sights, the beautiful buildings and monuments of this architectural paradise, and above all the parks and every visible touch of nature. The love of nature was inborn and grew with the years. It is likely, therefore, that he made many detours: strolling or 'wandering' was to be his favourite recreation to the end of his life. We may imagine him, too, visiting the historic places, the shrines of his heroes which lay more or less near his route—the birthplace of Schubert in the Nussdorferstrasse, the Schwarzspanierhaus, the houses in which Mozart and Beethoven had lived, though there is no record of his doing any sightseeing for its own sake.

We know that he was not a studious lad in the conventional sense. Nor was he a persistent reader, though somehow he acquired a smattering of literature which made him appear well-read. The truth is that he was, from an abnormally early age, a thinker and a dreamer. He meditated and cogitated, and reasoned things out. He revelled in the beauties of nature. And he indulged his imagination—a great part of the time in musical terms. All in all it was a 'creative laziness', the idleness which in Nietzsche's words is 'the beginning of all philosophy'. It is present in most thoughtful people, but it was prematurely so in Schnabel. Withal, he was a happy child, without great anxieties or restraints, without overweening ambitions or an undue sense of responsibility.

The result was that without a formal education he became one of the best educated men of his profession; that without reading he became one of the best informed; and almost without 'practising' he became one of the greatest of pianists of his time.

5. Debut and Awakening

IN January 1897 Artur's parents and sisters abandoned Bielitz and returned to Vienna, this time to stay. They had left him a precocious little boy; they returned to find him a man of the world— a premature adolescent with the intellectual and emotional attributes of an adult. He had developed at a prodigious rate in intelligence and in general knowledge, in his judgment of people and events. According to surviving ear-witnesses he displayed at fourteen many of the extraordinary traits of character which distinguished his professional career from those of his contemporaries. He was deliberate and somewhat self-assertive in manner, opinionated in his conversation, but good-natured and given to sly humour and puckish pranks. Although short and chubby, he already had that indefinable charm which made slaves of his admirers, especially those of the opposite sex. His almost exclusive association with older people, most of them 'intellectuals', had made him not only well-informed but critical— sometimes cynical—in his judgments.

He said good-bye to the 'academic' atmosphere of the Husserl household with its sabre-rattling students, and his education was now solely concerned with music—in the last two years of his apprenticeship. Once again he lived with his own family, housed this time in a modest flat in the Porzellangasse (IX. Bezirk), half-way between the Rossauer Lände military barracks and the walled-in park of Prince Liechtenstein's palace—a neighbourhood considerably nearer to the houses of his well-to-do friends. The Schnabel family fortunes do not seem to have been notably improved, but things were easier now that the children were growing up. Clara, the elder daughter, was ready to enter a career in light opera.

Artur had made tremendous strides, both in technical mastery and in developing that true understanding which gives life and meaning to the musical phrase. Already he had begun to acquire the beauty and the fine differentiation of tone which later gave such distinction to his playing. More and more during Leschetizky's classes he was called upon to demonstrate for the benefit of other and older students, thus becoming a consultant to aspiring pianists before he was permitted to give a concert himself. Indeed, the Professor persisted in regarding him as a musician and teacher rather than as a future virtuoso, but continued to be as exacting and as hypercritical as before, whenever it was Artur's turn to play. Artur was fully conscious of the fact that he was singled out for especially severe treatment, and many years later, when one of his pupils thanked him for being 'so lenient', he remarked somewhat bitterly: 'When I was young I had a very hard teacher, so I made up my mind always to be kind to my pupils.'

It is no wonder that in his middle 'teens young Schnabel was beginning to acquire a certain sense of superiority which at times he had difficulty in disguising, although he compensated for it by a show of humility—not toward his colleagues but toward the composers whom he was 'appointed' to serve. Since his co-students were nearly all adults, he felt that he had no real competitor, not even his old rival Mark Hambourg, since their repertoires were completely different. As for the two other Viennese *Wunderkinder* who had been held up to him as glittering examples, their names had already disappeared from the public prints. There remained only one very talented, charming little girl pupil of Leschetizky called Bertha Jahn, who was two years younger than he, and who was to make her debut about the same time. Schnabel spoke of her in after years with great admiration and affection, as someone too sensitive and precious to survive the struggle of a public career in a cruel world.

By this time Artur's reputation was growing locally among the profession and this resulted in another small source of revenue, for certain concert artists engaged him as accompanist and assisting soloist for their recitals, mostly outside Vienna. One of these was Camilla Landy, who had already acquired a European reputation as a *lieder* singer, and who was hailed by Viennese critics as 'a God-given talent and a great artist'. It was at Madame Landy's recital in January 1897 that Artur Schnabel made his first appearance before a metropolitan audience. According to the *Neue Freie Presse* he turned the concert into a 'sensation', for he 'amazed us with his singing tone and the—for his age—surprising warmth of his playing'. The critic estimated his age, despite his size, to be 'about sixteen', but in reality he was three months short of fifteen. Present at this surprising event was a really distinguished audience, including three royal princesses who naturally caught little Artur's smiling eye, and the spectacularly picturesque Mark Twain with his two handsome daughters.

Another artist who honoured him with her patronage was the aforementioned Rosa Hochmann, reputed to have been not only the most brilliant young female violinist of her time, but a petite and seductively beautiful brunette. Artur's senior by several years, she captured his fancy, which quickly developed into something more. It was not long before Rosa Hochmann became Artur's boyhood flame, and his association with her was certainly the first great romance of his youth. Incidentally, making music with Rosa in these impressionable years further stimulated Artur's love of ensemble playing.

On February 12th—two months before his fifteenth birthday—Artur Schnabel made his official Vienna debut, playing a recital in the richly ornate Bösendorfer Hall. His programme consisted of Bach, Beethoven, Schumann, Tchaikovsky, Chopin, Rubinstein, Moszkowski, Leschetizky and Edouard Schütt—a collection which betokens a generous promiscuity of taste on the part of his mentors, also perhaps a shrewd estimate of what the 'cultured' Viennese expected of a budding genius in those days. Rubinstein, Moszkowski and Schütt were popular favourites in the city of Schubert and Brahms, and the inclusion of Leschetizky was the burning of incense before a household god. There is no record of the encores he played. They may just possibly have included some waltzes by Schubert, the centenary of whose birth had been observed in sundry places a fortnight before.

It goes without saying that the response to Artur's offering was tremendous, and that the plump little lad in his blue velvet jacket and short trousers had to return innumerable times to bow, his raven locks falling over forehead and cheek. Hundreds of friends and co-students were present, including the nineteen-year-old Ossip Gabrilowitch, who had made his debut the year before, and of course his parents and sisters, patrons and teachers, in particular the white-haired Professor Leschetizky and the genial Dr. Mandyczewski. During the interval Artur 'received' in the green room. According to one eye-witness he stood in his corner 'as though fixed to the floor', extending his hand to all and sundry in the manner of a seasoned performer. His rich young friends, the Bondys, came in to congratulate him alone—without their parents. He greeted them with a dignified smile, without betraying any intimacy and without budging an inch from his chosen spot.

Reviewing the concerts of the month, the *Neue Freie Presse* had this to say about the event:

'The concert of the approximately fourteen-year-old pianist Artur Schnabel counts as one of the many triumphs which the Leschetizky School has recently achieved. The young artist—an extraordinary talent—has in a comparatively short time learned so astonishing an amount that he must already be reckoned as one of our notable virtuosi. With his gifts, his diligence and the excellent guidance which he enjoys it is only a matter of a very short time before he will arouse wide comment [*wird von sich reden machen*].'

The excitement was soon over and life went on much as before. The debuts of two Leschetizky prodigies (the other being his twelve-year-old friend Bertha Jahn) were soon forgotten in the swirl of a Vienna musical season which measured its performers, domestic and foreign, by the hundred. Anton Rubinstein, the prince of them all, had died two years before, but the succession included such figures as Eugene d'Albert, Ferruccio Busoni, Teresa Carreño and Moriz Rosenthal, who was deliriously applauded for his thundering octaves and *prestissimo* runs. The most popular of all, however, was a dapper middle-aged gentleman named Alfred Grünfeld, 'Imperial Court pianist' and the darling of Viennese society.

*　　*　　*

It is only natural that an attractive youngster, full of vitality, with Artur's gifts and his open-hearted generosity, would become a favourite and an easy prey to the affections of the easy-going and free-mannered Viennese. Feeling himself to be an adult, Artur donned long trousers and became the popular man-about-town—always, of course, on an 'advanced' intellectual level.

About this time he had what he considered the good luck of meeting some of the most promising young poets of the day—in a group of writers and artists, some of whom were already considered to be geniuses. This group included the whimsical essayist Peter Altenberg, also the poets Paul Wilhelm, Felix Dörmann and Hugo von Hofmannsthal (the future librettist of Richard Strauss), the painter Flora Wiesinger and the architect Alfred Loos. These were the 'young moderns' of the day, the spurners of tradition and convention, who dreamed of new and distant æsthetic visions and revelled in the playful pessimism of the time. Young and old, and especially young adolescents like Schnabel, participated in their fruitless arguments, endlessly discussing Tolstoy and Dostoievsky, Ibsen and Nietzsche—the best-sellers of the day. There were night-long debates on everything from positivism to occultism—and of course the artistic, moral and social decadence of *fin-de-siècle* Vienna.

This feeling of decadence was so strong that the best intellects began to distrust their own impulses and the validity of the values in which they believed. One of the escapes from this super-sophistication was *primitivism*—the cult of the 'noble savage' and the child. In this search for new sensations these flounderers turned from the esoteric to the exotic and from the exotic to the brilliantly trivial. 'From decadence to simplicity, and from simplicity to Hollywood,' commented Schnabel many years later—with the wisdom of hind-sight. At any rate it was fun to be among grown-ups, exciting to be older than one's age, though sometimes it led to excesses, or to a deep melancholy that had to be drowned in the heady young wine of Vienna. On one occasion at least poor Ernestine Schnabel, lying awake after midnight and worrying over the whereabouts of her errant son, was rudely roused by a group of young bohemians returning from a studio party to 'deliver' the tipsy youth into his mother's arms, this being the only recorded case of Artur's sowing of wild oats—possibly a case of living up to people far older but not notably wiser than himself.

★   ★   ★

The moral and æsthetic distempers of the intelligentzia had their counterpart in the political and social decadence of the Austro-Hungarian Empire. It was natural that a wide-awake youngster coming from a rather under-privileged environment, but having access to opulent homes abounding in comfort, fashion and luxury would be sensitive to the social injustices of a caste-ridden society like that of Austria in the last brilliant glow of the monarchy. The country was decades behind the more modern democracies and the constitutional monarchies of Europe, with regard to the elementary concepts of social advancement and economic justice. Universal suffrage was not enacted in Vienna till 1907. On the other hand, racial, religious and social discrimination were rife and Anti-Semitism was already on the march in Austria—decades before it played its gruesome part in Germany.

When Schnabel was thirteen years of age, Karl Lueger was re-elected mayor of Vienna on an officially Anti-Semitic programme, and 'patriotic' young hoodlums went about the streets bullying and sometimes beating children presumed to be Jewish. Nothing ever happened to Artur, but at times he was frightened, when he thought himself followed through the streets after dark. A mild liberal reaction, however, had already set in when he became interested in the social and political fabric of his native land.

There were violent discussions between the conservatives and the progressives among the intellectuals of Artur's acquaintance. But their verbal violence was not always convincing. 'The Viennese,' he recalled many years later, 'did not catch fire from the subjects they argued about, but from each other's enthusiasms.' And the enthusiasms themselves were apt to be spurious. For instance, the so-called modern design for a public building (which a few years later had become quite conventional) was the subject of passionate advocacy, because it was denounced as an 'outrage' in the Press. Conformity was the basis of official virtue. Yet no one objected to the laziness, the frivolity, the waste and the ostentation which were the chief remaining attributes of *noblesse oblige* in a dying social order. The Viennese were still too proud of their Imperial tradition, their glittering aristocracy with its titles and uniforms, the charm of their women, their wine and their songs (not those of Schubert, alas!) and above all their famous though threadbare gaiety. At the same time they affected a polite defeatism which on a future occasion was aptly expressed by the fictional World War general who reported that the situation was 'desperate, but not serious'.

Young people of Schnabel's generation heard the 'rottenness' of Austrian society, institutions, morals, art and literature denounced, day after day, by a modern Savonarola named Karl Kraus, widely known as *der Fackelkraus*, because of his editorship of a weekly paper called *Die Fackel* (The Torch). Kraus' ruthless pen spared none—neither powerful individuals, nor sacrosanct institutions, nor the Press. His books—*The Downfall of Culture, Morality and Criminality, Our Demolished Literature*—still constitute a cultural document on the decay of the Habsburg Empire. Kraus fought all manner of corruption, and mercilessly flayed the public idols of his day. At the same time he helped struggling young artists, promoted the works of poets and painters including Franz Werfel and Oskar Kokoschka and later on the composer Arnold Schönberg.

Whatever Artur read—or neglected to read—he certainly could not have missed the diatribes of Kraus. These violent outbursts of righteous indignation—or desperation—made a deep impression on the ripening adolescent, and the spirit of protest engendered by them was to remain a part of him through life. The smouldering discontent among his friends was bound to affect him just at the time when he felt that his apprenticeship was coming to an end, and when other young men on the threshold of professional life discovered that the future lay outside the boundaries of their native land. The decisive

element in his own restlessness was music—and the problem of how he
was to serve it in a healthier environment and a more promising field.

*   *   *

His great steadying influence in these years was Mandyczewski,
the wise and kindly scholar for whom he had a genuine fondness all
through his youth. It was with his help that he was able to explore
the inexhaustible treasure of the great masterworks—Bach, Mozart,
Beethoven, Schubert—for it was in Mandyczewski's library at the
Musikverein that he had access to the authentic texts, some of them
even before the great Complete Editions were published.[1] By delving
in these beautifully printed volumes of largely neglected classics he
continued to broaden his potential repertoire, while others of his age
were occupied in drilling their fingers to overcome the technical
pitfalls of Liszt and his progeny.

How much musical theory Artur really learned from Mandyczewski is uncertain. He himself has said that he never got beyond
the first principles of counterpoint, also that no one ever taught him
musical form or orchestration. However, it is a moot point whether
Artur ever learned *anything* in the conventional way. Essentially he
was self-taught, and his lessons were for the most part a give-and-take
process. Much came to him by intuition, and by direct study of the
masters. He began what he called composing before he could write
notes. Although he had not had any harmony lessons when he first
came to Leschetizky at the age of nine, he improvised correct harmonic
progressions with complete ease and a good deal of originality. When
Ethel Newcomb, a young American pianist, came for the first time
to play in Leschetizky's class and was told to 'modulate' between her
pieces according to the curious fashion of the time, she asked to be
excused, not having studied harmony. Leschetizky immediately
called on little Artur to improvise the interludes for her, which he
did 'quite correctly and beautifully'. Similarly, he found no difficulty
in reading orchestral accompaniments of concertos from the full score.

Artur had, of course, been writing music—in his own lackadaisical
manner—for years. Most of his efforts he destroyed. Now that he
had reached a kind of saturation point in interpreting the classics and
absorbing the more recent works of Johannes Brahms and his lesser

---

[1] The Bach, Handel, Mozart and Beethoven Complete Editions were issued
before Mandyczewski's time. Schubert's works, nominally edited by Brahms,
were completed under Mandyczewski's supervision in 1897; those of Haydn
were entirely edited by Mandyczewski; and those of Weber by his successors.

contemporaries, he began seriously to compose music—and to some purpose. The first fruits were three little piano pieces which he entered in Leschetizky's prize competition of 1897. The Professor, himself a composer of effective and brilliant though rather light piano music, wanted to stimulate the creative urge in his pupils. The three best pieces were to be chosen by a jury of well-known composers, but the final order of awards was to be voted by the assembled class after being performed by the young composers themselves. As usual in such competitions, the pieces were to be 'signed' with a literary quotation in place of the composer's name, which had to be submitted in a sealed envelope. When the entries were examined it was found that all three winning pieces were by Artur, who then graciously yielded two of the prizes to the runners-up. This triumph of the young 'musician who would never be a pianist' went a long way toward increasing his local reputation and raising his own self-esteem. The pieces, which were later published,[1] he promptly dedicated to 'my revered master, Theodor Leschetizky'.

[1] *Drei Klavierstücke.* Berlin, Simrock Verlag, 1898.

6. *Flight from Decadence*

THE Vienna of young Schnabel's time was, in musical terms, the Vienna of Brahms and Bruckner, of Hugo Wolf and the young Gustav Mahler. It was the last flowering of a culture which for a century and a half had spread the glow of a golden age. Like some other golden ages of the past, it became the pride of a generation which had little else to be proud of—the happy memory of a civilization in decay.

As a matter of fact, the heroes of this final phase had rather less than a hero's life. Brahms, the idol of a large and influential intelligentzia, lived a quiet productive existence in a Vienna backwater, while his works were published and performed mainly in his native Germany. Anton Bruckner wrote his nine symphonies in almost complete obscurity, and Hugo Wolf, utterly neglected and derided by critics and colleagues, ended his days in an asylum for the insane. The struggles of Mahler against an obtuse public had only just begun.

During all this time the music-hungry masses lay under the spell of the recently deceased Richard Wagner, while a frantic and senseless dispute between Wagnerians and Brahmsians divided the citizens into two hostile camps. But all parties were united in their adoration of the one genuine native Viennese composer, the waltz-king Johann Strauss!

Young musicians of Schnabel's calibre, on the threshold of their careers, may well have pondered their own situation in this reputed Mecca of Music, and may have doubted the validity of its reputation. Schnabel, always a sceptic, decided that it was undeserved, and that the old musical pre-eminence of Vienna had nothing to do with either its soil or its soul. The capital of the Habsburg Empire had simply been, for upwards of a century, the best European market for practising musicians, and this was due to a lucky combination of circumstances: first, the brilliance of its court, the wealth of its landed aristocrats, and the opulence of its ruling Church—environments in which music was an important function; and second, the fact that during most of this time it had no competition, for northern Germany was hopelessly divided into small and powerless fragments until its unification in the latter part of the nineteenth century.

The first Schnabel Trio, Berlin, 1902. From left to right: Alfred Wittenberg, Schnabel, Anton Hekking

The second Schnabel Trio, 1912.
From left to right: Schnabel,
Jean Gérardy, Carl Flesch

Carl Flesch and Schnabel at Rindbach, 1910

Now that the once mighty Empire was in a state of political and cultural decay, Austria, instead of attracting foreign talent, was being deserted by the talents it produced. The decline began with the rise of Prussia as the dominant factor in a new Reich; an aggregation of many states, with princely courts, all culturally ambitious, and many great and growing cities bulging with the wealth of new industries and an expanding world trade. The fulcrum of German culture had shifted to Berlin, the new federal capital, and the other great cities of the Reich. Germany had dozens of opera houses while the Austro-Hungarian Empire had three or four; dozens of orchestras and choral societies, a rapidly growing middle class, with a much wider distribution of wealth, and an intelligent industrial population—far more emancipated than that of most European states. Berlin, the booming capital of the most populous country in Europe, was a far better springboard for the artist than Vienna, or Paris, or London. Hence the slogan among the young Viennese, in music as in other professions, was 'go north, young man, go north!'

Yet there was still much to attract young Schnabel in Vienna. Since his successful debut he had now played in Budapest, Prague and Brünn. There had been sonata evenings with Rosa Hochmann and many rehearsals for the same. Between engagements there were still the gay Sunday parties at the Löwenbergs, and occasional escapades with the members of the international circle at Leschetizky's. To facilitate this stimulating comradeship, Artur accepted an offer of English lessons from Frau Baumfeld, the sister of his friend Franz Hutter, who remembers that Artur made surprisingly quick progress, but didn't get very far. Finally, there was the advent of Gustav Mahler as conductor of the Vienna Opera, which added new zest to those visits to the 'gods'. With the coming of this impassioned genius and reformer a new era was about to begin in Viennese musical life, closely coinciding with the death of Brahms.

Mahler, at thirty-seven, was not yet the controversial figure he later became, both as director of the Opera and as a composer, although his appointment by order of the Emperor seemed calculated to stir up a hornet's nest of Anti-Semitism. From the day of his debut Mahler was the hero of the young progressives to whom Schnabel, Schönberg and their friends belonged. His revival and rejuvenation of the Mozart operas, in accordance with new standards of stylistic purity, plasticity and dramatic vitality, kindled the wildest enthusiasm among the genuine Mozart lovers and particularly among the professional anti-Wagnerians.

Attending Mahler's first *Don Giovanni* Schnabel and three other Leschetizky pupils went delirious in their gallery seats, shouting bravos for Mahler till after the lights went out. They were the last to leave the theatre, and Artur, taking the score from a colleague, insisted on 'serenading Mozart in the Other World'. Accordingly they repaired to the Mozart monument in a nearby square, and intoned the quartet from Act I, rising to a mighty crescendo in the finale, when a burly Vienna policeman appeared and the Mozart worshippers barely escaped arrest. This was but one of many nocturnal escapades in which Artur along with much older colleagues played a rôle. Not all of them took place in such hallowed or even respectable surroundings as the Imperial Opera, but all of them had at least incidentally to do with music—either classical or romantic and always good, though sometimes 'light'. Many are the tales of intimates concerning the most unlikely places in which he played Schubert waltzes for the delectation of guests and 'personnel' until the small hours of the morning, thus proving very early in his career that music can soothe the most agitated bosoms as well as the savage breast.

The summer of 1897 Artur had spent in Zigeunerwald with his family, surrounded by various followers and friends. Rosa was one of them, and very much in evidence, making music with Artur while others listened. According to eye-witness accounts Schnabel's mother was fighting a losing battle against a bevy of female teenagers developing a sudden abnormal interest in music at the sight of Artur. In these idyllic surroundings, among woods, fields and mountains, it was inevitable that romance should flourish, and it did. The following winter was to be Artur's last with Leschetizky, and presumably also his last fling in Vienna. His patrons' subsidies would soon cease and his complete emancipation was therefore due. Important decisions had to be made, and the question of leaving Vienna was discussed with Franz Hutter and other adventure-minded friends.

At this point his friends the Bondys presented him with a welcome surprise: an invitation for Artur to visit their relatives in Berlin for a rather extended stay, with all expenses paid and a chance to look around. The Berlin cousins were the Cassirers, a remarkable and wealthy family of five brothers engaged in the timber trade, but all of them also more or less interested in the arts. Artur was overjoyed. On April 17th he would be sixteen years old, in other words an adult, according to his standards—and a few weeks later he would be on a voyage, all by himself, to a foreign land. There was just one source of regret: going to Berlin would mean good-bye not only to Vienna but to Rosa, its loveliest inhabitant. The musical flirtation which had begun so innocently had blossomed into full-blown love. But Artur was not one to brood over difficulties for long, and after all Rosa was a concert artist, too, with opportunities in the Big World outside.

*　　*　　*

Accordingly, after elaborate preparations which had occupied his mother and sisters for weeks, Artur set off on a journey which in those days took something like sixteen hours; and on a fine May morning of 1898 a dark, short but well-proportioned young man, rather elegantly dressed, in stiff wing-collar and fedora hat, arrived at the Anhalt Station in Berlin. No one was there to meet him, and a blue-smocked porter lifted his over-sized suitcase into an open horse-drawn cab. Artur leaned back and looked out on the busy station square with an air of owning the earth. The cab moved through streets of impressive proportions, then along a quiet tree-lined canal. The horse-chestnuts were in bloom, the scent of spring was in the air, and the whole town had a clean and orderly look which was excitingly new and strange. The size of the houses and the distances seemed immense after Vienna, and the horse, trotting comfortably over cobbles, took an eternity to reach its goal—the residential Joachimsthaler Strasse—which, as luck would have it, was closed for repairs.

However, a neatly uniformed maid approached the halted vehicle, made a curtsy and asked if this was Herr Schnabel. She had been sent by Artur's thoughtful host to the paviours' barrier with instructions to help him carry his luggage to the house. Artur, always alert for a pretty smile, considered this a good omen and responded by giving the cabby what he considered a magnificent tip, as behoved the honoured guest at a rich man's house.

The Cassirer household was enormous. All five brothers lived there with their families. The children, approximately of Artur's generation, were destined to play important rôles in the cultural life of Germany: one as a philospher, another as a publisher, a third as an internationally famous art expert who first introduced the French Impressionists to many European countries. Artur immediately sensed the atmosphere of well-being, refinement and good taste, and felt at home. He amused himself with the children and generally had a wonderful time. There was no obligation to work and—a novel experience—he was rarely asked to play the piano! Only the head of the house, Herr Eduard Cassirer, wore the customary middle-age beard—with the heavy dignity appropriate to it.

The Berlin of those days was a rapidly growing, bustling place with a somewhat glaringly *parvenu* look in its newer quarters, but retaining much of the charm of a typical old Continental capital. It had splendid shops, inviting restaurants and wide-open cafés with gay, awning-covered terraces extending on to the pavements. Traffic was still relatively quiet; horse-drawn vehicles were the rule, and the new electric trams still ran only on the main thoroughfares. Everywhere there was a feeling of prosperity, enterprise and solidity—with an apparent scarcity of poverty and slums. The growing trade and industry of Bismarckian Germany had made Berlin the most up-and-coming metropolis of Europe, and the most bumptious. The excessive orderliness and strictly imposed cleanliness might have displeased a Westerner, but young Artur, weary of the 'slovenliness' of Vienna, felt that he was in the promised land.

Only two things offended him: the large and vulgarly ornate apartment houses with their two entrances, one of them marked *Eingang nur für Herrschaften* (Entrance for Gentlefolk only), and the exclusive restaurants with signs reading *Weinzwang* (wine compulsory). In Vienna, with all its show of aristocracy and servility, there was an easy-going quasi-democracy which overrode class distinctions. And when it came to wine—why, everybody drank it, rich and poor, but nobody had to. These two Berlinisms were indicative of something vaguely disagreeable—the hard ostentation of the newly rich and the rigid rank-consciousness of the military state.

But there was nothing to deter a young bohemian in his quest of enjoyment, and Artur did it to the full. Relieved of all restraint, he explored the town, found friends or made them, sat in cafés till all hours, arguing, flirting, playing cards or billiards. He rarely rose before noon, sleeping off the previous night's adventures, and ignored the routine of a household which must have been punctiliously run.

As for the purpose of his visit, Artur had brought along his prize-winning manuscripts, and a letter of introduction to the publisher Simrock from one of the most lucrative clients of the house—namely Edouard Schütt, composer of piquant and very popular salon music, and one of the judges in Leschetizky's competition. The venerable Herr Simrock, head of a house that had been founded in the eighteenth century and now the sole publisher of Brahms, was inevitably a man with a long white beard. Cool and courteous, he looked at Artur's pieces and asked him to come back in a week. At the second interview he informed the sceptical young man that the pieces were accepted for publication, on one condition—the title (*Three Piano Pieces* and nothing more) would have to be changed. They would be called: (1) *Douce Tristesse*, (2) *Diabolique*, and (3) *Valse Mignonne*. The budding writer of 'absolute' music winced, but accepted his fate. Artur decided that he had not only acquired a publisher, but learned a lesson about publishers. His career as a composer had begun.

His next errand was to call on Hermann Wolff, the ruling impresario of Germany, presumably with an introduction from Wolff's Viennese counterpart, Albert Gutmann. Wolff was, as far as can be ascertained, the prototype of the entire tribe of impresarios, if one excepts the fabulous P. T. Barnum, who managed Jumbo the elephant and Jenny Lind. Wolff was unique in his profession. For one thing, he had studied music. For another, he had composed music. For a third, he edited the *Berliner Musik-Zeitung*. And finally he decided to become a manager because . . . he liked the company of artists! Wolff also founded the Berlin Philharmonic Orchestra and managed its concerts single-handed, as a private unsubsidized enterprise, until his death. He persuaded Franz Liszt, Anton Rubinstein, Joseph Joachim and Hans von Bülow that they needed a business manager (till then considered superfluous if not degrading). As the autocrat of Berlin's musical life he managed the German careers of nearly all the negotiable musicians, from Brahms to Tchaikovsky and from Sarasate to Adelina Patti.

It was inevitable that Hermann Wolff, too, should wear a beard, for to Artur dignity and wisdom went with beards. He took to Wolff immediately, though he described his attitude as 'curt—even sour' at the start. What impressed him was that 'without any words or fuss' Wolff started him on his public career. He didn't ask for a single photograph, or a single bit of 'publicity'. Artur had to play; that was all. With the advice of Wolff and sundry friends, it was decided that Schnabel should make his Berlin debut in the following autumn.

Meantime there was a little domestic difficulty: Artur, with his dilatory doings and undisciplined habits, had worn out his welcome at the Cassirer home. The head of the house notified him that his room would shortly be needed for a relative. But a more lenient younger brother made it up to Artur by inviting him to stay at a

comfortable hotel (with all charges paid). Artur afterwards boasted
that this suited him very well, since—just by chance, as it were—a
certain young person had arrived at the same hotel from Vienna.
So—for the rest of his stay—young Artur saw Berlin through even
rosier glasses than before. He returned to Vienna before the summer
set in, and was received by friends, relatives and teachers as though
he had encircled the world. And, in a sense, he had.

His first call was on Leschetizky, who received him with unwonted
cordiality—no longer as a pupil but as a guest and friend. The Professor asked him to play for the class on the very next Wednesday
night, as a visiting artist, so to speak. 'In reality,' Artur said dryly,
'there was no difference, except that I was not interrupted and criticized. After all, I had been playing for the class for years.' It was
about this time that Schnabel had been studying Brahms' B-flat
concerto, which was to become his most spectacular war-horse
during the early years of his public career. Usually, when concertos
were played in class, the Professor played the orchestral part on the
second piano. On this occasion he asked Artur's friend Heinrich
Gebhard to 'accompany', and Artur in turn accompanied Gebhard
in the D minor concerto by the same composer. It was a great occasion, and Leschetizky showed his satisfaction by patting both participants on the back, something that rarely happened. From now on,
the Professor regarded him as fully fledged.

Most of his time that summer was spent visiting—at various
mountain resorts of the Vienna region. The one thing he had missed
in Berlin was the mountains; he now realized how much they had
always meant to him. 'The mountains look down into Vienna,' he
used to say, and on every possible occasion he had gone out to look
up at them. His birthplace, too, was nestled in the foothills of real
mountains. Here, in these wonderful months of 1898, he indulged
his passion for walking and climbing, alone and in company—the
company of his first love. In these circumstances music became the
idealized synthesis of the more or less innocent delights of courting
and revelling in the delights of nature. 'For five weeks this summer,'
he explained in a September letter to Madame Brée, 'I didn't play at
all, but surely gained much in repose and security.' At the end,
however, he made up for his inactivity by working hard over the
programme for his coming Berlin debut. 'Right now,' he concludes
characteristically, 'I am practising very little, so that the pieces don't
come out better than good.'

Upon the family's return to Vienna, Artur experienced a great shock: he received the news that a very dear friend, Sigmund Panzer, had fallen to his death on a mountain tour. It shook him so deeply that he couldn't think of anything else for days. It was somehow symbolic that his leave-taking from Vienna should be associated with death.

PART TWO

YEARS OF FRUITION

7. Young Pianist in Berlin

IN September 1898, when Artur set out for a second time, it was for an indeterminate stay in Berlin. He had shaken the dust of Vienna from his feet and its cobwebs from his brain. His friend Franz Hutter had preceded him and was already the proud incumbent of a clerk's stool in a Berlin bank. Artur had armed himself with copious letters of introduction from various Viennese friends to influential relatives and friends in the German capital.

Once again his temporary foothold was the Cassirer house, whose head had forgiven Artur's unorthodox behaviour and whose entire family remained his faithful adherents for life. This time, however, he had planned a thoroughly independent and unfettered life. He and Franz Hutter soon found a cheap place to live in the Steinmetzstrasse—two furnished rooms in the flat of a shoemaker's family, just large enough to house the two, plus a grand piano graciously supplied by the famous firm of Bechstein. The house and the neighbourhood were shabby, noisy and rather depressing, though not too far from the cafés of the Kurfürstendamm—favourite haunts of the bohemians, artists and literati who daily settled the world's problems in endless discussions across marble-topped tables. It was a very great contrast to the opulence and fastidious refinement of his first Berlin abode. He was now on his own, and in hard contact with reality.

The atmosphere of Berlin made him feel that he had left not only Vienna but the nineteenth century behind him. Even in the comparatively poor environment of the Steinmetzstrasse one was conscious of a certain energy and alertness, an air of up-and-doing, and a feeling of confidence, as compared with the slackness and indifference, the jocular defeatism and precious morbidity which were part of the 'charm' of Vienna. There public life was still dominated by an effete aristocracy; in Berlin it was coloured by the mentality of the self-made man and the ruthless drive for success. Growth, enterprise, optimism were in the air. Corresponding to Austria's hereditary caste system, however, there was a rigid class distinction largely based on economic power and modelled on military rank. The social order was regulated by the Prussian ideal of obedience, but even though the middle and lower classes were obedient, they were not servile, as in Austria. More important, they had an increasing share in the good things in life, including the arts and particularly music. The masses of industrial and white-collar workers enjoyed a higher standard of living, better educational and cultural facilities and a far greater sense of security.

Moreover, Berlin as the federal capital was not the only centre of the country's cultural life. Artistic as well as industrial and commercial activities were decentralized. Munich, Dresden, Stuttgart and other state capitals had their royal or princely courts to subsidize theatres and concerts; great cities like Hamburg, Cologne, Frankfurt and Leipzig had their municipal Operas and musical institutions. Germany even at this time had more cities with over 100,000 population than any other country on the Continent of Europe. Indeed, many of these cities, with their own aristocratic and cultural traditions, looked askance at 'upstart' Berlin, an attitude which went hand in hand with a centuries-old dislike of 'colonial' Prussia. All in all, Berlin and Germany presented to the ambitious young artist a far more promising field than existed anywhere else in Europe.

On October 10th he gave his first Berlin recital in the Bechstein-saal, the smallest hall in Berlin but well suited for intimate music, and generally used by debutants. He was sixteen and a half, and in all essentials a man. His programme included some early Beethoven and pieces by Bach, Schubert, Schumann, Chopin and Brahms. The public response was friendly and even vociferous, as might be expected. The papers were cautious but spoke of his outstanding technical capabilities, his sureness of manner and his 'very respectable accomplishments in a purely musical sense'. The stern critic of the *Allgemeine Musik-Zeitung* said that though technically well grounded, he was 'not quite mature' (at sixteen!) but 'a very promising artist'. Later on he repeated the same programme at debut recitals in Munich and Leipzig, with equivocal and curiously contradictory results. In Leipzig he was acclaimed as the natural interpreter of the austere Nordic bleakness and heavy seriousness of Brahms, while he was said to have no access to the colourful, lilting sweetness and charm of Schubert. To the Munich critics he was 'obviously' the southern, Viennese type, wandering gaily and sentimentally through the woods and along babbling brooks. (These respective labels, by the way, stuck to him for years. For Leipzig he was too cerebral; for Munich, too sensuous.)

Two days after the Berlin appearance a young friend of Artur's, the Viennese violinist Max Wolfsthal, made a successful debut in the same hall, and during the following week the two gave a joint sonata recital which firmly established them in the public esteem. It may be mentioned in passing that within a fortnight Artur's charming Viennese *inamorata* Rosa Hochmann, already favourably known to Berlin, gave a more spectacular violin recital in the much larger hall of the Singakademie, thus demonstrating the superiority of feminine appeal. Whether she did this because, or in spite of, her friend Artur is not in the record. But there is evidence that the two young people were still in love.

The level of Berlin's musical life at this time may be judged by the fact that Eugene d'Albert, Ferruccio Busoni, Frederic Lamond and Edouard Risler were all giving piano recitals (Busoni an entire series illustrating the history of piano music from Bach to Liszt); that both Joseph Joachim and Pablo de Sarasate were playing the violin, and Lilli Lehmann was giving a series of song recitals—all during the same month. Arthur Nikisch was conducting the Berlin Philharmonic concerts, Felix Weingartner the Royal Orchestra concerts, while Karl Muck and Richard Strauss were the chief conductors of the Royal Opera. During the year of 1900 Richard Strauss became a permanent resident of Berlin, and conducted the first Berlin perform-ance of his tone poem *Don Quixote* (generally condemned by the critics as an 'ugly piece'). Among the young pianists, besides Schnabel, Berlin in the same season heard Mark Hambourg, the twenty-year-old 'pianistic titan', also Josef Hofmann, twenty-three, Ossip Gabrilo-witch, twenty, and Wilhelm Backhaus, fourteen. The competition was formidable, and on a high plane.

For any young man less self-possessed and independent than Artur this array of youthful virtuosi might have been discouraging. To him, however, they were not rivals, but travellers bound for a different goal. All of them, except little Backhaus, were being groomed for the world celebrity market, with America as the ultimate goal. Hofmann, indeed, was already the darling of the New World. Most of them had financial backing and the benefit of international pub-licity. There is no indication that Artur ever had any such ambitions. He had not been 'promoted' as a prodigy, and the stipend which had supported him during his apprenticeship had ended with his modest debuts under the ægis of Herr Wolff. He was simply expected to make his own way from the age of sixteen. Apart from any material considerations, however, he was at all times conscious of being different. As Leschetizky had said, he was a *musician*, and 'the music' was his sole concern. The music he chose to play was calculated to make this clear. From the very beginning his programmes consisted of works he wanted to play because he loved them or because they presented a particular challenge, and works he wanted to propagate because they were neglected or misunderstood. He deliberately omitted the more 'effective' and peculiarly pianistic pieces which relied upon brilliance, velocity and power. Even at this early age he regarded himself as the servant of music, and not of the listener.

He must have realized even at this time that life was apt to be difficult for an artist of his predilection; certainly not like the virtuoso's smooth series of unbroken triumphs, but full of problems to be solved and opposition to be met. At any rate he never coveted the life of the touring artist—a profession which did not appeal to his pedestrian habits and philosophical temperament. In later years he rationalized his choice by pointing out that the virtuoso was a phenomenon of the second half of the nineteenth century, while he was the belated offspring of a much longer period in which the musical profession was largely stationary, and the functions of performing, composing and teaching music were combined in one and the same person. At this time, without giving much thought to the future, he simply liked Berlin, and the idea of being a resident musician, ready to accept whatever might come his way.

★ ★ ★

At the beginning very little turned up, although the formidable Herr Wolff did what he could to spread his reputation—without the help of 'publicity'. He procured an invitation for him to play at the home of Count Hochberg, then the Intendant of the Royal Opera. On the programme was Mozart's D major sonata for two pianos, in which Artur's partner was the august and somewhat sardonic Karl Muck, then chief conductor of the Opera. This was, so far as we know, the first time he played Mozart in public since he made his juvenile appearance in a Mozart concerto at the age of nine. Whether he already considered Mozart the most difficult of all composers is more than doubtful; in any case he acquitted himself with ease, and he was soon engaged at sundry other musical soirées.

The most curious of these was at the palace of the Princess von Henkel-Donnersmark, who had the reputation of being somewhat peculiar, and certainly lived up to it on this occasion. She summoned the young pianist for a pre-interview and warned him, among other things, not to play any Chopin. 'My guests,' she said, 'are accustomed to the best, and might not like your Chopin interpretations.' (The

Princess was of Polish birth.) Young Schnabel was deeply impressed by the palace, if not by the Princess, and appeared at the concert dressed in his newly acquired evening clothes, his hair slicked down with Pinaud's *Eau de Quinine*. But he found himself and the other artists roped off from the audience 'like animals in a zoo' and forbidden to mingle with the noble guests. Nevertheless some of them conversed with him across the silken rope, and no one suffered in consequence.

This early experience with Prussian aristocracy aroused all of Artur's latent revolutionary instincts, and tended to make him shy away from the musical dispensations of the *haute volée*. Years later he learned that the affair had a sordidly comic aftermath. The peculiar Princess had deducted a hundred marks from his fee, explaining that she didn't like his music, and hated the smell of his hair tonic. Rather than argue about the lady's aristocratic objections, Mr. Wolff had quietly made up the difference out of his own plebeian pocket, and not till after Schnabel had become a celebrity did he learn of his manager's regard for a young artist's sensibilities.

Another proof of this managerial solicitude was to follow a year or so after the first, when Artur, still short of engagements, went on a tour of Norway as assisting artist to Willy Burmester, German violinist and the idol of audiences all over Europe. The tour comprised fifteen concerts within three weeks. Artur had never seen his partner before; when he did, he couldn't believe his eyes. Here was the tall, svelt figure of what he thought must be either a circus manager or a lion tamer, dressed with the exaggerated elegance of a tailor's mannikin. Burmester was probably the most 'decorated' artist of his generation, resplendent with orders from all the royal houses of nineteenth-century Europe. His popular success was fabulous and every one of his tours a triumphal procession. This time he played sonatas with Schnabel, who (thanks to Wolff's insistence) also performed a group of piano solos, after which the 'star' served up the evening's pyrotechnics, with the piano as a mere background. Once only did they play with orchestra—one concerto each. Burmester received the usual extravagant praise from the critics, one of whom said that Schnabel had degraded the lion (Beethoven) to a well-trimmed poodle dog.

Between concerts the eminent virtuoso taught his seventeen-year-old colleague two-handed poker, which noble pastime enlivened all their journeys between concerts. Here, too, Burmester exhibited his wonderful technique, with the result that he won about a thousand marks from Artur, approximately the total of his fee for the entire tour. When Hermann Wolff heard the reason for his young client's empty pockets he fairly exploded with anger and threatened him with the severance of their connexion. He then called Burmester on the carpet and made him disgorge. The two artists never played together again—either Beethoven or poker.

Under the strain of necessity young Schnabel took whatever engagements he could get, the most awful being in Potsdam, where he played a concerto with a military band! There were small concerts of the 'vocal and instrumental' variety in the provinces, usually in combination with other unknowns. Several were in drab little Prussian garrison towns where the officers' corps with their prim wives formed the cultured élite, and the N.C.O.s did the ushering in military style. In one concert a warrant officer counted the money during the first movement of Beethoven's sonata opus 101, at the back of the hall, clinking silver coins on a resounding china plate. Schnabel never forgot this episode as 'one of the most successful frustrations of an atmosphere' in his career and a supreme test of his powers of concentration. Despite these rugged pioneering efforts his impecunious state showed no improvement, and might have become painful but for the frequent meal-time invitations from sympathetic friends.

At this critical point Artur came to know, by way of Viennese introductions, a prominent publisher, a banker and a manufacturer, whose wives—all serious and accomplished students of the piano— asked him to teach them. This piece of good fortune tided him over the dry periods between engagements. Another helpful chore was the engagement to play twice a week for a wealthy young invalid who at a later time would probably have had to be satisfied with the radio.

*   *   *

The most important introduction he had brought with him from Vienna was directed to a middle-aged widow named Rosenheim and her son, a young chemist, later to become a professor at the University of Berlin. Mrs. Rosenheim was a native American, daughter of the German-American banker Hallgarten who had emigrated to the United States in 1848 and made a great fortune. After her marriage Miss Hallgarten returned to Germany and now, as a well-to-do widow, lived in the fashionable Tiergarten quarter with her bachelor son. The coming of the talented young Viennese, who combined with his great artistic gifts a genius for sociability, wrought a revolution in their staid though comfortable home. They both loved music and Dr. Rosenheim played the piano, but neither of them had any contact with professional musicians. They admired Artur because of his music and soon loved him for his character and personal qualities. He not only reciprocated their affection but was fired with the desire to enrich their lives.

With the memory of those charming, sociable and artistically rewarding Viennese parties at the Löwenbergs still fresh in his mind, he suggested the transplantation of the institution to Berlin soil. The idea was accepted with enthusiasm, and conditions proved to be ideal for the purpose. Artur already knew a number of young musicians, some home-grown, some Viennese, some foreign—who needed the conviviality and the spiritual warmth of such a home, and who welcomed the acquisition of a private platform for their art. There were violinists, pianists, singers, ensemble players and—most important —young composers whose works needed to be heard. There were amateurs as well as professionals, who would make music together for the love of it, and there were just music-lovers, writers and artists who made up an ideal audience. Berlin's fine and expanding conservatories were increasingly attracting foreign students and artists, and such house concerts were bound to attract an international group.

Thanks to Artur's talent for companionship and his taste and ability in devising programmes, the Rosenheim apartment was filled every Sunday, just as its Viennese prototype had been for years. Soon the Rosenheims were obliged to acquire a large town house and garden to accommodate the swelling crowd. While the great majority of performers were professionals, the characteristic and most agreeable feature was the informal mixing of professional and amateur, and the consequent attainment of genuine spiritual participation by those present. The performances reached a high degree of quality and variety, and a great many new works as well as new performers were first heard in this famous Berlin home. For upwards of two decades these cosmopolitan assemblies constituted one of the most stimulating forces in the musical life of the capital.

Artur's personal relationship to the Rosenheims became very close though hardly intimate. Eventually he came to fill a place which in other circumstances would be that of a younger son ; although in this case the 'father' and elder brother were combined in the one person—Dr. Artur Rosenheim, who was some ten years older than Schnabel. Although the two spent many hours, days and— during holidays—even weeks together, Artur continued to address

Dr. Rosenheim formally, and both used the formal pronoun *Sie* rather than the familiar *Du*. Artur visited the Rosenheims frequently during the week, playing for them, planning the programme for the following Sunday, and occasionally playing a quiet game of cards.

It may be said that Artur's social life and his professional activity were closely intertwined, and that both increased rapidly in volume and variety. Professionally he was fortunate in having a small number of extraordinarily talented and agreeable pupils, all older than himself, whose homes provided the kind of cultured environment to which he was accustomed. The husband of one of his lady pupils, Frau Anna Lehmann, was head of the Cotta publishing house (which first published the works of Goethe, Schiller and other German classics of the eighteenth and nineteenth centuries). Frau Lehmann had herself been a prodigy, a pupil of Moszkowski and Leschetizky, but owing to the prejudices of her socially prominent family she was prevented from following a professional career. The moment she heard Artur play, Frau Lehmann, then the mother of two children and one of the busiest hostesses of Berlin society, was galvanized into new artistic activity. She recognized him at once, as she later avowed, as the greatest pianist she had ever known, and begged him to teach her. From this time on Artur became a constant guest in one of the most distinguished literary homes of Germany. Herr Lehmann himself was a talented *littérateur*, and wrote witty comedies and parodies for home performances, with Artur as one of the actors—especially at Christmas, which he celebrated with the Lehmanns every year.

Quite a different aspect of his sociability was activated by his room-mate Franz Hutter, who had the reputation of being a 'wild fellow', at least among Artur's more sober friends. Both of the young Viennese bachelors were unattached and fancy-free, and revelled in their complete emancipation from family control and educational supervision. Much of their time was spent in cafés and other nocturnal haunts patronized by the intelligentzia of Berlin. In Vienna Artur's youthful roistering was done in private, for the listless loafing of the ubiquitous Viennese café sitters never appealed to him. Perhaps, also, he was too young. Now, in cosmopolitan Berlin he patronized the Café des Westens and other bohemian rendezvous far into the night—holding forth on weighty subjects such as politics and the scandals of the day. Artur delighted in shocking his listeners with extravagant absurdities concealing an essence of truth, with startling paradoxes and twisted syllogisms. He was a virtuoso in perpetrating bad puns, and composing those amusing couplets known as *Schüttelreime* (jumbled rhymes), for which he later acquired a dubious fame. He, Hutter and their compatriots, having played taroc in Vienna, now learned the German card game of skat, which was rapidly becoming the favourite pastime of musicians. Artur also was a fair hand at billiards, but this was a mere interlude to the more sedentary occupation of settling the current problems of politics, literature and the arts.

*　　*　　*

Artur's literary taste was undergoing the transformation that might be expected with the change of intellectual climate. In place of Austrian pessimism and defeatism, the air was filled with the optimism and self-satisfaction of an increasingly powerful and prosperous people. There was a great deal of arrogance and swashbuckling on the part of the supporters of the established order, as personified by the young Kaiser and the German officer class. But little of this, curiously enough, found its way into contemporary German literature. The predominant tone of writers was rather one of protest and warning. The greatest example of this was still Nietzsche, who was as tragically misunderstood by the pan-Germans of 1900 as he was by the Allied propagandists fourteen years later. There was a strong note of social protest in the dramas of Gerhart Hauptmann and of Frank Wedekind, whose bold exposure of vice and decadence was anathema to the moralists, as were the dramas of his Swedish colleague Strindberg. There was a bitter strain of protest in the polemics of Maximilian Harden, the editor and sole writer of *Die Zukunft*—an essentially conservative counterpart of Austria's Karl Kraus.

These were all subjects of lively discussion in Artur's group, and the favourite humorous weekly was, of course, *Simplicissimus*, which lampooned and caricatured all the events, acts and functions of government and society, in so far as they were considered harmful, dishonest or corrupt, with a peculiarly biting sarcasm and sardonic wit. The Prussian junkers, the profiteers and the philistines of the Kaiser's Germany were the favourite targets of its writers and cartoonists, who did not stop at an occasional bit of *lèse majesté*. Artur took great delight in this particular journal, along with the more genteel, literary and artistic *Jugend*—both of which were published in Munich.

Among the novelists who appealed to him were the romantic E. T. A. Hoffmann, the visionary Adalbert Stifter, and the realistic and bitter Otto Julius Bierbaum, some of whose verses he later set to music. He was still not a very persistent reader, but the range of his mental activity was extraordinary, and he had a more than average awareness of social and political developments, as well as the literary and artistic movements of the time. Like many other gifted people, he seems to have absorbed knowledge and information by a process of mental osmosis. His command of the German language, too, was remarkable for its rich vocabulary and its literary phraseology. He was inclined to talk, as the saying goes, 'like a book'. According to his own testimony, however, he continued to suffer from his own peculiar kind of indolence or 'alertia'. He worked very little at the piano, slept late in the morning and generally 'wasted time'. Nevertheless, his musical thinking was beginning to bear fruit in another direction, for he was again beginning to compose.

★   ★   ★

Once again, in the summer of 1899, Artur took a trip to Vienna to visit his family and friends and to spend another holiday near the mountains. It was to be his last for some years: indeed, the most compelling attraction, his youthful romance, had come to an end.

During this visit he made the acquaintance of a somewhat strange young man, his senior by one year, and exceedingly sophisticated if not mature. His name was Hanns Sachs, and like his medieval namesake, he was given to poetry. The son of a Vienna lawyer, he was obliged to study this dry science, but later turned to psychoanalysis under the direct influence of Sigmund Freud. At this moment, when Artur's creative desires were re-awakened, Sachs proposed to write for him an opera libretto based on E. T. A. Hoffmann's story, The Pot of Gold. Neither text nor music ever got beyond the first sketches, but Artur did eventually use one of Sachs' lyric verses (Das Veilchen an den spanischen Flieder) for a song.

Back in Berlin in the autumn, Artur prepared for two more recitals in the Bechsteinsaal, presumably financed by his friends the Rosenheims. In the first, Schubert's A major sonata, opus 120, was the principal item, along with compositions by Bach, Joachim Raff (curiously enough) and the four Brahms pieces (opus 119) which years ago had roused the ire of Leschetizky. Then, as if to propitiate his old master, he played a Siciliana all'antica by Leschetizky himself, and the Three Pieces of his own which he had dedicated to him, and which were about to appear in print. In the second recital he ventured to play Beethoven's Eroica Variations and was promptly rapped over the knuckles by one critic who considered that he was not yet 'ripe' for this particular work.   On the whole, however, he not only scored a resounding popular success, but earned the almost unanimous praise of the critics, who considered that he had gone a long way toward fulfilling the high hopes aroused by his debut.

8.   Romance in Rastenburg

IN January 1899, some three months after the sixteen-year-old Schnabel first electrified a Berlin audience with his playing of Schubert and Brahms, a tall and handsome young contralto earned her first Berlin laurels as a lieder singer—also with the emphasis on Schubert and Brahms. This was the dark-haired, black-eyed Therese Behr, a native of the Rhineland, who after a series of provincial triumphs was now taking the citadel of German music by storm. She displayed a gorgeous, velvety, dark-timbred voice which, together with an exceptional power of expression, caused the Berlin critics to compare her with the greatest lieder singers of the past. The editor of the *Allgemeine Musik-Zeitung* proclaimed that 'a genuine high priestess of the art has arisen once again'.

Neither the young singer from Mainz nor the youthful pianist from Vienna was conscious of the coincidence of their appearances. And neither of them had ever heard of the other when during the following winter they were engaged to appear together in a remote East Prussian town. The occasion was the first concert in a joint tour which offered its audiences a mixed bag of singer, pianist and violinist at a bargain price. It was one of those run-of-the-mill engagements which Herr Wolff's concert bureau arranged by the dozen every year. This one comprised seven cities of East and West Prussia, from Memel to Markrabowa, and the concert party consisted of Therese Behr, Artur Schnabel, and a violinist named Franz Schörg, pupil of Ysaye and *premier prix* of the Brussels Conservatory.

Artur and Schörg set out from Berlin and travelling all night reached Rastenburg, a grim, empty, snow-covered town, before dawn. On the way to their rooms in the typically drab hotel they passed a pair of ladies' snow boots standing outside a door. 'Look at the size of those boots,' said Artur with mock horror in his voice, provoking a snicker from his friend. Three hours later, in the breakfast room, they met the statuesque Miss Behr, who exhibited two rather small and daintily slippered feet, saying, 'Do you really think they're so big?' The young men covered their embarrassment by exaggerated laughter and a few moments later the three young artists were friends. Miss Behr mentioned the necessity of rehearsing her songs with the new pianist. But Artur, with characteristic abandon, suggested a sleigh-ride, to have a look at the Russian frontier, before they began. Presently a *troika* was speeding them through the crisp and sunny countryside toward the Russian border, which proved to be surprisingly far away, and they finally got back barely in time for tea and a quick once-over rehearsal for the singer and her strange but amusing accompanist—who would insist on playing his own compositions to her instead of the programmed songs! Despite this unexpected diversion, all went well at the concert, for Artur could sight-read not only the music but seemingly also the singer's mind.

Miss Behr was enchanted. In fact, the concert and the whole tour were one long *crescendo* flirtation that threatened to reach *sforzando* more than once. During concerts Artur noticed a curious little object near the music rack of the piano: a miniature porcelain figure of a roguishly grinning, squatting Chinese mannikin which, it turned out, had been surreptitiously placed there by Miss Behr. In the broad dialect of her native Mainz she called it *das Chines'che* (the Little Chinaman) and she had carried it with her everywhere, ever since she had acquired it under dramatic circumstances as a young girl. She swore that when placed on the piano at concerts it unfailingly brought good luck. It did so, of course, on this occasion—in more ways than one—and Artur loved it from the moment he experienced its mysterious powers.

When the concert party reached the beautiful city of Königsberg it encountered a colleague named Fritz Kreisler, whom Artur remembered from boyhood days in Vienna, and who now roused the young man's jealousy by asking Therese to let him—a mere violinist—accompany her on the piano at a future concert, a project which he actually realized the following year. However, when the six-foot Therese and the five-foot-four Artur arrived at the end of their journey, the romantic period had definitely set in. Since both lived in Berlin, and since Artur had urgently to show her some more of his songs, it was clear that they would see each other occasionally, to say the least.

The further outlook was none too bright. There were grave considerations and more than the usual obstacles to a possible match. There was as large a difference in years as there was disparity in inches: Artur was nearly eighteen and Therese twenty-three and a half. She came of a rather well-to-do German Protestant family, with a doting and watchful father who would certainly disapprove. There was also the difference of religion (or 'race') which would almost surely arouse parental opposition on both sides. And finally he was a virtually penniless youngster with extravagant tastes, prodigal habits and a dubious future, while she was a young lady of good conservative family, with a corresponding sense of responsibility, who as an artist had already 'arrived'.

A month later, in March, Therese Behr gave her second Berlin recital of the season. The programme, it was noted, was predominantly serious. The impact of her encounter with the all-too-young, impetuous and yet so appealing young pianist may well have been reflected in her singing. To quote one Berlin critic, 'the listeners were carried away by the inwardness and the warmth of her interpretations, so that after each song there was a demand to hear it again'. As for Artur, he was lifted into another world. Here was a great artist, expressing in another medium what he had striven to express in his—the spiritual elevation and the depth of meaning which in this particular kind of music is also conveyed by the text. Artur had come to love lieder as a child, particularly those of Schubert. Often, in a mood of overflowing happiness he had rushed to the piano, played Schubert songs by ear, while 'singing'—more correctly, shouting—the melody with his peculiarly uncouth immature voice, sometimes to the distress of the neighbours. Many years later he advised a class of students to devote some time of each day to 'communing with Schubert' through his songs.

To him the lied was 'the last, the most tender and the most individualized form of absolute music—yes absolute, for the words are merely a device to make the melody singable and therefore human'. In Vienna he had heard lieder from singers of varying ability, and often accompanied by himself. But he had never heard them projected with so much feeling, with such illuminating changes of tone and subtlety of nuance, such intensity of expression as now, from Therese Behr. He himself had tried his hand at writing songs for some time. He now determined to concentrate on this task, and to persuade Therese to sing them. A new chapter had begun in his career.

That summer, instead of going to Vienna, he accepted an invitation to visit his friends Dr. Otto Pringsheim and his wife at their country house in the Upper Silesian mountains. Here, in the quiet home of a scholar, Artur had the repose and the leisure that is supposed to favour creative thought. Here he immersed himself in the works of Richard Dehmel, Stefan George, Otto Julius Bierbaum, his friend Werner Wolffheim and other contemporary poets. And here he turned out (with a certain singer in mind) the first of the lieder which were later published as opus 11.

His principal recreation, as usual, was walking through the woods and fields, but this time it alternated with the Pringsheims' favourite one of tennis, and soon Artur became a fairly good player. Later that summer he paid a visit to his poetic friend Hanns Sachs at Innichen-Pustertal, in the Austrian Tyrol. The two young men were still talking about their operatic project, but Artur was at this time more interested in some romantic verses which Hanns Sachs had written and which might be suitable texts for songs.

*   *   *

Therese, as a well brought-up young lady of twenty-three, was spending the summer in Mainz with her family, which consisted of the parents, a brother named Hermann and a younger sister, Adele. Father Behr was part owner and artistic director of the celebrated firm of Bambi & Co., interior decorators, architects and makers of custom-designed furniture. He personally was responsible for the interior design of many fine buildings and some of the more famous German ocean liners of the time. Therese's brother was a conductor of the symphony orchestra at Breslau, and a composer of sorts. She herself was endowed by nature with a voice of phenomenal range, which misled her first teacher, the famous Julius Stockhausen in Frankfurt, to train her as a coloratura soprano! Her father then sent her to the Cologne Conservatory, where she had the wise counsel and assistance of the director, Dr. Franz Wüllner (father of that remarkable lieder singer, Ludwig Wüllner). From the age of seventeen she gave regular demonstration recitals at the Conservatory and a year or two later began her public career, singing in oratorios and recitals in most of the larger cities of Germany.

She made a first tentative Berlin appearance in 1898, when Otto Lessmann, a leading critic, discovered a flaw in her tone production and advised her to consult Etelka Gerster, the former prima donna of the Berlin Opera and later one of Germany's most successful teachers. In the course of a year the fault was remedied and Therese shone forth as one of Gerster's brightest stars. Her reappearance in Berlin in 1899 was the first of a continuous series of triumphs and the beginning of her career as a lieder singer of the first rank.

Highly gifted and excellently trained, Therese Behr interpreted the music she sang with an instinctive sense of phrasing and emphasis. She was essentially a musician and not just a singer, just as Artur Schnabel was first and foremost a musician and incidentally a pianist.

She applied her 'sixth sense' for musical expression not only to the songs but to instrumental music, where her critical ability came to be of value to others. With characteristic discrimination she selected for her partner at the piano not the usual type of accompanist but a pianist of real distinction, namely Alfred Reisenauer, who at that time was one of the leading German concert artists and a composer of some standing. Later in her career, Therese was selected by composers like Richard Strauss to sing first performances of their works, and Strauss even went to the trouble of transposing some of his songs (notably *Traum durch die Dämmerung*) specifically to suit her voice.

★   ★   ★

When Therese decided to study in Berlin she found a small apartment on the ground floor of a house in the Wichmannstrasse (Charlottenburg), where an older relative, Lili Walldorf, acted as her companion, chaperone and general factotum. Here Artur now became a frequent visitor, sometimes with his friend Franz, but more often alone. They made music together; studied together, planned programmes together and deepened their mutual admiration. Here Artur sent her his songs, accompanied by short and humorous notes and comments, and one by one she learned them for future use. Gradually she gained an insight into his personal difficulties, his failure to work hard, to make the best of his talents and fully to carry out the mandate of his genius. Very early in their acquaintance she exercised her maternal instincts, and at times scolded him roundly for his faults. His dependence on her increased with the years, and every separation from her was harder to bear than the last. At first it was she who was most frequently away on professional journeys, for she always had engagements while for long stretches he had none.

Artur was glad for Therese, yet jealous at the same time—not only because of her successes but because she had chosen another artistic partner before he himself appeared on the scene. Alfred Reisenauer, at forty, was after all a man with an established career, and here was Artur—far closer to Therese—sitting idly by. To make matters worse Reisenauer was said to be rather fond of drinking and not always reliable. At this point Therese, about to give a Berlin recital with him, asked Artur's advice. Could she continue to trust the man who at this moment was ill and unable to rehearse?

But how could Artur know, and how could he be objective, even if he knew? Therese suggested that he listen clandestinely to their next rehearsal and—in case of emergency—take over. Accordingly he and Franz Hutter staged a sort of Italian comedy, with both of them listening silently from an adjoining room. Alas! all went well—or fairly well. But by the time the recital took place Artur had determined there must be a change. The programme was a motley array comprising not only the classics but Tchaikovsky, Felix Weingartner, Hermann Behr and—Reisenauer, of course. Worst of all, the public devoured this mixture with gusto. The critics surpassed themselves and even went out of their way to praise Reisenauer for his 'courage' in acting as an accompanist and ignoring the foolish prejudice which considers accompanying a lesser art.

Artur was disgusted. 'There must be no further accompaniments by Reisenauer,' he shouted. And, understandably, Therese agreed. As it happened, Artur had given his own recital a fortnight before and scored his greatest success to date with a programme that was the very antithesis of Therese's with Reisenauer: Weber's completely neglected A-flat major sonata, the *Twenty-Four Preludes* of Chopin, and pieces by Bach and Brahms.

Shortly before the crucial recital with Reisenauer, Artur had introduced Therese to one of the Sunday gatherings at the Rosenheims. She sang, with him at the piano, Schubert's *Kreuzzug* and moved the assembled company almost to tears. The collaboration of the two artists and their complete absorption in the work was an unforgettable experience, and the deep impression they made was a clear indication of what should happen in the future. Each of them had reached a certain degree of accomplishment and public recognition; both had independently staked their claim as artists of rank in a certain field. There could be no objection to combining their efforts in making both kinds of music live again in the fullness of the composer's intention. In complementing each other, neither would detract from the other's domain: Artur would play works for piano and Therese would sing songs. It meant a new kind of programme planning: combining music for two different media bound by an inner unity to achieve a satisfying artistic whole.

That winter they worked together as much as circumstances permitted, exploring the wide reaches of song literature, studying whole cycles, just as Artur had studied the sonatas—from the original editions—and eliminating the extraneous matter, the misinterpretations and the 'expressive' nonsense of editorial hacks. Their first great encouragement came from an unexpected quarter—a music dealer and concert manager in Königsberg, where they had appeared together ten months before. This highly respected businessman, Otto

Hübner by name, was an amateur of music in the literal sense of the word, and had by his meritorious efforts raised the cultural tone of his community to a new level. Deeply impressed both by Miss Behr's singing and Schnabel's playing he had suggested that the two prepare Schumann's *Dichterliebe* and perform it in his city on a future occasion. He now repeated his offer for the coming spring. Had he perhaps guessed, when he selected the cycle entitled 'Poet's Love', that Heine's imaginary romance might nourish a real one? In any case the concert, set for March 26th, 1901, was destined to be more than a concert, or even an exceptional concert. It began with a Bach fugue, followed by Beethoven's *Six Sacred Songs*, and continued with Schubert's posthumous B-flat sonata followed by the entire *Dichterliebe*. It was without doubt very beautiful music superbly performed. Yet who would have thought that this programme would have a popular success in a provincial town and that the news of it would spread so that it would become a 'request' programme in several other towns? It did, and for years the so-called Königsberg Programme was performed innumerable times by popular demand.

Moreover, the programme became 'historic' in the two artists' lives. Under the spell of the music and the inspiration of the moment, they decided to unite not only their art but their lives. That night they became secretly engaged, and the date was engraved on what was later to be Therese's wedding ring. It was a truly moving climax to the season's work, and a mighty spur to new accomplishment. Artur, the 'lazy' youth, made a great resolve—to conquer the world for his Therese.

For reasons already indicated, the secret remained a secret, so far as the parents and the outside world were concerned. Only close companions like Franz Hutter learned what was in the wind. The two returned to Berlin and resumed their separate tasks for the present. Therese was off to sing in Beethoven's ninth symphony in her native Stuttgart, and Artur settled down to a new composition—a piano concerto with which he hoped to startle the public of Berlin.

Once again that summer Therese, closely guarding her secret, went home to her parents in Mainz. Left behind in Berlin by his beloved, Artur began to suffer the pangs of loneliness, perhaps for the first time in his life. He had never wanted for company, and had habitually worn his heart on his sleeve. Even his earlier adolescent love-affair had imposed no undue emotional strain. Now for the first time he had 'plighted his troth'. He had found his soul-mate, and the solace of this sweet and noble woman had filled his consciousness completely.

They had become partners in life and in art, to share each others' sorrows and joys, to surmount their difficulties and march together toward a single goal.

They were like two halves of a single sphere, and the pain of parting was well-nigh unbearable. Artur, the younger and more impetuous, appears to have suffered the most. He had made her promise to write him daily; his letters to her had to be sent surreptitiously or camouflaged in formal phraseology. Disconsolately he poured out his heart in songs, which he continued to produce in the pauses between the work in hand. At the end of June, at the peak of a Berlin heat wave, and waiting in vain for Therese's letters, his patience burst. He wrote her a woebegone epistle that mirrored the emotional crisis through which he was passing. Next day, having received two letters, he apologized for 'weeping in her lap'. He sent her his latest song, a setting of Theodor Storm's *Hyazinthen*, which he said was 'quite different' from his others and more difficult. But he felt sure it 'would suit her voice' and then plunged into a dithyramb about her singing. 'I would never have believed it possible that anything could become pure emotion so completely as your singing of [Schubert's] *Gretchen am Spinnrade*.' What seems to have overwhelmed him at this moment was a feeling of comparative impotence —the inability to create something that would be worthy of her stature as an artist. Even while working on his concerto he continued to grope for something which he visualized vaguely, a sort of hymn for a woman's voice with orchestra—but where to find the text?

About the middle of July 1900 he left Berlin for Kryschanowitz, the Silesian retreat of his friends the Pringsheims. Here he continued to work on the score of the concerto. At the end of August he writes to Therese that the work is completed and that he is to play it on November 17th with the Berlin Philharmonic Orchestra 'before an invited public [*geladenem Publikum*] in both senses'.[1] In the same letter he speaks of sending her several more songs, and refers to two joint engagements for him and Therese in Munich and Breslau. These were the first of many joint recitals on the model of the famous Königsberg Programme that the Wolff bureau was to arrange in Germany. The career of a great voice-and-piano team had begun in earnest, and so had a new chapter in the two artists' lives.

---

[1] A typically Schnabelian pun: the German word *geladen* may mean either 'invited' or 'full of fury'.

9. Early Struggles

THE season of 1901-2 was to prove an important milestone in Schnabel's career. He was now a professional musician in his own meaning of the word—a man who performs, writes and teaches others to perform or write music. Moreover, the word 'perform' was to be interpreted in the broadest sense. But despite all the excellent Berlin criticisms his provincial engagements were few and far between, partly because he was young and new and partly because he limited himself strictly to what he considered to be his assignment, making no compromise with the prevailing demand. Already he had the dangerous reputation of a 'specialist' in the lesser-known works of Schubert and the still not widely popular Brahms. His complete avoidance of the current favourites and of all bravura pieces was certainly not helpful to his manager, and his abhorrence of all showmanship and publicity did not increase his chances of success.

Ever since Leschetizky had labelled him a musician rather than a pianist, his chief preoccupation had been with the great romantic literature from Schubert and Weber to some of the profounder Chopin (especially the *Twenty-Four Preludes*), also certain works of Bach and the sonatas of Beethoven's middle period—music which at this impressionable age of the youth had the force of a religious experience. Now, at the threshold of manhood, his whole being was stirred by his love for Therese Behr, who personified his feminine ideal and who seemed to him to be a perfect instrument for the music he adored. The exploration of his favourite music with her was pure bliss, and writing songs for her to sing a constant spur to his imagination. He was still casting about for an appropriate text for an extensive work for solo voice and orchestra that was to be exclusively hers.

In October he was to accompany Miss Behr on a month's tour of the Baltic provinces, both Russian and German. It was to start in Riga (then under Russian sovereignty) and end at Marienwerder, on the Prussian side. Elaborate preparations were made and the two young people were thrilled in expectation of the journey into unknown parts, when suddenly there was a hitch. After spending hours and hours, day after day, in the ante-room of the Russian consulate, Artur was still waiting for a visa when the day of departure approached. The Tsar's government was very particular about admitting 'non-Aryan' foreigners (although the term was yet to be invented) to Russian territory. No pleas or pulling of wires were of any avail with the Tsarist bureaucrats, and Artur was so furious that he literally wept at being left behind. At the last moment a capable substitute pianist was procured at Riga, in the person of the Latvian pianist and composer Hans Schmidt (not to be confused with Artur's first Viennese teacher Hans Schmitt), who filled the Russian dates to the satisfaction of all concerned except Artur, who was twiddling his thumbs in his lonely Berlin flat, while Therese Behr experienced the most spectacular triumph of her early career. This reached its climax in the Estonian capital of Dorpat, where the students of the university lined her carriage route in gala array from the hall to her hotel and sang her a choral serenade. As soon as she returned to German soil Artur boarded her train and they finished the tour together in the neighbourhood of their first meeting twenty months before. Early in November they were back in Berlin for their first joint recital in the newly built Beethoven Hall, which was to be the scene of many years of happy work for both.

A fortnight later, the pair repeated their already famous Königsberg Programme featuring Schumann's *Dichterliebe* cycle and Schubert's posthumous B-flat sonata, performances which the critics regarded as 'beyond all praise'. The concert was generally regarded as an event, though few could have foreseen that these joint recitals would for decades to come be one of the most popular features of Berlin's musical life. In the course of that time the Behr-Schnabel team achieved a unique distinction throughout Germany and Scandinavia as model protagonists of the lied.

Before her departure for the Baltic tour, Miss Behr, in keeping with her rising position in the world, had taken a much larger and more representative apartment at the top of the same Wichmann-strasse house. When she returned she found the new abode furnished and ready, thanks to the ever faithful Lili, and presently she was joined by her young and exceedingly pretty sister Adele. She also found her old ground-floor flat occupied by Artur and his enterprising friend Hutter, who had been quick to seize this opportunity for acquiring a presentable bachelor establishment. The new arrangement, besides being very comfortable, proved to have great practical advantages. For the first time the two young men-about-town had a *ménage* of their own, complete with cook and maid-of-all-work.

There was a room adequate to house the Bechstein grand, and Artur could now teach his pupils at home and use his spare time for rehearsing with Therese, working on their joint repertoire when she was not on tour. Moreover, Therese could keep a watchful eye on his work, and his letters show that she did exercise some influence on the still lackadaisical young man. ('I am learning the [Beethoven] G major concerto *for you*', he dutifully reported.)

Artur certainly needed her discipline, for his own career was due for a new start. His generous friends the Rosenheims had arranged for the first performance of his own piano concerto with the Berlin Philharmonic Orchestra under its 'permanent' (i.e., routine) conductor Josef Rebicek, a most estimable musician. This was, of course, a semi-private affair, on a Sunday afternoon, calculated to give him the opportunity he had been waiting for—to play with an orchestra, perform his own composition, and make a somewhat bigger splash in the teeming waters of musical Berlin. Thus the nineteen-year-old composer earned the wildly ecstatic approbation of his numerous friends and followers, but only the most grudging and patronizing acknowledgment of the critics, who warned him not to get intoxicated by the applause, but rather learn from this first experience how to do better next time! Only the scherzo-like second movement was credited with having a chance for survival.

Cast in the conventional classic-romantic mould and following the symphonic four-movement pattern of Brahms, the work certainly had all the earmarks of youthful immaturity. Nevertheless it was a remarkable proof of talent for a young man who had never composed anything larger than a song or piano piece and who had never had an orchestration lesson in his life. Artur himself seems to have had no illusions about this concerto, for he promptly buried the score under a mounting accumulation of papers. There it was discovered twenty years later by his young disciple Eduard Erdmann, who insisted on reviving it with another Berlin orchestra as a hoax, disguising the composer's name under the transparent pseudonym 'Lebec'. Only one critic discovered the trick; the rest were more tolerant of 'Monsieur Lebec' than their colleagues had been of Herr Schnabel two decades before.

If Schnabel's concerto did not set the River Spree on fire, his playing of it certainly gave a new impetus to his reputation as a pianist. Of all the younger pianists appearing in Berlin at this time, none aroused such lively interest—as something new and different. The general impression was that here was not only a very great pianistic talent but a strikingly original musical personality. The growing opinion that he was an authentic interpreter of great music, gifted with unusual insight and great intellectual power, was strengthened by two further recitals, one of which included early Beethoven sonatas, the other devoted entirely to Brahms. There was, however, a certain air of superiority and even cockiness in his manner that evidently got on some critics' nerves. One patronizing scribe, Dr. Erich Urban, writing in the leading musical monthly *Die Musik*, felt bound to issue a 'warning' against

'the evil enemy who now awaits the favourable moment to take permanent possession of this young artist, so full of promise; namely superciliousness and self-adulation. . . . Like Zeus enthroned above mankind, Schnabel reigns over the works which have the honour to rise from beneath his fingers. When these creations are of gigantic proportions one may tolerate this haughty hovering above them, this contemplation from the angle of eternity. But such a stern and exalted attitude is downright ridiculous in pieces of charming modesty [*sic*] like Beethoven's A major sonata. . . . Here the appropriate approach would be Mozartian gaiety . . . and not this Schnabelian *pomposo*, by which one never knows who is more important, the player or the composer.'

Anyone who knew and heard Schnabel in his later years may recognize the germs of some of the critical reactions which often led to a complete misunderstanding of his character and his attitude, in which humility toward the works he played and reverence for their composers were the decisive elements. Even at this youthful age a psychologically inexperienced observer could be misled, by his almost forbidding seriousness and his excessive effort at concentration, into thinking him disdainful and proud. But even the testy Dr. Urban, who objected to 'the self-conscious depth of his shirt-front' and the dropping of the 'h' from the name Arthur as silly affectations, conceded that he 'grasped the spirit of a musical work with certainty and expressed it with unfailing decision'; also that he had 'a splendid, effortless and extraordinary technique' and that his tone was 'of exalted beauty, with pearly clarity in the runs, soft and singing in the cantilenas, and of metallic vigour in the forte'. What else was there to wish for?

Despite the fine notices in the Berlin papers, however, Artur was still virtually without provincial engagements in this fourth season since his German debut. His prospects, such as they were, now suffered a real blow, for the excellent Hermann Wolff, his manager and protector, died after a long illness in February 1902. To his junior partner, Herr Fernow, Artur was evidently just another young pianist among many. Nevertheless, like old Professor Leschetizky, this rather timorous businessman may have recognized that he was eminently a 'musician', and this may be partly responsible for what was now to happen.

*   *   *

One day Artur received a call from a much older colleague, the Dutch cellist Anton Hekking, who proposed to establish a Trio. Hekking, besides being a first-rate artist, was also something of a practical joker, and it was this incorrigible habit that had made him a freelance with time on his hands. Hekking had been instrumental in the founding of the Berlin Philharmonic Orchestra and had been its solo cellist for fourteen years, during which period he had exercised his curious sense of humour on many occasions—to the embarrassment of both conductors and players. One day at rehearsal, so the story goes, a strange and ghostly hum was heard, which turned out to be not of musical but of entomological origin. May-bugs were to be seen issuing from the *f*-holes of Hekking's cello, whose owner could not explain the phenomenon and finally found himself suspended by the orchestra which, he felt, owed him a better reward.

Now, having returned to his old stamping-ground after three tours of America, this seasoned performer with a keen flair for quality gladly followed Mr. Fernow's suggestion to take young Artur Schnabel as a partner in what turned out to be a unique artistic enterprise. As the third member of the ensemble, these two selected one of Joachim's best pupils, Alfred Wittenberg, a violinist noted for his ravishingly beautiful tone. The plan was to give Berlin music-lovers a popular-priced series of chamber music evenings, in the tradition of the former Bilse Orchestra, at whose popular concerts the audience sat at tables while beer and other refreshments were served. An initial series of ten trio concerts was announced for that spring to take place in the Oberlichtsaal of the Philharmonie—a spacious foyer adjoining the large Philharmonic Hall. The traditional tables were put in place, and the admission was (as at the old Bilse concerts) fixed at the uniform price of one mark (then worth a shilling). Beer was served between numbers, but this later became obsolete because the music itself proved to be sufficiently satisfying to the audience. The programmes were to consist ·of classical and, on occasion, modern trios, with solo pieces—instrumental or vocal—in the middle. Artur Schnabel, the junior member (just sporting his first moustache), took the leadership of the ensemble and full charge of the programmes as well. The first concert set the standard and pattern for the rest. It comprised trios by Beethoven (E-flat, opus 1, No. 1) and Schubert (B-flat), between which two masterpieces the individual artists played pieces by Josef Suk, Bach and Brahms respectively. Schnabel gave the final popular touch with a series of Lanner waltzes, played (according to the critics) 'with delicious grace and humour'.

The concert had a fantastic success, and the series caught on like wildfire. Subsequent evenings were usually sold out, and eventually the tables had to make way for additional listeners. The *Allgemeine Musik-Zeitung* ventured to hope that after this good beginning the new ensemble would become a serious factor in Berlin's musical life. This proved to be a prize understatement, for the concerts became an institution which lasted for years, and ceased only because the individual artists had become too celebrated to spare the time. After the first few years the Trio moved into the much larger Beethoven Hall. In the course of its existence it gave masterly performances of virtually the entire trio literature, besides solo and duo sonatas, with vocal solos by guest artists and occasionally works for larger ensembles. A considerable number of contemporary works had their first performances at these concerts.

Quite logically the Trio received its initial try-out at the Rosenheims. To Artur Schnabel these trio evenings meant first of all an extension of his social-musical activity beyond the select Rosenheim circle into the democratic region of cheap popular concerts. It gave him an excellent opportunity to prove the wide appeal of the choicest kind of great music, and an incentive further to explore the field of contemporary music, in which he was naturally interested all his life. In addition, these concerts and their preparation filled out a good part of his unemployed time, and this was an excellent tonic for his morale, for he was never one to spend his time practising, with no concerts to practise for.

Another boost to his self-respect came from the critic of the *Vossische Zeitung*, Dr. Max Marschalk, who not only wrote favourably about him as a composer but was willing to back up his opinion in a practical way. Marschalk was himself a composer and, being the brother-in-law of Gerhart Hauptmann, he had written the incidental music to the great dramatist's poetic plays. He and several associates had established a new music publishing house called Drei-Lilien Verlag, which now offered Schnabel a contract to publish all his output over the next five years. Artur accepted it with alacrity, refusing a more conservative proposal by the old Berlin firm of

Bote & Bock, to whose head he was introduced by Leschetizky, just
then on a sort of state visit to Berlin.

★   ★   ★

The old Professor, accompanied by the third Madame Leschetizky,
arrived in April—just in time to hear the Schnabel-Wittenberg-
Hekking Trio give their fourth concert to a sold-out house. Artur,
despite a preliminary attack of 'stomach cramps, terrible migraine,
etc.', was in fine form and afterwards reported to his Therese that
they played the Schumann trio with tremendous dash and success,
and that all the aforesaid ailments proved to be only nervousness,
'for as soon as I sat at the piano they were. finished'. It was an
auspicious reunion with his once so 'cruel' teacher.

For six solid days Artur acted as guide and host to the white-
haired Professor, attending a round of cultural and culinary festivities,
of which the most lavish took place in his own bachelor home.
Proudly he reported to the absent Therese: 'bouillon, lobster, fillet
beefsteaks, poularde, salads, marrons, California fruits, and—the
magnificent cigars for which I send you my innermost thanks.' Also:
'red wine, white wine, and sweet champagne (Veuve Cliquot),'
adding apologetically that 'Leschetizky likes it only that way.' They
were at table for three hours for this 'luncheon'. He and Hutter
accompanied the visiting couple to a play, a Wintergarten show
('boring'), a lunch at the Austrian Ambassador's, etc. But the climax
came on Sunday, when Artur introduced his old master at the Rosenheim party, and the Professor played Rubinstein, Chopin, and pieces
of his own. 'I had one of my greatest musical impressions,' writes
Artur; 'every bar an image; richness, form, colour, warmth, fire,
dash, life—in head and heart, in the fingers, the most sensitive finger-
tip nerves—all this and much more is in the playing of the wonderful
old man. Even his own shabby pieces impress one as exciting because
of his enormous vitality and his unique personality.' Thus Artur,
brimming over with enthusiasm for the seventy-two-year-old master
who 'treated him so badly' in the days gone by.

It is clear from his letters that in spite of no engagements he was
in high spirits, and that he was obviously in the swim. He reports
to Therese that the French violinist Jacques Thibaud (of whom both
were very fond) and his wife were in Berlin, and that Edouard Risler,
the great French pianist, has 'honoured me, the up-and-coming
young talent—with a long, comradely, charming and amiable chat'.
And if he were not so lonely for Therese, he adds ironically, his 'cup

Concert-Direction Hermann Wolff.

BEETHOVEN-SAAL.

Donnerstag, den 7. April 1904, Abends 7½ Uhr

Sechster (letzter) populärer Musik-Abend

der Herren

Artur Schnabel, Alfred Wittenberg
(Klavier)   und   (Violine)

Anton Hekking
(Violoncell)

unter Mitwirkung des **Vocal-Quartetts**

der Damen **Jeannette Grumbacher de Jong** (Sopran), **Therese Behr** (Alt)
der Herren **Ludwig Hess** (Tenor), **Arthur van Eweyk** (Bass).

Brahms-Abend.

PROGRAMM: Trio H-dur op. 8 (Neue Ausgabe). — Liebeslieder, Walzer für
4 Singstimmen und Klavier zu 4 Händen, op. 52. — Trio C-dur op. 87.

Eintrittskarten zu 2, 1,50 u. 1 Mark sind in der Hofmusikalienhandlung von
ED. BOTE & G. BOCK, Leipzigerstr. 37, sowie Abends an der Kasse zu haben.

BEETHOVEN-SAAL.

Donnerstag, den 14. April 1904, Abends 8 Uhr

CONCERT

von

Willy Burmester

unter Mitwirkung des

Herrn **Coenraad V. Bos.**

PROGRAMM: **L. v. Beethoven:** Violin-Sonate D-dur. — **F. Mendelssohn:** Violin-
Concert E-moll. — **J. S. Bach:** Chaconne. — **R. Schumann:** Aus fremden Län-
dern; Träumerei. — **J. S. Bach:** Präludium für Violinsolo; Air. — **J. P. Rameau:**
Gavotte. — **Padre Martini:** Gavotte. — **W. A. Mozart:** Menuett.

Eintrittskarten zu 5, 3 und 2 Mark sind in der Hofmusikalienhandlung von
ED. BOTE & G. BOCK, Leipzigerstr. 37, sowie Abends an der Kasse zu haben.

Programme of one of the early concerts of the
first Schnabel Trio, 1904

of bliss (?!) would be full'. What really bothered him was that Risler had 'so many engagements, and I have none—not one, although Leschetizky has had a talk with Fernow'—Fernow, whose efforts seemed to result in nothing better than hack work, such as 'accompanying aspiring singers who expect to have Therese Behr's success by hiring her accompanist'. Some of them even flattered him by choosing to sing his own songs. He took these chores because he felt he had to, and worked at them honestly, but he didn't like them.

Engagements or no engagements, Artur was not really suffering, what with lobster, poularde and Veuve Cliquot. Dinners, concerts, parties ('Friday at Madame Gerster's—performing Schnabeliana all evening'). His own twentieth birthday made him sad, but—

'I received [as presents] the *soi-disant* child of your own sensational trunk, for "tails" and linen only—a wonderful thing; also a very beautiful tie; stick and umbrella; loads of flowers! But what a bother to be the centre of things, and having to send so many thank-you's, especially when *you're* not here.'

All in all it may be said that at nineteen and twenty Schnabel was finding his feet in Berlin. Artistically and socially, if not economically, the professional musician was on his way.

★   ★   ★

This may be the appropriate place to take a look at the attributes which characterized the pianist Schnabel at this stage of his career. What immediately struck the knowledgeable Berliners was the beauty and variety of Schnabel's tone, the *Anschlagskultur* (cultivation of touch) which even to discriminating musicians was something new. He seemed to play, not with his fingers but 'with his ears', producing a finely differentiated scale of timbres and dynamics—within the tones of a melody as well as within the composite tones of chords. Young Werner Wolff (later a well-known conductor), who began to study with him at this time, has compared his treatment of the piano to Arthur Nikisch's treatment of the orchestra, which drew from it all the beauty and colour of the different instruments. Equally important was his poignant sense of rhythm, the delicate use of accents and the natural modelling of a phrase. Guiding both his tone and his rhythm was an instinctive understanding of the phrase, its inner meaning and its eloquence. Another feature was his perfect *legato*: he 'sang' his melodies, and never forced the tone beyond its natural capacity to produce vibrant sound. His use of the pedal was sparing and accurate, yet highly ingenious in exploiting the colours of the instrument.

He made at this time a rather free use of *rubato*, and tended occasionally to hurry a passage, but this was an involuntary physical reaction of which he was apparently unconscious. His runs were never a mere fast succession of notes: they were phrased, musically articulated and integrated with the melodic line. Finally there was already at this early stage a perfect intellectual comprehension of the structure of a work, and the subtle relationships of its various parts to each other. It was this, more than mere visual or oral memory, that enabled him to remember and reproduce so enormous a part of musical literature. For even in his teens this ability bordered on the phenomenal.

A casual acquaintance, the German painter Franz Wildhagen, has given us an example of this in recounting an incident of the year 1901. At that time both Wildhagen and young Schnabel were having their portraits painted in the studio of a prominent German artist, George Mosson—Wildhagen by Mosson's pupil Walter Bondy, and Schnabel by Mosson himself. He was being portrayed seated at the piano, and filled out the time by playing while the painter worked. Wildhagen ventured a number of requests for different pieces, which Artur unfailingly satisfied. Finally young Artur said: 'You seem to know so much about music; now *you* make the programme I am to perform here.' From then on, for two solid weeks, during two hours each day, the young pianist played whatever he was asked to, without once repeating himself! On being complimented by his listeners Artur, then nineteen, remarked with an air of objectivity: 'You know, I played just about as well as this when I was fourteen.'

10. Start of the Great Career

IT would have been abnormal if the course of true love had run smoothly, in these or any other two artists' lives. The very conditions of such dual partnership—of profession and affection—carry the seeds of discord within them. It would have been a miracle if the strains of the clandestine love affair between a still adolescent and struggling beginner and a far more mature and patently successful artist had not caused emotional and psychological conflicts. All available evidence shows that Artur Schnabel, at nineteen and twenty, between periods of spiritual elation, was subject to attacks of doubt and black despair, of self-abasement, and uncertainty as to his artistic validity, emotional sincerity and moral strength. Time after time in his letters he complains of his weaknesses of character, his inability to work, his incapacity to give his best to what he considered his appointed task. Time and again he measures his own 'artistic pretensions' against Therese's superior artistic powers.

'You,' he writes, 'have individuality of emotion; I only have individuality of style. What is the good of all this planned perfection, as against one single, sudden spontaneous bar? . . . Tonight I felt with horror that my piano playing is something dead, completely devoid of radiance and life. It's all so fine, so fine. Oh, I am surfeited with this *finesse*. Where are freshness, power, courage, audacity? . . . I can't let myself go; I haven't it in me.' There is no doubt he needed not only her love but her moral support, her belief in his genius, and the consolation she could give him in his pessimistic moods. Time and again in their periods of separation he poured out his heart, and invariably with the conclusion: 'We must marry!'

But she still hesitated. Much as she loved him, she had very definite misgivings about her suitability for this allegedly fickle young artist, who had the reputation of carousing in dubious company, and who had so fatal an attraction for the opposite sex. A painful example of this particular affliction occurred shortly after his move to the Wichmannstrasse house. This experience, added to Artur's instability, Therese's doubts, and fears of her family's opposition brought their relationship to a crisis, which culminated in Therese's offer to release him from his engagement. This he rejected vehemently and by the following spring they were closer to each other than ever before. Plans were made to break the news to Therese's family at a favourable moment and pave the way to marital happiness.

Artur was still seeking a suitable text for the projected work for voice and orchestra, and his friends had been searching the pages of German literature for months. In the summer of 1902 someone suggested Goethe's poem *Die Aussöhnung* (Reconciliation), and Artur promptly set to work. Once again he spent the better part of the summer with his friends the Pringsheims, and the composition was ready for performance at his second privately organized orchestral concert in Berlin during the following season. This summer's letters from Kryschanowitz are particularly affectionate and rather disconsolate. Superstitious like most performing artists, he begs Therese to let him have the Little Chinaman as a keepsake and a mascot to bring him the much-needed professional success. Indeed, the Little Chinaman appears to have been very busy that summer and autumn, for the following season opened far more auspiciously than any previous season in Artur's life. It may be said to have been the beginning of his great career.

The season of 1902–3 opened early with the resumption of the Schnabel Trio concerts to sold-out houses. This was now one of the hardy perennials of Berlin's musical life. Among the early guests were Therese Behr, singing songs by Schnabel, and the great Ferruccio Busoni playing the piano part in his own *Cello Variations* and giving way to Schnabel in the performance of his *Piano and Violin Sonata*. In October Artur played the Schumann concerto in Magdeburg— the first of many orchestral engagements in the provinces. Next the Trio went on a successful tour in eastern Germany which disgusted our young purist because of concessions made to so-called popular taste and the uncouth behaviour of his older colleagues. The first of his joint recitals with Therese was sold out far in advance and there was no longer any reason to doubt the drawing power of anything he undertook. Only his manager remained sluggish, until Artur precipitated an open row which eventually had its effect, but not until higher powers intervened.

The decisive factor was the all-powerful conductor Arthur Nikisch, idol of the German public, who after one interview with his young namesake engaged him to play the Brahms B-flat concerto (then regarded as the acme of monumental pianistic masterpieces and a crucial test of virtuosity) with the Berlin Philharmonic Orchestra playing in Hamburg, Germany's second largest city and Brahms' birthplace. As for Berlin itself, the all-important and much-desired orchestral debut had to be contrived by kind and generous friends, who simply engaged the Philharmonic Orchestra, conducted by Josef Rebicek, for a special concert at which Artur played not only the Brahms B-flat but also, *mirabile dictu*, the first Berlin performance of a concerto by Ignace Paderewski, the pianistic lion of the day. Between these two works Schnabel's own setting of Goethe's poem *Aussöhnung*, written for Therese Behr, was to be performed by her and the orchestra. This rather curious combination of offerings was evidently designed to prove the young artist's virtuosity, his interpretative powers, and his gifts as a composer at one fell swoop.

The concert certainly accomplished its purpose, in so far as the friends were concerned, although the critics had their reservations both about Paderewski and Schnabel as composers. But the *clou* of the occasion was obviously the Brahms. Here the Berlin pundits gave him good marks while saying that, measured by d'Albert's monumental performance, he did not quite exhaust all its possibilities. Schnabel, not yet twenty-one, took this success in his stride. When three weeks later he played the work under Nikisch, the effect was electric and the Hamburg press hailed it as an extraordinary performance. A still living and competent contemporary, then a piano student, reports that the 'completely unknown youth' threw every other pianist she had ever heard in the shade.

The ultimate judgment was given by the great conductor, for he immediately engaged the radiant Artur to play the B-flat concerto in that musical holy of holies, the Gewandhaus in Leipzig, also the Brahms D minor with the Philharmonic in Berlin. Both of those performances turned, as expected, into triumphs for the young artist, although one Leipzig critic took Nikisch to task for choosing a mere lad for so profound a work. He admitted his great talent and accomplishment; but one just couldn't be a Brahms player at that tender age! Nevertheless, such was the Leipzigers' love for their newly discovered genius that his appearances became almost *de rigueur* on subsequent New Year's Days—the traditional gala concerts of the Leipzig season ever since Mendelssohn was the conductor of the Gewandhaus Orchestra.

It was clear that with these three performances young Schnabel had 'arrived' in Germany. What is more, he had proved himself a worthy candidate for the hand of the woman of his choice, who in his eyes was a greater artist than he. Indeed, Therese had been making new conquests of her own. She had appeared in London as

CONCERT-DIRECTION HERMANN WOLFF, BERLIN W.

Montag, den 30. November 1903. Abends 7½ Uhr pünktlich

IV. Philharmonisches Concert

Dirigent: **Arthur Nikisch.**

Solist: **Artur Schnabel.**

PROGRAMM.

1. Ouverture zu der Oper „Genoveva" . *R. Schumann*

2. Concert für Klavier mit Begleitung des
   Orchesters No. I, D-moll op. 15 . . *J. Brahms*
   Maestoso.
   Adagio.
   Rondo (Allegro non troppo).

3. Idyllische Ouverture, Es-dur . . . . *E. N. v. Reznicek*
   (zum ersten Male).

4. Symphonie No. VIII, F-dur op. 93 . . *L. v. Beethoven*
   Allegro vivace e con brio.
   Allegretto scherzando.
   Tempo di Menuetto.
   Allegro vivace

   Concertflügel: **BECHSTEIN.**

V. Philharmon. Concert: Montag, 14. Dezember 1903

Dirigent: **Arthur Nikisch.**

Solisten: **Berthe Marx-Goldschmidt, Ernst v. Possart.**

Beethoven: Ouverture zu „Leonore" No. II. — **Schillings:** Hexenlied (zum
ersten Male). — **Weber:** Concertstück F-moll. — **Berlioz:** Symphonie
Fantastique (zur 100jährigen Geburtstagsfeier).

Das Verlassen des Saales nach Beginn des II. Theiles des Concerts kann — um Störungen während
der Symphonie etc. zu vermeiden — nur durch die rückwärtige Thür (bei den Stehplätzen)
bewerkstelligt werden.

Links: Programmbücher à 80 Pfennige.

Rechts: Programmbücher à 80 Pfennige.

Programme of Schnabel's first appearance as a soloist, at the
age of twenty-one, in the Berlin Philharmonic Concerts
under Arthur Nikisch

a soloist with the Hallé Orchestra under Felix Weingartner, and as the result of a notable performance of Beethoven's ninth symphony had become a member of an all-star Vocal Quartet [1] which was to play an outstanding rôle in Germany's concert life during the next few years. Again Arthur Nikisch had reserved the first appearance of the new Quartet for a Gewandhaus concert. The Quartet's obvious choice of a pianist and coach was of course Artur Schnabel, and so it happened that Nikisch and Schnabel appeared together, playing the four-hand accompaniment to Brahms' *Liebeslieder* waltzes at the Gewandhaus, to the great delectation of the Leipzig audience—a pleasant and amusing prelude to the young virtuoso's appearance as soloist some months later.

★   ★   ★

'There is a tide in the affairs of men which, taken at the flood . . .' For most young men in Artur's enviable position, it would have seemed, the time was now—to 'lead on to fortune'. Almost overnight he had become a favourite, not merely of audiences but particularly of conductors. For here was a young man who could be relied on to give a good and beautiful performance under all circumstances—if need be without rehearsal—and where is the conductor who doesn't need to economize in terms of rehearsal time? 'When I was young,' Schnabel used to say in his later years, 'conductors liked me because I needed no rehearsal; now that they *need me*, I make *them* rehearse.'

Be that as it may, his reputation now travelled beyond the German borders, and as a result he was invited to London by Dr. Hans Richter to play the Brahms B-flat concerto—some six weeks after he played it in Leipzig. He should have been thrilled at the thought of appearing in the world's capital with the famous Hallé Orchestra under its equally famous conductor. No doubt he was; and probably somewhat frightened, too; for he had never been outside the German-speaking empires, and was most conscious of what he called his monoglot condition. And when he first saw London, on a raw February day after a fairly rough Channel passage, the impression on the still barely mature though precocious young man must have been bewildering. His own word for it was 'colossal'.

The city, he thought, was not only grandiose but beautiful, and the people were both charming (*charmant*) and polite. But his lack of English made him feel awkward and less than naturally responsive.

---

[1] Its members were Jeannette Grumbacher, soprano; Therese Behr, contralto; Ludwig Hess, tenor; and Arthur van Eweyck, bass.

He was fascinated by the life, just as he had been by the liveliness of Berlin in comparison with his too easy-going native Vienna. But he was not attracted to it in the same way—as a place to live in and become a part of. It was too big, too strange, and there was no one to make him feel at home. He was to stay at a hotel—Previtali's in Arundel Street, patronized by generations of musicians—where he had 'two rooms with six windows' reserved for him at fifteen shillings a day (no meals). Such friends as he had were strangers in England like himself, but there were many—enough to be invited out for all his meals. The most congenial of them were the members of the Bohemian String Quartet (Hoffmann, Wihan, Suk and Nedbal), who came to call on him two by two. This was evidently a case of love at first sight and the beginning of a life-long companionship, although all four men were anywhere from ten to twenty years older than he. They talked and joked and planned all the music they would play together—and did—in the years to come. Finally the 'dear fellows' of what he called the Unshaven Quartet took affectionate leave by kissing him on both his pudgy cheeks.

By contrast with them he seemed a mere boy, with his delicate, downy moustache, his luxuriant black hair carefully parted on the left, his wing collar and cravat, his elegantly tailored clothes, his polite and fastidious ways. There is no doubt that he charmed everyone he met, and that he would have loved London as he was destined to do many years later, had it not been for its overwhelming strangeness, his homesickness for Therese, and—the cold. 'I don't exactly freeze here,' he wrote to her, 'but I am constantly cold—as cold in my fur coat as in my shirtsleeves.'

On the day of the concert he had the fright of his life. Driving to Queen's Hall in a hansom cab, with no idea of London distances and metropolitan traffic, he was terrified every time the cabby had to stop and wait—'eternities by contrast to my quickening pulse'. He arrived barely in time, thus escaping what would have been a disgrace, for, as he had just learned, the concert was to be attended by the Queen! His most vivid recollection was that Her Majesty sat at the end of the balcony, just behind him, and as the audience applauded after each movement, he had to make a complete volte-face each time and make a special low bow to her. At the end, after the sixth recall, he couldn't help feeling a little foolish. As to the performance, he said he played with much animation, that the orchestra produced beautiful tone throughout and that the cello solo in the slow movement of the Brahms B-flat concerto was 'wonderful'.

Criticisms in retrospect are sometimes more quaint than revealing, but in view of Schnabel's later position in England it is interesting to note that even then the leading papers were cautiously favourable and discriminating, without mentioning the artist's youth. The *Times* critic, who evidently had no liking for Leschetizky pupils, praised him for having 'preserved his individuality and his musical nature unimpaired'. Crediting him with 'almost ideal piano playing' he concluded that 'Herr Schnabel's success was unquestionable'. An enthusiastic writer in the *Musical Times* went all out in his admiration and astonishment:

'He not only played the beautiful work with consummate mastery but with the rarest insight into the master-mind that conceived it, and thus proved himself an artist of exceptional worth. The greatest piano concerto of modern times, it is also the most difficult, but Herr Schnabel might have been playing a simple sonatina, his demeanour at the instrument was so unaffected and natural and his superb piano playing so different from certain long-maned pianoforte lions who might be mentioned. *Ars est celare artem* indeed! . . . More legitimate playing we have rarely heard in recent years.'

Six days after this truly triumphant entry Artur gave the customary debut recital before a full Bechstein Hall and, in the words of the same paper, 'fully confirmed the good impression he had made'. He played the still wholly neglected Schubert A major (posthumous) sonata, which *The Times* surprisingly called 'one of the most beautiful sonatas of all time'; two early sonatas by Beethoven, Brahms's *Four Ballads*, opus 10, and some Schumann. This time the critic discovered that, like many young players, he was impetuous in rapid passages, but that he 'could evidently do whatever he wants in the way of technique'. The brilliance of his first reception had not been dimmed.

Less than two months later he was back in London, to give a second solo recital and a joint concert with Otie Chew, a violinist who had engaged him for a number of joint recitals in Germany some months before. The reasons for this connexion were obviously more economic than artistic, for the lady was hardly in his professional class. It is likely, however, that she was responsible for Schnabel's second visit to London, when he gave only one recital of his own and one with his unfortunate partner. 'It is true that she played better than usual,' he reported after the concert, 'but I just can't put the right spirit into it when I have to act the part of a steam-tug.' The critics were on the whole polite, but *The Times,* which only two months before had spoken of Schnabel's 'almost ideal piano playing', seemed to have become confused, for it commended Miss Chew while deprecating her partner! His own recital this time was poorly attended, though the small audience made up in enthusiasm what it lacked in numbers. 'I believe that my London success is already on the wane,' he commented rather wistfully, yet with a nonchalance which points to a remarkable disregard of the material interests at stake. The best way to explain it is, perhaps, that at twenty-one as at fourteen he was essentially a musician rather than a performer. Any latent ambition he might have had to become an international celebrity seems not to have entered his consciousness.

On his way home he dutifully stopped at Kiel to play Beethoven and Brahms concertos before a highly enthusiastic if provincial audience. It was the tail-end of the busiest season of his budding career. In the course of it he had played at least eight times with symphony orchestras, had given three Berlin and two London solo recitals, besides an indeterminable number elsewhere in Germany and Switzerland, also quite a few joint recitals with Therese Behr and with his *bête noire* Otie Chew. He had participated in over a dozen trio concerts, with programmes varying from Bach to Pfitzner, from Rameau to Vincent d'Indy, from Chopin to Rachmaninof! He had accompanied sundry singers (and resolved never to do it again) as well as the new Vocal Quartet. A number of his songs had been performed, some of them new, and in the intervening hours an increasing number of pupils had been instructed.

The reputedly indolent young man who had done all this had just celebrated his twenty-second birthday!

*   *   *

He knew, or must have known, that he was now an established success, and that wider and wider recognition was bound to follow. But what was uppermost in his mind and heart was Therese, his chosen and undoubted love and life companion. He had become, despite the disparity of their ages, her equal as an artist and competent to be her responsible partner and mainstay in the battle of life. Yet here they were, at the end of another year's work, departing in different directions instead of coming together for recreation, rest and planning for next year: he off to Silesia to visit his friends, she to her parents' home in Mainz. These enforced perennial separations were becoming ironical. They were a strain on both their nerves, and their still clandestine correspondence was becoming more and more painful. They had finally determined to make an end of this sham: Therese was to prepare her father and bring about a meeting with Artur. After all, he was now of responsible age, a young man with a growing reputation and a most promising future. The 'confrontation' seems to have taken place some time during the autumn of 1903 in Berlin, and after considerable correspondence Artur received a 'fairly conciliatory letter' from the old gentleman during the following July. In any case the secret was now out, and both parties were free to tell their friends. 'Now all I need to do,' wrote Artur, 'is to reconcile your father, then I can challenge the world!'

The news had reached Artur in Kryschanowitz and he lost no time telling his hosts the Pringsheims and the Jachmanns that he and Therese intended to marry 'next spring'. His letters to his fiancée, written during a mountaineering holiday with the Rosenheims, are full of ardour and happiness, optimism and boyish high spirits. 'I have you before me always, happy at last and therefore more dear and a thousand times more beautiful. All those superfluous tortures are finally at an end.' In his new feeling of triumph and derring-do he climbed the Ortler, one of the highest and most arduous peaks in the Austrian Alps, after having 'done' the Cimone a few days before. His health, which had been giving him quite a little trouble, was excellent again and his nervousness gone. He wrote to Therese that he and the Rosenheims had toasted the future bride in the best available champagne.

It was already late August, and on September 4th he had an engagement to play Beethoven's G major concerto—the one he always put off learning—in Baden-Baden. Nothing daunted, the whole party moved on to Karersee, near Bozen (Bolzano), hoping to get a piano for Artur to practise on. Seemingly the piano was no trouble, but when he got there they found that the resident German poet Ludwig Fulda was in the process of brooding over a *magnum opus*. So Artur and his Bechstein had to be installed in a hayloft over the carriage shed, and a few days later the G major was ready for performance at last. The public was duly appreciative and, to make his happiness complete, Therese came over from Mainz to hear it. It remained her favourite concerto for life.

11. Berlin at its Best

BERLIN during the first decade of the century was an extremely pleasant place to live in. It was a real metropolis, with all the amenities of modern life, but not yet the seething, monstrous inferno that noise and speed, brutality and greed were to make of great cities in the power age. Germany was at the crest of an optimistic wave, owing to the country's sudden prosperity and new importance in the world. This was also the heyday of the New Germany in 'shining armour' but before the sabre-rattling had begun to affect the people's nerves. Although there was considerable show of opulence on the part of the newly rich, the prevailing tone was set by the large and growing middle class, which preferred comfort to elegance, education and culture to frivolity and show. In the cultivation of literature, the drama and particularly music, Berlin was in the vanguard of Europe, and its educational facilities were attracting students from all over the world. Despite the stiff-backed Prussian aristocracy with its rigid social code, the morals and manners of the capital were definitely on the easy side.

Artur Schnabel felt at home in Berlin from the first. He was never homesick for the Vienna of his youth; he rarely visited it and didn't particularly like it when he did. He had no trouble making friends and quickly became surrounded by the same kind of people he had always attracted—intellectuals, better-class bohemians, artists, wealthy amateurs, and a sprinkling of aristocrats. The principal nucleus of his social activity was the Rosenheims' house, where by now a large segment of the musical profession and its devotees forgathered—especially the younger generation. Before very long he also came to know the Mendelssohns, perhaps the most distinguished musical family in Berlin, in whose houses the great figures of the older generation held court, among them Joseph Joachim, violinist and musical patriarch of the Brahms generation.

In Artur's time there were two Mendelssohn brothers, Robert and Franz, both bankers, whose families occupied neighbouring villas in Berlin's wooded suburb of Grunewald. Both families strove to maintain the tradition connected with the name of the great Felix, by the cultivation of the finest music in their homes. Robert von

Mendelssohn played the cello, his brother Franz the violin. They owned some of the finest Stradivarius instruments in existence. Both were excellent amateurs but Artur once remarked slyly that he had heard more exquisite tone produced on lesser instruments in his time. He often played sonatas with them, especially with Franz, in whose house he was the more frequent visitor. Their musical parties were more exclusive than those of the Rosenheims, and generally limited to the people who actually made the music. Guided by the venerable Joachim, the Mendelssohns were distinctly conservative in their taste, and reserved in their attitude to everything modern. However, the standard of performance was very high, although—or, as Artur maintained, *because*—both professionals and amateurs took part. Incidentally, Franz von Mendelssohn's charming and witty daughter Lilli, also an excellent violinist, married a highly talented composer and conductor named Emil Bohnke,[1] whose music was not exactly old-fashioned and who later, in his capacity as viola player, performed some of Schnabel's most modern compositions—though not in the Mendelssohn home.

Several times Artur played with the septuagenarian Joachim, whose style and attitude he then thought outmoded. Thirty years later it dawned on him that Joachim was not only the highest authority on chamber music but that he had been invariably right. Another occasional partner at the Mendelssohns was Eugène Ysaÿe, a wonderful artist whose playing made a great impression on the young pianist, though he realized that to Ysaÿe chamber music playing was just an 'excursion into unknown regions'.

With his first Philharmonic engagement under Arthur Nikisch young Schnabel entered the charmed circle created by Hermann Wolff and his remarkable spouse Luise, the fabulously capable, sagacious and at times sharp-tongued hostess of the 'Philharmonic dinners' at the great manager's house. These occasions dated from the very beginnings of the Berlin Philharmonic Concerts, originally organized by Wolff, who had selected Hans von Bülow as the first conductor and Nikisch as his successor. They took place immediately after the Sunday morning public dress rehearsal during the Philharmonic season, and usually occupied the entire afternoon, being always attended by the conductor and soloists of the concert and a diverse assortment of distinguished guests, including the internationally famous artists who happened to be staying in Berlin. The entertain-

---

[1] Emil and Lilli Mendelssohn Bohnke lost their lives in a tragic car accident in the 1920's, being survived by three lovely children.

ment on these occasions was, in Schnabel's words, a 'delight to body and soul: exquisite food and wines, a brilliant, stimulating and amusing group of people'. Among the regulars of this convivial assembly were, to name only a few, Eugene d'Albert, Teresa Carreño, Lilli Lehmann, Ferruccio Busoni, Karl Muck, Vladimir de Pachmann, Fritz Kreisler, Arthur Nikisch as a matter of course, and sometimes Richard Strauss. Discussion ran high but the tone was light, being as a rule set by the witty and jovial railleries of Herr Wolff and— later on—his widow and true successor, who was jocularly referred to as the 'Queen Luise' of the musical world.

It was here that Schnabel came to know the great figures of contemporary music and, indeed, the cream of Berlin's intelligentzia. The man who particularly impressed him was Busoni, both as a performer and as a composer. He was fascinated by his vibrant, incandescent personality, his penetrating intellect and his quick if somewhat impish wit. He was keenly interested, too, in d'Albert, who like Busoni had turned to composing but still held the heavy-weight title as *the* Beethoven player of his time. Schnabel was certainly less attracted by this rather grotesque figure than by Busoni. 'If Busoni and d'Albert had been combined into one,' he once said, 'the result would have been one of the greatest musicians of all time: for d'Albert was the raw material and Busoni the refinement.' As for Nikisch, the first great conductor to appreciate him, he found him 'more amiable than warm, always somewhat detached'. More-over, Nikisch was a passionate poker player, and ever since his first Norwegian experience Artur had avoided this particular sport. But he was completely devoted to the man who had done so much to advance his early career.

*　　*　　*

The musician who of all Frau Wolff's guests was to influence young Schnabel most powerfully was Richard Strauss. Artur admired him as a composer, notwithstanding the strong Wagnerian influence in his works; and he was soon to have an opportunity to appreciate his tremendous gifts as a conductor and an interpreter of the very music he himself loved most. He did not, however, agree with Strauss' social and political views, which at that time were not only conservative but in some respects reactionary. Strauss was an aristocrat of the intellect, very conscious of his own importance, and rather intolerant of a democracy which did not recognize the special claims of 'the superior brains'. He therefore was against the abolition of the three-class suffrage in Prussia, forgetting that it favoured the rich and the powerful regardless of brains. Yet Strauss was anything but Prussian; he was an easy-going Bavarian who hated militarism, and despite his German upbringing a cosmopolitan in his tastes, with a weakness for French culture, a special fondness for the Italian renaissance and the fabled glories of ancient Greece. To strangers he sometimes affected a rather spurious haughtiness, lighted up by flashes of a mildly sardonic humour. Like Nikisch, Strauss liked his daily card game, but he never touched poker and stuck grimly to skat, in which he was a dangerous adversary.

Artur took every opportunity of meeting his new idol, by accepting invitations to some of the opulent Berlin homes whose hostesses outdid each other in providing the great man with luxurious meals and the opportunity of playing skat for high stakes. Artur could hardly afford these steep hazards, but what he gained in return was beyond price. Without exception he lost at skat, but he won the privilege of walking the great man home to his hotel, and engaging him in highly esoteric and illuminating talks about their art. The balding, willowy six-footer. Strauss and the black-haired, dapper, stocky Artur strolling along the Tiergartenstrasse in animated argument must have been one of the rare sights of Berlin on these convivial nights. Strauss' favourite composer was Mozart, and it is more than likely that Schnabel's later predilection for Mozart received its greatest stimulus from these talks with Strauss. What is more, Strauss also had some very perspicacious things to say about the significance of Beethoven's dynamics, and this started a train of thought that led Schnabel to renewed and intensive study of this composer, which was to continue to the end of his career—with phenomenal results.

But these ambulatory conversations with Germany's greatest living composer had an even more direct effect on Schnabel's career. Strauss, then one of the chief conductors of the Berlin Opera, was being considered in competition with Felix Weingartner for the conductorship of the symphony concerts given regularly at the Opera House, as successor to the celebrated Dr. Karl Muck, who had returned to America as permanent conductor to the Boston Symphony Orchestra. The Wolff bureau, to promote the candidacy of Strauss, now organized a special concert with the Philharmonic Orchestra which would give the Berlin public a chance to hear him as a symphony conductor. And—evidently with the concurrence of Strauss—they engaged young Schnabel as soloist to play Beethoven's E-flat major (*Emperor*) concerto in an all-Beethoven programme ending with the fifth symphony. The success of this gala affair was terrific, as might be expected, since Strauss, when in the mood, was without a peer. Schnabel himself, speaking of it in retrospect, said the symphony was simply 'fulfilment'. 'No performance I have ever heard since—even by him—reached such a culmination.'

Needless to add, Strauss got the appointment. Artur's playing of the *Emperor* concerto—for the first time in his life—was certainly worthy of the occasion, and a great personal triumph. But his greatest satisfaction was the knowledge of having contributed to the success which lifted Strauss to the place where he was able to give the public some of its greatest experiences in symphonic music over the next fifteen years. (Three years later Strauss invited Schnabel to play the identical programme with him at the Berlin Opera House.)

The *Emperor* concerto with Richard Strauss was the climax of a season which comprised orchestral appearances in Hamburg and Cologne, Strassburg, Münster, and Kaiserslautern, where for the first time Schnabel played Liszt's E-flat concerto, then a favourite war-horse of all virtuosos. It is amusing to read in a letter written before the concert (in view of his later disdain of so-called technical diffi-culties) that he was 'very fearful' of the result. 'If the instrument is a bad one, I am lost.' But it evidently wasn't, for he played the concerto 'as easily and effortlessly as I had never dared to hope'. For the rest, he played three Berlin recitals which in some ways foreshadowed the kind of programme repertoire he was to develop in his mature years. The first consisted of four sonatas, by Schubert (B-flat, posthumous), Chopin (B minor), Weber (A-flat) and Beethoven (C major, opus 2, No. 3); the second of sonatas by Brahms, Beethoven and Schubert; and the third of a Bach partita, the Schumann *Humoresque*, and the *Mood Pictures* of his friend Josef Suk.

This was the last season of the original Schnabel Trio, for the restless Anton Hekking had once again flitted to America, which gave Schnabel the opportunity of varying the fare and playing the Brahms horn trio and the clarinet quintet. On another occasion he had an opportunity of playing with the French violinist Henri Marteau and the Belgian cellist Jean Gérardy, who later took Hekking's place in the reborn Schnabel Trio. But the high point of the chamber music season for Artur came with the Berlin visit of the famous Bohemian String Quartet, those 'four fascinating men' whose blend of great simplicity with great vitality he never tired of praising. They played an entire programme of Dvořák and another of Brahms, each time with Schnabel's collaboration in one or two works. These concerts and four joint recitals with Therese Behr rounded out his biggest year's work as a performer to date. He was winning favour as a composer, too, for not only Therese Behr but at least one other very good singer (Hertha Dehmlow) sang groups of his songs which, for a wonder, won high critical praise.

The last of the Schnabel-Behr recitals, given in the Singakademie, one of the largest halls in Berlin, comprised some songs which subtly confirmed the rumour that had long been in the wind—that the pair were about to become man and wife. When Therèse sang Hugo Wolf's *Mein Liebster ist so klein* (My Sweetheart is so Small) with a twinkle in the direction of her accompanist, the audience burst into joyous laughter followed by tumultuous applause.

                        ★   ★   ★

Artur Schnabel was in the final weeks of his bachelorhood, and was having what is commonly known as the last fling. Franz Hutter, the 'wild fellow' who had been his room-mate these six years and more, was himself in the throes of a tender attachment, and incidentally on the way to affluence in the publishing business. Two other boon companions, Willy Tiktin the lawyer and Werner Wolffheim the poet, were soon to follow his example. They and several others who had been drawn by Artur's magnetic personality still visited the old haunts and argued away the time until the small hours; for the world, seen from the angle of Berlin, was becoming more 'interesting' day by day. This was the year of the first Morocco crisis and the Germans had reason to become more nervous as they watched the gyrations of their politicians and the megalomania of their youthful Kaiser. Among the group who met in the cafés of the Kurfürstendamm and the comfortable apartments of Charlottenburg were writers like Karl Ettlinger the humorist, Max Marschalk and Oskar Bie, painters like Walter Kurau, George Mosson, Otto Dix and Eugen Spiro, whose sketches of Artur and his musical friends in action adorned the pages of the current periodicals; and young musicians like Gottfried Galston, Richard Buhlig, Bruno Eisner, and his pupil Paul Goldschmidt, whose tragic malady was to end in suicide in the first year of the war.

It was still a wonderful time in Berlin: new directions in literature and the theatre; the impressionist and post-impressionist movements in art; revolutionary ideas in politics, punctuated by explosive speeches in the Reichstag, and the biting satires in *Simplicissimus*—altogether a seething cauldron of ideas, good and bad, but in any case better than the 'flabby pessimism of the Viennese'. Artur liked the Berlin scene and the rôle he played in it.

There was just one little fly in the ointment: he might still be called up for military service. He had remained an Austrian subject, and was obliged to report annually to the medical examiner at the consulate. Thus far he had been regularly deferred, thanks to a little diplomatic influence, ostensibly because of a somewhat eccentric toe! But you never could tell—and the European skies were getting dark around the edges. On the other hand he had been taken notice of by royalty, and had been 'commanded' to play chamber music with Prince Frederick Wilhelm of Prussia—an indifferent amateur violinist but an expansive and bibulous host—in his castle in Silesia. Not to be outdone by her future husband, Therese Behr was made a 'court chamber singer' by the Grand Duke of Baden a month before the marriage.

'I had a very good time during my first ten years in Berlin,' Schnabel used to say much later, when speaking about his career. This sentence helps to explain something that has often puzzled his friends. How was it possible, after the truly spectacular successes of his early twenties, that he did not embark on the usual round of artistic triumphs in the international field? Other outstanding pupils of Leschetizky, approximately his contemporaries—Mark Hambourg, Ossip Gabrilowitch, Ignaz Friedman and others—were conquering continent after continent, while the 'musician' among them remained in the unexciting backwater of Berlin, playing chamber music, teaching, accompanying and writing songs for his future wife. At sixteen he had set the Berlin critics by the ears, at twenty he had played with Nikisch, at twenty-one under Hans Richter in London and at twenty-two with Strauss in Berlin, each time with resounding success. Yet he stuck to his chamber music and didn't return to London for twenty years.

He sometimes explained his reluctance to travel abroad by pointing to his linguistic handicap—the inability to converse with the natives of foreign countries. A more likely reason was his virtual lack of worldly ambition and his absorbing concern with himself in relation to his art. He was still growing internally, developing emotionally, still learning—in an environment that was eminently congenial to him, where he was appreciated and listened to, not only when he played but when he talked—a constitutional necessity to him throughout his life. Until further notice he had chosen a comparatively stationary, studious and sheltered life which satisfied his desire to be a musician in the complete and traditional sense of the word.

★   ★   ★

The marriage of Therese Behr and Artur Schnabel—the tall contralto and the short pianist—took place at a Berlin registrar's office in June 1905. Therese's father had offered to give her away in Berlin instead of the family's home city of Mainz since both the young artists were busy filling engagements right through spring. Therese had just sung Beethoven's *Missa solemnis* at Bremen while Artur had played his *Emperor* concerto at Münster, so Beethoven was the divinity that presided over their union. But it was Papa Behr who presided over the feast, held in the bride's apartment with a jolly crowd of friends around a groaning board. It was a hilarious and interminable meal —with jocular speeches and dubious doggerel on the fame and future of the happy pair—a liberal flow of oratory lubricated with wines and champagne, expertly provided by the Rhenish father of the bride. Immediately after, the couple went south for their honeymoon, and eventually to Vienna, where Therese was taken into the bosom of her husband's family, and shown all the sights that had been familiar to Artur since childhood—from the Hofburg and the Opera to the *Wurstelprater*, centre of the traditional gaiety in three-quarter time of which Vienna held the undisputed monopoly. Also she was introduced to Leschetizky, the white-haired 'Herr Professor' in his rambling villa of the 'Währinger Cottage', to receive the blessings of this nuptial veteran—now in his fourth round of married bliss.[1]

On the return trip they met Papa Behr at Salegg in the Dolomites, where Therese—wearing bloomers—was initiated as a mountaineer when the party climbed the Similaun, over 10,000 feet high, and all got glacier burns in the process. By early autumn Artur and Therese were back in Berlin, in their own home, taking part in concerts and teaching on a really large scale. Therese was still a member of the Vocal Quartet, but Artur had dissolved his popular Trio in expectation of a more widely spread activity.

---

[1] At a subsequent visit after the birth of Schnabel's first son, Leschetizky mistakenly congratulated Artur on his 'baby girl'. When told that 'it's a boy', the septuagenarian exclaimed : 'Too bad, I had hoped to become your son-in-law one of these days!'

12. *Partnership for Life*

THE Berlin home which Hans Jachmann and his wife found for the newly married couple was a huge twelve-room flat of truly heroic proportions. Herr Jachmann was a grand-nephew of Richard Wagner, and evidently thought in Wagnerian terms. The Jachmanns, staid and kindly people, had on several occasions been Artur's summer hosts in Friedersdorf. Now, as near neighbours, they were eager to be helpful to the Schnabels in their new abode. Their choice turned out to be so suitable that Artur and Therese remained in it for twenty-eight years, and left it only when Berlin and all Germany had become impossible for them to live in.

But while they were there it was perfect, both as to comfort and convenience. The house was in the Wielandstrasse, quite close to the Kurfürstendamm, one of the main avenues of the highly 'bourgeois' section of Charlottenburg. It was in easy walking distance of the Hochschule für Musik, some of the principal theatres, and the zoo, which in turn adjoined the Tiergarten—Berlin's finest park. Moreover, it was close to all the pleasant haunts where Artur was wont to spend his leisure hours. The flat itself consisted of two huge rooms suitable for studios, the larger of which easily accommodated two Bechstein concert grands standing side by side in the centre, with a slender pedestal bearing a bronze replica of the well-known Greek figure of the Dancing Faun between them.

This room was used by Schnabel for playing and teaching, and by the family for general sociability. Three of its walls were lined from floor to ceiling with bookshelves which eventually housed a very impressive library. This bright, high-ceilinged room, combining spaciousness with comfort and cosiness, was in time to become familiar to hundreds of musicians and students from the four corners of the earth, as the scene of great dispensations of beauty and wisdom, of friendly gatherings and cheery hospitality. Another, somewhat smaller studio, far enough removed to be out of earshot, was used by Therese Schnabel for her teaching.

There were of course the usual drawing-room, dining-room, boudoir, guest-room and nursery, not to mention the 'offices' presided over by Lili Walldorf, who now became housekeeper and

99

general secretary for the new 'firm'. Eventually there was the usual Victorian ménage, complete with cook, maid and nurse, for it was expected that the family would in due course expand.

The pattern of the young couple's life was virtually determined by this omni-commodious abode and the already established routine of their profession. Both devoted some hours each day (except when absent from Berlin) to teaching, and with Artur this was of very flexible duration. The more a student absorbed the more time he got—and as with Leschetizky it was rarely under two hours. Eventually the lessons were given in 'class'; that is, the teaching was done individually but in the presence of all the pupils, who were expected to listen and learn. When this became the custom, the lessons would begin after the midday meal and last more or less indefinitely into the evening hours. They were, however, subject to the teacher's own schedule: while he was away for concerts the pupils would wait.

In the preparation of his own concerts he was still the undisciplined procrastinator and the irresponsible tempter of fate. In his youth, time and again, he often dawdled through the day of a concert, playing billiards right through the afternoon, then would rush home to dress, drink several cups of black coffee and arrive at the hall just as the audience got seated. Now, with a well-regulated home, there was less excuse for this haphazard behaviour, but he always treated each concert as an adventure rather than a routine event. Although he knew a large part of the literature of the piano by heart, his programmes were limited to what might be regarded as his 'specialities', and works that he thought were unjustly neglected.

He still stuck to Brahms and Schubert as his *pièces de résistance*, and next to them the rarely played sonatas of Weber and the less hackneyed works of Schumann. He was rather reluctant about adding more Chopin and even more so about Liszt, though his technical equipment was equal to all demands. When he finally ventured to play Liszt's B minor sonata in Berlin, he surmounted its notorious difficulties with spectacular ease. 'That Schnabel can play Beethoven, Weber and Schubert we have long known,' wrote one critic, 'but that he would come up trumps with Liszt's sonata . . . surprised his admirers. We never heard it presented by any known pianist in such towering majesty.' More remarkable was his avoidance of the later Beethoven sonatas until his middle twenties, evidently because of a feeling of inadequacy or immaturity. Only now, in his twenty-third year, did he feel able to do a measure of justice to the devotional eloquence of opus 109 and the soul-stirring profundities of opus 110. Of Mozart he played no sonatas as yet (having 'mastered' them as a child and, as customary, discarded them as an adult), and only one concerto, the popular D minor. Rather than experiment in public with masterpieces whose deeper secrets were still beyond him, he filled out his programmes with lesser or even despised pieces like Mendelssohn's *Songs Without Words*. But whatever he unearthed was presented with such conviction, seriousness and meticulous perfection that it struck his auditors as a discovery, which in a sense it was.

This almost niggardly economy of choice combined with the utmost fastidiousness explains, in part at least, why this already very popular pianist played so relatively few recitals. For one reason or another he gave no recitals of his own in Berlin during the first few years after his marriage, although he and Therese Schnabel continued to delight the Berlin audience with their joint presentations of piano pieces and lieder in ever new groupings. In other German cities he would play recitals only when engaged outright—perhaps eight or ten times a year. On the other hand, he was in increasing demand by orchestras for the particular concertos he was known to play with such mastery: the two Brahms, Beethoven's E-flat and G major (also more recently the C minor), Mozart's D minor and very occasionally Liszt's E-flat. On these occasions he usually 'brought down the house', and often he was forced to add encores, a practice he came to abhor in later years.

The song-partnership with Therese, begun when the two young people were first engaged, was cultivated even more intensively now that they were man and wife. The critics had begun to find that Frau Schnabel's voice had lost some of its lustre, but all agreed that her art of interpretation and her emotional intensity had reached even greater heights. Above all, the spiritual unity and the fusion of the two musical temperaments were as nearly perfect as could be wished. In the early years of their marriage they explored together all the songs of Schubert—some six hundred of them—also those of Schumann, Brahms and Robert Franz. More recently they had performed a great deal of Hugo Wolf, Peter Cornelius, even some Tchaikovsky, and certain contemporaries like Erich Wolff. Significantly, Schnabel had withdrawn his own songs from their repertoire and, in fact, had stopped composing songs—an indication of a radical change in his attitude to the latest developments in contemporary music.

In the winter of 1909–10 they performed for the first time Schubert's cycle *Die Winterreise* in their Berlin series of concerts. It was a hazardous undertaking for a woman to sing this intensely romantic song cycle, set to a series of poems which so obviously are the outpourings of a love-sick youth, and which in the realistic public's mind called for a man's voice. Besides, Frau Schnabel's voice had been greatly reduced in volume as the result of illness. Nevertheless the impression made by the performance was overwhelming. Paul Bekker, one of the most intelligent and severe of German critics, wrote that her ability to grasp the spirit of a work and to convey it by the sheer power of suggestion was so irresistible that all the usual demands of the listener seemed to disappear. Interestingly enough, he compared her style and mastery of expression to those of Ludwig Wüllner, who despite vocal shortcomings was the most impressive male lieder singer of his generation. In the course of the next few years Therese and Artur Schnabel presented all the song cycles of Schubert in a manner which exhausted their full dramatic power and musical qualities, and exercised an almost hypnotic influence on their listeners. From this time on the joint recitals of 'the Schnabels' had become a feature of Berlin's musical season which filled the Beethoven Hall at least four times each winter.

★   ★   ★

Besides his solo appearances and the joint recitals Schnabel frequently participated in various chamber music ensembles, an activity which continued to give him particular pleasure. The first Schnabel Trio having been dissolved, the gap it left was in part filled by the great Bohemian String Quartet, which had 'adopted' Schnabel as its partner for piano quartets and quintets—chiefly those of Beethoven, Schumann, Brahms and Dvořák, and an occasional performance of Schubert's *Trout* quintet (with the help of a local double bass). Every year the 'Bohemians' came to Berlin, usually for several concerts, and each time they teamed up with Schnabel for a part of their programme. In the spring of 1908 he joined them for a short tour of Spain—his first foreign journey since his memorable trip to London four years before. It was a rollicking experience with the 'dear fellows' and their wonderful musical temperaments and lively ways. The tour was a real personal success for Schnabel, and as a result he was invited for another tour of Spain and Portugal, this time with his wife as a partner, singing—of all things—Schumann's *Dichterliebe* with German words.

On his way to Spain he filled an engagement in Brussels, to play the first Belgian performance of Brahms' B-flat concerto—a rather grim experience, to judge from his letter to Therese: 'The solo cellist was impossible, the conductor hurried me, the violins played sloppily —and yet the orchestra sounded beautiful, at least after the second rehearsal.' All in all, what with recitals, chamber music and orchestral appearances Schnabel was now kept as busy as he wanted to be. Therese on her own account filled a goodly number of engagements —as recitalist, as soloist in choral and orchestral concerts, and as a member of the Vocal Quartet (which incidentally had acquired a new tenor, Paul Reimers). Economically speaking their joint incomes were quite adequate to the demands of the rather opulent establishment, particularly with the revenue from an increasing number of pupils.

They were, of course, surrounded by a host of eager friends, ready to help them in the inevitable initial complications of domestic life. The first adversity was Therese's long and psychologically trying illness in 1906, as the result of a miscarriage, which prevented her leaving Berlin for several months, while Julia Culp filled her place with the Vocal Quartet. Artur stayed by her side for most of the summer and spent a part of his enforced idleness composing. There was no vacation, but they made up for this the following year when they spent their first real summer holiday alone, for even their honeymoon had been largely monopolized by their two families. In order to enjoy what they should have enjoyed alone, they repeated the identical itinerary, going to Vienna, climbing in the Dolomites, and sojourning in Munich—without relatives. Here their most inspiring experience was the rediscovery of Mozart's operas as performed in the pure, expressive style of Mozart's day, under the guidance of Felix Mottl. Both Artur and Therese had been so completely absorbed by instrumental and song literature that this contact with the dramatic side of Mozart came as a new discovery, and they determined to exploit it to the full.

Accordingly they patronized the Berlin Opera more frequently the following winter, to hear not only Mozart but Wagner and Verdi —particularly the latter, who remained one of Artur's favourite composers for life. During the first winter of their marriage Richard Strauss's opera *Salome* had had its first Berlin performance. So fascinated were they by this powerful dramatic creation and the scintillating kaleidoscope of new sounds, that they listened to it seven consecutive times! What this did to Artur's creative urge is difficult to guess. It is a fact, however, that after one more rather half-hearted essay in the neo-romantic idiom of his youthful pieces he stopped composing for close on eight years. His swan song of what he later deprecated as his juvenile period was a set of three pieces published in 1907 as opus 15 by the Drei-Lilien Verlag. It consists of a *Rhapsody*, a *Nachtstück* and a sequence of *Waltzes*, which are still influenced by Brahms and Schubert, while the piano style is rather more full-blooded than in his earlier pieces and songs. A real advance can be detected in these waltzes, which are both vigorous and tender, and the final one—in strict canon—is a brilliant *tour de force*. It is more than likely that the rather innocent world of his early composing collapsed under the impact of Strauss' *Salome* and the audacities of the Viennese atonalists. In any case he was so preoccupied with his performing and teaching activities that his intellectual energies were fully absorbed.

*   *   *

The Schnabels were now thoroughly settled in Berlin, and it may well have seemed to both of them that this would be the routine for the rest of their lives: a comfortable home, a respectable number of engagements in Berlin and Germany, with an occasional trip abroad, a satisfying round of teaching, and an interesting circle of friends in one of the most stimulating cities of the world. Nothing could be more serene and regular. All they now needed, as a relief from their perennial ramblings, was a settled summer home—preferably in the mountains—which had become a necessity for both.

They had no difficulty in making up their minds, for in the summer of 1908 they had been invited by Therese's friend Jeannette Grumbacher (the soprano of the Vocal Quartet) and her husband to their villa on the Traunsee, one of the loveliest lakes of the Austrian Salzkammergut. Here, in the little village of Rindbach, a colony of musicians and music lovers had already established itself. The most magnificent of the country houses there belonged to the Mendelssohns, and one of their guests was that charming singer, Julia Culp. Another colleague, the violinist Carl Flesch, was settled with his family nearby. The Schnabels had fallen in love with the place—the mountains, the lake, the picturesque Austrian peasant houses, and the fragrant woodland walks.

In August 1909 their cup of happiness was filled to overflowing by the birth of their first son, Karl Ulrich, so obviously his mother's child. During Therese's pregnancy Artur had gone prospecting, and found a villa which seemed ideal as a retreat and a place for fruitful summer work. As it happened, the presence of Carl Flesch also provided a new opportunity for chamber music. They arrived with the new baby in the summer of 1910 and would—for all they knew—come for years and years.

★   ★   ★

Without a doubt the most important result of the Schnabels' adoption of Rindbach as a summer refuge was Artur's association with Flesch, who was henceforth to play an important part in his career. This remarkable artist was his senior by more than eight years, and already recognized as an outstanding virtuoso as well as one of the leading violin teachers of Europe. He was Hungarian by birth and education, but later became a pupil of Marsick at the Paris Conservatory, whom he recognized as his real master. He was a first-rate musician and an experienced chamber music player, a man of strong intellect and firm character, well read, well informed and a brilliant raconteur. For five years he had been professor at the Bucharest Conservatory and five years more at the Amsterdam Conservatory. In 1908 he aroused unusual attention with five historical violin recitals in Berlin and decided to establish himself in the German capital. There he soon came to admire Artur Schnabel and proposed that they play sonatas together. At the time the Schnabels came to Rindbach he was planning to edit and annotate Mozart's piano and violin sonatas for the Peters Edition and suggested that they do it together. Thus the summer of 1910 gave them an opportunity to know each other better as artists: the result was a very rewarding collaboration and a friendship which was to last the greater part of their lives.

The collaboration began with two sonata recitals in Berlin which comprised works by Brahms, Schubert, Mozart and Joachim Raff. They were exceedingly well received and the result was a number of engagements in other German cities. In addition, the two artists teamed up with the well-known Belgian cellist Jean Gérardy for a trio and sonata concert which drew a capacity audience to Berlin's largest hall, the Philharmonie. It was quite frankly a 'popular' concert, with a programme of favourite items—something that Schnabel later looked upon as a deplorable catering to the mob—which included besides two Beethoven trios the *Kreutzer* sonata (opus 47) and the piano and cello sonata in A major, opus 69. At any rate it gave all three players the opportunity to show themselves as brilliant virtuosi as well as ensemble players of the first rank. It also started something that was to last until the first World War broke it up, namely the second Schnabel Trio, more illustrious if less informal and 'pally' than the first. It regularly sold out the Berlin Philharmonie two or three times a season, and it culminated in an unforgettable series of seven concerts comprising all the Beethoven trios and trio variations, all the Beethoven piano–violin and piano–cello sonatas, plus the cello variations. The last concert given by the Schnabel–Flesch–Gérardy Trio was in the winter of 1913–14, ending with a performance of Mendelssohn's trio in D minor. Before another season of the Trio could be announced the Germans had invaded Gérardy's country, and his colleagues never saw him again.

It was in the musical colony of Rindbach that Artur Schnabel came to know Erich Wolfgang Korngold, the prodigy composer whose name had been trumpeted through the world as that of a new Mozart. He and his father, the distinguished music critic of the Vienna *Neue Freie Presse*, were the Schnabels' neighbours in the summer of 1910, just after young Korngold had written his second piano sonata in E-flat. There is no doubt that Korngold, at thirteen, was not only a phenomenally gifted composer but that the sonata in question was a remarkable work, well worth performing. Speaking about it nearly forty years later, Schnabel called it 'still a most amazing piece'. Never afraid of doing the unusual, he decided to play the work in public, and did so during the following season in young Korngold's home town of Vienna, as well as in various other places. Aside from the objective estimate of its merits (which it got), one would have expected only favourable comment on Schnabel's gesture in the Press. There appeared, however, several malicious innuendos regarding his motives—in view of the fact that Korngold senior was at that time the most influential critic in Austria. The gossip that went around is best summarized by an imaginary conversation in which a colleague asks Schnabel whether Korngold's sonata is 'rewarding', to which he replies: 'No, but his father is.' Schnabel paid no attention to the rumours and not only continued to play the work, but he and Flesch also played young Korngold's violin and piano sonata (written in 1912) at their regular recitals in Berlin.

Later on Korngold, as is well known, wrote several very successful operas, of which two (*Violanta* and *Die tote Stadt*) were performed in more than forty opera houses, including the Metropolitan in New York. Still later he settled in Hollywood and engaged in the lucrative occupation of writing for the screen. Schnabel never ceased to be

The third Schnabel Trio, 1915: From left to right: Carl Flesch,
Hugo Becker, Schnabel

Schnabel in 1925

Therese in 1925 at the
height of her singing
career

fond of him and was convinced that he was 'unhappy, making all that money' and that he would 'surely give it up'.

Schnabel himself was still far from making money in Hollywood proportions. He was obviously quite content with the moderate income of a professional musician living and working in Germany. Nevertheless, his tastes were—if not extravagant—definitely aristocratic. Among his friends he was even considered a spendthrift, for he believed in enjoying the good things of life—generosity, good clothes, a good table and good wines, riding first class in trains and living at first-class hotels. When twitted about his egalitarian and quasi-socialistic sympathies for the working class while doing himself so well, he usually replied that he believed not in levelling down but levelling up. In Schnabel's utopia *everybody* was to ride first class!

Incidentally, his family was increasing; in February 1912 the second son, Stefan, was born. Artur, to keep the pot boiling, was busy all summer editing the Mozart violin sonatas with Flesch.

PART THREE

YEARS OF TRAVAIL

13. The Professional Musician

THE period between Schnabel's marriage at the age of twenty-three and the birth of his second son seven years later had seen transition from youth to maturity, in appearance as well as reality. Outwardly, in 1905, he had still been the boyish-looking, wavy-haired young man-about-town with the fetching come-hither smile, a deliberate air of elegance and a decided sprightliness of manner. Seven years later he presented the compact, serious, forceful figure of an obviously important person, whose handsome, mobile features and deep, grey eyes immediately commanded attention and respect. His hair was now half-cropped and there was just a suggestion of droop in his flourishing moustache. As always, he was neatly dressed and well-groomed, with a tendency to quiet and even sombre formality. The change in appearance reflected the transformation of the man—from the light-mannered bohemian to the responsible *pater familias* and the conscientious artist and teacher, filled with the importance of his task and the seriousness of his mission. It was the difference between the high-spirited starter and the dedicated worker toward the ever-distant goal.

Apart from his work, the principal influence in his development was his marriage, which despite inevitable difficulties and adjustments was completely happy from the start. It brought him a new assurance of validity, a sense of security and, with the birth of two children, fulfilment. His love for Therese deepened with their intimacy and so did his admiration of her character and her sound judgment in matters of art. In the letters of these early years of married life he never tires of reaffirming his love, his loneliness during their frequent separations and his almost pathetic solicitude for her and the children's well-being.

His sense of responsibility and duty as a parent increased his diligence and his concentration on work. At the same time his many contacts with older men of intellectual stature deepened and broadened his outlook on the world. Professor Rosenheim tried to interest him in the physical universe beyond his 'too anthropocentric' mentality, which was almost exclusively concerned with human beings, their aspirations and destinies. He learned about Einstein's theory of relativity (first published in 1905) and Rutherford's experiments in radioactivity, but his general apathy to science resisted these disturbing encroachments.   His intimate friend Hanns Sachs, one of the early disciples of Sigmund Freud, lectured to him on psychoanalysis, but his uninhibited moral outlook, coupled with his strict ethics and an almost Spartan sense of duty made him suspicious of what seemed to him an easy escape from personal responsibility.

Most of his friends were musicians, but among them also were writers, scientists, painters and at least one authentic philosopher, Professor Ernst Cassirer, the son-in-law of one of his earliest bene-factors in Berlin.

The tenor of his own thinking and the content of his reading were broadly philosophical, but unlike his father he was free from the talmudic scholasticism of the Jewish religion.   He was a rationalist in the tradition of Spinoza, believing in the divinity of all things as they are manifested in Nature, to which he was drawn since early youth.   He was vaguely familiar with Kant's *Critiques* and with Schopenhauer's pessimistic philosophy.   But he was more attracted to Nietzsche's exaltation of the individual, the superman who rises above the earthbound herd to the higher regions of the spirit.   He was, like most of his generation, strongly influenced by the theories of socialism, and as he grew older he reacted more and more violently against the brutal materialism of the industrial age, against the economic exploitation of nature, science and art, and against the social injustices of modern civilization.   As he watched the deterioration of a society which, he thought, regarded human beings primarily as factors in the expanding system of mechanized life, he gradually came to accept the utopian dreams of the radical Left.   At this time, however, he was still optimistic and affirmative in his outlook, an easy conformer to the rules of polite society, a gay and eager epicurean enjoying the conventional pleasures of life.   He was essentially an idealist who believed in the Goethean formula of the identity of the good, the true and the beautiful.

Much of his spare time during the early years of his marriage was taken up with the collection of music and books—the works of the masters from Bach to Schubert in the recently issued monumental Complete Editions; the classics of German literature from Goethe to Nietzsche, German translations of the great non-German writers from Shakespeare to Shaw, Molière to Flaubert; Ibsen, Dostoievsky, Tolstoy and many other modern Europeans constituting the intellec-tual arsenal of the enlightened post-Victorians.

How much of all this he ever read is uncertain. He was never an assiduous reader, except of newspapers and certain periodicals, but he came to know the contents of more books than the average educated person—by the simple process of reading copious reviews. He also had the ability to extract the essence from a printed page at a glance—by a sort of selective sight. If compelled by curiosity to know all the contents of a forbidding tome he would not hesitate to depute the task to his wife, and ask her to give him a 'digest' of the story or the argument. In almost any assemblage he would give the impression of a very well-read man, when as a matter of fact he lacked the patience for long application to anything but music. 'I have done little else all my life,' he once said in public, 'but *think in music.*' Yet the literature he read contributed greatly to his intellectual development. Although he had little taste for fiction, he was interested in contemporary writers like Thomas Mann, whose *Die Buddenbrooks* appeared in 1905, and his older brother Heinrich Mann, whose series of novels collectively entitled *Das Kaiserreich* constituted a bitter and ruthless social criticism of Germany society. Although not especially addicted to the theatre, he occasionally saw the plays of Gerhart Hauptmann and Frank Wedekind, of Ibsen and Shaw, and later the expressionistic dramas of Georg Kaiser and the satirical comedies of Karl Sternheim. This was the period of Max Reinhardt's first triumphs in the legitimate theatre, and Schnabel admired his work, however much he came to deplore his ultimate 'descent to Hollywood'.

Most of his wide knowledge and information, however, he derived from conversation. He was an inveterate talker, and his favourite recreation was walking with a willing listener or a lively debater. He attracted all sorts of people, and some of them naturally were experts of one kind or another whose brains yielded worthwhile facts. He made friends easily, especially on his journeys. On the other hand, he enlisted the fervent loyalty of numerous admirers and followers who accepted his word as law. 'By inclination I am talkative,' he once explained, 'but I have used much less time for words than for tones, and this may be the reason for my habit of expressing myself in an aphoristic manner. Also I have no talent for systems and methods—no analytical mind.'

* * *

Inevitably the increasingly widening orbit of his travels broadened his outlook and eventually made him a true internationalist, although at this time he was definitely and proudly German (professing no affection for his native Austria). Up to his marriage he had left Germany only three times—once on the Burmester tour of Norway and twice for very brief trips to London. Now he revisited Vienna, Budapest and Prague, and played there periodically until the first World War. But he never quite overcame his aversion to the Viennese audience which, he said, contained 'too many talented Philistines'. From 1907 onwards he visited—alone or with his wife— Belgium, Switzerland, Sweden, Spain and Portugal; and a little later he became a regular guest in Zurich and Basle, both very musical cities with excellent orchestras. And in 1910 he played for the first time in Riga, the difficulty of a Russian visa having been surmounted at last.

The Latvian capital made an indelible impression on him, for it was the most cosmopolitan, international and vivacious place he had ·ever seen. The population then consisted of an interesting mixture of Latvians (mostly of peasant stock), German businessmen (who had been a constant element since Hansa times), Prussian aristocrats living on their landed estates, and Russian administrators and soldiers who had ruled the country for two hundred years. There was also a very flourishing Jewish middle class consisting of merchants, doctors, teachers and lawyers. This blending of races and communities gave the city a unique fascination or, as Schnabel put it, 'oscillation'. What interested him most, of course, was its highly developed musical tradition, the Opera House where Richard Wagner (and more recently Bruno Walter) had been chief conductor, and the orchestra which was, as it happened, in the throes of a 'pin-prick' strike. This had a rather peculiar effect on his playing of the Brahms B-flat concerto, in which two precocious and subsequently famous youths made an unexpected first appearance. Fritz Busch, then employed as a conductor's assistant, volunteered as a substitute French horn player (with comical but literally painful results), while his brother Adolf, an incipient virtuoso on holiday, could not resist sitting in with the first violins.

In the autumn of 1911 Schnabel made his first visit to Russia proper, which consisted of appearances in St. Petersburg, Moscow and the picturesque ports of the Baltic provinces. He gave recitals with programmes of a surprisingly varied character, including such items as Liszt's *Sonnets of Petrarch* and *Au Bord d'une Source*, and even played Liszt's E-flat major concerto under Willem Mengelberg, the conductor of the Amsterdam Concertgebouw Orchestra and at that time a regular guest conductor in both Russian capitals. He also met for the first time Sergei Koussevitzky, then in the initial years of his conducting career. Both of these men were destined to collaborate with Schnabel on many notable occasions in the future. Generally speaking, Schnabel stuck to his chosen assignment on his first Russian tour—the great romantic masterpieces, with a somewhat increased concentration on the earlier Beethoven. But late as his thirty-first year he told an inquiring pupil (Lee Pattison) that he did not feel ready to play all of Beethoven in public. Yet he had been working on Beethoven sonatas and teaching them to pupils, for many years. With him the mastering of a great work, fathoming its depths and unravelling its mysteries, was a continuing process, a never-ending voyage of discovery. What he considered ready for performance at one stage would often not satisfy him at the next. And it was this absence of finality which made him refuse to record his performances until he had passed the half-century mark.

At this period of transition to maturity he still felt tentative about the later sonatas. It was in 1911 at Hamburg that he first played a complete Beethoven programme of five sonatas. Including the final two (opus 110 and opus 111), as well as the A-flat major, opus 26 (with the funeral march), the gay G major, opus 31, No. 1, and the C-sharp minor, opus 27, No. 2 (known as the *Moonlight*), it presented a sort of cross-section of Beethoven's *œuvre*. It was a task which challenged his greatest powers and invited dangerous comparisons with older contemporaries like Lamond and d'Albert. The success of the concert was tremendous and the critics were even more extravagant than usual in their praise. He repeated the programme in Berlin, with similar results. Yet he did not play another all-Beethoven programme for several years, adding very gradually to his knowledge of the sonatas. Not till 1927 did he venture to play them all.

Although Schnabel was now well on the way to being an international figure as a concert pianist, he never lost sight of his threefold mission as a professional musician: performing, composing, and teaching. Teaching had been a regular occupation ever since his boyhood days in Vienna when Leschetizky advised some of the older pupils to enlist little Artur's help—musically rather than technically—in overcoming difficulties of interpretation. He had resumed teaching from the moment he first settled in Berlin—again by giving technically advanced players the benefit of his example and advice. From then on he was rarely without pupils who would utilize his free time between concerts. Now that he and Therese had acquired proper studios it was evident that teaching would become a major part of their work. As for him, it had become a necessity, not merely for economic but artistic reasons. He obviously loved teaching. To him it was just another creative activity, and an opportunity to exercise his musical and forensic gifts.

Schnabel summarized his attitude to teaching in these words: 'It is the teacher's business to introduce his disciples to actual music-making, or music realization, from the initial steps on a restricted plane to the loftiest flights within the musical cosmos.' But, he added, 'the teacher who gives the final courses is not the one who should give the first, even if he could. You don't employ a mountain guide to teach a baby to walk.' It goes without saying that this intensive pedagogical activity, this guiding of the student to the 'loftiest flights' was bound to have an important effect on himself. It widened his already phenomenal knowledge of musical literature, reaching far beyond the regions which he cared to travel as a performer, and it deepened his understanding of the masterworks which he found, even in middle age, to be not yet completely within his reach. Teaching to him was what practising is to most artists. In teaching others, he also delved for himself; one might say he argued himself into the very core of a work. It was the complete intellectual understanding and emotional absorption of the masterworks that gave him the sovereign command and the confidence of his late years.

It has often been said that Schnabel never taught what is known as 'technique'. It would be more correct to say that he expected the purely physical requirements to be attended to in advance, in the interests of economy and (so to speak) good form. He had very rational ideas about the development of one's faculties for the key-board—principles which had become generally accepted since his youth. But he abhorred the purely mechanical drill of achieving dexterity by means of exercises without reference to the music that was to be played. When he said, 'I don't know how [to teach technique]; others can do it much better', he simply meant that at this stage of his career he was not interested in technique as such: the problem was how a certain *musical* effect was to be achieved, not how the achievement was to be come by most easily. 'Let us not make piano playing too easy', he would sometimes say, or—with reference to a given passage—'Let us make this a little difficult'; the purpose being always to achieve the utmost truth of expression, a desire which cannot be satisfied without genuine effort.

Whatever he may have told his pupils in earlier years about 'relaxation', about using the weight of arms and shoulders rather than muscular force or impact, the decisive guide was always the ear. Once he spoke jocularly of cultivating an 'affectionate relationship between the cushioned finger-tips and the keys'; and he never ceased stressing the necessity of acquiring a perfect *legato*—an absolute continuity of singing tone. But his most constant admonition was 'First hear, then play!' and this applied not only to tone but to the rhythm, the shape of the phrase, the expression—in short, the music. 'Musical ideas (in performing as well as composing) must,' he insisted, 'precede the appearance of the music itself. The performer must labour *mentally* to comprehend the finished piece of music which he undertakes to transform into sounding reality—not only as an arrangement of tones but as a formed and organized expression.'

The supreme aim of Schnabel's teaching was that the music be understood, loved, and thereby truthfully performed. As in his own playing, the piece was his sole concern: one might say that he taught the *piece*, rather than the pupil. When he had reached the summit of his powers as an artist, he still exercised the highest function of the teacher—as the servant of music. He might reach the desired aim by explanatory words, by actual example, or by the power of suggestion: the result was all that mattered. 'The process of artistic creation,' he said, 'is from inwardness to lucidity', and so was the process of his teaching.

What he had to say to the pupil dealt primarily with the content of the work, the musical fabric, its emotional or spiritual content, its æsthetic qualities and its structural characteristics; and secondarily with the problems of actual performance—the *Vortrag*. He urged students again and again to study musical form, to get the feeling of periods (and especially to discover the irregular ones) as the basic unit of expression.

The choice of the work to be studied was always the pupil's. He brought to the lesson what he had prepared, usually without advice or previous knowledge of the teacher. The lesson was always individual, but all the other students were free to listen if they wished, and profit by what they heard.

Invariably the lesson began with a complete performance of the work by the pupil, playing from memory, while Schnabel listened, giving close attention to the printed text. (Once, when the pupil used Schnabel's edition of the Beethoven sonatas, he quipped, 'You'd better let me have it; I wouldn't like to contradict myself!') Then followed a short lecture—some descriptive remarks about the work, its essence, or a broad analysis of its architecture, or just some striking features which might have escaped the pupil's notice. Whatever it was, it focused attention on the *work*, and it usually established a pleasant community of thought and purpose—in a friendly atmosphere of exploration. Usually at this point Schnabel said something so illuminating, arresting or even challenging, that it was not easily forgotten. Sometimes a sentence, or a single word, might light up the meaning of the piece, or change the pupil's attitude toward it, as on one occasion, after a too tame finale of Schumann's *Carnaval*, Schnabel simply underscored the word *contre* in the title: *Marche des Davidsbündler contre les Philistines.*

Then the real instruction would begin: while the pupil played the work a second time, Schnabel, sitting at the other piano, would illustrate, shout directions, explain a poignant turn of the harmony, correct the modelling of a phrase, or whisper inner meanings to justify his point. Whenever necessary he would interrupt and demonstrate by playing the bar, passage or period, and make the pupil repeat and repeat till he had grasped the meaning, the importance of a modulation, a sequence, an inner voice, an imitation or a subtle motivic relationship—the things which gave the piece its character and brought it to life. Not until the pupil had understood a given passage and mastered it in the indicated manner was he permitted to proceed. The purpose was to achieve the truest expression of the composer's thought in every passage, and its relationship to the whole. Often it was a gruelling process, for nothing less than perfection was the aim.

The peculiarly impressive quality of Schnabel's teaching lay in his ability to suggest images and evoke the mood of a piece by imaginative, non-technical words and phrases—a line of poetry, a glimpse of nature, a tender sentiment, a suggestion of pageantry or drama: anything to touch the pupil's sensibility and rouse his inner feeling— 'from inwardness to lucidity'. Sometimes he would fit improvised words to a melody in order to point its character, solemn or devotional, gay or roguish, passionate or sentimental. Again and again he would correct a wrongly phrased theme by simply setting it to words, with the comma in the right place. So fertile was he in inventing literary parallels (mostly in German) that some pupils wrote them down for their private collections of Schnabeliana. One of them recorded Schnabel's running commentary on a medium-length Beethoven sonata, the transcript of which takes up more than fifty typed pages!

His explanations and commentaries were often spiced with sudden bits of humour, paradoxical commands and random quips. 'Think twice, play once!' was a favourite admonition at the start of a critical passage. After one of his exhortations he might say by way of encouragement, 'It's warmer on the heights than it seems to people in the valleys.' A pupil playing Schumann's C major *Fantasie* who overshot the mark in a wide keyboard leap was consoled with, 'That's all right; once in a while one must miss at this place, otherwise people wouldn't know how difficult it is!' A young lady pupil who ran into trouble by nervously rushing a rapid passage was told to 'just play slowly in a fast tempo'. Another, who wanted to 'adapt' a widely spread chord to her small reach was told to 'try breaking your hands!' Schnabel rarely showed impatience, but would quickly turn it off into a pleasantry. 'I can *show* you how it is done,' he once said in mock despair, 'but the talent you have to bring along.'

The amount of mental and emotional energy expended by Schnabel in the course of a single lesson (usually anywhere from two to five hours in length) would have worn out any normally vigorous person. But he was phenomenal in his intellectual capacity as he was in sheer physical endurance—so long as his interest was sustained, which was always the case when great music was concerned. The study of a Beethoven sonata or a work of similar length often consumed two entire lessons. When the work was finished, the pupil was presumed to have everything he needed for its performance. He was not expected—or asked—to play the same work for Schnabel again. Thus, with pupils bringing fresh additions to their repertoire to succeeding lessons, the number of works covered in the course of a teaching period of, say, from four to eight weeks, would constitute a very considerable portion of piano literature, classical, romantic and modern.

It is not to be supposed, of course, that Schnabel taught only the works he played in public. He tolerated the works of every school, including the French impressionists, whom he did not greatly admire, but whose works he played in class (sometimes at first sight) with complete mastery and with great fluency and fidelity to style. To the astonishment of the young moderns he also taught and demonstrated, with little or no preparation, the works of contemporaries from Schönberg to Hindemith. These excursions into the present he thoroughly enjoyed and encouraged more and more, and no doubt they stimulated his own creative impulses anew.

The high endeavour which characterized the Schnabel lessons created a rare spirit of camaraderie, suffused with the infectious energy and good humour of the master himself. Schnabel gave himself up completely to the task in hand and often worked himself up to a fever of musical excitement. He is remembered by numerous former pupils as being generally cheerful and courteous and, except for rare flurries of temper, exceedingly kind. Some older pupils came to him year after year—even after they were well started on their public careers. There came a time, however, when he felt a student was, or should be, off the leading strings. To such he would say: 'You must make your own music now', by way of good-bye. But his work with the young people remained a perennial joy throughout his life.

★   ★   ★

The third function of the 'professional musician', namely that of composing, had been virtually dormant for several years. Since 1906, the year in which he wrote the *Three Pieces*, opus 15, Schnabel had not composed a note of music, so far as we know. This might be explained by the increasing demand on his time as a performer and teacher, or by his own remark that probably 'the urge wasn't strong enough', were it not for later developments in Schnabel's life. These indicate that the urge, though submerged at times, was always alive. Proof of this was the powerful impression made on him by Richard Strauss's *Salome*, soon to be followed by *Elektra*, and various other works which foreshadowed a new and radical turn in musical creation. The subsequent years, though barren of actual production, were nevertheless years of fruition in Schnabel's career as a composer, in preparation for what was to come.

Arnold Schönberg, the revolutionary genius whom Artur had known slightly as a boy in Vienna, had in his latest works abandoned the accepted harmonic structure of classic and romantic music, as well as the whole apparatus of post-Wagnerian pathos, for a completely new style and a new concept of musical æsthetics. His *Three Piano Pieces*, opus 11, and his *Five Orchestral Pieces*, opus 16, the despair of the traditional musician, had caused violent reverberations throughout the musical world and divided it into two parts—the few who hailed Schönberg as a great and daring innovator and the many who decried him as a charlatan. As soon as Schnabel saw these works he realized that a new day had dawned and that, for better or worse, the hyper-romantic effusions of his middle-aged contemporaries had lost their validity for the future. In 1911 Schönberg settled in Berlin, where he completed his *Textbook on Harmony*, and where in the following year he wrote and produced one of his most successful works, *Pierrot Lunaire*. About that time Schnabel renewed his acquaintance with the great musical iconoclast who found it difficult to make a living, and during 1913 he was in a position to give him some material assistance. The lengthy and frequent discussions between the two men, which extended far into the nights, robbed the busy pianist of sleep and rudely disturbed his peace of mind.

The fascination of the new freedom from the conventions of diatonic harmony and the 'tyranny' of the bar-line was such that Schnabel now repudiated everything he had hitherto produced—not without protest from Therese, suddenly bereft of all her 'very own' songs. But he plunged into the work of experimentation, made her study the new composers, and finally convinced her that the future of music lay in the still unexplored regions of free expression.

After months of soul-searching and tribulation he began work on a setting of a long poem by Richard Dehmel entitled *Notturno*, for voice and piano, in a free and mordantly dramatic style which broke completely with everything he had ever done before. It would be strange, in the circumstances, if Schnabel had not been influenced by Schönberg—at least intellectually—just as it would have been impossible for Wagner not to be influenced by the innovator Liszt. And superficially at least his *Notturno* is reminiscent of the texture of Schönberg's song-cycle *The Hanging Gardens*, though in substance there is no resemblance whatsoever. Free from all melodic, harmonic and rhythmic restrictions (even the bar-lines are absent) this lengthy rhapsodic improvisation is so enormous a step into the future that its birth pangs must have been equivalent to a psychological and emotional crisis, which explains that it was not actually brought to paper till 1914. It was written for the still hesitant Therese, whose art had been so closely identified with Schubert, Schumann, Brahms and Wolf.

It has been performed by her at various times with varying response, and it is still considered a 'problematical' work. Whatever its ultimate value, it forms a milestone in Schnabel's development and an important factor in our estimate of him as a musical pioneer.

14. *Playing Out the War*

IN January 1914 Schnabel made his second visit to Russia, following an invitation from Sergei Koussevitzky, who had in the meantime founded his own orchestra. In both St. Petersburg and Moscow he played the D minor concerto of Brahms, a composer then still unfamiliar to most Russians. It was a brilliant success. Reporting to his wife he wrote that he had never before played the concerto so well and with such freedom. He met many important people, made friends with Alexander Glazunof, hobnobbed with Bruno Walter and other German colleagues and made plans for future Russian tours.

Returning to Berlin in high feather, he resumed his recitals with Therese, presenting the most ambitious programmes they had yet given—all-Beethoven, all-Schumann, Brahms, Liszt, and all-modern. The halls were full and the critics indulged in veritable dithyrambs of praise for the 'blessed artist pair'. Schnabel and Flesch rounded out their season's activities with a programme of contemporary sonatas— a *tour de force* which drew a crowded house long after the normal end of the season. Between his Berlin concerts Artur dashed off to other cities, giving examples of what a Dresden critic called 'the most mature mastery in piano playing' to be heard. He appeared as soloist with all the more important orchestras in Germany, gave recitals, joint recitals with Carl Flesch, and trio concerts with Flesch and the new member of the Schnabel Trio. The place of Gérardy had been taken by an excellent German cellist, Hugo Becker, and the new ensemble was immediately in demand.

Schnabel was now thirty-two years of age, and definitely on the broad highway to fame. Engagements poured in as never before. The name of Schnabel was also beginning to figure in the foreign press, and his overseas pupils were spreading his fame abroad. There was no doubt that in the autumn he would go to Russia again, and that his international career was about to expand.

But neither Schnabel nor his friends had the slightest inkling of what was brewing on the horizon of world affairs. In June, while he was quietly working on his *Notturno* and planning a holiday in the

Dolomites (instead of the usual teach-and-play vacations of recent years), the dream was suddenly shattered by the news that the Austrian heir-apparent had been murdered by Serbian revolutionaries at Sarajevo. Within a few days it became clear that Austria was determined to go to war to avenge the deed and that the German government was standing firmly behind its ally. Legally the Schnabels were Austrians and listed as foreigners resident in Germany. As both countries were involved in the crisis there was nothing to be done but stay in Berlin and await events. He and Therese were swept along by the winds of patriotic propaganda: like other political innocents they believed that Germany was encircled and that a 'war of defence' was inevitable. When the inevitable happened, crowds of frenzied Berliners thronged Unter den Linden and converged on the Imperial Palace to demonstrate their loyalty—Artur, Therese and their neighbours among them. Presently the Kaiser made his 'I know no parties, I know only Germans' speech and Schnabel suddenly discovered his own German patriotism. Hitherto he had not joined anything more serious than the German Alpine Club; now he became a member of the new Deutscher Verein—an association of loyal liberals aiming to advance the cultural unity of the German people.

But what next? What would happen to people such as he—an Austrian civilian in Germany and an avowed pacifist? Would he be permitted to go on making music? Would the easy-going Austrian officials continue to defer him from year to year, or would he, too, be called up for military service?

As the war fever rose it was seen that music was an important factor in sustaining the people's morale. Beethoven in particular was listened to with an almost religious devotion. In the first winter of war Schnabel and Flesch played all the Beethoven violin sonatas to full houses. The E-flat major (*Emperor*) concerto, like the *Eroica* symphony, became a musical ritual with patriotic overtones. Artur played it at the ceremonial opening of the new People's Theatre (Volksbühne) in Berlin, in the ancient Gürzenich hall in Cologne and at other strategic places. His popular success rose to new heights. The war actually proved a stimulus to more genuine participation by an increasingly devoted public. This seemed all to the good so far as the fate of musical artists was concerned. Besides, everybody thought the war would be over—very soon. Germany at the head of the Triple Alliance would score a quick triumph over the encircling 'Entente'. . . .

The first break in Schnabel's optimism came in the spring of 1915, when the Germans, in a pathetic attempt at cultural propaganda, sent some of their best artists abroad. He himself was booked for a recital in Milan—his first professional visit to Italy. It was in April, the very month when this dubious ally of Germany was negotiating the secret treaties which were to bring their country into the war on the Allied side. To his utter surprise the Italians were quite openly unfriendly and their Press attacked him as a 'representative of German militarism!'

The next shock came in Brussels, where he had gone as soloist with the Berlin Philharmonic Orchestra under the leadership of Felix Weingartner. In his political naïveté he had expected a Belgian audience at this concert in the Théâtre de la Monnaie. But the house was filled solidly with German uniforms: Belgium was an occupied country and no civilian was allowed near the place! The following autumn he had to give recitals—by official arrangement—in neutral countries like Holland, Switzerland and Sweden, for the German Foreign Office had a great belief in music as a medium of persuasion. His reception was anything but friendly and some critics were downright insulting. Dutch critics called his playing the embodiment of Prussianism, 'a page out of Kant or Hegel' and 'the boredom of perfection'. An Amsterdam paper, noting the neat precision of his runs, said that he played like 'a convict counting peas'.

The only redeeming feature of these cultural sorties was a purely material one. In his semi-official capacity he was able to get scarce and essential foodstuffs sent to Berlin through diplomatic channels. This was a vital consideration, for in the second year of the war the Germans were already beginning to be rationed and the Schnabel family, with two growing boys, was naturally suffering with the rest. As the war wore on their privations increased, and their earnings dwindled as the German mark lost its purchasing power. These hardships, and particularly the lack of coal, soon took their toll in health. Early in 1916 Schnabel succumbed to severe rheumatism and neuritis in the shoulder, which incapacitated him for three months and made him doubt his ability to resume playing. The family went to Freudenstadt, a Black Forest resort, where he was treated with physiotherapy. To complete the Schnabels' misery, both boys contracted the measles.

In this state of enforced idleness Schnabel turned to his favourite indoor 'sport'—composing—which he had not been able to pursue since the outbreak of the war. He wrote a quintet for strings and piano, consisting of three long movements, which must have occupied him for a number of weeks. This score has puzzled students of his compositions, because it seems to indicate a retrogression from the advanced modernism of the *Notturno*. It was, in fact, Schnabel's last attempt to sail in the wake of contemporary neo-romanticism. In it he essays an ultra-chromatic and overcrowded counterpoint and produces a bewildering complication of powerful sonorities. Perhaps this work—a highly intellectual product—reflects the state of mind he must have been in, compounded of the frustrations of wartime, illness, anxiety and the uncertainties of the future.

At this moment there came, like a bolt from the blue, a peremptory summons for Schnabel to be examined—this time by the Germans— as to his fitness for military service. He had felt fairly safe, since the German Foreign Office had requisitioned him for 'cultural propaganda' and services such as playing for hospitalized soldiers and the Red Cross. But this time he wasn't dealing with diplomats but with military bureaucrats who saw no reason why a mere artist should be spared. Creating spiritual values by making good music, they frankly told him, was well enough in its place but fighting for the country was more important. Hoping to make short shrift of their victim, German officials now requisitioned Schnabel's dossier from the Austrians and they—accommodating as ever—just couldn't find it. But finally Schnabel had to appear before a medical examiner and once again exhibit his poor toe. 'Ah,' said the kindly man, 'no doubt you find it difficult to walk?' 'Difficult to walk, indeed!' answered the proud mountaineer. 'I have climbed the Similaun, the Ortler, the Zugspitze. . . .' Hardly were the words out of his mouth when he realized that he had probably forfeited his only chance of not serving in the ranks. However, being a quasi-foreigner and a prominent artist, there were still possibilities. 'Some of your colleagues,' he was told, 'have volunteered to serve the Fatherland's cause by pledging a portion of their earnings for war bonds.' Relieved at the prospect of escaping the nightmare of fighting—particularly for a cause that he felt was no longer his—Schnabel with magnificent irresponsibility pledged a sum beyond anything he was likely to earn in wartime, to the utter consternation of his wife and friends. In order to make good his pledge he was obliged to contract a debt which grew inexorably throughout the duration. The bonds, of course, were destined to become worthless after Germany's collapse.

For the remainder of the war Schnabel was kept in perpetual motion, playing more concerts than ever before, and getting poorer and poorer in the process. The following summer of 1917 the family spent in Berlin, unable to afford a vacation. Ironically enough,

Artur was being hailed everywhere he appeared as an 'incomparable artist', applauded with 'wild enthusiasm', and thanked for giving 'indescribable pleasure' to the public. On the other hand he was exploited for benefit performances of various and sometimes dubious kinds. To him the height of ignominy was reached when he was asked to appear, dressed as Franz Schubert, and play in the synthetic Schubert operetta known as *Das Dreimäderlhaus* (alias 'Lilac Time') under the patronage of the Crown Princess Caecilie. Only by pulling all possible wires and vowing that he would rather go to war, after all, than take part in this degrading masquerade was he graciously excused.

Another benefit concert, which might have been the most disheartening event of all—except for Schnabel's tenacity and stubborn belief in his creative powers—was a Benefit Concert for German War Refugees from foreign countries. It was one of a series of contemporary concerts and consisted entirely of his own compositions. It comprised the *Notturno*, sung by Therese Schnabel, the recently composed piano quintet, and as an *hors d'œuvre* the *Rhapsody* for piano from his opus 15, played by himself. Three more disparate works by one and the same composer would be hard to imagine. The programme would have been a heavy dose for all but the hardy souls who, fortified by unlimited faith, insist on listening to modern music as a duty. Part of the audience fled before the end; the rest applauded politely. The critics not only tore the concert to pieces but indulged in long discussions on the psychological aspects of the Schnabel 'case'. How can a great artist, and so fine a distiller of the classic spirit, they wondered, write such 'ugly' and unnecessarily modernistic music? Quoting Schiller's *Don Carlos* the senior Berlin critic wrote: 'Either you lied then, or you lie now.' Schnabel's disgusted retort was that perhaps he lied both times! What he felt after this really terrible experience is not on record. It probably confirmed him in his determination to be a composer; but it could hardly have mitigated the unhappiness of these years.

The economic stringency of the Schnabel family was somewhat relieved in the fourth year of the war by a windfall—a Scandinavian tour sponsored by the Danish piano house of Hornung & Möller. The enterprise was an unqualified success and laid the foundation of Schnabel's great and lasting popularity in the Scandinavian countries. He was re-engaged for a second tour (with Therese) in the spring of 1918, and for a third just after the war. The great advantage of these tours was the chance of getting some nourishing food for the family and the fact that the fees were paid in a hard currency, since the German mark had begun its downward course of inflation.

*   *   *

In the summer of 1918, which the entire Schnabel family spent in the Baltic Sea resort of Dievenow (while the children were recovering from whooping cough), Artur wrote his first string quartet. This work, despite its conventional key signature (D minor) was a decisive step in the direction of atonality and free linear counterpoint. It was also his most impressive creative achievement up to that time, boldly following the path of ultra-modern expressionism which he first essayed in the *Notturno* of 1914. This quartet, hitherto his longest in duration, was destined to have a decisive influence on his career. Henceforth composition was no longer a mere pastime or sport, but for some years to come his major concern.

For the present, however, he was still predominantly a successful and hard-working pianist, whose fame had spread throughout central and northern Europe, and was beginning to be noted in more distant lands, as the first World War was nearing its end. The final month of the war found him still touring the western provinces, witnessing the debacle of the German army and the beginning of the people's revolt. His first reaction to the outbreak of revolutionary disorders in Germany was an immense feeling of relief. He was delighted to hear both the teenage soldiers and the old civilian guards who shared his train compartments on their way to or from the front talk loudly against the Kaiser's régime. One night, in Bonn, when the members of the Schnabel Trio were consuming a meagre hotel supper after their concert, the head waiter came in to announce quite simply that the revolution had broken out, just as though he were reporting that it had begun to rain. The revolution *had* in fact broken out in various isolated spots—in Kiel, Hamburg, Bremen, Munich—and soon all Germany was to be ablaze. The three artists left Bonn and went their separate ways. Schnabel ran right into the seething cauldron at Cologne. Utter chaos reigned. With difficulty he made his way eastward, having been lifted bodily through a compartment window into a train bursting with riotously happy soldiers dashing for home. After this physically painful though hilarious experience he eventually arrived in the city of Cassel—just in time for his next engagement. There he heard the Kaiser's abdication announced to a vast crowd in the city square. 'It was absolutely indescribable,' he recounted later. 'These thirty thousand people cheered—and acted—as though a

golden future was about to dawn.' That night the city was in complete darkness, and not a wheel turned in the streets. Yet he played
his recital to a crowded and jubilant house, lit only by a few flickering
candles.

Two days later he was home in Berlin. It was November 18th:
the republic was being proclaimed and Therese took the boys
to hear Humperdinck's *Hänsel and Gretel* at the Opera House—as
though it were Christmas Day. The German monarchy had ceased
to exist.

Life still went on and concerts continued as usual, for neither war
nor revolution could kill the thirst for music. But the people's misery
deepened from day to day, and food was scarcer than ever, since the
'hunger blockade' continued for another eight months. Despite
everything, this dark and hungry winter witnessed some of the finest
performances in the Schnabels' career. In a joint recital during the
week of the Spartacus rebellion they gave an all-Schubert programme consisting of almost unknown sonatas and songs. Whatever Schnabel did to weather the storms of war, whatever com-
promises he had to make with his pacifist conscience, he never departed
from his self-imposed artistic code. His programmes were as true
to his inner demands at the end as they were at the beginning.

In accomplishment and in spiritual resources he was infinitely
richer than five years before, when all the world seemed to beckon
to him. But materially he was as poor as ever. What was more, he
now faced the debt of many thousands which he had contracted in
order to obtain his release from military service. Without his faithful
and generous friend, Dr. Arthur Rosenheim, he would have had to
go back on his pledge, with unimaginable consequences. Now,
after his home-coming, the Rosenheims were the first to welcome
him at a family feast—with the best that a wartime larder and a well-
guarded cellar could provide. At the height of the party, Dr. Rosenheim, following a touching little speech of welcome, quietly slipped
an envelope to Therese, by this time moved to tears. In it were the
promissory notes, torn and cancelled, representing the loans with
which Artur had purchased his safety during the war.

*   *   *

The war had made Schnabel politically conscious. He had met
many people in commanding positions, and he had watched the hopeless misery and the confusion of the masses. When Kaiserism was
destroyed and democracy took its place he, like millions of others,

thought that the days of exploitation and class struggle were over. Yet within two months the brutal conflicts between Right and Left broke out anew, and two idealistic if misguided leaders, Karl Lieb-knecht and Rosa Luxemburg, were brutally murdered by the military in the streets of Berlin. A like fate befell Kurt Eisner, the first republican premier of Bavaria. And this was but the beginning of a thousand acts of violence whose victims included such men as Matthias Erzberger, leader of the Catholic Centre party, Walter Rathenau, Maximilian Harden and hundreds of the country's best men. The bitterness of this post-war year burned deeply into Schnabel's con-science and influenced his thinking for many years to come.

15. 'The Happiest Years'

'THE years from 1919 to 1924,' Schnabel once told an audience of students, 'were the most stimulating and perhaps the happiest I ever experienced.' To most of the people who, like him, were obliged to spend them in post-war Berlin, this would be hard to believe, for they would remember the immediate post-war period in Germany as one of the most painful and turbulent of their lives, to be surpassed only by the bloody years of the Nazi tyranny which had yet to come. It was a time of revolution and counter-revolution, of political terror, physical and mental suffering such as has rarely been experienced by any nation in modern times. In the wake of the greatest defeat since the Napoleonic wars, it saw the collapse of an economic and social structure based on principles and premises which were no longer valid, and the widespread abandonment of moral and ethical concepts regarded for centuries as immutable. This short period encompassed the ruin of the most stable and solid segment of German society and the abandonment of the vaunted middle-class virtues of honesty and thrift. It was a period of under-nourished children and frustrated youngsters, of hunger and poverty, disillusionment and despair. These few years saw the Spartacus rebellion, the abortive Kapp Putsch, the occupation of the Ruhr, the nightmare of runaway inflation resulting in the liquidation of lifetime savings, the evaporation of security and the widespread disruption of family life.

And yet, within this period Germany witnessed an intellectual and artistic revival unparalleled since the Romantic period. While the physical and material fabric of the nation seemed to be crumbling, new æsthetic and spiritual values were being created. New forms and concepts of literature, painting, architecture and music came to the fore and were either applauded or heatedly discussed. Modernistic and controversial novels and plays, defying generally accepted conventions, were avidly read, seen and heard, if not unreservedly approved. New methods of stage production, paradoxically enhanced by the economic restrictions of the time, gave new vitality to the contemporary theatre. Modern 'dance recitals' and readings of controversial poetry became as popular as the satirical vaudeville and the

MS of part of the second movement of Schnabel's Sonata
for Violin Solo, composed in 1919

political cabaret with its stinging satires on state and society. Contrary to expectation, Germany after the war had not fewer but more theatres and concert halls than before; and the working-classes had greater access to music and cultural entertainment, partly through the levelling effect of nation-wide poverty, partly through reforms instituted by the new republican régime. The formerly royal, ducal and princely theatres and opera houses were now the people's property, subsidized by the several states of the Reich.

What this meant in a country so culturally decentralized as Germany may be gathered from bare statistics. Germany had at the end of the first World War fifty-four operatic theatres and ninety orchestras, of which more than half were of full symphonic strength. In addition there were numerous choral and other local musical societies which engaged the concert artists of the period. Altogether this was a musical market second to none in the world.

In Berlin a second opera house (the Deutsches Opernhaus) had been opened in 1912. A third was added in the immediate post-war period by the reconstruction of the old Kroll Theatre. More significant of the period was the development and expansion of the People's Theatre (Neue freie Volksbühne), established shortly before the war to enable the working-classes to see good plays and hear high-quality concerts by the simple device of purchasing tickets *en bloc*. Schnabel had quite early in his Berlin career co-operated with the Volksbühne by giving concerts for it. In 1915 the organization completed its own magnificent theatre, designed for plays and concerts. Schnabel played at the first musical event of the newly opened theatre, and many times thereafter.

One of the leading spirits in this organization was Leo Kestenberg, a pupil of Ferruccio Busoni and an educator of unusual distinction, with original and even revolutionary ideas on the teaching of music in the schools. Immediately after the revolution, when the first Social Democratic régime was established, Kestenberg was placed in charge of musical affairs in the Prussian ministry of education, and in this capacity reformed the entire system of musical instruction, from elementary school to conservatory, corresponding to the university level. He also advocated and instituted a system of licensing private music teachers on the basis of professional qualifications or examination. Schnabel was in complete sympathy with this reform and supported it in the public prints. It was Kestenberg who nominated Schnabel for the honorary title of Professor, as the last to be given this rank by the Prussian state.

Kestenberg appointed, as director to the Berlin High School of Music, the Austrian composer Franz Schreker, who was then thought by some leading German critics to be a second Wagner, and, as his assistant, the eminent musicologist Georg Schünemann. Kestenberg was largely responsible for modernizing and raising the standards of this state-operated conservatory, thus enhancing the status of Berlin as a centre of musical education. Incidentally he also helped to bring Busoni back to Berlin after his self-imposed exile in Switzerland, and had him appointed to an important teaching post in composition at the Prussian State Academy of Arts.

Schreker, the new director, brought with him from Vienna some of his most talented pupils, including Ernst Křenek, then twenty, and Alois Hába, famous as one of the first composers in quarter-tones. Another young genius to appear in Berlin about this time was the twenty-five-year-old Paul Hindemith, who was to become professor of composition at the Hochschule a few years later. Still another was the highly gifted if somewhat eccentric Eduard Erdmann, a native of Latvia who quickly earned distinction both as pianist and composer —and as a vigorous exponent of the ultra-modern school.

It was to the advent of such lively and genial young colleagues that Schnabel ascribed much of the happiness of these dynamic Berlin years. If, as he liked to say, he had in his earlier life associated exclusively with his elders, he now made the most of this close and stimulating contact with youth. However, it was a highly precocious, and super-sophisticated youth he ran into—the avant-garde of a generation that had burned the bridges of the nineteenth century behind it. These youngsters were completely uninhibited by the romantic tradition and the 'decadent' respectability of their elders. To them Schnabel was the singular phenomenon of a middle-aged intellectual who delighted in the antics of the young, an artistic grandseigneur who could be as radical as the best—or the 'worst'—of them. He respected Schönberg and admired his intellect, but he loved the Křeneks and the Erdmanns who in turn admired him. Not only did they respond very willingly to his ideas; but he, too, found that contact with them proved reciprocally productive. They came to him at least one evening a week, played their compositions or listened to his own, and discussed each other's music till three or four in the morning.

Modernism had long been a challenge; now it became a faith and a sort of freemasonry of art. A New Music Society had been formed by the conductor Hermann Scherchen who, characteristically, had formulated its tenets while a prisoner of war in Soviet Russia. A new fortnightly journal, entitled *Melos* and edited by Scherchen, became the organ of the new *illuminati* and, thanks to the progressive Professor Kestenberg, Scherchen was later made a lecturer on contemporary music at the Hochschule, thus gaining official recognition for the young revolutionaries' ideas. Factions developed, of course, and every new work was discussed with all the fervour and bitterness of partisanship. The more moderate wing of the moderns infiltrated the staid old Allgemeine deutsche Musikverein (General German Musical Association), founded by Franz Liszt and at this time headed by Richard Strauss, which had hitherto ignored the young radicals in its annual festivals. The radicals were now organizing their own festivals, first in the little South German town of Donaueschingen (under princely patronage) and later at Salzburg, where they joined forces with their Austrian colleagues and eventually with their contemporaries in a dozen other countries.

Schnabel was interested in all these activities but still kept himself aloof, as one who was generally considered an outsider by the militant professionals of the modernist camp. His known contribution to music in the new idiom was still limited to the *Notturno*, written in 1914 and performed just once during the war. The last month of 1919, however, saw the first performance of his string quartet in D minor, written at Dievenow during the last summer of the war. Excellently played by the Premyslav Quartet in Berlin, it had a decidedly mixed reception, but according to one—perhaps partisan—reviewer the 'hissers' were defeated by the 'intelligent listeners'. Most of the critics turned their well-worn thumbs down; some clever ones detected a suspicious relationship to Schönberg (whose name was anathema); but one hardy non-conformist hailed the work as truly revolutionary in its novelty, as an expressionistic rebirth of romanticism and the last word in freedom of melody and rhythm.[1]

In Schnabel's own mind, however, this work was already superseded by a still more daring adventure—the result of another concentrated creative period at Dievenow during the summer of 1919. This was the sonata for violin solo, a non-stop five-movement work of nearly an hour's duration which still stands alone in its particular category, both for its monumental proportions and the ingenuity of its formal integration. Discarding all conventional harmonic and rhythmic conventions (as well as bar-lines), it is held together by a

---

[1] Oskar Bie, critic of the *Börsenzeitung* and eminent writer on music and the theatre.

continuous process of thematic development from a single melodic germ, through a prodigious variety of evolutions, culminating in a final fugue. This incredibly difficult piece achieved something of a *succès de scandale* when it was performed by Carl Flesch with complete technical mastery and musical understanding in November 1920 at a concert of the New Music Society in Berlin. Most of the critical comments were negative, some hostile and even insulting. One noted scribe concocted. a clever but untranslatable pun impugning the composer's sanity by twisting Hans Sachs' poetic comment on Walther's Prize Song in *Die Meistersinger*:

> *Dem Schnabel, der heut' sang,*
> *dem war per Vogel hold gewachsen.*

Nothing daunted, Schnabel dashed off, as a wedding present to a favourite pupil, his most deliberately brilliant composition for piano, a *Dance Suite* consisting of a series of short movements in dance rhythms (foxtrot, waltz, etc.) and interludes with programmatic titles—'Encounter', 'Wooing', 'Suspense', 'Affirmation'—altogether a sort of latter-day reflection of Schumannesque romanticism. This charming trifle (comparatively speaking) was first performed by Eduard Erdmann during the winter of 1921, and though partially successful with the audience found little more favour with the critics than its predecessor.

Incidentally, the Berlin critics' reactions to these three problematical but indisputably serious works were more than a personal attack; they were part of the general outcry of the æsthetic guardians against the young radicals' assault on the public's ears which had begun with Schönberg's opus 11 and 16 before the war. It was especially bitter in the case of Schnabel, whom these same reviewers had extolled for years as the ideal interpreter of the classics and who as a pianist had shown no partiality for the ultra-modern school. They resented his defection from the ranks of the regulars as much as they detested what he now produced.

Yet there was a notable if small number of musicians who recognized the element of greatness in Schnabel's venturesome flights of fancy, and some forward-looking critics like Oskar Bie who freely acknowledged his 'inner freedom', his imagination and strength of will. There were, moreover, some encouraging antidotes to the journalistic poison poured out in Berlin. In May 1920 Schnabel's *Notturno* had two remarkably successful hearings, at the Mahler Festivals in Amsterdam and Wiesbaden, both times sung by Therese, with himself at the piano. The first string quartet had fairly successful performances in Dresden and other German cities, and in the following year it was selected for the German Tonkünstlerfest of 1922 in Düsseldorf, where, little more than two years after its rejection by most of the Berlin press, it was overwhelmingly acclaimed by the assembled élite of German musicians and critics, and immediately accepted for publication by the Universal-Edition of Vienna.

In the spring of 1920 Schnabel, convinced of the authenticity of his creative gifts, announced that he would abstain from playing in public during the following season in order to devote himself exclusively to composition. This, his first bit of deliberate publicity, came as something of a bombshell to his admiring audience. The ultra-conservative *Allgemeine Musik-Zeitung* printed the notice with the comment that this news would be 'received by the musical public with considerable alarm'—an obviously barbed compliment in view of the recent events. In any case Schnabel's desertion of the concert platform was bound to be a painful loss.

Indeed, it would not be too much to say that as a pianist Schnabel by this time had become not only an idol of the public but a national institution. His recitals drew full houses wherever and whenever he played. He was applauded by the public and lauded in the press for the pleasure he gave, for the ideals which he represented and reflected in his programmes, and for his almost fanatical sense of duty to the composer. In particular, he was becoming recognized as an authentic interpreter of Beethoven, both in Germany and in Scandinavia, where he had recently resumed his earlier experiment of playing five of the master's sonatas (including the last) in one concert. Moreover, he was widely respected as one of the few outstanding musicians who cultivated the various departments of his art with equal ability and devotion.

In the conditions obtaining in pre-war Europe all this would have made him not only famous but affluent. In impoverished, chaotic post-war Germany it only imposed unusual hardships. He and his companions travelled in dilapidated, crowded, unheated railway compartments through the length and breadth of a country racked by strikes, riots and rebellion. In Kiel, in the midst of a Spartacus rising, Schnabel played in utter darkness because of sabotage to the power plants. In Frankfurt, French occupation troops paraded their tanks and guns to the blare of military bands while the Schnabel–Flesch–Becker Trio played Schubert and Brahms to the suffering audience. In city after city he played concertos to half-starved and music-hungry audiences under a variety of young conductors then gradually rising to fame—for negligible financial returns. All in all, he had done more than his duty to the German audiences in these years, as indeed he had done throughout the war.

But despite these hectic efforts he and Therese were barely able to keep the family in modest comfort, for the soaring prices threatened the economic existence of the artist as well as the other professional classes. Fees did not remotely keep step with the vertiginous rise in the cost of living. Yet a part of the German public and even some of his colleagues resented his decision to make a 'creative pause', and some ascribed it to the most sordid of motives, since he continued to accept a few comparatively lucrative engagements in Scandinavia. In the circumstances these were just enough to keep the Schnabel household above water and provide a frugal country vacation for the growing sons. Thus they spent the summer of 1920 as paying guests with their formerly well-to-do friends the Jachmanns in Friedersdorf, since they, as all middle-class people, were also feeling the pinch.

Nevertheless, after a considerable struggle with his conscience, Schnabel stuck to his resolve. To escape the distractions of Berlin life he went to the little Austrian village of Mühlheim, not far from the Bavarian border, where he had accepted the hospitality of a Viennese acquaintance in a plain but comfortable country house. Here, in a winter landscape framed by the mountains of Salzburg and Berchtesgaden, he found solitude and other prerequisites for inspiration. To Therese, who would now have to bear the brunt of their economic burdens, he wrote:

'My glimpse of the future is compounded of courage and fear, confidence and doubt. Self-reliance alternates with the lack of it from hour to hour. Is what I am doing a necessity or a frivolous subterfuge? Is surfeit or hunger the propelling force? The end-product alone can give the answer.'

Therese had always been a firm believer in his creative gifts. She had loved every song he had written, and she had performed them all in public with complete conviction and incidentally a great deal of success. But these trifles he now regarded as the sins of his youth. He stopped her singing them, while he started out on new and uncharted seas. Till recently Therese had had no ear for the 'contemporary' idiom, and only after long and painful persuasion, followed by diligent study, had she fought her way through to an understanding of this new language of the rising generation. Now that she was convinced of the inevitability of radical change it was

she who encouraged Artur in his pioneering. With him she believed
that he must interrupt his public career and seek new inspiration in
retirement. And all this in full knowledge that it would mean a
cruel break in the perennial series of joint appearances with him,
which had recently reached a new climax of popularity with their
first performances of Schubert's most popular cycle, *Die schöne
Müllerin*, in Germany and in Scandinavia. With complete confidence
and high hopes for his search of fulfilment she sped him on his way.

His departure meant good-bye for an indefinite time to his German
audiences and to his long and happy public collaboration with his
wife, with Carl Flesch and with his Trio. In January, for the first
time in twenty years, Therese gave her joint recitals with another
partner—Artur's intimate friend Bruno Eisner, an excellent pianist
and like him a voluntary exile from Vienna.

*   *   *

The Mühlheim refuge, in the dead of winter, seemed hardly ideal
for creative work: a thoroughly bourgeois household, rooms filled
with discarded old-fashioned Viennese furniture, with an elderly
third-class piano and a well-worn billiard table as the chief means of
entertainment. The family was agreeable and unobtrusive, tre-
mendously respectful and enchanted whenever Schnabel touched
the keys (playing an occasional sonata with the son of the house, an
amateur violinist). There was a typical Austrian peasant housekeeper who provided typical Austrian country meals. The one
grievous lack in tobacco-hungry post-war Austria was cigars, for
Schnabel had become a passionate cigar smoker—even while working
—but in one way or another a few were smuggled across the border
from Germany. The landscape was wet and dreary at first, but
beautified later by a veil of snow. And always there were the distant
mountains and the idyllic walks along the river Inn. Nature, the
indispensable feeder of his imagination, was casting its subtle spell.

The flow of inspiration was slow at first. He filled his time with
walking, reading and teaching himself English out of a book. After
five days he had begun his second string quartet. He reported to
Therese that 110 bars were written and he had regained the necessary
concentration. After another week he wrote that he hoped to finish
the first movement during his stay. 'I am not hurrying,' he wrote,
'for I want to consider everything carefully before I set it down. . . .
I do hope that when I bring you the fruit of my solitude you will
not think it a complete failure.' After still another week he feels

Huberman, Casals, Schnabel and Hindemith rehearsing in the Hotel Bristol for the Brahms Festival, Vienna, 1933

On the balcony at
Tremezzo, 1934

Tennis at Tremezzo, 1934

With a group of pupils at Tremezzo in 1935, including, on
Schnabel's immediate right, Betty Humby (Lady Beecham)

that the quartet will be 'quite beautiful; above all, beautiful *in sound.*' Near the end of the fourth week the movement was finished—about 300 bars long, taking eighteen minutes to play. It had, he wrote, 'a long breath, strong build-ups, passionate climaxes, and its character is sometimes wild.' But no proper ideas occurred to him for a second movement and after two sketches he abandoned the attempt. It was not until late in the following summer that he continued the work, at Gaschurn, a tiny village in a high valley of Vorarlberg, where he spent a few weeks with his family and two American friends, and where inspiration came on lonely tours through endless valleys, and on steep climbs across glaciers to rocky peaks.

★   ★   ★

In the months preceding his voluntary exile a good many things had happened which seemed calculated to turn him from the newly chosen path. One of the largest German publishing houses, the Ullstein Verlag, had gone into the business of publishing reprints of the great musical classics in a series called *Tonmeister-Ausgabe.* It now proposed to Schnabel that he prepare a new annotated edition of the complete piano sonatas of Beethoven. This offer appealed to him very strongly, since he had come to realize the inadequacy of the various current editions and their frequently misleading or inaccurate interpretations of the original text. It would mean, of course, years of arduous work to be done alongside his teaching and other activities. He accepted the task with the proviso that it would be done thoroughly, at his own pace and convenience.

About the same time an American concert manager, Sol Hurok, proposed a tour of the United States for the ensuing year. This had come about through the intervention of one of Hurok's artists, the famous violinist Mischa Elman, who had visited Berlin some time before and admired Schnabel's playing. The conditions of this offer, however, were not satisfactory and this led to protracted negotiations through another intermediary, namely Schnabel's old friend of bachelor days, Franz (now Francis) Hutter, who had become a department head in a large publishing concern in New York. These negotiations went forward while Artur was deep in the Austrian countryside, trying to concentrate on composing. They dragged on for many months, during which he became thoroughly disgusted with the exigencies of the concert business as conducted in America. Eventually a contract was signed, thanks to the resourceful Hutter, providing for a limited number of concerts during the winter months of 1921–2, the very time which he had wished to devote to composition. Under this contract Schnabel was obligated to use the Knabe piano exclusively on his American tours—at least during the next seven years.

These prospects were indicative of Schnabel's growing international reputation, although he had hardly set foot outside Germany since the war. In a large measure this was due to his teaching and to the success and influence of some of his American pupils. Ever since his early twenties some foreign pupils had come to him in Berlin, where he ranked as one of the two or three leading artist teachers of the time. Young Americans like Guy Maier and Lee Pattison (later a successful duo-piano team) and Edward Ballantine, composer and instructor at Harvard, had spread his name in the United States. One American, the beautiful and gifted young Mary Boxall Boyd, had become his preparatory assistant. Now that the war was over, American and British pupils began to flock to Berlin—and to Schnabel —again.

When he returned from his mountain retreats in the spring and again in the autumn of 1921, he stuck to his resolve not to play in public in so far as Germany was concerned, meantime preparing for his American tour. On the very last day before his departure he was engaged in coaching his disciple Eduard Erdmann in the performance of his *Dance Suite,* which the rambunctious young Latvian had planned to perform at a Berlin recital in January.

★   ★   ★

But there was still another surprise in store in this year of surprises. In the midst of the frantic session with Erdmann, the bell rang and a winsome young woman in her early twenties was shown into the ante-room after announcing herself as the daughter of Artur Schnabel and an outstanding lady violinist, whom he had not seen since his teens!

Schnabel's reaction to this startling piece of news is a matter for speculation. Possibly he was too deeply engrossed to take it in. The maid had not ventured to disturb him, and the young lady was kept waiting in the little reception room until her patience was near to bursting. When he finally entered the room all doubt as to her authenticity was quickly dispelled. The resemblance was striking: face, eyes, and chin—the whole figure of the diminutive Elisabeth (nicknamed Ellie) was a miniature of Artur. She was his daughter without a doubt, though only seventeen years younger than himself.

Moreover, she revealed that besides being her father, Artur was also the grandfather of a two-year-old boy. Having inherited her talents and temperament from both parents, Ellie proceeded to demonstrate them at the keyboard by playing a composition of her own. All in all, she was so charming, vivacious, and obviously gifted that very soon the entire family were captivated, including the two boys when they met her after Artur's return from America. Therese, who might have had pardonable reservations, took Ellie to her heart as the daughter of the family. From that moment she became a new factor in the domestic life of the Schnabels. It was the most unexpected but by no means unwelcome contribution to 'the happiest years' of Artur's life.

At the risk of impairing the continuity of our story, the following explanatory facts might be added at this time. The young lady had been adopted and brought up in the family of a very well situated Austrian industrialist, and had married the son of the house. She was brilliantly gifted in music, as might be expected, and had already given proof of her talents by producing a number of compositions of various kinds and playing some of them to her delighted father. Later she was to become a devoted student of ecclesiastical music. She composed cantatas and liturgical music, as well as an opera and other secular works, under her professional name Elizabeth Rostra. In 1928 she moved to Berlin and became a welcome and lively member of the Schnabel circle. After the second World War, which she spent in Paris, she emigrated to Canada. Her son, J. Christopher Herold, in turn inherited her linguistic and literary gifts.

16. American Interlude

STILL under the influence of the emotional experience occasioned
by the appearance of Ellie, Schnabel left for Hamburg to embark
on the *Manchuria*, a slow, unfashionable American liner bound for
New York. He might have been travelling in the deepest incognito,
for the plain folk who made up the ship's company obviously had
never heard of him. Moreover, he spent the first few days in bed,
suffering from a sore throat and low fever. When he recovered, he
was out in mid-ocean. After ten days' battle with the elements the
ship arrived in New York harbour in the late afternoon during a
typical American blizzard which all but obliterated the famous New
York skyline—his first American disappointment.

Schnabel was met by his old friend Francis Hutter, and sundry
acquaintances. Hutter had conducted all the negotiations concerning
Schnabel's New York appearances and the subsequent American
tour which, it seemed, was still in the promissory stage.

Within three hours of his arrival in New York, well-meaning
colleagues dragged him off to the most bizarre musical event he had
yet experienced—a testimonial concert for the composer Moritz
Moszkowski, reported to be ill and destitute in Paris. Fifteen famous
and near-famous pianists appeared on the stage of Carnegie Hall
simultaneously, playing on fifteen pianos of five different makes.
They played singly, two-by-two, and all together while the eminent
Walter Damrosch conducted them from the rear of the stage. As
the *pièce de résistance* they performed the several movements of
Schumann's *Carnaval* in rotation, the *Préambule* and the final *March*
being played by all fifteen in chorus. Among the stars of this
performance were Wilhelm Backhaus, Harold Bauer, Ossip
Gabrilowitch, Ignaz Friedman, Joseph Lhévinne, Germaine Schnitzer
and Elly Ney. Prodigious sums were collected in donations, by the
sale of autographs, and other money-raising devices—enough to keep
several starving musicians in affluence for years. Sceptic that he was,
Schnabel was not exactly impressed by this typically American
demonstration of sentimental generosity—with free publicity for all.
His comments are not on record. He had been warned in advance

that in America he must never make an ironical remark—a temptation he obviously could not resist.

His own debut a few days later was in dismal contrast to that gala demonstration. It came on the afternoon of Christmas Day, which happened to fall on a Sunday. As might have been expected, only a handful of dedicated followers plus a rather pathetic assortment of post-prandial free-ticket holders (euphemistically described by one reviewer as a goodly number) turned up in the cavernous spaces of Carnegie Hall. They listened with surprising concentration to what was then regarded as a heavy programme, consisting of Schumann's C major Fantasy, a posthumous sonata by Schubert, and the F minor sonata of Brahms. As usual he gave no encores, but there was enough applause to cause *Musical America* to complain about the unpleasant impression created by a 'certain element' indulging in repeated displays of demonstrative enthusiasm.

Only a corporal's guard of critics turned up. The *New York Times* printed no review of the concert, but devoted a half-column to an evening concert which Chaliapin gave to a vast audience in the Hippodrome. The *Tribune* carried an unsigned paragraph in six-point type stating that Schnabel's technique was imposing and his interpretations 'admirable'. Only one eminent critic, Deems Taylor of the *New York World*, made bold to say that Schnabel belonged in the first rank of living pianists; that there was beauty and character in his tone; and that he 'produced the most arduous effect with that ease and dignity which are among the marked signs of a really great artist'. The editor of the *Musical Courier* resented what he considered Schnabel's superior attitude, and his exacting programme, presumably calculated to tell the audience what they ought to want. This was followed by an editorial advising Mr. Schnabel to 'be sensible' and cater to the American audience in 'selling his wares'.

Altogether this result was not surprising if one considers that there was virtually no advance advertising of Schnabel's coming, that he had opposed all newspaper publicity, and that his name was generally unknown except among his colleagues, his former pupils and a few people who had heard him in Europe before the war. He had made no gramophone records and had ignored the musical trade journals, which now returned the compliment in kind. With characteristic stubbornness he had determined to treat the United States like every other country in which he had appeared, without regard to its vast size, its frankly commercial attitudes, and the highly developed machinery of promotion which had become indispensable to success. His own reaction to his first appearance was normal. 'I played,' he wrote home, 'as well as I could in so far as the . . . instrument permitted. My success appears to be considerable."

His optimism faded rather suddenly after the next recital, three weeks later at Town Hall. This was to be the real test: an all-Beethoven programme consisting of four sonatas including opus 110 and opus 111, plus the *Thirty-Two Variations* in C minor, which, curiously enough, he had been warned by colleagues not to play.[1] It was a kind of programme he had been playing in Europe for years, and he refused to believe that Americans would not appreciate it. But the hall, although much smaller than Carnegie, was only half full. Schnabel had given strict orders that no free tickets be given out except to a few fellow-musicians. Among them were Backhaus, Lhévinne, Gabrilowitch, Casals and some others—quite a galaxy of stars. According to his own report, he played his best. The listeners, he felt, were deeply stirred. But next day the papers seemed determined to convince him that he had failed—*versungen und vertan,* like Walther in the first act of *Die Meistersinger.*

The facts, however, don't quite bear him out. It is true that the *New York Times* merely reported the concert in a line or two, but H. E. Krehbiel of the *Tribune,* an acknowledged Beethoven authority and editor of Thayer's *Life* of the master, wrote: 'The tones of Beethoven, as played by Mr. Schnabel, detached themselves from the instrument and became embodied beauty, vitalized by feeling.' The others were either equivocal or cautious in their comments. Schnabel came to the somewhat hasty conclusion that conditions were unfavourable for his kind of music-making, and that America was not for him. In a fit of depression he wanted to cancel his third recital, and only the intervention of his old friend Gabrilowitch prevented this irrational step.

The concert took place ten days later, on a Wednesday afternoon, he wrote, for the benefit of 'the ladies who don't happen to be playing bridge'. This time he deliberately chose what he considered a popular programme—Weber's A-flat major sonata, the four Schubert impromptus, opus 90 and Chopin's B-flat minor sonata. But the ladies—bridge or no bridge—stayed away in large numbers and only

---

[1] According to a story told in Beethoven's biographies the master, hearing the daughter of the piano-maker Streicher practising this piece, asked what it was, and on being told it was his own work, exclaimed: 'What an ass I was to write it.' This had caused a certain American critic to call it a mediocre work and it was thought unwise to ignore this dictum of recognized authority.

an inner circle of devoted partisans attended, including most of the eminent pianists then in New York. Half the audience crowded into the artist's room afterwards to shake his hand. 'I now enjoy,' he wrote ironically, 'a high reputation among about one hundred denizens of this city of eight millions. Nearly half of them are my former pupils and the rest are European colleagues.'

The *Times* and the *Tribune* were silent about this concert, having done their stint on the previous one; only the *New York Herald* opined that he was a 'piano interpreter of high rank'.

Materially, Schnabel's American prospects were shrouded in darkness. There were few engagements, and fewer still at the fees which he had stipulated. The energetic Mr. Hurok, who had done so well for Mischa Elman, and was doing so magnificently for Chaliapin (advertised as the 'highest paid artist in the world'), professed great difficulty in placing the reputedly too serious Artur Schnabel in the smaller cities, where people were said to be afraid of sonatas. All the experts of the concert business tried to impress him with the fact that he must appeal to the 'tired business man'. Schnabel replied that 'my only employer is the art'. He would not change his programmes in any way.

However, this was not the only difficulty. Schnabel, though famous in Europe, was simply unknown to the general public in America and had not been advertised with the usual epithets and slogans used in the promotion of celebrities. Besides, there was at this time in America a superfluity of pianists of various grades and types, whose names and pictures were spread across the billboards of the country and the pages of the professional Press. 'I feel,' he wrote, 'like an owl which has flown to Athens without really being an owl.'[1] Homesickness, annoyance and a general sense of futility combined to make him disgusted with the whole American adventure, and he tried unsuccessfully to find ways and means to cancel the tour without breaking his contract. A successful trip to Buffalo and Detroit, where he played Brahms' D minor concerto with the orchestra under Gabrilowitch, was the only pleasant interlude in a long period of 'unemployment'.[2] However, he stayed and even fulfilled his

[1] 'Owls to Athens' is the German equivalent of 'coals to Newcastle'.

[2] By a completely fortuitous coincidence, this concert turned out to become historic in a curious way. The Detroit *Free Press*, owner of a local radio station, experimentally picked up the concert and broadcast it to a far-flung radio audience. Thus Schnabel, who resisted radio transmission and all mechanical reproduction for many years after this widely publicized event, became an unwitting pioneer in the broadcasting of good music.

contract to make what he called 'Ampico preserves', record rolls for
the Knabe-Ampico pianola. This, he punned, was the only method
for him to play a rôle in America.

*   *   *

Despite all disappointments and the obvious disharmony between
Schnabel's inflexible principles and the social climate of America (a
'mixture of violence and indifference'), there was no lack of friendly
sociability and comradeship. Great artists like Richard Strauss, the
skat partner and musical mentor of his twenties; Ossip Gabrilowitch,
his class-mate of the Leschetizky years; the composer Paolo Gallico,
an intimate of pre-war Berlin days; respected colleagues like Fritz
Kreisler, Ignace Friedman, Joseph Lhévinne, Ernest Hutcheson, David
Mannes and 'that wonderful man Casals'—all these were good com-
rades and kindred souls to whom he could pour out his heart without
fear of being misunderstood. He was never lonely, in fact he was
rarely alone, as he wrote, 'except in bed or in my bath'. Day after
day he dined at the houses of friends, old and new, 'in order to increase
my clientèle', but more likely to hold forth on politics, art and the
decay of modern society.

He had been warned before coming to America never to criticize
American taste or customs, never to be sarcastic about popular heroes,
never to mention communism; but he did all these things to his heart's
content, often with a sharp tongue, and his caustic witticisms gained
greater currency than his words of praise. His favourite parlour trick
was to play a contrapuntal mélange consisting of such popular
favourites as Rachmaninof's C-sharp minor *Prelude,* Paderewski's
Minuet, Dvořák's *Humoresque,* and Kreisler's *Caprice viennois* under
the title 'United Pets of America'.

Moving among the polyglot musical fraternity he actually met
very few native Americans, but many whose recently acquired
Americanism made them super-sensitive to criticism of all things
American. He was a little too fond of clever repartee at the expense
of eager businessmen proud of their products. When the Ampico
man boasted that the instrument was capable of reproducing 'sixteen
nuances, from pianissimo to fortissimo', he answered, 'Too bad! *I*
happen to use seventeen.' These things combined to make him less
popular than he might have been, and aroused a certain hostility in
circles that might have proved useful in a material sense.

But there is no doubt that as an artist he gave all that was in him.
Each time he played, according to his testimony, he played to his

own complete satisfaction. 'A new feeling of self-delectation,' he wrote to Therese, 'has come to me now. I hope I shall never lose it again. Quite recently I had a presentiment that my piano playing will not change materially from now on: a sort of consciousness of maturity, a realization that I shall no longer have to struggle for it, but garner it like a fruit. . . . In consequence I enjoy it so much more than in the past.' It is remarkable that this sense of maturity as a performing artist came to him in America, in an environment and under conditions which he considered unfavourable to artistic achievement. It is as though his very resistance to all external factors had made him concentrate all the more on the essence of the music, on playing 'as though for himself alone'. 'But,' he continued, 'this condition makes it quite impossible for me (I feel this irrevocably) to resume the virtuoso career in the previous proportions. For merely to enjoy makes a man mean. And to persist in an occupation which no longer poses a problem would lower me to the level of a mere seller of finished goods. In contrast to this [piano playing], my composing is in its budding stage; and I would like, during the next fifteen years or so—if it be my lot to live them—to work and strive to discover whether it can come to fruition.'

Accordingly, when Schnabel returned to Germany in the spring of 1922 he was more than ever determined to dedicate all his efforts to the ultimate purpose of composition. It was now two years since he had announced his intention not to play in public in Germany till further notice and devote himself to composition. He had made good his threat so far as Germany was concerned: his American excursion was primarily an effort to support this resolve and prolong it. Concerts in impoverished and inflation-ridden Germany would in any case not have been profitable; and the American tour, though financially disappointing, might see him through another creative period. Even as it was, the amount of dollars earned represented a considerable sum when translated into German currency, and he managed to add to it by filling a few extra engagements in the hard-currency countries of Scandinavia and by his usual teaching activity during the spring. Moreover, he had reason to be encouraged by the resounding success of his first string quartet at the German Tonkünstlerfest in Düsseldorf that June—a splendid vindication for the recent rejection of his *Dance Suite* by most of the Berlin critics, when played by Eduard Erdmann during Schnabel's absence in America. Be that as it may, Schnabel arranged to spend most of the summer composing at the lovely Austrian lakeside village of Rindbach, where he and Therese had passed so many happy and active summers in the pre-war years. The old 'Villa Schnabel' was no more, but the family found a most comfortable refuge in the Mendelssohns' beautiful country house, left vacant that year. Here he continued work on his second string quartet (finished a little later at Eger) and also composed his only piano sonata, which was to be performed by Eduard Erdmann before long.

All this time there had been much argument and correspondence concerning his return to America for a second visit, in order to retrieve the 'failure' of the first. Hurok was attempting to book a coast-to-coast tour for the second half of the season 1922-3. Schnabel did not give his final consent until November, and at the same time he wrote to Therese that 'it will surely be my farewell visit'. Moreover, this time she would have to accompany him to make the trip more bearable. The decision to have another try was made in view of a most dismal economic outlook in Germany. The slow depreciation of the currency, which had brought increasing hardship to salaried and professional classes, now continued at a frighteningly accelerated speed. And, as always, Germany's misery was accompanied by increased social and political strife.

The prospect was dark indeed when Artur and Therese embarked for New York shortly after Christmas, leaving the household in the charge of the faithful Lili Walldorf, and the children in the care of their one-time nurse Luise. Both boys, aged thirteen and eleven, were now at school in Berlin, and the elder (Karl Ulrich) was well advanced as a piano student of Leonid Kreutzer, at the Hochschule für Musik.

★   ★   ★

Schnabel's second arrival in America was certainly more auspicious than the first. Quite a number of friends were on hand to greet him and his wife when the *President Fillmore* docked in New York. Manager Hurok reported he had booked a tour of about thirty concerts for him—from New York to California. It had a noble and successful beginning under the auspices of the Society of the Friends of Music, whose president (Mrs. J. F. D. Lanier) was to become one of his most loyal friends in America. It was an all-Beethoven concert conducted by Artur Bodanzky,[1] at which Schnabel

---

[1] Artur Bodanzky, following a distinguished career in Austria, Germany and England, came to New York as conductor at the Metropolitan Opera in 1915 and acted as musical director of the Friends of Music from 1917.

played the G major concerto and the solo part of the *Choral Fantasy*, opus 80, a work so rarely performed in America as to have the effect of a novelty. This time the *New York Times* gave him at least a respectful notice, saying that he 'caught and truly portrayed the spirit of Beethoven's work', while H. E. Krehbiel in the *Tribune* emphasized his 'great beauty of tone' as well as his 'impeccable technical finish'.

Later in the season he played with the New York Philharmonic Society under Willem Mengelberg, the Boston Symphony Orchestra under Bruno Walter, and the New York Symphony under Walter Damrosch. In this last concert he was joined by his two already famous American pupils, Guy Maier and Lee Pattison, in Bach's triple concerto.[1] Travelling across the continent Schnabel played in all the important cities of California, the Mountain States and the Middle West, swerving as far north as Montana and as far south as Texas. Contrary to the fears of managerial experts, the response almost everywhere was excellent and in the chief cities it was little short of triumphant. The critics in most places were enthusiastic and in some ecstatic. Yet everywhere, without exception, Schnabel played his customary programmes, consisting entirely of sonatas and other large cyclical works, or complete groups of works by the great classic and romantic composers. He made no concessions to so-called popular taste and sometimes seemed to take a puckish delight in playing long, unfamiliar works in musically backward communities, as if to prove that music knows no social or educational boundaries. He never allowed himself to be hurried by restlessness in the audience and he was not the least bit rattled when a large part of his Colorado Springs audience walked out one by one during the twenty-four *Preludes* of Chopin.

Nevertheless, he had no greater sense of satisfaction in his activity than he had experienced on his first visit to the United States. Many years later, when recalling this period of his career, he said that he had been very unhappy on this tour, that he had only a moderate success and 'certainly didn't deserve more'. That this is not to be taken literally is clear from contemporary accounts and criticisms, and also from what follows. 'It may be,' he said, 'that my approach to musical life in America was a wrong one, and so I was somehow

---

[1] By a curious coincidence a little girl aged ten named Helen Fogel played her debut recital on the same evening in Æolian Hall. Unknown to Schnabel at the time, she became his pupil many years later, and his daughter-in-law in 1940. As Helen Schnabel, she is still one of the best interpreters of his piano pieces.

frustrated. . . . I disliked, and I still dislike the star system, and I believed and still believe that I belong to a department of music to which most of the popular performers of this period did not belong. Therefore I didn't do as well as I might have in other circumstances.'

Added to his sense of frustration in failing to penetrate the hard crust of American indifference were the minor annoyances caused by semi-primitive local conditions, sketchy arrangements and instruments imperfectly adjusted to his needs. In many respects large parts of America were still 'raw' in artistic as well as human relations. What struck him in the West was what had struck Charles Dickens in America some eighty years before—the indifference and carelessness, the lack of reverence and respect for art, while going to incredible lengths in the worship of *artists*, that is, the well-publicized celebrities or stars. The people were everywhere cordial and grateful enough, but those who dealt with the artist personally were just a little too business-like for his taste. In Helena, Montana, where the Schnabels arrived in a blizzard, he learned that the concert in the next port of call had been cancelled, because the local society had disbanded for lack of funds. In a northern California town he gathered, from a newspaper headline, that he—Artur Schnabel—would not arrive because of a snowstorm, so the concert was 'postponed'. The actual fact of his presence caused no apology, only a change in schedule which sent him scurrying off to San Francisco the same night. Perhaps the most bizarre result of American 'carelessness' was when he saw his picture—at the age of about twenty—in a San Francisco paper with a strange name under it and the legend that he was 'wanted' for murder!

The vast distances, the vagaries of the climate, the inadequate provisions for strangers unfamiliar with the country—all this constituted a combination of natural and organized discomfort incompatible with the atmosphere in which art could thrive. On the other hand he was charmed by the hearty egalitarianism which he experienced in many places. The best example of this was a Vienna-born waiter in Colorado Springs who invited the Schnabels for a ride in his own motor-car to the top of Pike's Peak—as a friendly gesture to a former compatriot!

The climax of his discontent came on the return journey, in Chicago. Here the piano developed a sticky key in a critical passage of the Brahms D minor concerto. He refused to go on and signalled to the conductor (Frederick Stock) to stop. After some delay he finished the concerto on another instrument raised from beneath the

stage. Schnabel regarded this as a hint of fate. He admitted freely
that this accident could happen to any piano, and he did not blame
the makers. But he had already made up his mind to sever his
connexion with the Knabe firm. Actually it was not the piano at all
but himself and his reaction to America that had reached the breaking-
point. If the Knabe people would not release him, he would simply
not return to the United States for the remainder of the seven-year
contract. This is exactly what happened in the event. He and
America didn't get on together; as he had predicted, this was to be
his last visit—at least for some years.

But there were other and deeper reasons for his decision. He
was tired of the repetitive occupation of the touring performer. His
repertoire, highly selective as it was, no longer exhausted his capabilities, nor did it satisfy his creative instinct. He was no longer 'enjoying'
his work as he had done the year before: he would have to widen his
horizon to yet unexplored regions of musical re-creation. And this
called for intensive activity rather than extensive tours.

Schnabel's second American tour ended at the Mannes Music
School in New York, in four intimate concerts of the kind he really
liked, with not a hint of celebrity glamour or virtuosity about them.
The first was a recital of some personal favourites, from Bach's *Italian
Concerto* to Schumann's *Davidsbündler*; the second consisted of
Schubert's *Winterreise* with Therese Schnabel; the third was a four-
hand programme (mostly Schubert) with Ernest Hutcheson, and the
last an all-Beethoven sonata programme by himself.

An artist of somewhat less elevated standards, with a less rigid
sense of obligation to his 'employer', and slightly less exacting with
himself and his audience might well have been gratified by his
accomplishment and the impression he had made. But he was
inflexible in the artistic demands he made upon himself, and in his
own judgment he had failed. When, if ever, he would see America
again was a secret in the lap of the gods. As to his own immediate
future his decision was made. As to America, we now know that it
was about to go through one of the most hectic, materialistic and
distracted periods in its history, the build-up to the tragic climax
of boom-and-bust followed by the sobering experience of the great
economic depression. To people gifted with 'second sight' it may
have seemed providential that Schnabel stayed away from a country
so disinclined to inwardness and reflection as was America in the
roaring 'twenties.

17. *Adventures in Atonality*

WHEN in the depth of the winter of 1920–1 Schnabel took refuge in the little Austrian village of Mühlheim in order to explore his own creative resources, he had just four adult works to his credit: that is to say, compositions written in his thirties, and separated from what might be called his creative adolescence by a decade mainly devoted to his expanding career as a concert pianist. One of the four, the piano quintet of 1915, was cast in the accepted post-romantic mould of the pre-war period; the other three were in the free chromatic or so-called atonal idiom of which Schönberg had been the early pioneer, and which Schnabel developed into his own personal style. These three 'revolutionary' works comprised the *Notturno* for voice and piano, the first string quartet, and the sonata for violin solo, written respectively in 1914, 1918 and 1919. All of them had been performed in public and had been received with varying degrees of critical abuse by the conservative majority and with more or less cautious approval by the more progressive or adventurous few.

With this bold experiment Schnabel had come to a parting of the ways. His future course lay in the development of new resources in the field of linear counterpoint, freed from all the fetters of the traditional harmonic laws and conventional rhythmic patterns, but also from the new theories of atonal music promulgated by Matthias Hauer and later adopted by the Schönberg circle. He would have nothing to do with the 'isms' of the recent past. 'Nothing is so stale,' he used to say, 'as the ideas of the day before yesterday.' But he was never averse to real beauty—even of the old-fashioned sensuous kind.

Beautiful or not, he knew perfectly well that his kind of music would encounter the implacable hostility of the Old Guard and almost total lack of comprehension on the part of the general public. That had been the fate of his first string quartet, which later experienced a complete reversal of opinion. The second string quartet, of 1921, was a complete break with the past. In it he adapted the relentlessly dissonant counterpoint of his most advanced contemporaries to an

almost bewildering density of tonal texture. An outstanding characteristic of this work is the ingenious integration of its three movements by the invention of ever new thematic ideas related to one
basic theme first stated in the introduction. This fantastic wealth of
ideas, crowded and sometimes telescoped together, raised the question
in many minds whether Schnabel's music was not wholly cerebral
and beyond the musical perceptiveness of the average person. This
quartet was to remain problematical for years to come. When first
performed in Berlin (in 1924) the critics were inclined to reserve
judgment, while conceding the beauty of some of its melodic material.
Many were troubled by the difficulty of comprehending the music
at a first hearing. 'One's first impression,' wrote one reviewer, 'is
diverted into *intellectual effort* by the interesting content much sooner
than would be the case in later hearings.'

Here, indeed, is the basic difficulty which applies to much contemporary music: it requires so much mental strain on the part of
the listener that one or even two hearings are rarely enough to clear
the way for æsthetic enjoyment.

Undeterred by such material considerations, Schnabel was remarkably happy in his new creative activity. While he could not afford
to suspend his concert appearances indefinitely for the sake of the
financially unproductive task of composing, he devoted his summer
holidays from 1921 to 1925 to composition and the rest of the year to
playing and teaching. As these were for the most part lean years, the
Schnabels spent their summers accordingly—in the inn of a tiny
mountain village of the Vorarlberg, in the Mendelssohns' villa at
Rindbach or at the Jachmanns' house at Friedersdorf in Silesia, where
the third and fourth string quartets were written in 1923 and 1924,
also his string trio in 1925.

*   *   *

The third quartet turned out to be the most accomplished chamber
music work to date, showing a remarkable advance over its predecessors in both content and form. According to Ernst Křenek it
is one of the truly great works in the contemporary idiom. The
composer's distribution of the material has become much clearer, the
tonal texture less crowded and the articulation more incisive. Again
the opening theme dominates the whole work. The thematic material
is rich and widely varied, but unity of design is accomplished by a
technique which is very much Schnabel's own: motivic features
appear again and again in musical complexes of heterogeneous

character. The three movements, played without a break, are shorter than in the earlier quartets, varied in mood, fanciful and at times amusing. Schnabel's good humour, while working on the piece, shows itself in a surrealistically distorted waltz passage superscribed '*Mit Gemüt, etwas schmalzig*', to which he adds one of his typical home-made rhymes:

> *Aus der Kunst*
> *wird auch nur Dunst*
> ('Even art goes up in smoke').

But the end of the movement is serious again and reflects a peculiarly personal sadness.

This work had to wait seven years before it was performed by the progressively minded Kolisch Quartet in Berlin. By this time Schnabel's reputation as a composer, in Germany at least, had risen to the point where he was always respectfully listened to and intelligently discussed. One courageous critic, fond of fanciful imagery (Oskar Bie), apostrophized him as a master of form and likened the music to 'an almost planetary circling of sound images'. If only for the record, it is worth quoting this passage written in 1931 about the man who fifteen years before was dismissed as persistent but untalented: [1]

'Beethoven's last quartets were described for decades as eccentric, bizarre and unplayable. Today the academicians grovel before him in the dust. Will Schnabel's music have a similar fate? I for one am sorry for those who wish to decide this question now, by whistling on their hollow keys.'

As this reference implies, the whistlers and hissers were still in evidence whenever Schnabel was performed.

Two more works came out of Schnabel's summer workshop in Friedersdorf, the fourth string quartet in 1924, and a string trio in 1925. The quartet has no strikingly new features; in fact it reverts to the congested polyphonic texture of the second, but shows many ingenious contrapuntal devices. The first movement—a kind of fantasia—conforms to Schnabel's peculiar kaleidoscopic style, in which several short motifs are used to form different contexts. The second is of the slow scherzo type, and the beginning of the *finale* is one of the rare instances in which Schnabel employs strict fugato-like imitation. Later this gives way to his usual manner of tightly

[1] Rudolf Kastner, critic of the Berlin *Morgenpost*.

packed contrapuntal continuity. (The work was not performed till many years later in New York.)

The string trio, by contrast, is much more transparent and concise, and seems to betoken the composer's desire for greater clarity and directness of expression. Vigour and expressive effect are achieved through clear and purposeful design rather than abundance of material. Its slow second movement has a virtually diatonic two-voice subject of great beauty, combining stateliness with other-worldly serenity. This work, practically unnoticed for ten years, was finally chosen by the Austrian section of the International Society for Contemporary Music to be performed in Vienna in 1936, less than two years before Hitler's annexation of Austria made an end of all 'musical bolshevism' in Greater Germany.

Vienna was not only the cradle of atonalism and the citadel of musical radicalism in the inter-war period but also the city in which Schnabel had grown up in the autumnal days of Brahms, Bruckner and Hugo Wolf. Schnabel had remained aloof from the movement and the organization which had been promoting advanced contemporary music. He had been curiously shy about his own creative accomplishments, had not performed any of his own works in public since the 'romantic' days of his youth, and was hardly known as a composer outside Germany. It was therefore an unusual event when the Viennese section ventured to give the first performance of a work by a renegade Austrian composer who was being acclaimed by audiences throughout Europe and America as one of the greatest pianists of the time.

The Viennese showed no more than respectful appreciation of their fellow-citizen and the critics were reasonably objective. The *Freie Presse* hailed him as a 'creative musician of power and originality', whose polyphony tended to out-Reger Max Reger—a not altogether unintelligent comparison. They were not shocked, of course, by the bold harmonic structure which 'often leaves the bounds of tonality', for even the hardiest Viennese critic was by this time inured to the atonal extravaganzas of the post-Schönberg generation. Schnabel himself was not present; in fact he rarely attended performances of his works until the last decade of his life.

Nor did he make any strenuous efforts to get them performed— or published. Indeed, he seldom even tried his works over on the piano except for colleagues and intimates—or disciples who intended to perform them. Whenever he was asked about his reluctance to play either his own works or novelties by other composers, he maintained that the playing of new works was the particular duty of the younger generation—a euphemistic explanation if ever there was one.

*   *   *

The early 1920's were, with the exception of the last decade and a half of his life, Schnabel's most productive years. They were also the most significant, because within the limited time available to him he developed his own characteristic mode of expression. In the intimate yet discursive medium of the string quartet he projected his musical thoughts in their most personal and trenchant form. Only once, in the piano sonata, did he depart from his favourite vehicle in these years. It is curious, and almost unique, that a great pianist-composer, who communicated so much of the world's finest music through the medium of his instrument, should write so little for that instrument; but this is just another paradox in Schnabel's nature. He began writing for the piano in his youth, plunged into chamber music in early middle age, became a symphonist in the last decade of his life, but made only a very occasional gesture in the direction of the piano, usually to please a favourite young colleague. Thus, the *Dance Suite* and the piano sonata were written with Eduard Erdmann in mind: indeed, there was hardly another pianist alive who would have tackled their diabolical difficulties but this impetuous, somewhat uncouth yet highly intellectual young artist.

Erdmann was a child of the Baltic regions, a Tarzan-like figure with long arms, huge angular shoulders and abnormally large hands—a rather unexpected aberration in a family of professors and philosophers. A greater contrast could hardly be imagined than that which existed between him and the small, handsome and always perfectly groomed Schnabel, whom he adored. Gifted both as pianist and composer, he embraced the revolutionary creed of the Schönberg circle and became a brilliant exponent of contemporary music. It was he who insisted on Schnabel's writing 'something for the piano' so he (Erdmann) could play it.

When Schnabel finally produced this 'something' (in 1923) it turned out to be a sprawling five-movement tone-structure of forty-five minutes' duration, which remained his last piano work for twenty-five years. It is hardly a sonata by the accepted definition, but Erdmann nevertheless suggested that it be entitled sonata, 'first because of its dimensions, second because of its weight, and thirdly—why not?' Like most of Schnabel's compositions it is not only of vast design but full of imagination, of passionate and even vehement expression, yet not without tender and strangely ethereal moments. It is ultra-chromatic and ultra-dissonant throughout, with only rare lapses into traditional harmony. In 1924, it was submitted to the jury of the I.S.C.M. by its German section and was accepted for performance at the International Festival in Venice the following year. Erdmann played it at the Teatro Fenice to a predominantly Italian and unsuspecting audience which, after being subjected to more than an hour of contemporary novelties, had had its patience stretched to the breaking-point. It listened with admirable decorum until the end, when a stentorian voice (later identified as that of a well-known Spanish cellist) emitted the single word *basta*! There was the usual mixture of applause and hissing.

Neither Erdmann nor Schnabel were in the least perturbed or surprised. The incident remained notorious and was duly embellished in the telling. Years later Arturo Toscanini, when Schnabel was introduced to him, remarked with a gentle terror in his voice: 'Tell me: are you really the Schnabel who wrote that terrible piece I heard in Venice?' Schnabel was delighted to acknowledge himself the culprit. The two nevertheless remained friends, although their attitudes to music were essentially different and their paths rarely crossed.

With the completion of his string trio Schnabel in 1925 stopped composing for nearly six years. He himself gave no reason for this strange hiatus, but implied that other preoccupations, such as the work on his edition of the Beethoven sonatas, may have intervened. In his spoken reminiscences he simply said: 'And then I stopped composing.' It is true, of course, that these were among the busiest years of his life, comprising a great many concert performances and the memorizing of an enormous volume of music he had not previously played in public. In any case he liked to speak of himself at this time as an 'amateur composer' or to say that composition was to him 'a kind of sport'. What he meant to convey, surely, is that he composed for love rather than for payment, popularity, or fame.

The fact that he used the seasons of recreation and outdoor living for the exercise of his creative faculty was both practical and characteristic of Schnabel. He drew inspiration from the countryside—the flowers, the trees, the sky, the majesty of the mountain peaks, all of which was by the subtle alchemy of imagination transmuted into tone. He adored the mountains above all: the gentle woodland path, the steady climb, the pause in some idyllic spot, the final ascent and the vista of the distant peaks: the mystery of the vaguely longed-for Beyond and the solace of present achievement—all these were symbols of the transcendental universe which he found mirrored in the great masters' works and which he hoped to reflect in his own. Amateur composer or just professional musician, he could now in the middle of life look back with a degree of satisfaction upon a considerable body of mature works.

He had reached a point of rest in his creative development. It was time for a pause, while he exercised his faculties in other areas of musical art.

18. Return of the Prodigal

THE year 1923 was a year of tragedy for the German nation. It began with armed occupation, passed through political terror and ended in the economic ruin of the country's middle class. Ten days after the Schnabels sailed for America the French army marched into the industrial region of the Ruhr to enforce the payment of reparations. In consequence of a well-organized 'passive resistance' currency inflation was deliberately permitted to get out of hand, and the result was financial chaos and widespread hunger and misery. This in turn brought the dangerous growth of violence and armed repression —a foretaste of more sinister events yet to come.

One of the most astonishing facts of this fantastic period was that ordinary people, swept along by the inexorable current of fate, were still able to continue their customary occupations in virtual ignorance of the unprecedented catastrophe that was to overtake them. It was as though the experiences of the war had dulled their powers of perception and inured them to misfortune and suffering. The usual tasks were done, daily duties performed, enjoyment and recreation provided as usual: plays were performed, music was made and works of art created in a fever of activity seemingly stimulated by the abnormal and bizarre events of the day. Berlin's music-lovers in these days enjoyed unforgettable performances of Beethoven and Mozart in the Philharmonie and the two opera houses, even while food riots raged in East Berlin and the country was in a state of siege. News of political murders, of civil war in Saxony, of the 'Black Reichswehr', the sinister 'Organization C' and the Hitler-Ludendorff beerhall *putsch* made no impression on the people while their constant daytime preoccupation was the rapidly accelerating decline of the mark.

At the time of the Schnabels' departure for America in 1922 the already inflated mark had stood at 7,000 to the dollar. When they returned, less than four months later, it was several millions to the dollar. Soon it began its mad plunge through hundreds and thousands of millions until the printing press was unable to keep pace with the speed of inflation, and so-called basic figures subject to varying 'multipliers' took the place of regular prices. Two years later, when the currency was stabilized, paper marks were called in at the rate of a billion to one!   One of the effects of this operation was that the savings of ordinary people were swept away in one great holocaust, while the big producers, speculators and war profiteers had accumulated vast amounts in terms of real values and goods.

Schnabel, who had lost his savings during the war, now lost them a second time.   Years later he spoke of this runaway inflation as the maddest period he had ever lived through.   In his reminiscences he related the following tragi-comic episode.   After one of his recitals he had to hire a porter to carry home the proceeds—a suitcase full of paper marks.   In order to lighten the load he stopped at a delicatessen shop to buy a sausage, thus converting dwindling currency into a solid investment.   But next day he read in the paper that—for once— sausage prices had gone down.   Such were the uncertainties of life!

Schnabel was notoriously innocent in matters of finance.   Usually, after filling engagements abroad, he had immediately exchanged his hard currency earnings into marks, which then proceeded to dwindle in value until very little was left.   How much he managed to salvage out of his American surplus is not known.   However, there is in his letters not a trace of complaint about financial difficulties, and the Schnabel household went on as before: on a necessarily spacious yet modest scale, with two growing boys at school and the usual number of dependents and personnel.   On the other hand, Schnabel's mode of life was definitely economical.   Devoid of superficial pride, he rode on trams and buses (when not engaged in his favourite exercise of walking) and indulged in few luxuries except cigars.

Having now renounced his American prospects till further notice, he decided to resume the full activities of the professional musician once again in Germany, where he had not played in public for more than three years.   But first, during the pleasant month of May, he revisited his home city of Vienna for three concerts in a row.   The first was with orchestra and the last an all-Beethoven recital for which, he was pleased to report, there was great demand.   The enthusiasm of musical Vienna for its native son, the intelligent participation of the audience and the genuine warmth and affection shown him by a host of old admirers was a pleasant experience for one who had always taken a dim view of the musical taste of the light-hearted Viennese. This revival of youthful memories and friendships, not forgetting the reunion with his parents and other relatives, seemed to give a new fillip to his ambition as a performer.   Moreover, his growing inter- national fame had brought many foreigners to these concerts, including some aspiring young artists who then and there decided to become his pupils. Among them was a young British pianist, Marguerite Macintyre, who was to form an important link with his future English public.

Altogether, he was so impressed with the beauty and charm of his old 'decadent' Vienna that for a few moments he toyed with the idea of settling there with his family. In this distinctly nostalgic mood he played his very best, as he wrote to Therese, 'although I have left the *Männchen* [his little Chinese lucky charm] behind in Berlin.'

In the autumn of 1923 he made his grand return to German concert life in Berlin. The Berliners had not liked his turning his back on them, for Berlin was after all the city which could claim to have 'made' him. But the Berlin critics were still the same who had written most of the bad notices about his ultra-modern compositions, and there had been just a hint of pique in his curt notice of non-appearance. But the rancour had been forgotten. He had come back from America, the fabled land of riches, more famous than before. Offers of engagements poured in from all parts of Germany, from Austria, Scandinavia and even Soviet Russia.

★　★　★

Despite the bad times a new and vigorous wind was blowing in the musical world of Berlin. The death of Arthur Nikisch in 1922 had closed a long, often brilliant but generally 'traditional' era. Nikisch had been Schnabel's first great sponsor and a revered friend to the last. ('Happy man,' wrote his one-time protégé when he learned of his death; 'he was privileged to go while still near the summit.') His passing made way for two gifted younger men: Wilhelm Furtwängler, who succeeded him as conductor of the famous Philharmonic Concerts, and Bruno Walter, who was engaged to conduct a new series of concerts with the same orchestra, sponsored by the old firm of Wolff & Sachs.[1] Many people thought that Walter, a native Berliner and Furtwängler's senior by ten years, should have become Nikisch's successor. However, shortly afterwards, he became the musical director of Berlin's Municipal Opera, while retaining his own Philharmonic series. In 1927 still another rising star was to join the Berlin galaxy. This was Otto Klemperer, successively chief conductor of the Cologne and Wiesbaden opera houses, who was now

[1] Hermann Wolff, the firm's founder, who had sponsored the original Philharmonic Concerts, brought Hans von Bülow to Berlin as their first conductor, and Nikisch to succeed him.

engaged to direct the second house of the Berlin State Opera (the so-called Kroll-Oper) and to conduct its regular symphony concerts.

These three highly gifted men, Walter, Furtwängler and Klemperer, were the outstanding conductors of their generation in Germany, and each of them brought a distinctly fresh personal and forward-looking element to the scope and quality of musical performance in Berlin. Schnabel's return to the concert platform at this moment seemed providential, for his ideals were close to theirs; he had played with all three, and had long been in lively communication with the two who were newcomers to Berlin. He had, in fact, 'discovered' Furtwängler many years before as conductor in Lübeck, and he had closely watched Klemperer's career for years. Both of them were among his ardent admirers. Their coming, as well as Walter's, made life in Berlin more attractive to him than it had been in recent years.

His first two orchestral reappearances were with Walter and with Furtwängler (in Beethoven and Mozart concertos). In each case the public's reaction was in the nature of a personal homage for both soloist and conductor. Schnabel's own first solo recital—in a crowded Philharmonic Hall—released a great wave of enthusiasm and the final number in an all-romantic programme, Schumann's *Davids-bündler*, made people rise in their seats. This was preceded by a four-hand recital with his friend Bruno Eisner and a joint recital with Therese Schnabel—all within a few weeks. Berlin was determined to have its fill of Schnabel. But his most spectacular and unusual appearance was in a performance of Schönberg's *Pierrot Lunaire* with an *ad hoc* ensemble comprising Marie Gutheil-Schoder (a star of the Vienna Opera), Boris Kroyt, Gregor Piatigorsky (then a recent refugee from Soviet Russia) and leading wind-players of the State Orchestra, conducted by Fritz Stiedry, of the Berlin State Opera. This was the first post-war performance of this difficult and still problematical work, and it proclaimed Schnabel's sympathy with the Schönberg school of contemporary music. It was the first and last time he publicly participated in the performance of an ultra-modern work. The result was a triumph for the absent composer and for all participants.

In all these appearances the critics were extravagant in their praise of Schnabel while the faithful Berliners gave ecstatic ovations to the Prodigal Son, and their plaudits were echoed throughout the country, whenever he appeared.

About this time economic conditions in Germany, having reached their lowest ebb, underwent a radical change. The mark was stabilized in November 1923, which meant that artists' fees at least returned to a realistic basis. They were no longer paid in huge bundles of worthless paper, but in the newly established currency, and soon compared favourably with fees in hard-currency countries. On the other hand, concert tickets became suddenly expensive, as everything else, and audiences shrank in consequence.

Nevertheless, it had once again become worthwhile even for foreign artists to appear in Germany, and this brought about a radical change in the musical life of the country. While the change was salutary in that it enhanced the quality and variety of the offerings, it also had its painful aspects, for it temporarily excluded large sections of the musical public from participation. All this was part of Germany's readjustment to world economy—the so-called era of fulfilment, with its Dawes Plan, its balanced budget and the facing of hard realities arising from national defeat. The predominantly educated class of *rentiers*, the civil servants and small business and professional people were the immediate sufferers, and next to them the industrial workers, with shockingly low wages in a time of rising unemployment. The people's misery had its repercussions in virulent party strife, the growth of political reaction and the rise of para-military formations. Internationally it revived old hatreds and created new suspicions, gradually allayed by steps toward *rapprochement* such as the evacuation of the Rhineland, the Geneva protocols, the Locarno and Kellogg Pacts.

Against this background of shifting and portentous world events, artists and *entrepreneurs* in the entertainment world projected a variegated and spectacular display of talents and ideas, many of them of high artistic quality, ingenuity and splendour. Orchestras and ensembles vied with each other in the performance of classics and startling novelties, and stage directors devised new styles of decor and methods of lighting and production. No less than three opera houses, all state or municipally subsidized, now competed in variety of repertoire, excellence of performance and popular appeal. There was an aggregation of singers—Jeritza, Dux, Lehmann, Leider, Kemp, Onegin, Jadlowker, Josef Schwarz, Richard Tauber and many more —rarely to be heard in a single city at one time, and a degree of discipline in ensemble which has hardly been equalled since. New operas by Richard Strauss, Ferruccio Busoni, Franz Schreker, Hans Pfitzner, Kurt Weill and others (not forgetting Ernst Křenek's controversial *Jonny spielt auf*), alternated with stylized revivals of half-forgotten Verdi and re-studied productions of Mozart masterpieces, in which conductors like Walter, Klemperer and Stiedry emulated the inspired innovations of the late lamented Gustav Mahler.

Schnabel, always interested in genuinely artistic efforts and new creative manifestations, revelled in this local renaissance. He frequented the opera and the theatre, indulged his growing love of Verdi and the old love of Mozart, whose transcendent genius was newly revealed in these modern productions, conscientiously recreated in the spirit of the composer and without the upholstered trappings and inflated interpretations favoured in pre-war days.

He was interested, also, in the concerts of modern works by the International Society of Contemporary Music, including the first Berlin performance of Stravinsky's *Sacre du Printemps* and works by Serge Prokofief, Alban Berg and other moderns. At a somewhat later period he even acted briefly as chairman of the Society's local group. Altogether, these were stimulating times: to many it seemed the swan-song of a dying culture; to Schnabel and his young friends it was Berlin at its best.

★   ★   ★

One of the international events that left their mark on this period of German history was the somewhat notorious Treaty of Rapallo, which had been concluded between defeated Germany and Soviet Russia in April 1922. This by-product of the abortive Genoa Conference had restored trade and normal relations between the two countries under the very noses of the victorious Western Powers. It was severely criticized in the West, and violently opposed by nationalist circles in Germany, whose foreign minister (Walther Rathenau) was murdered two months after the event. Whatever its political significance, the Treaty of Rapallo made it possible for German artists to appear once again in Russia, as they had done habitually in times past. And two years later Artur Schnabel was one of the first to be invited.

He had, of course, not seen Russia since Tsarist days, ten years before, and he was very curious about the changes wrought by the revolution, especially as they affected the country's cultural life. When he went to Moscow and Leningrad in April 1924, Lenin had been dead only three months and the inevitable struggle for power had not yet been resolved. The New Economic Policy ('Nep') was still in force and many signs pointed in the direction of a reconciliation with the West. The Soviet government had been recognized by Great Britain and Japan, and economic co-operation with Germany was in full swing. Schnabel rather naïvely imagined that his invitation might be due to his well-known liberal political views, which caused some of his conservative friends jokingly to call him a Bolshevik. Actually, one of his outstanding characteristics was a rather cantankerous opposition to the shortcomings of the established order, regardless of parties and politics, and he had been very outspoken about the post-war behaviour of German industrialists, speculators and war profiteers. However, when he got to Russia and its proud proletarians, his 'aristocratic' side came to the fore. 'It seems,' he reported afterwards, 'that they hoped to embrace me as a *tovarish*, but apparently I did not react as expected.' Indeed, the post-revolutionary conditions in contrast with the 'good old' Tsarist days were in many respects distasteful to this product of an effete Viennese bourgeoisie. 'In Tsarist times,' he commented, 'I saw examples of misery only in the lower classes, which now did not seem very much happier than before; but the wealthy people, who were once amiable, gay and attractive, were ever so much more miserable now.'

The concerts were, of course, organized by a government department with a central office for all Russia in Moscow. An official had been detailed to 'keep Schnabel company'. He spent most of his time in the society of this sociable bureaucrat, originally a dental worker, now a musical master of ceremonies. Schnabel was to play, first in Moscow, then in Leningrad, but he suddenly learned that Moscow had postponed the concert for four days. 'And what about Leningrad?' asked Schnabel, worried about not getting there in time. 'Oh,' replied the former dental worker, 'the central office will arrange all that.' So the artist spent most of the four days in the outer office, watching people come and go. They were 'so happy to be allowed to use telephones and other gadgets for the first time in their lives' that Schnabel enjoyed himself by just watching them.

It was the same at the theatre, where he spent his idle evenings. There was so much acting going on in the auditorium, by people enjoying the new experience, that it was more exciting than the drama on the stage.

In this theatre, packed with people, Schnabel gave the last of his four Moscow concerts. As always, he had made his programmes without regard to his listeners, who in this case were almost all industrial workers. He played five sonatas, just as he might have done in sophisticated Berlin. The audience sat silently through each piece, but the applause broke out with almost indecent urgency immediately after the last note. This noisy response, he discovered, was not meant as approval of what had been given, but as a demand

for more. 'The people want a reward for their patient suffering of
the unusual; they want familiar favourites as encores.' Accordingly,
after Beethoven's sonata, opus III, with its soft reverential ending,
the gallery began to shout 'Campanella, Campanella!'—fully expecting
him to oblige with Liszt's scintillating show piece which had been the
standard encore of the only other pianist they had heard that season.
Schnabel, provoked into opposition, determined to give no encores
whatsoever.

There was much else in the new Russia to quarrel with: old and
tired pianos, ugly halls, concerts starting an hour late and interrupted
by half-hour intermissions. But in general there was not much
difference between the bad manners of audiences, whether they were
capitalist or communist, west or east. Yet in Leningrad, the old
Tsarist capital, the inhabitants seemed somewhat closer to western
culture. And there were still many charming people, some of them
distinctly *ancien régime* and very conservative in their musical taste.
Alexander Glazunof was still the grand old man of Russian music,
and still convinced that certain notes in the scores of Beethoven and
Schubert must be misprints, because 'they are so unexpected'. Schnabel also heard the nineteen-year-old pianistic wonder, Vladimir
Horowitz, whom he counselled to get out of Russia.

The Russian critics, judging from what they wrote, were not
only as dogmatic as any other breed, but doctrinaire as well. One
Moscow scribe wrote that Schnabel's interpretations might be all
right for the bourgeois world, but it was clear that the revolution
had not had the slightest effect on his conception of that great revolu-
tionist, Beethoven. Two days later, his Leningrad colleague, still
labouring under the impression that Schnabel was a comrade, wrote
that his rhythm suggested 'the battalions of labour marching against
the bulwark of capitalism!' In retrospect Schnabel decided he was
not a success in Russia—at least not in Moscow. Nevertheless the
place certainly fascinated him and the Soviet public presented a new
kind of challenge. In any case, as we shall see, he was destined to
return there on three occasions between 1925 and 1928.

Presently he was back in Berlin, surrounded by his family and his
pupils in the studio—teaching, playing, talking, gesticulating while
smoking his inevitable cigar. But it was no longer the large, multi-
national class of ambitious youngsters that had crowded the studio
in recent years. They had dwindled to a small, impecunious though
highly talented group of seven. The foreigners had departed, since
Germany was no longer the haven for people from sound-currency

countries who could live on next to nothing in the paper-mark economy of the inflation years. Its currency stabilized, Germany had ceased to be a 'shoppers' paradise' for people with dollars, pounds, kroner or francs. Those who remained of Schnabel's pupils were not able to pay his fees. All the same, they were being taught.

Teaching had always been an important factor in the Schnabels' household budget. Now, by the force of circumstances, it had become a charity. Neither Artur nor Therese could bear being parted from these gifted youngsters whose whole future was bound up with the help and inspiration they derived from their precious lessons.

At this critical moment the Berlin High School of Music repeated an offer which Schnabel had persistently rejected—to teach a class of advanced students, or what is commonly called a master-class. This time he accepted, but on conditions of his own choosing: he was to teach a maximum of seven scholarship pupils, to be chosen by himself. The teaching was to be individual, but with all members of the class present. The teaching periods were to be chosen to fit in with his concert career—in other words, the schedule and rules were to follow the pattern that Schnabel had followed through the years. The only difference was that he gave the lessons in the Hochschule, though at hours to suit his convenience, if necessary outside school periods—even at night. The seven chosen scholars were, of course, the students whom he had been teaching free. Now he was to be paid a handsome stipend—by the state. It was an equitable bargain, for the prestige of Schnabel's name was worth all the administration could pay. But it was liberal, too: there was no discrimination as to nationality, and several of the favoured pupils were foreigners, ranging in origin from Latvia to the United States.

Hitherto Schnabel had always refused to work for an institution, and he had boasted that he never would. When twitted on his inconsistency in accepting the post he gave a very simple excuse: 'I decided that, after all, a sour apple is better than no apple at all.'

PART FOUR

THE GREAT ARTIST

19. New Light on Beethoven

ARTUR SCHNABEL will always be remembered as one of the great interpreters of the genius of Beethoven as manifested in his works for the pianoforte. Through most of the nineteenth century Beethoven was revered principally as the great master of the symphony and the creator of a vast body of large-scale orchestral and vocal works. Of his piano sonatas, increasingly appreciated by discerning musicians as the more inward and intimate expression of this titanic genius, only the earlier ones achieved general popularity and particularly those which were distinguished by sometimes spurious subtitles such as the *Pathétique,* the *Moonlight,* the *Appassionata,* etc. These became the favourites of both professional pianists and amateurs in the Romantic period, while the bulk of the thirty-two were largely overshadowed by the more 'colourful' works of composers such as Schumann, Chopin, Liszt and others who consciously exploited the sonorities of the modern piano. Not until the days of Hans von Bülow and Eugene d'Albert were all the Beethoven sonatas played in public, and even then the all-Beethoven programme was a great rarity.

Like other young pianists, Artur Schnabel in his youth studied the better known Beethoven sonatas, and no doubt explored the lesser known as well. His special preoccupations, however, were first Brahms, then Schubert and Schumann. Not until his middle thirties did he become more profoundly absorbed with the Beethoven sonatas, and not until his forties did he present all-Beethoven programmes, although he had long played all the five Beethoven concertos and most of his chamber music—trios, violin sonatas, piano quartets—in public.

The decisive impetus came when he accepted the task of preparing a new annotated edition of the Beethoven sonatas for the Ullstein publishing house in Berlin. It was then that his imagination was fired anew by the beauty, the emotional and spiritual content of these works. It was then that he discovered how much of their inherent power and subtlety of expression was not realized by most performers of his generation. Schnabel's work on the Beethoven edition got under way while he was still intensively occupied with his own problems as a composer. His second, third and fourth string quartets, his own piano sonata, the *Dance Suite*, and possibly the germination of his string trio all date from the years during which he edited the Beethoven sonatas. Thus his approach to this work was that of the composer as well as the performer. He was concerned primarily with revealing the musical structure and the organic development of each movement; secondarily with the technical problem of playing it. His emphasis on the essence of the music, its emotional and poetic content, was what had always given Schnabel's playing its characteristic quality. Consequently his overriding purpose as a teacher, and now as editor, was to guide the student to a more profound understanding of the composer's thought.

His fingerings and other technical directions, therefore, were intended to ensure the correct articulation and expression of a given passage, and not merely to facilitate its execution. Sometimes he felt that the very difficulty of a passage was essential to its realization: that is, the struggle to achieve was part of the music itself. However, if a passage called for tenderness or lyrical expression, the fingering must be such as to *invite* a singing tone. All his directions were meant to clarify or emphasize the composer's own intention. But since they were suggestions rather than directions, he had them printed in small type—smaller than the composer's own marks of expression. The tempo markings in his edition were strictly Beethoven's own; but inevitably there were subtle variations within these tempi. These were intended to convey the natural pulse of the music as Schnabel felt it, but again his indications appear in small type. In his early years Schnabel was sometimes criticized for his rather free tempi, a natural reflection of his youthful feelings. In principle he was a firm advocate of strict time, and severely critical of sentimental retards. He was, however, master of a very subtle *rubato* which gave his playing its vivid, improvisational quality within the bounds of essential rhythmic fidelity. This, too, was reflected in his optional markings, which aimed to stimulate the student's own expressive functions, within the limits of the composer's intentions.

Strict adherence to the composer's will as expressed in the original text was at all times his supreme command. He abhorred the many so-called 'revised' editions issued at intervals since the works were first published. Many of these, borrowing from each other and compounding the sins of previous generations, were encrusted with what Schnabel called 'a century and a half of interpretative mud'.

Schnabel himself followed the text of the scholarly Complete Edition published during 1864–7 on the basis of the original texts (*Urtext*) which he must have known since the early days with his teacher Mandyczewski in the Vienna archives. In doubtful passages he had recourse to the original Beethoven manuscripts or facsimiles available, for the most part, in the Prussian State Library in Berlin. Schnabel explained the process as follows:

'I tried to get hold of as much of the original as possible—manuscripts, copies corrected by Beethoven himself, also the first and second editions, of which Beethoven had seen the proofs. In cases of discrepancies between the MSS. and the early editions which he had seen in proof I decided in favour of the printed version because Beethoven was not always too careful in his manuscripts, knowing that he would see the proofs.'

He found that many of Beethoven's markings had been misunderstood or presumed to be errors by previous editors, and that many so-called aberrations, including certain inter-harmonic pedallings, were the deliberate intentions of a bold innovator. He concluded that, contrary to appearances, Beethoven was a meticulous worker and precise in his expression marks and directions to the player. Schnabel himself had followed many of these disputed markings for years, likewise certain tempo indications commonly regarded as impossible, and thus had found the key to many a 'cryptic' passage.[1] He recognized Beethoven not only as the climactic finalist of the classical period but as the boldest of all innovators—a clairvoyant pathfinder to the future. His edition, therefore, was bound to become very largely a record of his own journey of discovery as an active interpreter (though he deprecated the use of the word) of Beethoven's works.[2]

[1] All the pedal markings except the very few which Beethoven himself inserted in the later sonatas are, of course, Schnabel's recommendations. He proceeds from the premise that Beethoven left pedalling to the discretion of the player; it was part of the instrument, which is played 'with hands and feet', and the amount depended on the acoustics and the mood of the player, who is expected to employ the pedal *ad lib*, except where the composer's own markings make it obligatory. 'These markings have to be observed *under all circumstances*', said Schnabel; 'they are an inseparable part of the music itself. There are only 20 to 30 pedal marks in all of Beethoven's compositions for the piano—comprising about 1000 pages. Their effect is what we now call impressionistic sonorities (as for example in the long-held pedals of the *Waldstein* sonata). They are unexpected, fantastic, adventurous.'

[2] All metronome markings, except where Beethoven himself provided them (in opus 106), are Schnabel's own choice, but are intended to be no more than suggestions.

The actual work of editing the thirty-two sonatas was to occupy varying portions of his time over the greater part of five years. They were first printed separately and appeared in instalments during the years 1924–7, and were later re-issued in two volumes by publishers in the United States, Great Britain and Italy.[1] They have been widely and increasingly used by teachers and pianists all over the world. Schnabel did not make any claim to finality or infallibility for his edition. He regarded it simply as one man's contribution to a continuing effort to arrive at the ultimate truth. The immediate effect of this intensive study was on himself: a fresh realization of the immensity of this inexhaustible treasure.

★　　★　　★

As a pianist Schnabel had come to Beethoven gradually, playing the sonatas as he came to understand and love them. Now for the first time he recognized fully their collective significance as the greatest body of compositions in the literature of the piano, and as the most intimate revelation of Beethoven's thoughts—a personal confession unparalleled in all music. His slowly growing desire to play them all in one continuous series now came nearer to realization. But it was not until the completion of his edition, which coincided with the hundredth anniversary of Beethoven's death in 1927, that he was able to fulfil his wish.

For the present he continued, as he had done for years, playing Beethoven together with the works of other composers, but the emphasis was gradually shifting away from the romanticists (always excepting Schubert) to Beethoven and still later also to Mozart. This trend was faintly perceptible in the concerts he gave in Germany before his second trip to Russia, where this time he gave six concerts in nine days and was reported to have left 'the deepest impression imaginable'. Returning to Berlin in February 1924, he played a Beethoven programme (five sonatas including opus 54, 110 and 111)— a recital which to one discerning critic was a revelation of new emotional and expressive powers. This was the kind of programme which pointed the way to a pattern which was to become familiar in future years.

More precise and descriptive than the fleeting impressions of the contemporary critics is the objective analysis of a fellow-pianist, Claudio Arrau, who, though not a pupil of Schnabel, was an excep-

[1] Simon & Schuster, New York; Oxford University Press, Oxford; Edizioni Curci, S.R.L., Milan.

tionally keen observer of his work. In his recollections published shortly after Schnabel's death he wrote (in *Musical America*):

'Remembering how Schnabel played Beethoven, two things particularly stand out in memory—his grasp of the whole character of every sonata and his divine way with the slow movements. With all the sonatas, from the very first one—in which Beethoven is already Beethoven and a master, and which is therefore entirely definite both in shape and construction and in essential character—to the final op. 111, where Beethoven is the seer transcending all human struggle, Schnabel became a seer himself in his grasp of the component details and the sum total of this colossal literature.

'In a period when playing fast often seemed to be the sole goal of piano virtuosity, Schnabel paid no heed and showed his courage by making the slow movements really slow. Strengthened by conviction and concentration, he played them slower than anyone else had even imagined to be possible. Absolutely unforgettable was his way of slowing down still more at the end of such movements, a slowing-down that created a dramatic atmosphere and tension that were both impressive and unique. This was evidence of a deep, inner repose that most musicians attain only late in life, if ever, but that he possessed to a rare degree from the beginning. . . .

'His performance of opus 54 shows that he did not follow his own edition and markings slavishly, but gave himself freedom to follow the inspiration of the moment. To a rare degree he maintained both a balance of the means required to do things as he conceived them and a balance between intellect and intuitive emotion. Many artists have one gift or the other. But in Schnabel there was a remarkable synthesis of knowledge, intelligence, intuition, emotion and technical means. Schnabel's importance as an artist stems from the importance of the message of Beethoven's music. In the thirty-two sonatas Beethoven created a whole cosmos. In their totality, they form an immense epic of man's struggle and suffering and ultimate victory of the spirit. Schnabel, uniquely, was man and artist enough to meet all the demands of this staggering outpouring of genius.

'In these last sonatas Beethoven developed a language for the initiated, a language of a symbolic and esoteric character never more strongly pronounced in any works of art before or since. Because Schnabel was one of the few initiated who understood and spoke this language he was able to bring the Beethoven of this period nearer to contemporary comprehension. No greater realization could come to any artist.'

*   *   *

It is interesting and revealing that Schnabel, while in the midst of his Beethoven studies, and while preparing himself for the monumental task of playing the entire thirty-two sonatas in Berlin, deliberately turned aside to take a fresh look at Mozart, a composer whose works for the piano he had hardly touched since the days of his childhood when he, like most beginners, was given Mozart to

'cut his teeth on'. He recalled, with something like horror, how at
the age of nine he had been made to play the master's D minor concerto as a proficiency test for the benefit of his Viennese sponsors.
'Children are given Mozart,' he used to say, 'because of the quantity
of the notes; grown-ups avoid him because of the *quality* of the notes,
which to be sure is elusive.' This surely could not be said of himself,
for throughout his career he had played the piano parts of Mozart's
chamber music—violin sonatas, trios, quartets, etc. But it was
nevertheless true that he had made his remarkable career first with
the romantic masters, including Brahms, then with Beethoven, and
that in his adult years he had thus far not publicly played Mozart
sonatas. As regards Mozart's piano concertos, it is even doubtful
whether he, any more than the mass of his pianistic colleagues, had
more than a bare knowledge of the existence of this greatly neglected
treasure, and certainly not a full appreciation of its worth.

Now, in his early forties he had suddenly chosen to play the
D minor concerto again in his old city of Vienna, where he had
played it at the age of nine, but this time in juxtaposition with
Beethoven and Brahms. Whatever may have been his primary
reason for this choice, it was also an opportunity to prove his growing
conviction that Mozart was not only one of the greatest of the great,
but that his music was the most difficult to 'realize' in performance.
It is doubtful whether his Viennese audience agreed with him, for it
was his playing of Beethoven's *Emperor* and Brahms' B-flat concertos
that invariably brought him the greatest applause. But in his later
years Schnabel spent an inconceivable amount of time and effort in
convincing sceptics of the supreme mastery and profundity of Mozart,
and in impressing students with the difficulty of playing his works.
To drive home his point he would sit at the piano, smoking a cigar
and looking nonchalantly around the room while tossing off the most
notoriously perilous passages of the Brahms B-flat; and then by
contrast summon the greatest concentration and care in producing a
cantabile passage from a Mozart concerto, whispering '*this* is difficult!'
By endless argument and example he inveighed to the end of his days
against the long neglect of Mozart's works.

But even more by playing them. The Vienna concert of 1923
and its immediate sequels in Berlin and elsewhere were but the
beginning of what eventually became a crusade. In the same season
he began to play Mozart sonatas in his recitals, beginning with the
familiar one in B-flat major (K. 333) and the four-hand sonata in
F major (K. 497) in a recital with Bruno Eisner. The next year or

two he was very largely absorbed with Beethoven, as we shall see; but even in the Beethoven centennial year he played the great C minor Fantasia (K. 475) and the C minor sonata (K. 457)—performances which have remained unforgettable. Unfortunately they have not been perpetuated on gramophone records.

It was after he had finished work on his Beethoven edition that he seriously investigated the lesser-known Mozart concertos. And, as with Schubert and Beethoven, the discovery made him a pioneer. From that time onward he was wont to add at least one new Mozart concerto to his repertoire every year until he had played some twelve of them in public, and many of them a number of times.[1] Later in life he often made the inclusion of Mozart concertos a condition of his acceptance of orchestral engagements, and in after years he played two or even three Mozart concertos at a single concert. Exacting and meticulous as he was at rehearsals, he was never more so than when Mozart was involved, and he often insisted on three or more orchestral rehearsals—until he was assured that the orchestra's performance was commensurate with his own and, if possible, that the orchestral players really enjoyed it! Mozart, he insisted, was inconceivable without love—on the part of all participants.

In all cases where authentic cadenzas of Mozart's own were available, Schnabel usually played them. In the D minor concerto he used the ones which Beethoven wrote for it. For the C minor he wrote his own, and was widely criticized by people who believed that a cadenza must be written in imitation of the composer's style.

Of Mozart's sonatas Schnabel played at least ten in public, so far as our records go; possibly several more. Privately he played them all. It is certain that he loved them all, though as in the case of Bach may have thought some not suited to large modern halls. However much he admired, venerated and loved Beethoven, it is sure that his love for Mozart never diminished but increased to the very end of his life. He never ceased to respond to the strength, nobility and spirituality of his musical thought, never failed to be moved by the beauty and tenderness of his melodies, and never ceased to be fascinated by the originality and subtlety of his harmonies. When he played Mozart he was swept along by the inherent vitality of the music, the vigour and grace of its rhythm. Often his face

---

[1] These included, besides the familiar D minor (K. 466) and C minor (K. 491), the G major (K. 453), F major (K. 459), C major (K. 467), A major (K. 414), A major (K. 488), B-flat (K. 595), and the two-piano concerto in E-flat (K. 365), which he played with his son, Karl Ulrich.

lighted up in almost child-like wonder at the ethereal quality of certain passages.

Again and again in later life he inveighed against people who thought of Mozart as something less than profound, while admitting his charm, his supposed simplicity and graceful 'rococo' character. 'Mozart is not for candlelight,' he once said when someone suggested eighteenth-century period trimmings for a concert. 'He is the sun.' Schnabel was convinced that such mistaken and belittling ideas about Mozart were partly responsible for the inadequate performances of his works, and for their neglect during the nineteenth century and even later. When pupils came to him with the idea that Mozart was comparatively 'easy', he would point out the fact that Liszt's rhapsodies are mostly well performed, but Mozart's sonatas scarcely ever.

★   ★   ★

Schnabel's intense concentration on Beethoven and his re-awakened interest in Mozart happened to coincide with a fresh attempt to extend his concert activity to England—stimulated no doubt by the urgings of his British pupils. He was now approaching forty-three, and he had not visited the British Isles since his memorable London debut at the age of twenty-two. It seems almost incredible, in the light of later events, that more than twenty years should have elapsed seemingly without any thought of returning to the scene of one of his more spectacular youthful triumphs, and without any invitation that might have tempted him. The truth is that the dapper young man who appeared under Dr. Richter and bowed to the Queen in the Queen's Hall had been completely forgotten. Many stars had risen and set in the interim, the war had intervened, and Schnabel had achieved a continental reputation—in Europe and America—without repercussions in England. Now at last he came back very modestly to play two recitals in the tiny Æolian Hall in Bond Street, booked on his behalf by the London agents of Bechstein's, with the hope of stimulating the British sale of their pianos after the setback following the war.

The first recital attracted about one hundred people—at the height of the London season in April 1925. With tongue in cheek Schnabel reported home that it was an 'artistic success'. At the second he played a programme of Beethoven sonatas, including the *Appassionata* and opus 110 to an only slightly larger audience, but he received excellent reviews in the Press. H. C. Colles wrote in *The Times* that Schnabel 'provided the most vivid and stimulating playing heard in

London for some time' and ended by saying that 'Mr. Schnabel must play Beethoven to us again.'

Unfamiliar as he was with the English passion for understatement, Schnabel may not have been duly elated. Other papers wrote favourably and the *Musical Times* exclaimed: 'For once we have intellect and emotion in perfect assimilation.' Since none of the London critics seemed aware of the eminent position that Schnabel held on the Continent or even remembered his previous appearance in England two decades before, one must credit them with uncommon and independent judgment. The significant fact of the matter was that Schnabel's immediate though unspectacular success in England was made with the sonatas of Beethoven. Yet hardly anyone seems to have known that he was then in the process of bringing out his own edition of Beethoven's sonatas, and that he was becoming recognized in Germany as one of the great interpreters of the master.

Be that as it may, Schnabel's more optimistic friends and followers predicted a brilliant future in England, and some enterprising managers thought there might be commercial possibilities, for one of them offered to engage him for a 'celebrity concert' in the Albert Hall. When told that it held 7,000 people, Schnabel refused. 'If I am not yet a humbug,' he remarked, 'I certainly don't want to become one now.' He knew that at this stage of his career it would not be he but the sensational advertising that would draw a crowd. Also he was frightened by the reputedly queer acoustics of the hall. (Years later he used to joke about it as the hall in which 'you only hear half, but that half you hear twice.') Despite his own rather prickly pessimism about his prospects it was clear that the professionals had taken his solid qualities at their worth, though as might be expected he had partisans and enemies from the start.

From his first moment in England he was surrounded by a band of ardent admirers, including his pupils Norman Wilkes and Marguerite Macintyre, and some of England's most popular artists, such as Myra Hess and Irene Scharrer, the violinists Yelly d'Aranyi and her sister Adila Fachiri (nieces of the late Joseph Joachim). After his first concert a group of congenial people gathered at the house of Sir Robert and Lady Mayer, founders of the famous Children's Concerts, to make him feel at home. His simple, unassuming conviviality, personal charm and ready wit captivated nearly everybody, while his rather truculent independence engendered a curious hostility in a small but vocal opposition. But it was clear that fortune was on his side. Moreover, he had fallen in love with England, with its people, its ravishing countryside, with the serene dignity of London and the friendly atmosphere and leisurely tempo of English life.

As a result he was back in England, after another spell of composing and a busy autumn of concerts on the Continent, to give a further Beethoven recital—this time at the Queen's Hall, 'top-heavy' with musicians, music-lovers and students who made up in enthusiasm what the orchestra stalls lacked in numbers. This time the programme comprised five Beethoven sonatas ranging from the hackneyed C-sharp minor (the *Moonlight*) to the great C minor, opus 111. Once again *The Times* critic led a chorus of praise, while Walter J. Turner, writing in the *New Statesman*, discovered he had 'never really heard opus 111 before'.

Returning once again to London late in the year he played still another Beethoven programme, culminating in the colossal opus 106, *für das Hammerklavier*, which he had only rarely played in public before. This concert was, he confessed, a kind of self-examination— or soul-searching—which should decide whether or not his now maturing plan to play the entire thirty-two in a single series during the Beethoven Year of 1927 would be realized. Evidently the decision was in the affirmative, for after the concert he wrote to Therese: 'Now I am glad. I look forward to the Thirty-two with joy.' Of the concert itself he said that it went well—'the smaller sonatas without blemish; opus 106 excellent excepting some minor inaccuracies and unclear details.' This probably referred to the final fugue, which makes almost superhuman demands on the player. Schnabel himself once doubted whether it was fully realizable, that is to say with technical perfection, textual clarity and adequate power of expression. It is probably beyond anything that the pianists of Beethoven's time could have mastered with the instruments then available, and it may well have been conceived in one of those transcendent moments when human aspiration outruns earthly realities.

This crucial Schnabel recital, given in the Grotian Hall in Wigmore Street (destined to become a total victim of the blitz) was outwardly not a conspicuous success. Perhaps people were kept away by the fog or frightened away by the weightiness of the programme. For Schnabel himself it was a source of deep satisfaction. He felt that he had come closer to the sources of Beethoven's inspiration than ever before, and had succeeded more nearly in conveying his experience to others. In a letter to Therese he wrote:

'For years I have learned my lessons as the result of my discontent; today at long last I am learning them from the degree of satisfaction I am able to garner from my performance. Does this mean that I have become less exacting? Or more accomplished? In any case I like playing better than I used to, and I certainly can play better than I did. The impression I made— on a very intelligent audience—was very interesting: tense, lost within themselves, many of those present may have experienced something like a glimpse of the Unknown.'

Schnabel had seldom expressed himself so positively about himself or his work. Indeed, this new mood suggests an important psychological change: he had reached a certain point in his development, and this in turn was to change his outlook and his estimate of the future. The new sense of confidence, of accomplishment in understanding and performance, meant that his reproductive or re-creative activity could now absorb all his energy and—for the time being—give him artistic satisfaction. It meant, in the sequel, that he was content to make another pause in composing: during the ensuing years he would play, interpret, teach, while strengthening his own creative faculties from within.

It is clear that Schnabel's reception in England and his own reaction to it signalized an important turning-point in his career. A new degree of intellectual maturity and spiritual serenity had been reached. Outwardly there was no apparent change. He would continue to live in Berlin as the professional musician practising his art in a gradually expanding circle of influence. But in his mind London would always remain associated with one particular achievement: his closest active approach to Beethoven and the public's acceptance of it.

20. *The Beethoven Year*

IN his forty-fifth year Schnabel had reached what might be regarded as the pinnacle of his career as a performing artist. At the meridian of his life he had attained a degree of accomplishment and artistic satisfaction that is given to few. But in his case it would be more appropriate to say that he stood on a high plateau from which as an experienced mountaineer he could glimpse still higher ranges—up to the ultimate and perhaps unattainable peaks. At any rate it was a point of rest at which, in a rarefied atmosphere, he could confidently survey the clear outline of the tasks that still lay before him. All this had nothing to do with what is commonly called success, a thing that might be measured in quantitative terms and of which at middle age he was destined to have a great deal. It had less to do with the area of influence and the number of people he could reach than with the degree of spiritual elevation and intensity of experience he could induce, and most of all with the fulfilment of his obligation to his 'employer'—that composite deity personified by Beethoven, Mozart and their peers.

The degree of that sense of duty is measured by his deliberate renunciation—for an indefinite time—of all direct creative endeavour which had given him such great satisfaction in the past five summers; and its justification was registered in the joy which he experienced in that concert played to a mere handful of people in a small London hall late in 1926, culminating in Beethoven's opus 106 which he described as a personal test of himself. Here he felt, perhaps for the first time, the inner joy of authentic re-creation and the satisfaction of having moved his hearers so profoundly that they were 'lost within themselves'.

It seems providential that he arrived at this point on the very eve of the 'Beethoven Year', which marked the hundredth anniversary of the master's death. He had already contributed to Germany's nation-wide celebrations of the event in the autumn of 1926. But of all these pious observances perhaps the most sincere and the most exacting was Schnabel's performance of the thirty-two sonatas in seven consecutive Sundays in January and February 1927, a project which he had harboured for the past three or four years and which to his knowledge had never been attempted before.

Very appropriately it took place in the simple and dignified auditorium of the Volksbühne in the working-class section of Berlin. Here 2,000 people assembled at each concert to enjoy these works in an attitude of concentration and reverence without the usual trappings of a gala event. They sat in a darkened hall as Schnabel, in plain workaday dress began to sound the quiet, contemplative opening of the D major (*Pastoral*) sonata, opus 28, followed after a short pause by the great A-flat major, opus 110, and they responded in a rising crescendo of appreciation to the end of the final *pianissimo* chord of opus 111, when after minutes of silence the rising tension of the seven-day experience was released in a veritable tempest of applause.

Schnabel had designed the seven programmes to comprise four or five sonatas each, in a non-chronological order which alternated works of different periods and varying moods.[1] It evidently proved æsthetically satisfying to him, for he saw no reason for changing it in later repetitions of the series. The feat of memory would, of course, be stupendous for any but the most gifted musicians, but that aspect never troubled Schnabel, with his enormous command of musical literature.

The public response to this great homage to Beethoven was, as might have been expected, tremendous. The critics were enraptured, and there was hardly a note of dissent. They acknowledged it to be the principal event of the musical season. 'Indescribable,' said Dr. Hans Fischer in the *Allgemeine Musik-Zeitung*, 'this accuracy of execution, this noble submission to the will of the creator, who eludes interpretation by external means. One left with the sense of having heard Beethoven himself.' It must have given Schnabel a genuine sense of gratification (triumph would not be the right word to apply to this devoted servant of music) to see to how profoundly he had moved, thrilled and enlightened his audiences. He was never completely satisfied, but if this year of 1927 was a year of fulfilment, the Beethoven series in Berlin represented the greatest single achievement of his career to date.

He was, of course, appropriately elated by the achievement, but he took it in his stride, teaching and editing between concerts when not preparing for the next. Nor did he rest on his laurels. Three

[1] The seven programmes as played by Schnabel will be found in the Appendix, p. 327.

days after the series he was playing the Beethoven G major concerto in Bremen, and a week later he was again in Leningrad and soon after in Riga, where he and the local orchestra commemorated Beethoven on the anniversary of his death. This was followed by another Beethoven recital, where he had to play the *Hammerklavier* sonata on an unresponsive piano. 'This piece, as I imagine it,' he complained, 'is to be approximately realized only on absolutely reliable instruments.' In Leningrad, too, he played the same almost unrealizable piece—on an especially imported Bechstein, but with overstrained hands, while the Adagio was accompanied by a coughing audience of 3,000. He was once again at war with himself: the conflict between his desire to perform only for duly prepared audiences, and 'the necessity to keep alive'. Worse still: here was 'a public which is willing and capable of the most powerful impressions, but which is shamefully held down by the artists'. And this in a country where the profit motive was not supposed to exist! He was 'determined not to go on much longer'. But the cultivated bourgeois atmosphere of Riga and the Scandinavian capitals brought a timely change of mind.

Back in Berlin he found a summons to Italy, where he had not played since the dark early days of the war, when artists from Germany and Austria were unwelcome, and he had not been anxious to repeat the experience. But a different wind was blowing in Italy now, and Schnabel's Beethoven playing had become a European legend. He must come, wrote the Italian manager, and play the *Emperor* concerto in the Augusteo, erected on the foundations of the Emperor Augustus' tomb! Italian audiences, however, were not as well disciplined as some others, and were likely to shout for encores at inappropriate moments. To guard against this a 'No encore' sign was prominently displayed during the performance. He gave recitals both in Rome and in Florence and the reception was as good as might be expected. Schnabel's own reaction to these cities, on the other hand, was ecstatic. Anticipating the æsthetic feasts that awaited him, he had persuaded Therese to accompany him, and like a newly married couple they spent five delectable weeks in Rome and Florence—an interlude in their busy professional life to which they were to look back with longing for years to come, until inevitably they were drawn to Italy by the fateful course of events.

*   *   *

The new Berlin season opened as early as September with a

concert of the Staatskapelle under Otto Klemperer, who had at last been transferred to his new Berlin post. As Bruno Walter and Wilhelm Furtwängler had done on their coming to the capital, Klemperer chose Schnabel as his first soloist, playing the Mozart D minor concerto. The Beethoven observances were over in Germany as elsewhere, and Schnabel may be said to have contributed as much as any European musician, playing Beethoven from London to Leningrad and from Hamburg to Rome. The new Beethoven sonata edition was on the market in Germany, and the British and Italian editions were soon to follow—enduring monuments to Schnabel's devotion to the master. Moreover, from now on every year would be a Beethoven year for him, and in some countries, notably England, he was in danger of being labelled accordingly.

However, before the year was out he was able to report on what he called 'the greatest pianistic success of his entire career'—and not with Beethoven but the B-flat concerto of Brahms, as soloist with the Royal Philharmonic Society at the Queen's Hall (November 17th). It was his first opportunity of playing to a house-filling and very representative English audience since that long-forgotten occasion when as a mere youngster he played the very same concerto in the very same hall in the presence of the Queen. The conductor this time was Oskar Fried, familiar to him from Berlin, a curiously assertive but able individual who could on occasion rise to real brilliance. This performance, with a strange and unimpressed orchestra and a notoriously 'troublesome' soloist, spurred Fried to extraordinary efforts. The effect was electric, but the hero of the encounter was Schnabel. At the end of the concerto, the entire house rose and shouted—a most un-English demonstration.

Before this spectacular triumph, Schnabel had taken part in a so-called Super-Concert in Croydon, at which Maggie Teyte sang French ditties and a popular bass roared 'Simon the Cellarer'. Advertised as 'the world-famous Schnabel', he contributed a long and unfamiliar Schubert sonata by way of 'punishment', and was surprised to reap the loudest applause. 'Another gratifying confirmation,' he commented, 'of the righteousness of the fight for the liberation of the listener from the fetters of the cowardly *entrepreneurs*.' He was never so happy as when he could fight the dragon. By contrast, a fairly easy programme of standard classical and romantic pieces, sponsored by an æsthetic coterie of musical epicures known as the Pianoforte Society evoked only mild response. Nevertheless, it may be said that from now on Schnabel had the great London public at his feet. He responded by giving them his best. Never at any time did he make the slightest concession to what is commonly regarded as the popular taste. He never underestimated their artistic capacity and intelligence. In the course of years he played to them the known masterpieces for the piano in programmes of heroic pro-portions. He never catered to cheap sentimentality or the love of more power and brilliance. He never gave a single encore or other-wise encouraged the hero-worship of his admirers. Yet he managed to appeal not only to the serious and intelligent amateur and the seasoned professional but to the young and youngest generation of listeners. Indeed, the chief purpose of his next visit to London—two months later—was to keep a promise given to Sir Robert Mayer to play at one of the Children's Concerts at the Central Hall, West-minster.

The Robert Mayer Concerts for Children had been started some five years before and had achieved a high degree of popularity, thanks very largely to high-minded and intelligent direction. With the help of generous subsidies and later on the support of local government bodies, the enterprise eventually spread to twenty-five or more cities in Great Britain. At this time, however, they were still confined to London. Their purpose was to make first-class symphonic music available to the thousands of music-minded and musically gifted children who were excluded from the regular symphony concerts by the exigencies of metropolitan life, by regular school hours or by lack of means. They differed from the usual juvenile offerings in that they presented only complete though judiciously selected works in unadulterated form. The only concession to youthful immaturity took the form of short and amusingly explanatory talks by the con-ductor, Dr. Malcolm Sargent, who even in those days had a flair for dealing with children and a natural ability to stimulate their imagination.

Schnabel, usually sceptical of all devices to arouse interest in music by extraneous means, was immediately interested when he learned that the music would not be tampered with, that the children would be accompanied by parents or teachers (adults not admitted unless accompanied by a child!), and that groups of selected school-children would come duly prepared for what they were about to receive. He himself took his engagement very seriously, and gave a performance of the still rarely heard Mozart concerto in G major (K. 453) in a programme also comprising orchestral works by Mendelssohn, Schubert and Weber. The hall was packed, the children sat in breathless silence and knew enough not to applaud between movements. The response at the end was thunderous, and Schnabel had to promise an early return.

In consequence of this appearance another new cultural enterprise was to emerge which has since become a custom in many cities, especially in America. This was the London Museum Concerts, founded by Edward Makower, a trustee of the London Museum, occupying Lancaster House in the heart of St. James's. Here both young and old music-lovers were able to listen to chamber music and recitals by eminent artists in the more informal atmosphere of a home, sitting in comfortable chairs and on the steps of the grand staircase instead of stiff rows of seats. Schnabel was to be one of the first to play in these delightful 'house concerts', reminiscent of old Vienna days.

A few days after the memorable Children's Concert, Schnabel played for a private audience at a beautiful London town house, the home of the Courtauld family in Portman Square, which contained the now famous collection of impressionist paintings owned by Samuel Courtauld, head of the British rayon industry. At this time the Courtaulds were particularly interested in music, since Mrs. Courtauld had undertaken to revive and finance opera at Covent Garden, which had suffered a sad decadence as the result of the first World War. This somewhat hectic and none-too-happy experience soon came to an end and Covent Garden passed back into professional hands. Schnabel made the acquaintance of the Courtaulds at the house of mutual friends, where he completely captivated these sensitive and generous people by his conversation, his views on art, his political and social speculations and his increasingly pessimistic opinions concerning the materialism of modern life. 'Sam' Courtauld, member of an old county family and a fabulously successful industrialist, was at heart an idealist, a socially conscious citizen in the best English tradition, and a rather shy and introspective person. His private indulgence was the acquisition of masterpieces of the French impressionist and post-impressionistic schools of which he was a wise and passionate connoisseur. These treasures, and the classic Adam mansion which housed them were later bequeathed to the public. At this time they made a background to one of the most cultured and tasteful households presided over by one of London's most gracious hostesses.

'Lil' Courtauld was a charming and warm-hearted woman who, though reared in 'society', preferred the company of artists and intellectuals, and whose love of music was as ardent as her husband's love of painting and poetry. Schnabel's exalted conception of the artist's duty to art was in such obvious contrast to the paste and cardboard exhibitionism of mediocre opera that his coming to London wrought a decisive change in her attitude to music as a public function. It confirmed her real purpose—to improve and broaden London's musical life and to make it accessible to more people in all walks of life. Through Schnabel she learned of similar enterprises—the workers' concerts of the Berlin Volksbühne and the Friends of Music in New York. She determined to enlist his help and advice. The private concert which she engaged him to give in Portman Square for her friends marked the inception of a project which was to redound to the benefit of thousands of Londoners. Schnabel, curiously enough, reacted rather grumpily to the very opulent but somewhat crowded surroundings of a private house, charged an especially high fee, and was most discontented with his performance. But the heart-warming nobility of his hosts, their sincere love of art, the stimulating company and the serious discussion after the concert, lasting until the small hours, completely reconciled him and opened up a new vista of fruitful activity.

Schnabel did not return to England till the next year, which was one of the busiest in his career, but he had occasion to meet the Courtaulds abroad. And although illness and other difficulties postponed the fruition of Mrs. Courtauld's ideas, an intensive correspondence developed between them on the project of a new series of concerts, while Sir Robert Mayer contributed his help and advice toward the project, which was to provide one of the most stimulating episodes in London's artistic life.

*   *   *

Despite his preoccupations in other parts of Europe, Schnabel's ties to England were becoming even closer, and the small band of intimates who surrounded him in London began to be an important factor in his life. An early and eager addition to the group was Walter J. Turner, who from his first meeting with Schnabel became his most faithful and pugnacious champion among the writing fraternity. Turner was a thin, dyspeptic-looking man in his middle forties with piercing eyes and a permanent chip on his shoulder. He was an extreme idealist, ultra-critical and categorical in his opinions, which he voiced without any restraint either in conversation or in his writings. He was highly regarded as a poet and only slightly less so as a very fanciful, satirical and highly unconventional novelist. He was born in Australia, where his father had been a cathedral organist and had imbued him with a rather fierce love of music. For some years he had been writing musical criticisms for the *New Statesman*, which were as non-conformist and considerably more cantankerous than the prevailing tone of this weekly. He enjoyed disagreeing with other writers, and when he took up the cudgels for Schnabel he went out on the longest accessible limb, as can be seen by the following extract from the *New Statesman*, written after Schnabel's first Queen's Hall recital:

'Mr. Schnabel is one of the finest pianists I ever heard, or ever expect to hear. There was no fuss in the Press next day, and this was perfectly appropriate and characteristic; so much so, indeed, that it is with a certain misgiving that one mentions Mr. Schnabel in print at all, since nowadays publicity is not for great men but for simulacra who will take whatever shape their publicity agents suggest as advantageous to them.'

No one ever applauded Schnabel more sincerely than Turner, but it was difficult for him not to poke someone else with his elbow in the process. Withal he was a sincere and lovable person, with a dry wit and a certain acrid charm. He had lost his heart to Schnabel, approved not only of his music but his ideas, whether good or just provocative. Schnabel returned his friendship, appreciated his talents and his books and always liked his company. In the summer of 1928 Turner joined the two Schnabels and a group of friends on a joint holiday in the French Alps. The party stayed in a small hotel at Argentières which affords a grandiose view of Mont Blanc and the entire chain of snow-capped peaks and glaciers above the Chamonix valley—the kind of landscape Schnabel delighted in because it suggested the infinite and the unattainable. He was in his most relaxed mood, ready for all-day tours, with or without guide, climbing and plodding up the long stretches of hillside, moraine and ice-fields to the bare rocky summit beyond. All the company were dressed for the occasion in the conventional mountain garb, except Turner the individualist, who came along in duck trousers, tennis shirt and sneakers, defying convention as well as the human endurance imposed by weather and altitude. Day after day the discussions went on— about music and literature, philosophy and the decadence of society. Schnabel, slow and methodical, was the seasoned mountaineer, never exhausted, his eyes on the path, pausing for every view, discoursing on the vast polyphony of nature and the harmony of green valleys, snow and sky.

One day a car drove up the valley, bearing the two Courtaulds in search of their friend. The discussions now became practical: regarding both music and London's musical life. Plans were laid, arrangements made and invitations extended for 1929, when the Schnabels were to stay at Portman Square for the period of Artur's first extensive British tour.

September came and the party broke up, all its members going their several ways. Artur, after brief visits in Switzerland and Bavaria, was back at his high desk in Berlin reading proofs, and at his piano preparing for the most arduous and varied season in his concert career.

21. The Schubert Year

PREOCCUPIED as he was during the early 1920's with the music of Beethoven, Schnabel nevertheless rejected any attempt to stamp him as a Beethoven specialist—or for that matter a specialist of any kind. To him there was no qualitative difference between the handful among the world's composers whom he regarded as the truly great. He deplored all attempts to grade the immortals: Bach and Beethoven, Mozart and Schubert, Mendelssohn and Weber; and it was only by their best that they should be judged. To him they were divinities in a most exclusive heaven, to which all may aspire but few have gained admittance through the centuries. If, as a performer, he was partial to any kind of music it was that which he felt to be 'transcendental'—a quality which was not to be explained, because it existed in regions beyond human understanding, but which by its mysterious spiritual powers could move the human soul to blissful experience. Beethoven's music accomplished this in nearly all his works; but so did Schubert's on a somewhat lesser scale but in the same degree.

For Schnabel it was a happy coincidence that the centenary of Schubert's death came so close to that of Beethoven's. To him this poignant juxtaposition indicated both a duty and an opportunity. For if Beethoven was the great hero of his middle years, Schubert had been the great love and the great discovery of his youth. Indeed, Schubert's works had been rarely absent from his recitals and especially the hundreds of programmes he performed jointly with Therese.

The Schubert Year of 1928 came at a time when Schubert was still regarded by the world at large as the great song-writer but not as one of the greatest all-round composers, and even Liszt's valiant championship of 'the greatest poet among musicians' had not eradicated the distinction. In Schnabel's youth, even in the city of Schubert's birth, most of the works that Schubert wrote for the piano were still known only to certain scholars. These men were even then laboriously putting together the first complete edition of his works under the supervision of Schnabel's theory teacher Mandyczewski. When the seventeen-year-old Schnabel played Schubert's posthumous A major sonata at a Berlin recital, it was obviously a surprise to the critics, and when he played other Schubert sonatas throughout the first half of his career, they were still virtual novelties to the public. Although the response was always favourable, few of his colleagues ever ventured to perform these works until his own pupils followed his example.

Long before this, of course, Schubert's *Impromptus, Moments Musicaux* and numerous dances had become popular throughout the world, not to mention his only frankly brilliant display piece, the *Wanderer Fantasie*, which Liszt thought fit to transcribe for piano and orchestra. But his most important works for piano, the sonatas, were still virtually unknown, while most pianists were lured by the romanticism of Schumann, enchanted by the melancholy sweetness of Chopin and fired to heroic efforts by the powerful bravura of Liszt.[1] Schnabel felt that this neglect was not so much the fault of the public as of the performers and the critics who persisted in underestimating Schubert as a symphonist and an all-round composer. He himself argued against this widespread opinion. His contention was that Schubert's melodies were instrumentally conceived, and best adapted to instrumental music, as can be seen from his marvellously idiomatic chamber music works.

Although very reluctant to express himself in print, he inspired an article on 'The Piano Sonatas of Franz Schubert' published under his name in the *Musical Courier* of New York at the beginning of the Schubert year. In it he said:

'Schubert's inspiration never needed the external stimulus of poetry or circumstance, though poetry often released the spring of inspiration that was constantly welling up within him. The songs were a musical by-product of the principal business in hand, which was invariably a work requiring free and continuous creation.

'Having cleared our minds of this common error of regarding Schubert chiefly as a melodist, we should re-examine his piano sonatas and discover, first of all, their intensely dramatic content. To convince ourselves, we need only to look at the posthumous sonata in C minor which vibrates with passion and emotion almost throughout its four movements; or the second movement of the (also posthumous) sonata in A major, in which he employs a wholly new kind of expression, for the "discovery" of which his nineteenth-century imitators were able to take the credit; or, for that matter, the A minor sonata of 1826, opus 143.

---

[1] As an example of the widespread neglect of Schubert as a composer for the piano, be it recorded that even so great and versatile a musician as Serge Rachmaninof stated to the author in 1928 that he had no knowledge of the existence of any Schubert sonatas!

'The depth, versatility and multiplicity of that expression appears limitless and reaches its greatest power in the development sections of his sonatas. Here we have the true dramatic conflicts, with fresh surprises at every turn, to arouse our wonder and admiration. If we find these long, and lacking in continuity, it can only be because we are looking for a conventional classical "working out" instead of a thrilling story in which every note has its psychological purpose. Unless, moreover, we understand the delicate relationships which vitalize Schubert's text we may often mistake a subtle variant for a mere repetition, or, if it be a repetition, be unaware of the psychological reason underlying it.'

It was almost exactly twenty-eight years since Artur and Therese Schnabel had first performed Schubert songs together. From the beginning Artur regarded these works as symphonic in character, with their expressive elements equally distributed in the vocal and piano parts. The complete and integrated interpretation of the musical and dramatic substance gave their performance an emotional impact that has rarely been equalled in lieder singing. Now, in the course of the Schubert centennial they restudied these works in the light of their ripe understanding and the high accomplishment they had reached at the height of their career. At the same time they were able to relive their long artistic life together in a manner which had special significance for them and their numerous admirers.

That Schnabel should take a pre-eminent part in Berlin's Schubert centennial was therefore a foregone conclusion. That they would both share equally in this effort was eminently fitting. Their contribution to the Schubert commemoration consisted of a series of six joint recitals, in February and March 1928, which drew their audiences from various parts of Germany as well as from abroad. These unforgettable concerts included no less than ten of the fifteen piano sonatas including, of course, the three posthumous ones, also such lesser-known gems as the 'little' A major, opus 120, the A minor, opus 42, and the B major, opus 147; also the *Wanderer Fantasie*, the rarely played *Three Piano Pieces* of 1828, the two sets of *Impromptus* and the *Moments Musicaux*. Among the vocal works presented were the three great song cycles, *Die schöne Müllerin*, *Die Winterreise* and *Schwanengesang*, and other poetically integrated groups, such as the Goethe *Mignon* songs and many of the most characteristic single lieder and ballads—altogether more than one hundred items. Here was a truly monumental exposition of Schubert's works, so arranged as to grip and fascinate the listener with ever-increasing tension to the end. The undeniable physical limitations of this no longer youthful singer were completely obliterated by the technical mastery of her execution and her power of dramatic expression. Each cycle or group of songs was a genuine experience. This, in the words of Alfred Einstein in the Berlin *Tageblatt* was 'the highest possible integration of interpretative powers applied to deep and sincere feeling'.

As for Schnabel's playing of his life-long favourites, he had rarely been as happy, as completely in command of himself as on this very special occasion. There was not the slightest leaning toward sentimentality: it was as though one moved freely in sunlit space with an unendingly distant view. 'This Schubert cycle,' wrote Rudolf Kastner, the critic of the *Morgenpost*, 'will continue to live as a spiritual treasure in the memory of all who experienced it.'

For the average musician this massive presentation would have been a prodigious test of memory, coming so soon after his presentation of Beethoven's thirty-two sonatas. But the congenitally 'lazy' Schnabel did it without apparent effort, and continued to fill miscellaneous engagements as before, while teaching his pupils' repertoires ranging all the way from Bach to Prokofief and Ravel. That same winter he varied his programmes by adding Bach's *Italian Concerto* (he was very sparing in his playing of Bach's clavier music on the modern piano), some Mozart sonatas and the A minor rondo (K. 511), Weber's A-flat sonata, Schumann's *Kreisleriana*, *Humoresque*, etc. He also played the Mozart G major concerto (K. 453) for the first time with the Berlin Philharmonic under Bruno Walter, and Beethoven's cello sonatas with the young and greatly gifted Emanuel Feuermann, whom he first met early that year in Leningrad, and whose talent and musicianship he greatly admired.

This, by the way, proved to be Schnabel's last trip to the Soviet Union for some years, for no apparent reason except that other and greener pastures absorbed his attention increasingly. In later years he rationalized it by saying that some of his Russian friends suffered so much that he could not stand it any longer. At the same time he found the Leningrad orchestra 'immeasurably improved', the musicians delighted with his playing of a Mozart and a Brahms concerto, and the audience deeply impressed. But he also commented that a whole evening of Schubert was a 'hard blow for audiences in which the majority are ignorant and yet prejudiced.'

Nevertheless, he continued to celebrate Schubert wherever he could: he gave two all-Schubert recitals for his old friends, the citizens of Riga, brought still another Schubert sonata to his new friends in London (having already played them four), and carried the gospel of Schubert to Italy in the spring.

The Italian experiment came in the course of a short tour with his old friend Carl Flesch. They gave piano and violin sonata recitals in Rome, Naples, Siena, Florence and Milan. Here—in Italy's musical capital—Schnabel played a solo recital which included the Schubert A major (posthumous) sonata, designated on the programme as the 'first performance in Milan'—a century-old novelty! Next day he reported that the work had made a deep impression, while the rest of the programme (all sonatas) did not fare quite so well. 'The Italians,' he wrote, 'are still accustomed to applauding after every five minutes of music by way of relaxation, and of this I cheated them.' Nevertheless, the concert was rated a great success. A writer in the most important newspaper, however, reported that Schnabel had the greatest technique extant but was 'not very musical'. This may have been one of those critics of whom he said 'that they know everything better, but nothing well.'

In Florence he and Flesch played in the 'entrancingly beautiful' hall of the Pitti Palace and had an appropriate artistic success. While his own star was certainly rising in Italy, he felt that it had not risen very far. Also, he was not as happy as he had been the year before, when he and Therese enjoyed Italy together. His present companion was a very old partner whose qualities he was always ready to admire but who in discussions with the hyper-idealistic Artur kept his feet a little too solidly on the ground.

Schnabel found Italy to be ravishing yet disappointing.

'As far as I can tell at this point [he wrote], it lacks that indispensable spirituality which is nourished by need, doubt, suffering and longing—the longing which can never be wholly satisfied at any given stage of attainment. The other qualities—gaiety, serenity, clarity, integrity, will-power, impetuosity —are discernible and tangible; but they leave one wishing for perfection through refinement and diversity.'

All this was as much a reflection of his mood as it was a criticism of a country which later he came to love more and more. To its natural beauties he had already lost his heart, and especially to its mountains.

'The mountains are here among the people, yet beyond them. Man can't hurt them. A few of them may have railways built on them. But no one can level them, utilize or otherwise exploit them. One may gaze at them, conquer them by climbing, by personal effort, and so feed one's pride, enrich one's memories and affirm one's identity with nature—the ultimate refuge of mankind.'

     *   *   *

Schnabel was at this time in the full flush of his physical powers, a short, compact but by no means corpulent man, with a moderately large, well-rounded head and an habitually serious yet engaging countenance. He had a lush crop of moderately short hair, still only slightly mottled with grey, and a neat, business-like moustache. Nothing about him corresponded to the popular idea of an artist, though his keen responsive eyes and sensitive mouth reflected a quick mind and an affirmative attitude to life. His movements were deliberate and his walk leisurely, his facial expression alert, mobile and frequently lighted up by a radiant and infectious smile. His keen sense of humour and readiness for fun were rarely obscured except when seriously preoccupied with his work. He had no trace of the proverbial absent-mindedness of the professor, or the bohemian attitudes of the artist. Indeed, the superficial impression was that of a man of affairs—in any case a solid citizen, with an uncompromising taste for neat and very conservative dress. One detail of old-fashionedness remained with him to the very end: he refused to wear a white waistcoat with his 'tails'.

The quality which sooner or later impressed itself on everyone was his unobtrusive and irresistibly magnetic charm. When not in one of his pessimistic or sharply critical moods, or on one of his periodic rampages against the contradictions and incongruities of what he considered this greedy and brutalized world of the mechanized age, he was good-humoured, often gay and rather fond of his own brand of joke: with a decided preference for puns and—often bilingual —plays on words. He was an indefatigable talker, mildly didactic, especially in matters of art, inflexible when discussing ethical principles or artistic standards.

All through his adult life, Schnabel was a highly conscientious and dutiful husband and father, though not unsusceptible to female charms. He was deeply concerned with the future of his children and a generous provider for his ageing parents, less fortunate relatives and dependents. His conventional and outwardly unadventurous habits were those of the highly respectable middle-class citizen. He was orderly and systematic in the German manner—a natural reaction to the Austrian *Schlamperei* with which he became disgusted in his youth. Indeed, in his attitudes and habits he was more German than Austrian, and he only objected to being taken for a German when the word acquired the dreadful connotations of Nazism.

He was always a liberal in politics, and long sympathetic to social democracy, yet essentially aristocratic in his tastes. Indeed, with all his modesty and frugality he was essentially a *bon vivant*. He was only mildly interested in the theatre (with a notable exception in favour of operas by Mozart or Verdi), much less so in the cinema (with exceptions in favour of Charlie Chaplin and the Marx Brothers), and not at all in the radio and all forms of mass-produced entertainment. In fact he was hostile to all kinds of art substitutes. He had no taste for professional sport but was a keen and competent tennis player. His principal social pastime, aside from conversation, was a game of cards, usually bridge, which became his favourite in later years.

Schnabel had a fair knowledge of literature, mostly German, some French, and in his later years English. He now spoke all three languages (German and English with an almost phenomenal vocabulary) and his letters showed an unusual command of aptly contrived expressions and a fastidious choice of words. He gave the impression of being a more than commonly well-read man, and his library suggested the book-lover of wide knowledge and taste. Actually, Schnabel spent comparatively little time in reading. His wide acquaintance with people in different walks of life was one of his major sources of knowledge, and he liked to cultivate his friendships separately rather than in groups. Going for strolls with a friend, a pupil or a companion of some sort was one of Schnabel's favourite ways of enjoying his leisure hours. In later years, as his eyesight became progressively impaired by illness, these methods of absorbing information became more and more the rule.

But all through middle age Schnabel was blessed with thoroughly good health and vitality, troubled only with occasional neuritis in one of his arms, with nervous headaches and sleeplessness induced by emotional or mental strain, none of which was outwardly discernible. There is no record of his having missed a single engagement before his middle sixties. Until that time he was a passionate mountain climber, physically—as well as ideally—always striving toward the heights.

22.   On the Road to Fame

IT may be said that in his later forties Schnabel was beginning to acquire a truly international reputation for the first time in his life, but it was a reputation of a very special kind. He had long been famous in the Germanic countries, and accepted as a celebrity in Soviet Russia. He was admired in England and respected in the United States. He was beginning to be known in Italy and by hearsay even in France—as a protagonist of Beethoven and Brahms. But his primary appeal was to the cultivated music-lovers: the serious-minded, the professionals, the students and the connoisseurs formed the core of his audiences. Even in Berlin, where he was a prime favourite with working-class organizations, his audiences usually included a sprinkling of musicians—conductors as well as instrumentalists, teachers and writers. Generally speaking, his audiences made up in quality what they might lack in numbers.

This, of course, was largely due to his refusal to woo the masses by playing down to his audience or by the usual methods of publicity. He strictly forbade 'papering' the house even in cities where he was still new. For many years now he had refused to give encores, because he carefully constructed his programmes as a well-balanced whole which could not be added to without detriment to its design. (To the innocent inquirer he would explain that he considered applause a 'receipt' and not a 'bill'.) In general, he refused to regard the wishes of the audience or consider its right to call the tune. He was perhaps the first pianist in his generation who bluntly and consistently said that he served the composer and no one else. And he explained his comparatively narrow choice of composers by asserting that it was determined by what he called his assignment. He still considered himself to belong to a particular type of musical performer, devoted to clearly defined tasks which were not generally or adequately fulfilled by others. Why should he play what so many others did so well, when there were so few who could, or would, do justice to the immense quantity of indisputably great music—much of it neglected? It was this kind of music, more exacting and difficult than any other, that he had made his speciality. 'I only play music that is better than it can be played,' he would say. In other words, he never claimed anything more than that he aspired to an ideal which could be approached, but rarely if ever attained.

There could be no quarrel with his aspirations, and few people doubted his sincerity. But one might well question the rigidity of his standards, or the exclusion of many works of real quality even though of easier appeal. He denied, for instance, the assertion that a César Franck or a Debussy had any claim on his talents as a performer, though he did not refuse to teach their works to others. Admittedly great composers in their particular field, like Liszt, some of whose works he gladly played in his youth, he put aside in later years. Chopin he gradually dropped from his programmes, and even Brahms, an early favourite, was later all but discarded—with the exception of the two concertos.

Again, it was difficult to understand his attitude with audiences which stood on lower and sometimes radically different cultural levels from his own. He doggedly insisted on treating them alike, regardless of nationality and social or educational background, not because he thought they were equally prepared to absorb the unadulterated master works but because he felt that nothing else should be expected of him, any more than a minister should be expected to preach anything but the Word of God.

Always a good European and a thorough-going internationalist, Schnabel was curiously single-minded when it came to musical taste, in which he followed the most fastidious Germanic standards—which he himself had helped to establish. He expected these to be accepted wherever he went and made no allowance for differences of temperament, cultural traditions, levels of education and capacity to appreciate. Once in Soviet Russia he deplored the necessity of having to play for 'unprepared' audiences; yet he refused to modify his programmes and continued to play late Beethoven sonatas to people who were shouting for Liszt's *Campanella*. Though duly forewarned, he insisted on playing Beethoven's opus 111 in his first Liverpool concert, and cheerily reported that 'only a few people left the hall'. He was often annoyed but never intimidated by the behaviour of his audience.

The most extreme case of this stubborn adherence to his programme came in 1929 on his first extensive tour of Spain. Fresh from his triumphal success in London with a programme culminating in Beethoven's *Diabelli Variations* he insisted on playing this colossal and unfamiliar work in Seville. The unsuspecting society matrons and the eligible señoritas with their swains, who regarded the concerts of the very select Spanish musical societies as a rare but legitimate opportunity for courtship, could hardly be expected to maintain silence during a fifty-five-minute non-stop masterpiece. But neither the persistent chatter nor the yowling of a pair of cats off-stage and the variegated noises of a neighbouring café prevented Schnabel from going through with this gruelling task of concentration, though he later admitted that for the first time in his career he had omitted some of the prescribed repeats! One may well ask whether this kind of artistic masochism was calculated to elevate his listeners, to test his own will-power, or to placate his 'only employer—the art'. It is even more questionable whether these pioneering efforts materially improved the musical life of Spain. The important thing to realize is that he firmly believed it was his duty to try.

Nevertheless he derived evident satisfaction from the ten concerts he gave in the course of only fourteen days, ranging from Valencia to Oviedo and Bilbao via Madrid. Everywhere, he reported, he had to play 'against the public', but the most successful concert—which means where *he* was most nearly satisfied—was in the smallest town, León. He definitely felt that here he made a very deep impression at the end. For the rest he found his consolation, as usual, in nature: in the very beautiful Cantabrian Mountains and the uninterruptedly blue sky. And he regained his spiritual calm while admiring the 'ineffable beauty, power and grace' of the Alcazar.

Generally speaking, Schnabel found it more difficult to win audiences in the Latin countries than among the Nordic and Slavic peoples of the Continent. We have already spoken of the varied reaction of the Italians before they accepted him with enthusiasm. On the other hand he himself had taken virtually no initiative in their direction. At a time when his name was already well known throughout Europe and the United States, he had never once been heard in France. He had visited Paris several times *en route* and had fallen in love with it as everyone does, but he had not received or solicited an invitation to play there until 1929, when a Berlin agent had arranged an engagement with the comparatively new Orchestre Symphonique de Paris, on his way to Spain. The conductor was the very able Louis Fourestier and the piece was Beethoven's E-flat concerto. There were not many people present, but Schnabel reported that the performance was 'the best I have thus far achieved', a very important statement considering the source. The Paris press took virtually no notice of the concert; only the conscientious Clarence Lucas, then Paris correspondent of the *Musical Courier*, reported that Schnabel's 'authoritative manner, his broad, noble style, rich tone and subtle modifications of tempo made his interpretation memorable.' It also gave great delight to his hearers, for Lucas reported that he was recalled a half-dozen times. Yet there were no further repercussions and the arbiters of French musical life were seemingly asleep. It was five years later before they woke up.

Before the end of this unusually adventurous season Schnabel made a quick trip to Vienna, played in one or two South German cities and then made for home, to resume his 'life with the young pupils, which always refreshes me', as he wrote in a letter to Mrs. Courtauld. This time the refreshment was to have a climax in the form of a second concert by Schnabel pupils at the Hochschule, which aroused the admiration of the Berlin critics to an uncommon degree. It should be mentioned, too, that Schnabel's own son Karl Ulrich, whom he had not taught regularly but who probably learned more from him than from anyone else, was beginning to be heard, not only as a pianist but as a composer in the latest 'linear' style.

A happy event of that spring home-coming was the visit of Arturo Toscanini to conduct a series of operas as a guest of the Berlin State Opera. Schnabel dived with gusto into the mellifluous stream of Italian operas, and he and Therese enjoyed themselves for several weeks without let or hindrance until Artur, half-inebriated with Verdi melodies, cried 'Halt! I've had my fill!' He continued to admire Toscanini for his marvellously expressive conducting of Italian opera, but he was never convinced that the famous *maestro* fully succeeded in recreating the substance of the great classical symphonic works.

*   *   *

Throughout the early months of the year Schnabel was much preoccupied with Mrs. Courtauld's plan to create and sponsor the new series of orchestral concerts in London, mainly for the benefit of wide segments of the public which had hitherto been almost excluded from the enjoyment of great music in first-class performances. The ultimate purpose was to raise the general level of English musical life by establishing a new and exemplary series of concerts, orchestral and other, and to appeal to as wide an audience as possible. To ensure a really high standard of performance there would have to be first-rate conductors and soloists and—most important—an adequate number of rehearsals, regardless of cost. The programmes were to be chosen on the basis of quality alone, without national bias, and with the secondary object of broadening the existing repertoire by performing works recognized abroad but not yet heard in England. As musical director Mrs. Courtauld chose Dr. Malcolm Sargent, hitherto the conductor of the Robert Mayer Children's Concerts, and the series was to be known as the Courtauld–Sargent Concerts. But the most potent advice as to programmes and performers was to come from Schnabel, who had given the first impetus to the idea. The work of organization was left entirely in the hands of Mrs. Courtauld and her very able assistant, Miss Cecily Stanhope.

Plans were discussed in a lively correspondence between the two principals in the spring and summer of 1929. Schnabel proposed as conductors for the first four concerts, besides Sargent, Bruno Walter, Wilhelm Furtwängler and Otto Klemperer. He had also recommended most highly Dr. Karl Muck, a 'very great master, whose reliability, maturity and unselfish devotion are not equalled by any living artist', but for one reason or another this wish was not fulfilled. Schnabel himself was to appear at two of the concerts, playing two and three concertos respectively, and he proposed Carl Flesch and Gregor Piatigorsky as additional soloists, also Paul Hindemith in a work by himself.

There was, of course, opposition from local quarters, and the irrepressible Turner valiantly counter-attacked in the *New Statesman*. But the only serious shadow that lay over the enterprise was Mrs. Courtauld's ominous illness, which apparently abated during the subsequent months. Schnabel himself had not been entirely well of late, complaining of rheumatism and intermittent neuritis—his 'occupational disease'. In his letters to Mrs. Courtauld he cautioned abstinence from certain foods and stimulants, even smoking—advice which he was obliged more and more to follow himself.

But his one great cure was fresh air and the beneficent beauties of nature, so in July he was off to the mountains again with Therese and some of his English friends. This time they stayed at the Eggishorn, where the view of the Bernese Alps with the towering Jungfrau, Mönch and Eiger were spread before them as sensationally as the Savoy Alps had been in Argentières the year before. Late August saw him in Italy, sea-bathing at Forte dei Marmi and visiting various friends, alone, at Ascona and a little castle on the Lake of Constance. He was socially, as always, in great demand. Early in October he was back in Berlin, playing the Mozart E-flat piano quartet and the Dvořák A major quintet—two of his favourites— with the Kolisch Quartet, which on this occasion gave the first performance of his own third string quartet. It was the first work by him to be performed in several years. One of his most successful to

hnabel with Stefan, then playing the part of Lord Willoughby in the Old Vic's
Richard II. London, 1934

ith Karl Ulrich and Stefan,
anning a motor tour of
France

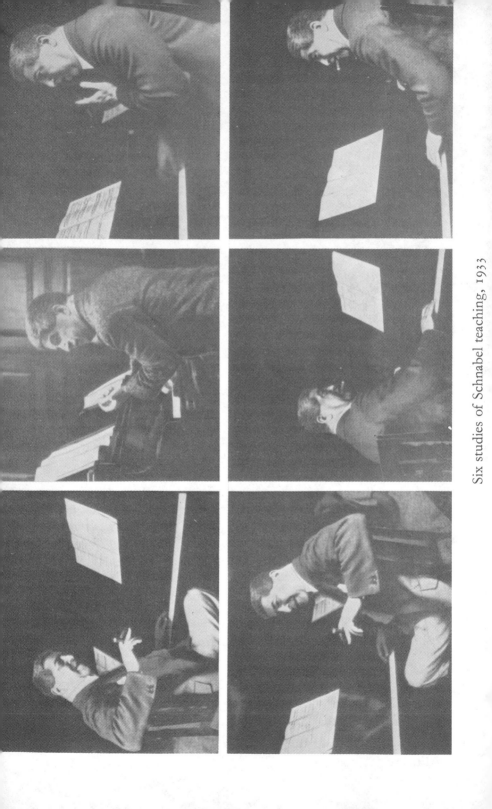

Six studies of Schnabel teaching, 1933

date, it received a more than respectful hearing. No doubt it also aroused new creative longings in himself—after a four years' pause. But the time was not yet: his reputation as a performing artist was only now approaching something like world fame. And he was still not fifty, the age at which he once had promised himself to terminate his pianist's career.

23. Success in England

BY the autumn of 1929 the preparations for the Courtauld–Sargent
concerts had been completed. The plan was not to compete
with existing institutions but to create a new audience from largely
untapped sources by means of a new organization, the Concert Club,
which drew its members from the personnel of large concerns,
department stores, commercial houses, banks, government offices,
and professional bodies. Mrs. Courtauld simply submitted her plan
to a number of business and professional leaders for advice and help.
The response was completely positive. Announcements were made
to the various concerns by their own managements, inviting member-
ship in a group to be affiliated with the new Club. The members
would have the privilege of subscribing to one or two seats for the
first series of four orchestral concerts at very low cost. Only a very
small number of seats was retained for public sale on the evening, in
order to prevent hard feelings. When the series was fully subscribed,
a waiting list was started for the next season, and eventually a repeat
performance was to be provided for the expected overflow.

The result was that the Queen's Hall was virtually sold out, with
almost no newspaper advertising. At later seasons the concerts were
given in duplicate, which reduced the inevitable deficit and made the
concerts very nearly self-supporting. It is pleasant to recall that the
idea had a wholly favourable reaction in the Press.

The first concert was a triumph rarely equalled in the Queen's Hall.
Schnabel played the Beethoven G major and the Brahms D minor
concertos and the London Symphony Orchestra under Malcolm
Sargent contributed Mozart's G minor symphony. The atmosphere
was electric and at the end the listeners, including large numbers who
were new to this kind of music, stood up and cheered. The Press
burst into a pæan of praise which belied the well-known British
reputation for understatement. 'A new chapter in the history of
music-making was opened in Queen's Hall last night,' said the *Daily
Telegraph*. 'Never before had an audience of this precise character
been drawn together to listen to fine, serious music played in a fine
way.' Other papers, metropolitan and provincial, daily, weekly and
monthly, hailed the concerts as a public boon.

The critical estimate of Schnabel was summed up by H. C. Colles of *The Times*, who said that the remarkable thing about his playing was its 'all-inclusiveness'. 'One pianist may give us the poetical quality of Beethoven, another his intellectual power, while a third will emphasize his vehemence or his tenderness. Herr Schnabel welds all these qualities and many more.' And Ernest Newman of the *Sunday Times* reinforced this by pointing out 'his complete mastery of all aspects—form, display and emotion.' Perhaps the real measure of his popularity was given when the *Daily Express* announced that he was now 'the most fashionable' pianist playing in London!

A few of the more perspicacious observers also noted that the orchestra under Malcolm Sargent seemed to play a new rôle. The *Saturday Review* had this to say on the subject: 'Herr Schnabel is not the man to treat a concerto by Beethoven as a work for pianoforte solo with orchestral accompaniment. The work is seen as a whole, to which every instrument must contribute its proper share.' People close to him were particularly aware of the significance of this remark, for he was notoriously as meticulous about the orchestra's playing as he was about his own—a fact which could become embarrassing to the kind of conductors who resent 'interference' from the soloist. Schnabel's tendency to 'take over' at rehearsals had become notorious, and this inspired a good-natured cartoon portrait by the British artist Edmond Kapp entitled 'Schnabel and the Conductor', but showing *only* Schnabel at the piano.

Schnabel had, of course, been consulted in the choice of the youthful Sargent as the musical director. Here was a highly gifted musician and one not yet too 'set' in his ways to take counsel from an older man. Sargent had a difficult rôle, placed in juxtaposition with such distinguished elders as Bruno Walter and Otto Klemperer, and he acquitted himself remarkably well. He quickly became an important figure in English musical life and (as Sir Malcolm Sargent) was destined to achieve both national and international fame.

The second Courtauld–Sargent concert was no less felicitous than the first. This time Schnabel played three concertos, Mozart's D minor, Beethoven's C minor and the B-flat major of Brahms. 'It is impossible to say,' wrote the critic of the *Observer*, 'in which Mr. Schnabel was the greatest; we liked them all.' Mozart lovers like H. E. Wortham of the *Daily Telegraph* found that 'the utmost extravagance of epithets would not convey the ease and the sureness that marked Schnabel's modelling of Mozart's phrases,' but the most vociferous applause of the audience followed the Brahms B-flat. 'In big-muscled music like this he is without equal,' said Ernest Newman, who injected the first sour note by criticizing the orchestra's 'commonplace work' in certain places. 'For a Schnabel a concerto is a spiritual experience that has been brooded over in silence for years,' he remarked, 'for an orchestra a concerto is just an engagement.'

The wonderful success of the Courtauld-Sargent concerts is now a chapter of musical history. They revealed to thousands of Londoners a new facet of culture and gave to many a new interest and an unforgettable experience. More than that, they had a salutary effect on the quality of music-making in general. 'There is an all-round improvement this season,' commented the *Daily Mail*, in speaking of the new enterprise, 'proper rehearsing is adding a new interest to music in London.' But there was bound to be some resentment when the *Daily Express* credited Mrs. Courtauld with having accomplished 'what the B.B.C., with its strong educational inclinations, might have done,' and pointed out that while her concerts packed the Queen's Hall from floor to ceiling, the B.B.C. Symphony Orchestra played to 'row upon row of empty seats'.

It was inevitable, too, that the extravagant adulation of Schnabel in some quarters should arouse dissent in others. Walter J. Turner, of course, rode his snorting steed to battle in the *New Statesman*, and elicited a vicious counter-attack from a writer in *The Nation* under the heading of 'Schnabel and Schnabelolatry': 'The inevitable has happened,' it began. 'Quite a number of intelligent people are beginning to discover reasons for *not* regarding Mr. Schnabel as the greatest pianist of the day. It is a natural reaction against the outpourings of gush with which the undiscriminating admirers have deluged a great reputation. Unhappily the effects of revulsion fall not upon the Schnabelolators but upon their idol.' It is a comfort to realize, in retrospect, that this turned out to be a false alarm, and that he continued to be held in undiminished reverence in England for the rest of his life.

During that very season he appeared half a dozen times in London alone within less than two months, and without any diminution in the public's response. The critics, hardly less enthusiastic than before, now went in for discriminating comment, some of which—in so far as it is reflected on the *composers*—he took very much amiss. For instance, he was furious when Schubert's *Drei Klavierstücke* (1828) were treated by some critics as mere trifles. But it was never the comment on his playing that annoyed him; it was the derogation of the great masters and the lack of intelligent appreciation on the part of people who should be leaders of opinion. The year before, a Liverpool critic had called Beethoven's opus 111 a 'boring sonata'. The result was that next time there was a smaller but exemplary audience, listening in rapt silence to the even more difficult opus 106. Schnabel was delighted when the same critic now called him 'the Einstein of music', adding that Einstein 'probably had more romantic feeling', and he promptly sent a message to the great scientist, apprising him of this back-handed compliment.

As regards his own compositions, he was used to the critics' abuse in Germany, and was not surprised to read the poor notices of his first string quartet when the Hungarian String Quartet played it in London in January 1930. What mattered to him was that he himself liked the work—'better than before'. He had not heard it in years, and characteristically had shown no interest in it after it achieved its decisive success at the Düsseldorf Festival eight years before. However, the London critics were at least respectful, and expressed a desire to hear the work again. One of them, F. Bonavia, writing in the *Musical Times*, called it a 'remarkable piece of work, which had moments of great beauty.'

It goes without saying that Schnabel, like most really great artists, was his own severest critic. He never tried to cover up deficiencies, and was as unhappy about what he considered undeserved praise as he was about unintelligent blame. His letters to Therese are full of precise reports on the quality of his playing. Commenting on his contribution to a Robert Mayer Children's Concert at which Queen Mary was present, he said it was a 'very mediocre' performance and could only partly be explained by the acoustical conditions of the hall.

★   ★   ★

It was in Manchester that Schnabel made his most profound impression, the Manchester of Hans Richter, the Hallé Orchestra and the Free Trade Hall—according to Schnabel the 'only heated hall in England'. Appearing twice within a fortnight, he had what he himself called a 'fabulous success'. At his recital he played three sonatas—the Schubert posthumous C minor, the Mozart F major (K. 332) and Beethoven's *Hammerklavier*. Neville Cardus, sensitive and erudite critic of the *Guardian*, was delighted with his 'truly symphonic reading of the Schubert', but devoted the major part of his extensive criticism to the Beethoven, which is worth quoting for some very perspicacious remarks about Schnabel's 'life-giving rhythm'.

'Here we are at the source of Mr. Schnabel's greatness. There are pianists who are his equals in piano playing; none can excel him as a builder of significant form. Form with Schnabel is not a matter of external phrase-making and balancing: it is the consequence of an internal rhythm—the coursing blood of musical energy shaping from within outwards and inevitably.'

Cardus found that he played the fugue of the *Hammerklavier* sonata 'titanically, discovering from some stormy depths within himself a new strength that cast out of mind one or two hints of laboured portentousness felt earlier on,' and concluded that he was 'the biggest-minded pianist of the day'. But Cardus's own objectivity led him to add that he missed in him the 'note of magic' and 'the element of strangeness which belongs to beauty and poetry'—not in order to find fault but 'to mark Schnabel's style and psychology'. It was this speculative quality in Cardus' writing that intrigued Schnabel: he was never against intelligent criticism and never attracted by mere praise, though there is little doubt that he disagreed, and none whatever that he won the argument in the end!

Schnabel was immediately attracted to this man as one who sought to penetrate the inner mysteries of music, and who exercised his convictions regardless of personal sympathies. The two were soon introduced to each other, and a warm friendship sprang up between them that lasted to the end.

★   ★   ★

As he came to know the provinces and eventually filled engagements in all parts of the British Isles, Schnabel became more and more disturbed by what he called, in a sweeping generalization, 'conditions'. This might include anything from draughty halls to bad acoustics, inconvenient local customs or plain indifference. In general, he found people 'not properly equipped for the road to art—and not aware of the existing shortcomings.' This might be shown by insensibility, or apparent lack of respect for art and artists, in contrast to the high development of social ritual and punctilio and the strict British observance of the rules of sport and fair play. In the last analysis he blamed the artists themselves for being too unexacting. 'Perhaps,' he wrote, 'they are not really satisfied, but they certainly lack the fighting spirit to improve the environment where it hampers or depresses them.' As an artist Schnabel was rarely satisfied, and under the skin of the artist there was also the pedagogue and reformer. As such he held a pathetic belief that talking about things would mend them.

To him, playing in English halls always remained a very special kind of experience: 'Often their owners arrange an artificial blizzard on their platforms. This is very hard on the performer, while the audience, in jerseys and overcoats, combine the zest of fresh air with the pleasure of music.' From Bristol he reported that when he began to play his fingers became as cold as icicles, and he saw the potted palms on the platform waving 'in a wonderful wind'. Five years later he returned to find the same auditorium converted into a luxurious 'hall of mirrors' at a cost of £40,000. But here was the same wind that had been going through it before all that money had been spent! Once, in Glasgow, he arrived in a thick fog, which had penetrated to the hall when the concert began. 'It was so thick,' he reported, 'that I couldn't see the audience. But I knew there was one, for I heard it cough.'

The English themselves know all about their weather, of course, for they have long made it a leading subject of conversation. Schnabel's complaint, like Mark Twain's, was that they did so little about it. When asked by a newspaper reporter how he liked the English climate he answered that he thought the outdoor climate agreeable, but the indoor climate was such that all the pianos suffered from colds.

Eventually he became accustomed to the weather, but he never became reconciled to certain other time-honoured customs. The most unforgettable encounter with tradition occurred one Saturday night in Oxford, where his concert took place in a hall not far from the tower of Christ Church College which houses Old Tom. When he began his second group of pieces the great bell began to toll. Thinking it must be striking nine, he waited, hands in lap, but the 'clock' went on and on—until he had counted seventy-five strokes and the audience couldn't hold their laughter any longer. For they knew what he didn't: that this was Old Tom striking 101 times, in honour of the hundred original students plus one. There was no provision for relaxing a rule once established by pious tradition, and Beethoven was effectively silenced by *force majeure*.

This incident, to Schnabel, was almost matched by the knitting and tea-drinking ladies of Folkestone, where he was booked to play a recital in the hall of a hotel atop the cliff. The piano was decorated with flowers, 'as for a funeral', and the tea service with accompanying noises was threatening to continue right into the concert, until the manager came and told Schnabel he might 'kick-off' at five. But the programme had to be curtailed by one sonata because the dinner hour

'could not be disturbed'. Schnabel finished but was so depressed that
at the end he waited in his subterranean artist's room to recover his
spirits, and barely escaped being locked in for the night.

Despite 'conditions', the vagaries of the weather and the peculi-
arities of people, Schnabel achieved an exceptionally close contact
with the reputedly reticent English; and he took particular pleasure
in making himself accessible to all sorts of people, dissidents as well
as admirers. Once a Manchester tram driver who had studied piano
asked and received permission to attend a rehearsal. Schnabel liked
him and afterwards invited him to every rehearsal and every concert
he gave in the town. In the course of years the ardent follower saved
up money to purchase a first edition of one of Beethoven's works
and presented it to Schnabel as a token of his gratitude. Some years
later, during his series of Beethoven concerts a rather testy London
amateur wrote Schnabel a letter criticizing his interpretation of certain
sonatas. Schnabel answered the letter and invited his correspondent
to come and talk it over. They argued every point at issue, while
Schnabel illustrated at the piano. In the end he persuaded his man,
who henceforth came to every concert and remained as faithful as
only a convert can be.

*   *   *

One of the most important results of Schnabel's success in England
was that certain important people in America were now determined
to bring him back, regardless of material obstacles. His old contract
with the Knabe Piano Co. had now expired, and negotiations for the
only other piano in question, the Steinway, had been going on, thus
far without success. Influential friends, such as Mrs. J. F. D. Lanier
(president of the Friends of Music), had tried their best, but the
Steinway policy was that Steinway pianists were to play no other
piano anywhere in the world, a condition which Schnabel refused to
accept. Nevertheless there was a growing demand for him, especially
on the part of certain conductors, including Artur Bodanzký, Ossip
Gabrilowitch and Sergei Koussevitzky, of the Boston Symphony
Orchestra.

In 1929 Koussevitzky was planning a Brahms Festival with the
Boston Symphony to take place the following spring. He invited
Schnabel to be the principal soloist and, since the Steinways were
still adamant, arrangements were made with the Berlin house of
Bechstein to send two of their concert grands to America, also the
necessary technicians to service them. To make the trip worth while
for Schnabel, two more concerts were planned for New York.

Schnabel accepted with mixed feelings, hoping for the best, and the contract was signed while he was at the peak of his English success.

In March 1930 he sailed on the *Aquitania* from Cherbourg, after a short and pleasant stop in Paris on the way. He still carried with him the unhappy memory of his previous American experiences, and a rather confused resentment against New York, which he remembered as 'a huge railway station surrounded by a million windows'.

As soon as he arrived in Boston, all this was forgotten. The town, the atmosphere, the people, all reminded him of England. 'It is New *England,* after all', he commented in his first letter home. This time, moreover, he stayed with friends, at a lovely country house in Milton, Massachusetts, the home of a former pupil and a prominent member of Boston society. 'The people who "spoil" me here,' he wrote, 'are very different from those I knew before: there are no *parvenus,* no musicians with a worm's view of life.' They were well-bred, hospitable, quiet yet spirited, reticent yet warm-hearted folk. The house he lived in was 'exactly what I would have wished'.

The Boston audience turned out to be equally congenial and the occasion was as auspicious as could be imagined. Schnabel took part in three all-Brahms concerts with the orchestra, playing both concertos, and in a chamber music concert with the Burgin String Quartet, at which he also played the *Piano Pieces* opus 119, and accompanied the contralto Margaret Matzenauer in Brahms songs. All the concerts were gala events and the response was extraordinary—even for him. 'At one stroke,' he reported, 'I was singled out from all my colleagues to occupy a place apart.' Regarding his performance he merely remarked that he played 'as well as I am able to play', which was the highest self-praise he ever indulged in. He was delighted with Koussevitzky—an 'exalted artist'—and the Boston Orchestra was 'simply beyond comparison'.

The upshot was that Schnabel, who seven years earlier had been received with polite but moderate approbation, now appeared to the Boston critics as a phenomenon beyond their powers of description. His technical resources were 'inexhaustible'; he was 'the virtuoso, the musician and the poetizing interpreter', and (according to H. T. Parker of the *Transcript*) he 'summoned a tone so limpid, soft and bright, so edgeless, so luminous that it gave no hint of an instrument of hammers and wires'. What the eminent critic discovered, like other analysts before him, was Schnabel's very particular sense of rhythm—'an underlying and unfailingly plastic rhythm that informs

the entire concerto and binds it together as an organic whole'. Also
he was struck by his sense of continuity—'an unfolding unity and a
concentrated progress that were new sensations of the concert hall'.
By common consent, Schnabel was the great figure of the festival.
When during the following week he played the Beethoven G major
concerto another critic said that it had 'a loftiness and authority'
which made him question whether he had ever really heard it before.

Shortly after this the Boston Symphony played its regular weekly
two concerts in New York and Schnabel again was the soloist in
both Brahms concertos. Present were the usual Boston Symphony
subscribers, with a few outsiders, and there was no general publicity.
But W. J. Henderson, the veteran critic of the *Sun*, allowed that
Schnabel had undoubtedly grown since he last visited New York.
'His performance last night was memorable', he wrote. 'He not only
interpreted Brahms but he played the piano as only a master can.'
Most of the daily press wrote in a similar vein, and the musical weeklies
chimed in.

This time Schnabel found New York, in the brilliant radiance of
spring, more agreeable than eight years ago. It is just possible that
the rosy glow of his new success had softened the edges of what he
saw. He still did not understand this city and its inhabitants with
their 'superior, super-casual outlook on life'. There were no grandiose
proposals from managers, and he refused the offer of a single recital
in New York. But the Boston Symphony people were delighted
with his success and immediately invited him for another festival in
the spring of 1934. His complete capture of America could now be
only a matter of time. He was, as he wrote to Rita Macintyre, 'in
every respect satisfied and overjoyed'. Although he never gloated
over a mere material success, the plain fact is that he had now triumph-
antly established himself in the two most important musical market-
places of the world—London and New York.

★   ★   ★

No sooner was he back in Berlin than he rounded out the year's
happy events by resigning his professorship at the Hochschule. In
his recollections, many years later, he gave as his reason the growing
nationalistic tendencies of the faculty. Be that as it may, he had
begun to find the job irksome, and he could now well afford to give
it up. It was not that he loved teaching less, but that he loved his
freedom more. He could continue to teach as, when, and whom he
liked—in his own home. Just then he was busy playing chamber

music with his once more reconstituted Trio, consisting of himself, Carl Flesch and Gregor Piatigorsky. He nicknamed it 'Arti, Vati and Piati' (Vati being the German diminutive for *Vater*). In May the Trio appeared in the Berlin Philharmonie and was greeted with jubilation. They played Mendelssohn, Schubert's E-flat trio, Beethoven's *Schneider Kakadu Variations* and a new *Trio Fantasie* by Ernst Křenek, one of the few radical contemporaries with whom Schnabel saw eye to eye. The study of this work had no doubt stimulated his own desire for renewed creative effort, and he immediately began sketching a new sonata for solo cello.

This, the first stirring of creative activity in five years or more, was not to bear fruit till the following year. In the interim, however, he was prompted to begin another string quartet—his fourth—during the course of a varied holiday with his wife and his London friends which began strenuously at Arolla, some 6000 feet high in the Valais Alps, continued in the relaxing air of the Adriatic coast, and ended in the Palazzo Barbaro in Venice. There as the guest of a wealthy patroness of music, Mrs. J. F. D. Lanier of New York's Friends of Music, he experienced the sybaritic existence of a grandseigneur. Reflecting none of the luxuries and frivolities of his environment, this work marks a return to the rather congested style of his second quartet. The kaleidoscopic first movement uses several themes in ever-changing contexts to form a continuous fantasia, and a slow scherzo-like middle movement leads to a tightly-packed contrapuntal finale. It is one of the less accessible of Schnabel's quartets.

By contrast with it, the sonata for 'cello solo which he had sketched in the hurly-burly of the past Berlin season, to be completed the following year, has all the melodic beauty, lightness and clarity that might be expected from a single-voiced essay in free fantasy. This unique work is much shorter and less extreme than the violin solo sonata of 1919, and its expressive style rises to great melodic beauty and clarity. The first of its three movements develops ever new aspects from a single motif. This is followed by a characteristic *ostinato* in perpetual motion, which leads to a slow, poetic discourse and a finale which combines three contrasting ideas—the last ending in a pizzicato figure suggesting a Gregorian chant.

This work was eventually finished in the tragic European summer of 1931. He was fated not to resume composing till 1935—the beginning of his most consistently productive final years of his life.

24. Triumph Amid Tragedy

WHEN the Schnabels returned to Berlin after their Italian holiday in September 1930, an ominous change had taken place. There had been a general election, and as a result the Nazis emerged for the first time as a major political party, with 107 Reichstag seats in place of the twelve they held before. The immediate result was a crescendo in their raucous behaviour and a new tone of arrogance and hysteria in their Press. That this could be the turning of the tide leading to national disaster and to personal tragedy for millions did not for a moment enter the minds of the average intelligent but politically not clairvoyant citizen. But everyone must have been aware of the increasing economic misery of the people, due this time not to inflation but to loss of employment, high taxation and languishing trade—a portent of world-wide depression. Poverty was everywhere; but in Germany it was aggravated by the sinister exploitation of popular distress through the machinations of political adventurers whose diabolical aims were as yet not fully understood. While inept officials tried to prop up a tottering democracy by means of emergency decrees, a fanatical 'leader' stirred the flames of violence out of the embers of the people's wrath.

Artur Schnabel, intensely preoccupied with his widening field of activity, seemed scarcely aware of the ominous implications of these developments. His own great successes outside of Germany during the previous season, and especially his triumphs in the important cities of England and the United States, had shifted the fulcrum of his career away from Central Europe to the English-speaking world. As the result of his rapidly increasing following in foreign lands and his ever-widening circle of friends, his personal orientation was becoming more and more international, and his former linguistic limitations had long since been overcome both in regard to English and French.

His immediate attention was centred on the very promising second season of the Courtauld–Sargent Concerts in London, and the projected repetition of the music festival in Boston, a most promising springboard for a more widespread conquest of America. In the circumstances it was natural that he saw life through somewhat rosier spectacles than Therese, who was closer to the incidents of everyday living in Berlin, and who vaguely sensed the dangers ahead. Trying to reassure her he wrote from London: 'I know that it is difficult to breathe freely in Germany these days. All the more one must resist infection. I hope you will have regained your balance when I return and can stand aloof from the nauseating realities of the time.' Still, he himself may have been 'whistling in the dark', for his complaints of insomnia and his recurring neuritis were probably signs of worry.

But all this was swept away in the swirl of fresh successes and the wonderful prospects opened by the Courtauld–Sargent concerts. Mrs. Courtauld, whose illness had given much cause for concern, appeared fresh and strong again, active and inspired to carry on the work so well begun. Largely thanks to her, the second Courtauld–Sargent season promised to be a brilliant success. The concerts were double-subscribed, so that they would be given in pairs, with the Queen's Hall completely filled twice for each programme. Schnabel was to collaborate in two of these pairs, in October and January, both conducted by Dr. Malcolm Sargent. At the first, Schnabel performed Beethoven's triple concerto with Carl Flesch and Gregor Piatigorsky, and he also played the clavier part in Bach's fifth *Brandenburg Concerto*. The second concert constituted a new test of versatility, for it comprised three concertos: Schumann's A minor, Mozart's in C major (K. 467) and Beethoven's in E-flat. The response to these concerts, both by public and Press, was magnificent. Since Schnabel's name was by now virtually sacrosanct in England, the inevitable critical darts—gentle enough—were aimed at his colleagues or at the works. (Schnabel was particularly furious at the critic who called a movement of the *Brandenburg Concerto* 'the most boring in the entire literature'.)

The biggest popular success was, of course, the *Emperor* concerto, but what gave Schnabel the greatest happiness was the Mozart, which at these concerts of course had the benefit of unlimited rehearsal. 'Mozart five times,' he reported to Therese, 'each time more lovable [*immer lieber*]!' In the words of W. M. McNaught (in the *Evening News*) the performance was 'Mozartean in all the usual senses, and it had besides an intimacy and confidence that were an adornment of Schnabel's own.' Schnabel was at the top of his form, and enjoyed himself hugely, most of all perhaps in a trio concert he gave with Flesch and Piatigorsky which culminated in Schubert's great trio in E-flat. When the critics treated it as less than a great masterpiece he decided that there must be 'a rule against enthusiasm' and a tacit understanding that 'soul-shaking is not for English gentlemen'. But for the English audience he had nothing but praise: 'the listeners here,' he wrote to Therese, 'are as one can only wish them to be.'

★   ★   ★

Next to the British, the Swiss had always been among the most exemplary audiences, so he had every reason to expect an excellent result when he went straight from London to put the citizens of Zürich and Lausanne to the test with Beethoven's *Diabelli Variations*. As expected, its reception by the public was good; one Zürich critic, however, declared the work to be 'a third-rate concoction, with hardly a trace of genius'. In Lausanne, alas! he had very few listeners, because his concert coincided with the appearance of 'another transcendentalist', namely Krishnamurti, the Indian advocate of asceticism and dispenser of 'mass-produced happiness'. Schnabel was so sorry for the unlucky concert manager who had so fatally overestimated the power of Beethoven in this unequal contest that he returned half his fee. What really depressed him, however, was his experience in Geneva, where he played Weber's *Konzertstück* in an orchestral concert alongside of Ravel's *Bolero*. This 'shoddy' piece, according to Schnabel, was greeted by the Press as the work of a young Fortinbras, while poor Weber aroused only the critics' pity. All of which seems to show once again that there is no accounting for tastes. Even in the supposedly cultured German city of Munich the *Diabelli Variations* were dismissed by one writer as 'a very weak piece, though strongly executed'. Nothing was so calculated to rouse the ire of a man who believed that great music is always better than it can be played. But then we must remember that Schnabel never quoted a criticism unless it made him angry. The good ones he threw away.

What mattered to Schnabel and what determined his good humour on this journey, as always, was the degree of inner satisfaction he was able to derive from his work. And at this particular time he felt that he had reached a new phase in his development as a performing artist. Rarely satisfied as he was with his performances, even when they were successful, he now was sufficiently pleased with his playing to put it on record. In a letter to Mrs. Courtauld from Frankfurt at the end of 1930 he wrote:

'The concerts were satisfactory as a whole and on the line which for me is the only bearable one, inspired exclusively by musical motives. . . . I felt distinctly an important progress in my work; I am now much freer than two years ago . . . and with that consciousness, or—better—sudden awareness of a change, I reacted with deep gratitude to nature which permitted me the attempt to approach such spheres.'

To anyone who knew Schnabel, his severity in self-criticism and reluctance to self-praise, this confession is both revealing and significant. It means that he had reached a point sufficiently near perfection to be regarded as definitive. And it is especially interesting that this came two years after he had achieved the peak of public recognition with his complete cycle of Beethoven sonatas, at a time when Mozart was the new and ultimate star in his heaven, and—last not least—when he was seriously thinking of recording his playing for posterity.

The new sense of accomplishment and satisfaction was, it appears, communicated to the public wherever he went—through Switzerland to Italy and southern Germany—for he reported that 'the atmosphere in all the concerts was the proper one, concentrated, tense, sincere and simple: no affectation, no false solemnity, no false familiarity; the audiences silent, attentive and, as it seemed, happy to be impressed through their own activity'. The letter, by the way, was written in English, a sign that Schnabel's emancipation from the area of Germanic culture was making great strides: he was becoming 'international' in more ways than one.

On the material plane this was reflected in the widening orbit of his professional travels. Early in the new year (1931) he was again in England, filling engagements in London, Oxford, Manchester and smaller places (including one famous seaside resort where he felt that music was just 'a tree in the desert'). In London, the Queen's Hall was packed again for his recital of Beethoven and Brahms. And here, too, the response of the audience was the same as on the Continent— listening with rapt attention, in an atmosphere of complete devotion. From London he went to Warsaw, to Hamburg, to Greece, and thence to the Middle East. This he rather regarded as a pleasure trip, and accordingly took his wife along. The fact is that he was now in demand in many strange places, and Turkey was one of them. He played with orchestras in Istanbul and Ankara, and gave ten recitals there and in the provinces. No one took the trouble to keep the Press reviews, so it is difficult to know how he impressed these exotic audiences with his offerings of Mozart, Schubert and Beethoven, occasionally varied by Schumann and Brahms. On the return journey he appeared in Athens, home city of his future friend and champion Dimitri Mitropoulos and famous for its highly cultured upper class. Here Artur and Therese revelled in the wonders of nature and the arts of man, spending many hours among the sculptured miracles of the Parthenon. Returning homeward via southern Italy, they stopped for a brief but radiant holiday at Ragusa on the Adriatic Sea, where they met their younger son Stefan, happily and definitely liberated from school, with news from home. It was the happy end to a season of outward triumph and inward satisfaction, though not unmixed with illness and forebodings of unhappy events to come.

★   ★   ★

The first indication that all was not as well as could be in the best of all possible worlds came from the city of Artur's youth, where Austria's largest financial institution, the Vienna Credit-Anstalt, failed in May. Although Schnabel may not have suspected it, this was the crash heard round the world, and the beginning of a chain reaction which left no European country untouched. In quick succession leading banks closed their doors in Germany—a country now so nearly bankrupt that only an international moratorium could forestall its collapse. Mass unemployment and destitution spread through Europe, a counterpart to the Great Depression in the United States.

Schnabel, still in the heyday of his English popularity and, happy with a new invitation to America, looked into the future with confidence. Moreover, he now had awaiting him in England a firm offer of a gramophone contract which, if accepted, could go far toward making the family's future secure. Adding to the happy outlook, Karl Ulrich Schnabel had recently secured his first engagement in England, with prospects of more to come, while Stefan with full parental blessings was preparing for a theatrical career. It was therefore a carefree family that went to the Dolomites that summer, to meet their English friends in a remote mountain village with the quasi-anatomical name of Obergurgl for a holiday of climbing, to be followed by a fortnight's refresher at Francavilla in southern Italy. Here the family ran into a patch of very bad luck, which to someone more superstitious than Schnabel might have been regarded as an omen of worse to come. After climbing up to a resort in the Neapolitan Appenines, 'Karuli' drank of the impure local water and fell violently ill with a most painful dysentery that lasted for weeks. Therese, who undertook to nurse him, became infected, and at that same moment Artur was laid low by a severe attack of neuritis. Since no proper medical facilities were locally available, the family finally took refuge in the salubrious resort of Merano in the South Tyrol. While convalescing Artur actually finished his sonata for cello solo, begun the previous year.

It was at Merano that Schnabel got the full impact of the ominous world situation. Early in September Great Britain abandoned the gold standard, and shortly after devalued the pound sterling by about thirty per cent. In America the financial and commercial panic had deepened into a depression which gradually assumed the proportions of a national disaster. Unemployment ran into many millions and affected professional people as well as industrial workers, concerts and theatres as much as shops and factories.

But it was not until the Schnabels returned to Berlin that Artur realized how these events would affect his own fortunes, and when he did he was simply puzzled. When told of the devaluation of sterling he calmly suggested that his fees be paid him in dollars. When he received a cable from America notifying him of the indefinite postponement of the Boston Music Festival he resented it as a personal affront.

It was undoubtedly a hard blow. He had arranged his whole year with this important engagement in mind, and his plan was now 'a shambles'. As the magnitude of the calamity bore in upon him, he fell into deep pessimism—not only about himself but the state of the world. In a letter to Sir Robert Mayer he saw no way of preventing the collapse of the old order, but regarded it with a morose equanimity. Writing to Ernst Křenek he envisioned a near apocalyptic downfall—not only of Germany but of our much-vaunted and 'consistently betrayed' civilization.

In the midst of the general misery there now came a poignant note of personal tragedy. Harriet Lanier, one of the two feminine idealists who had given him so much encouragement by their artistic pioneering, died on her sixty-fifth birthday in New York. Her death meant not only the loss of an old and valued friend but probably also the end of the Society of the Friends of Music which she had founded and which had done so much for the musical life of America. The news reached him in London, while he was rehearsing Beethoven's *Choral Fantasy* with Malcolm Sargent and the London Symphony Orchestra. This was, by a melancholy coincidence, the very work of which he and Artur Bodanzky had given a memorable performance for Mrs. Lanier's Friends of Music eight years before. The London performance, in one of the Courtauld–Sargent concerts, inevitably took place under the shadow of the sad event, further deepened by the knowledge that Mrs. Courtauld was once again haunted by the lingering illness of recent years, which now was to prove incurable. Yet no one knew that this was destined to be the last concert 'Lil'

Courtauld would hear. The long arm of fate reached out and dealt
its shattering blow on Christmas Day 1931, when she succumbed—
after a sham recovery—to her cruel disease.

Schnabel was not in London when it happened. After some
orchestral engagements in Switzerland he had gone home to Berlin
for the holidays. The news came unexpectedly; only two months
previously he had submitted to her the programme of the only piano
recital he was to give in the Courtauld series of 1932 and at her
special request: Schubert's posthumous sonata in B-flat, Mozart's
sonata in D major (K. 311) and the *Diabelli Variations*. In mid-
January he was back in London to play it, in her memory, at the
Queen's Hall. Samuel Courtauld, not wholly unprepared for the
tragic event, gave a noble example of fortitude and generosity: the
concerts were to be continued as a memorial to his wife; and the
mansion in Portman Square was to be dedicated to public use as an
Art Institute. Most of the priceless paintings in it were eventually
bequeathed to the nation and now hang in the Tate Gallery. Only
a few of his favourites were, for the time being, removed to the
small Mayfair house which he now made his home. He and Artur
remained firm friends for life. When Schnabel completed his first
symphony (1938) he dedicated the score to his friend Samuel
Courtauld—one of the few dedications he ever indulged in—and
Courtauld considered this the greatest honour which had ever been
bestowed upon him.

★   ★   ★

About this time, as the direct result of his English popularity, a
new dimension was added to Schnabel's influence in the world. For
it was in England that he was finally persuaded to make gramophone
recordings of his interpretations. It is one of the most revealing facts
of his career that despite many tempting offers this phase of his
activity did not begin until he approached the end of his fiftieth year.
Fundamentally he rejected the idea that a musical performance should
be reproduced in rigid permanence, since by its very nature it could
only be a transient approximation of the composer's vision. To him
its very essence was its aliveness, its mutability, the continually unfolding and never-ending revelation of beauty—a part of man's
striving toward the ideal. Everything static, immutable and final in
musical activity was to him barren—in his own word, *kinderlos*.

His own performances he regarded simply as one man's approach
to the creator's meaning, and therefore neither final nor valid as a
permanent model. When the gramophone people asked him

21. XII. 1931

Liebste Marion,

diese Zeilen, um Dir und
Euch ein frohes Weihnachtsfest
und ein gutes neues Jahr zu
wünschen, das, wie schlecht es
immer rundherum, in der
sichtbaren Wirklichkeit gehn mag,
doch aus der eigenen Güte und
dem sonst noch vorhandenen,
unabhängigen, (sozusagen krisen-
festen) Glücks-Vorrat geschaffen
werden kann.
    Es war sehr schön bei Euch; ich
habe mich vollkommen wohlgefühlt
und bin dauernd dankbar.
    In Liebe Euer alter Artur.

Schnabel's handwriting. Christmas greetings to the
author's wife from Berlin, 1931

whether he didn't think the machine good enough for him, he said quite simply: 'It is I who am not good enough for the machine'—a remark that could easily be misunderstood. What he meant was that no performance, however good, was good enough for eternity. A truly live performance was bound to be different from any other; indeed, no two of his were ever quite alike, for every one was a new experience.

All this had been argued a dozen times—with gramophone representatives and with persuasive friends. The promise of financial reward did not tempt him so long as it involved a compromise with his convictions. Economic necessity, which in the dark days of depression became imperative, may well have played a part in his consent at least to make a test recording. But his final decision came with his own recognition of a new freedom in his playing and a still nearer approach to identity with the composer, especially in the case of Beethoven.

To some extent Schnabel was always a fatalist, and fate at this moment appeared to him in the shape of a little man called Fred Gaisberg, who was the artists' representative of the Gramophone Company (H.M.V.). Mr. Gaisberg caught him at the psychological moment: when he was thrilled anew with the idea of playing the entire thirty-two Beethoven sonatas in London. While rejecting once again the usual suggestion of recording an easily saleable selection of well-known pieces he now made an all-or-nothing proposal to record the whole set of Beethoven sonatas, plus the five piano concertos, and this was eventually accepted. In tackling this unprecedented project the Company resorted to the plan of selling the records by subscription, through a newly organized Beethoven Sonata Society, which in the event turned out to be a great success. But the decision was not an easy one. 'I shall never forget the look on the faces of the directors when I told them,' reported Mr. Gaisberg in his memoirs, naïvely thinking that he had snared the great Schnabel with a 'fat guarantee' and convinced him that 'one could combine his ideals with the machine'.[1]

On the day following the Queen's Hall recital in memory of Mrs. Courtauld, Schnabel made his first gramophone tests. Reporting home he said that the first records were 'ugly in sound' but were musically satisfactory—a seemingly curious distinction for a man who was praised throughout his career for his beautiful tone. But he always subordinated the purely sensuous element to the musical and

[1] F. W. Gaisberg, *Music on the Record* (1942).

emotional content of what he played. Beauty of sound was automatic with him—a part of his nature. What happened is that he had reconciled himself to the inevitable and was determined to solve the problems which existed; and it must be admitted that among other things he and his engineers eventually achieved a remarkable degree of tone fidelity. Early in February he signed his contract, and so began what he once called the most painful experience of his life.

Staying at a friend's house in St. John's Wood he took his daily walks to the His Master's Voice studios—his 'torture chamber'—in the Abbey Road. 'I felt as though I were being harried to death,' he wrote. 'Everything was artificial—the light, the air and the sound, and it took a very long time before I could make the gramophone people adjust some of their equipment to music, even longer to adjust *myself* to the improved equipment.' According to all accounts he became a terror to the engineers and quickly acquired the nickname of 'the charger'. But after a while he himself reported that he 'became more indulgent and didn't ask so much', and later wrote:

'This is not an agreeable activity. But since I have discovered that I may yet learn a great deal from it, and since the result is in reality none of my business (!) I feel somewhat relieved. This discovery is not, as I believe, a manœuvre of self-deception. Learn I certainly can, though it will be a strain.'

It must be understood that he was—as always—not merely learning but forcing others to learn. He rejected out of hand the contention that recordings must be made within a certain limited range of dynamics, and he decided that this was one of the main reasons for the smooth but un-plastic, impersonal recordings of performances by artists who certainly could play better than they sounded on records, and for the pale and partial reflections of great masterpieces that already crowded the market. 'If there is a discrepancy between man and machine,' he said, 'then the machine must be adjusted to the man not the man to the machine.' It is this that caused his engineers to lose sleep, but in the end they met on common ground, and the entente between them—in the course of ten years—became an artistic collaboration of the most sensitive kind. 'He was a great man,' goes the saying in His Master's Voice. 'We've seen none like him.'

But in this first year of recording he suffered unspeakably, and his letters are masterpieces of self-castigation. Speaking of this 'accursed *Verplattung*',[1] he says:

---

[1] A typically Schnabelian *double entendre*, i.e. disc-making, which can also be interpreted as 'flattening out'.

'For twenty years I have refused to be part of this destruction by preserva-
tion. Now I *know* I can't play well enough to want to remain forever on
the same level. The coupling of the unceasingly changeable man with the
permanently insensitive machine is wrong. It is mankind using its intelligence
for self-destruction. . . .'

'My body is too weak for this process. I was close to a breakdown and
almost wept when on the street, alone. . . . My conscience torments me:
this is the surrender to evil, treason against life, the marriage with death.'

But in plain words he explained the practical limitations of the
recording process thus: 'It is almost impossible to play with the
mechanical exactitude which is required for a definitive, never-to-be-
changed performance without sacrificing some measure of concentration and freedom' (i.e., spontaneity). He admitted that the problem
was attractive, but nevertheless it 'remains a lie. Man cannot be
deprived of his soul; and the machine cannot be given a soul. The
boundaries between them cannot be effaced.' [1]

Yet soon after all this he reported quite cheerfully that more than
forty records had been made and that the Company was 'enchanted'.
'One of its minions,' he slyly gloated, 'will arrive at our home in a
fortnight and unwind the whole dance of death.' By the middle of
March 1932 eight sonatas and two concertos were ready, and soon
they were selling remarkably well. They were, as is generally known,
unprecedented in the degree of fidelity and expressive quality achieved
with the means then available. The physical and emotional effort
expended in this period must have been enormous, especially when
we consider that between recording sessions he filled important
engagements from Berlin to London and Manchester.

Before many records were released Schnabel had the urge to
escape from this painful make-believe into reality—by playing the
entire thirty-two sonatas in London, as he had done five years earlier
in Berlin. When he did so the following October and November
the Queen's Hall was entirely sold out for the seven recitals, the
public's enthusiasm rising with each concert. The Press was absolutely
unanimous in its judgment of this phenomenal performance. Perhaps
the critic of *The Times* (Dyneley Hussey) came closest to a rational
summing-up in saying that Schnabel 'combines in a remarkable degree
the knowledge of the scholar with the passion of the artist'. 'This

---

[1] It is to be noted that all Schnabel records were made before the invention
of tape recording. A great deal more spontaneity is possible when the player
knows that corrections can, after all, be made without repeating the entire
performance of a work.

urgency, this absorption in the onrush of the music,' he continued, 'is just what makes his playing the decisive, great and commanding artistic achievement it is.' Even Ernest Newman had no reservations. 'I could wish for nothing finer,' he wrote in the *Sunday Times*, and 'I do not see what more there is to ask for.' The *Daily Telegraph* called the concerts a miracle and the *Referee* characterized Schnabel as 'a virtuoso on whom has fallen the mantle of a prophet'.

25. Farewell to Germany

IN the Germany of 1932 events were marching on with the iron tread of fate. Industry stagnated and millions suffered semi-starvation; the government went through the travesty of further elections, and all the while the lurid spectre of Adolf Hitler rose more threateningly on the murky horizon of politics. But all was quiet in Berlin when Artur Schnabel returned on April 1st to teach waiting students, rehearse a concert with the Staatskapelle under Klemperer, and celebrate his own fiftieth birthday—once his datum-line for retirement from the concert platform. There were two anniversaries in Berlin that year—that of the Philharmonic Orchestra and that of Artur Schnabel himself. He had already played with the Philharmonic under Furtwängler in January; now the Staatskapelle wished also to honour him as its soloist. A most festive and climactic programme was chosen: Beethoven's E-flat concerto and the ninth symphony, which one of the papers called 'a grandiose document of humanism born in the great revolutionary era'. Schnabel—a revolutionary in his own way—was given a great ovation, within a few days of the election in which Hindenburg became president in a neck-and-neck race with Hitler. Masses of letters poured into Schnabel's study congratulating him, and every politically decent newspaper carried a tribute to the artist to whom Germany owed so much. He thanked his correspondents with a characteristic paragraph sent to the Press:

'A fiftieth birthday has one advantage. It gives one the chance to learn whether or not he is expected merely to receive but also to *give*. Happy to know the answer, I thank all those whose friendly and affectionate words have told me that they receive—and expect—what I have to give. I can wish nothing better for the future than the continuation of this happy exchange.'

But his real 'thank you' came in the form of a piano recital in the Philharmonie, consisting of Mozart, Schubert and Beethoven, with the *Diabelli Variations* as the climax. Never in his life did the critics seem so impotent in trying to express the ultimate in praise; never was a public so stormy in its ovations. The papers headlined it as 'Artur Schnabel's Great Day'. Hardly less festive was a special Philharmonic concert, this time for the Red Cross (now in a period

226

of great need), at which Schnabel played Mozart's C minor concerto
under Fritz Stiedry's direction, followed by Schubert's C major
symphony. Again a great and touching tribute by public and Press:
'We are proud that he belongs to us,' wrote Berlin's most popular
paper, the *B. Z. am Mittag*; 'grateful that he has returned.'

Returned to what? That very month of May the senile general
who now figured as President of the Republic dismissed the con-
stitutionally chosen Chancellor Brüning and replaced him with his
favourite, the notorious Colonel von Papen. The fate of German
democracy was sealed, and soon there would be no place for such men
as Schnabel, Klemperer, Stiedry and Bruno Walter in the country
which had given birth to Bach, Beethoven and Brahms.

The Schnabel family, in a subdued mood, spent their usual
mountain holiday in Switzerland this time—at Pontresina, close to
Italy—where friends visited them from England and Germany and
joined them in the modest walking tours that now took the place of
the strenuous ascents of former years. On a visit to Lake Como they
came to know the beauties of Menaggio and other lakeside villages,
one of which was later to become their second home. In late
September Artur was back in Berlin, once more teaching his class of
young pianists, but before the end of October he was in London
giving his Beethoven cycle (as already related) and making a second
batch of recordings. This time, for greater convenience, he occupied
bachelor quarters in Portland Place and later was joined by Therese,
who had been invited to record a number of Schubert songs with
her husband. She had not given public concerts in recent years, but
in January 1929 she had sung Schubert's *Schwanengesang* cycle in
London to a small invited audience of music-lovers and professionals.
Her artistry, sincerity and emotional power were still the same, and
the technicians at His Master's Voice took the opportunity to capture
her remarkable interpretations for posterity.

★   ★   ★

When the Schnabels once again returned to Berlin, yet another
general election had just taken place, and resulted in a temporary
setback for the Nazis—enough to make optimistic liberals breathe
easier; but it was only the tragi-comic prelude to one of the ghastliest
chapters in modern history. Schnabel, still oblivious to the imminence
of danger, yielded to renewed demands for his services. Early in
December the Berlin Philharmonic Orchestra under Bruno Walter
gave a Brahms concert as a sort of 'curtain-raiser' to the approaching

Brahms centenary, and Schnabel played the solo part of the D minor concerto—'a performance of well-nigh unsurpassable power', to use the words of the *Allgemeine Musik-Zeitung*. And not for a moment did it occur to him to alter his season's plans, comprising a repetition in Berlin of his famous Beethoven sonata cycle—seven concerts, widely spaced from early January to late April. This was to be followed by a Brahms Festival in which he, Bronislaw Hubermann and Gregor Piatigorsky were to play most of the master's chamber music with piano.

The Beethoven recitals this time were given for the general public in the large hall of the Philharmonie and, for the first time, Schnabel permitted them to be broadcast. The response of the Press, with the notable exception of the racially-biased papers, was even more ecstatic than during the first Beethoven series, five years before. Every applicable superlative was marshalled to describe the unprecedented mastery and the profound penetration achieved by the great pianist. The sold-out houses and the increasing manifestation of real enjoyment by the audience attested to the undiminished devotion of the German people to their pianistic idol.

On the political level a perilous situation was developing as Schnabel's series progressed. General Schleicher was forced to resign as chancellor after three weeks' rule to make way for Adolf Hitler. This event was greeted with the ear-splitting shouts and demonstrations of the 'revolutionary' mob. As the Nazi régime was being consolidated, the idea that 'non-Aryan' music should no longer defile the German air became a fixed policy. Accordingly the last three of Schnabel's Beethoven recitals were not broadcast. After the end of the series two solemn-faced bureaucrats of the German Broadcasting authority (one of them a former pupil of Schnabel) called and thanked him ceremoniously; then with understandable embarrassment announced that the projected appearance of non-German soloists at the Brahms Festival would not be possible. Schnabel cut them short with the following classic retort: 'I may not be pure-blooded, but I am *cold*-blooded. Good-bye!'

And it was definitely good-bye. Schnabel never played another note in Germany during the remainder of his life. Ironically enough, now that he had overcome his aversion to broadcasting, more Germans were able to hear him than ever—from abroad. Already in February, between his Berlin recitals, he had gone to London to play Beethoven's *Emperor* concerto with the B.B.C. Symphony Orchestra under Adrian Boult. He was in England again in April,

playing Beethoven's piano and violin sonatas with his fellow-exile
Hubermann, and in May he went once more to play the Brahms
B-flat concerto in London and to receive an honorary doctorate from
the University of Manchester. There he had of course to deliver
the customary dissertation—usually reduced to polite rhetoric in the
case of performing musicians. But Schnabel took nothing lightly
that had to do with music, and on this occasion he prepared a master-
fully written essay entitled *Reflections on Music*, which was a microcosm
of his whole philosophy of music as an essential part of human life
and happiness. It began with the words 'Let there be tone' and
ended with Schopenhauer's dictum that 'music is the universe once
again'.[1]

During Schnabel's April stay in London he worked many hours
in the 'torture chamber' of Abbey Road, making additional records,
and by the middle of the month he had completed altogether fifty
double-sided discs of Beethoven sonatas. It is amazing that he could
find the concentration, the energy (his arm was again bothering him)
and the peace of mind for all this varied and absorbing work, while
the Nazis' disgusting brutalities continued to threaten the existence
of civilized society at home. Besides his professional work he now
had to ponder the problem of his future base of activity—outside
Germany.

Moreover, as the result of continued efforts by his friends in New
York, negotiations were under way for an American tour in the
autumn of 1933. Steinway & Sons had at long last consented to
furnish and service his concert grands in the United States, without
any conditions regarding Europe. Marks Levine and George Engles
of the N.B.C. Artists Service in New York had convinced themselves
that the fame of Schnabel in Europe and particularly in England,
reinforced by the phenomenal public acclaim in Boston and New
York during his short visit in 1930, was as nearly a guarantee of success
as even a hard-boiled American manager could desire.

*   *   *

Until now there had been no decision that the Schnabel family
would abandon their Berlin home. Germany, Berlin and the
Wielandstrasse had been immutable facts in their lives for a generation:
the place where they lived, worked, taught, raised their children and

[1] The essay, written in German but delivered in English (translated by César
Saerchinger), was published by the University of Manchester Press and later
by Simon & Schuster in New York.

had their cultural roots. Although their passports were Austrian, Germany, for better or worse, had been their country.

Both their sons were now at the age of discretion, which they exercised in various and somewhat unwonted directions. Karl Ulrich (still 'Karuli' to his friends) was twenty-three and already profession-ally active, earning the cash needed to subsidize his rather eccentric pastimes by playing, accompanying and teaching. He was a tall and typically Germanic figure with soft features and a wayward blond lock dropping over his forehead. His sophisticated, dogmatic, ex-travagantly imaginative mind was obviously derived from the solidly German maternal side of his ancestry; Stefan, two years his junior, who resembled his father both in looks and temperament, was light-hearted, easy-going, roguish and witty—a born comedian with a quick eye for the girls. He had passed his school-leaving exams and was now studying to be an actor at Ilka Grüning's Dramatic Academy in Berlin.

The sprawling Wielandstrasse flat was still in its florescence as a meeting-place for the younger generation, swarming with youngsters of both sexes learning to sing or play, and with friends of the two vital and gregarious young men who strained its facilities beyond all justifiable limits—with new-fangled enterprises and scientific games. Barely out of his teens, Karuli had filmed an extravaganza of surrealist adventures and hair-raising exploits in the interior and exterior spaces of the house and roof, pressing family, friends and unsuspecting retainers into service as 'extras' at the apparent risk of life and limb. In less active periods of the year the twelve rooms and corridors were turned into road-beds and shunting-yards for the trickiest of electric railways with the most problematical time-tables devised by Karuli and his only slightly less juvenile friend Paul Hindemith (in his spare time a viola player and an already well-known composer). Stefan fancied unorthodox adolescent amusements and nocturnal sorties on motor-bikes, until his theatrical instincts found a more legitimate outlet in the dramatic school. At twenty-one he was a promising actor and a successful but suddenly 'ineligible' candidate for junior rôles at the Hamburg Municipal Theatre. This certainly was an in-dication that the situation in Germany was becoming untenable, even for a Schnabel.

In the end it was the perspicacious and sceptical Karuli who urged his parents to leave the country—if only for a time. Schnabel was still in England when the news of the Reichstag fire shocked the civilized world. He got back to Berlin and his family in time to watch the barefaced farce of yet another election which the Nazis were bound to win by dint of intimidation and violence. On March 23rd the Hitler dictatorship was formally established, a week later came the national boycott of Jewish business firms, and soon after that the retirement of Jewish civil servants, teachers, doctors and lawyers by decree. Writing to Lady Mayer, Schnabel reported rather cryptically on what was euphemistically called the 'national revolution', the implications of which he had evidently not yet grasped. Early in April he was again in London, watching the burgeoning trees, shrubs and flowers of Regents Park from the windows of a furnished flat in Park Crescent. He had wanted to bring Therese with him this time, but Stefan fell ill with jaundice and needed a mother's care. Besides, it was she who had to superintend the pulling up of stakes in Berlin.

The die was cast. It had been decided that the family should go to Italy in May, to occupy a little villa in Tremezzo on the shore of Lake Como, where Artur had been prospecting the summer before. This simply furnished little house—named Villa Ginetta—on the hillside above the Grand Hotel, with a wide view of the lake and the mountains, and the use of the hotel tennis courts, was just what Artur needed. It was to be his summer home and his classroom for years to come. But at this time it was regarded as a temporary refuge, for no one was fully convinced that matters would not come right again in Berlin. (The flat had not been dismantled and the staff was still intact.)

The exodus was to be made by motor-car, and Artur collected copious advice on what kind to purchase, only to be reversed by the younger generation in Berlin, which now took charge. In a German-built Fiat, filled with primary necessities from music to tennis rackets and cine-cameras, the two almost totally inexperienced chauffeurs took themselves and Mama Therese on the three-day journey through the Tyrolean Alps, up the Inn Valley, through the Engadin, down the steep spirals of the Maloia Pass to the narrow shore road along Lake Como—into a new country and a new life. Soon they were joined by Stefan's schoolmate Peter Diamand, who had been engaged as secretary and general factotum of the new establishment and who now proceeded to notify the loyal pupils waiting to join the class.

'We have been driven into Paradise!' Schnabel exclaimed when he finally reached this delectable spot, after another month's seasonal activity abroad.

At no time in this hectic period did Schnabel betray the slightest excitement or anxiety. He played his concerts, made his records, gave his lecture in Manchester and attended the elaborate academic party given in his honour by the University. He proudly sported his Mus. Doc. and revelled both in the honour and the festivities. On May 10th he spent five hours rehearsing Brahms programmes with his colleagues, and a few days later he turned up in Vienna for the opening concert of the Brahms Centennial Festival.

The atmosphere in Vienna was hardly more cheering than that of Berlin, but somehow different. Conditions were miserable and there were beggars in the streets. The Nazi virus had penetrated to the lower shifts and people were getting their signals mixed in peculiar ways. A little old woman coming into the restaurant where Schnabel was lunching with friends offered tiny bunches of lilies of the valley for sale, and thanked the purchasers by shouting 'Heil Dollfuss!'

Schnabel obviously enjoyed his reunion with the gentle Pablo Casals, whom he had not met since his first New York visit twelve years before. In a cosy Viennese hotel room they rehearsed, with Hubermann and Hindemith, the sonatas, trios and quartets of Brahms which were to comprise three concerts of Brahms' chamber music, in leisurely fashion—with Schnabel smoking his inevitable cigar. The concerts went well, and were duly appreciated by capacity audiences, but a curious feeling of nostalgia lay over the proceedings, induced perhaps by thoughts of an earlier and better springtime, almost forty years back, when the little Artur trotted along with his elders to the Vienna Woods, and answered with a strong affirmative to old Brahms' unfailing questions: 'Are you hungry?' and 'Have you had enough?' But a more immediate cause of the subdued atmosphere was the memory of what had been going on in Germany, and the bitter reflection that in the city where thirty years ago he *first* played the B-flat concerto with Arthur Nikisch he might never play again.

Now, in Vienna he played both piano concertos, and Hubermann and Casals played the violin concerto and the double concerto, all under the baton of Wilhelm Furtwängler, who had come expressly for the purpose from Berlin. He was not as yet a state councillor in the Nazi régime, but he was known to be in good repute in the 'highest' quarters—one of the few really great hundred-per-cent Germanic conductors and no doubt the greatest artist among them. To Furtwängler this was a crucial occasion. He was a patriotic

German, presumably not a Nazi and possibly as liberal and idealistic as anyone there. But he was determined to stay in Germany and work from within for the one thing that mattered to him—to keep the well-springs of music pure. He had already shown some courage in holding the small group of Jewish musicians in the Berlin Philharmonic against racial attacks. On this day, as the most representative German musician in Vienna, he determined to make a great gesture. At the supper following the final concert he invited Schnabel and Hubermann to be the first soloists of the Berlin Philharmonic's next season—and the first under the Hitler dictatorship! He had obtained official sanction for what he was suggesting, and he urged them to accept in advance, in order to set a precedent which would open the door to all other artists of non-German (i.e. Jewish) blood. Evidently under severe emotional tension he turned to his old friend Schnabel for a reply.

The answer had to be 'No', of course, though Furtwängler had been more naïve than tactless in making the request. He had really meant it to be a personal tribute as well as a sincerely patriotic gesture in the cause of art. His face blanched when he heard Schnabel's answer, quickly echoed by Hubermann. The two men parted, not to meet again until many years later, when both were old and grey. In the intervening years the world had gone up in flames.

★   ★   ★

The summer at Tremezzo was a great success from the pedagogical point of view. Many pupils came from various countries, to be taught, to listen and be listened to, and to hear drops of wisdom fall from the master's lips. It was a resuscitation of the Schnabel classes of an earlier period—at Rindbach in the Salzkammergut. Schnabel was older and far richer in experience and accomplishment, mellower and more serene as a teacher, counsellor and friend. The little room on the ground floor of the villa hardly held more than the two grand pianos, hence the assembly overflowed on to the terrace with the doors wide open to the dry and sun-drenched morning air, with hardly a rainy day in a month. The pupils, all quartered in little hotels in Tremezzo and the neighbouring villages, gathered around with their pieces prepared, or to listen to their colleagues, sitting or squatting, admiring and absorbing—in a rare spirit of camaraderie. The pianos had to be brought from Milan and a whole caravan of them trundled along the Milan–Como road. Schnabel, of course, had two excellent Bechstein grands as before. Lessons as usual lasted from three to five hours or more, beginning at eight in the morning. The end came when the task was done, regardless of the clock.

In off-times Schnabel would play tennis, stroll with his little canine companion Mackie, and occasionally climb the nearby hills. On rare occasions there would be a boating party and picnic on a nearby island. It was an idyllic existence for most, though no doubt there were heartbreaks, disappointments and jealousies as in any conglomeration of young and ambitious people. But there were many moments of great happiness, festive evenings with supper at lakeside inns with moonlight reflected on the water, to the sound of gay laughter and the signs of budding love. Tremezzo will always be connected with Schnabel in the memories of disciples from many lands, and of those natives who watched the goings-on with unobtrusive indulgence. They continued from year to year until the brutal hand of war made an end of this idyll of artistic endeavour in 1939.

In August, when the temperature on Lake Como usually becomes oppressive, the pupils scattered and the Schnabel family spent a few weeks at Selva in the Val Gardena, where they had the company of a few intimates, including Fritz Stiedry, the conductor, of Dr. Fritz Fischer, another German friend, and Artur's pupil Lili Kraus, who had been helpful in finding the Tremezzo house for the family. As there was now no early likelihood of living in Germany again, it was decided that Therese and Stefan should make their home in London for the winter, while Karuli returned to Berlin to liquidate the huge flat and provide for the eventual disposition of the furniture, the shipping of music, books, pictures and personal effects. Artur was booked to sail from England for his autumn tour in America, which was to open with a New York Philharmonic concert under Bruno Walter. Just nine months before, these two had appeared jointly with the Berlin Philharmonic, neither of them suspecting that they would give their next concert together as exiles in America. It was 'farewell to Germany' for both.

Feuermann, Schnabel and Szigeti
at the May Festival in Ann Arbor,
Michigan, in 1940

Therese and Artur at Gascon
Ranch, New Mexico, in the
summer of 1943

Schnabel rehearsing with members of the American String Quartet in
Los Angeles in 1945

PART FIVE

'CITIZEN OF THE UNIVERSE'

26. Towards a New Life

ON a warm and pleasant September day of 1933, Schnabel and his younger son Stefan were merrily motoring northward from the Lake of Como across the Swiss Alps and into the wide, wide world. The two travellers, having crossed the St. Gotthard Pass, were refreshing themselves at a lakeside inn at Brunnen, after taking a look at ancient Schwyz, with its three stark granite peaks, rising like sentinels of fate out of the smiling plain. This strange, mysterious bit of mountain scenery was to remain one of Artur's favourite spots in the world. 'Here,' he once remarked to Therese, 'I should not mind having my burial place.' But today father's and son's minds were far from death, as they sat down to tea and cakes, and to send their 'loving thoughts' to her at the Villa Ginetta back in Tremezzo. They were thinking of their own and the family's future, now that they had been torn from their moorings and set adrift in strange waters.

For Artur it was to be a life of still greater movement than heretofore, of travels across continents, of ever-widening influence and activity. For Stefan it meant building a career as an actor in a strange country and a strange language, an arduous climb from the bottom rung of the ladder; for Therese, separated from her devoted flock of pupils, the task of re-establishing herself in a new and unfamiliar metropolis. The problem of temporary living quarters in London was shortly to be solved. Dr. Malcom Sargent was slowly recovering from an illness and was obliged to live abroad for a year: his very commodious house in Kensington was placed at the Schnabels' disposal, complete with servants, piano and library—a truly wonderful find.

Leaving Stefan in charge of arrangements, Schnabel was free to sail for America in the pleasant company of Otto Klemperer, an early refugee from Nazi Germany. A few days later he was welcomed by a happy band of old friends and young pupils in New York, where his prospects were now far brighter than ever before. His new agents had booked him for twenty-odd concerts within two months—from New York to Texas—and as soloist with a number of orchestras, including the New York Philharmonic Symphony, the Boston Symphony, and those of Chicago, Cincinnati, Minneapolis and St. Louis. By contrast with his former arrivals, he was now received as an acknowledged celebrity, and everything augured well for a genuine success. There were various honorific invitations, including one from the White House, but he declined them all and concentrated on his main task. Only one thing worried him this time: the new and to him still unfamiliar Steinway piano. 'These steeds,' he commented, 'are of the Paderewski breed—not made to canter in my paddock!' He found them 'terribly loud' at first, and the keys too 'fast', but this difficulty was sure to be adjusted—progressively—thanks to clever technicians, tuners and specialists in artistic temperament.

His opening appearance, with Bruno Walter and the New York Philharmonic Symphony in Beethoven's G major concerto, was a perfect collaboration of two sympathetic souls and the two erstwhile Berlin friends celebrated a genuine double triumph. According to Lawrence Gilman, writing in the New York Herald Tribune, Schnabel 'gave us an example of what piano playing can be in the hands of a completely self-effacing master'. These were bold words in a city which all the great living virtuosi now made their platform, but where self-effacing masters were probably rarer than anywhere in the world. This time the Press went all-out in its praise of Schnabel, and spoke of his playing as a kind of revelation. Critics who either had not heard him on his previous visits or had failed to recognize his real significance now exhausted their æsthetic vocabulary in describing his qualities. What must be taken into account in estimating this change is the fact that the New York public of 1933 was musically more mature, and far more sensitive to the genuine but less spectacular kinds of music-making than the metropolis of the Roaring 'Twenties. He himself had reason to be surprised by this unanimous appreciation and he enjoyed it to the full.

This time no critic objected when he made his first recital an all-Beethoven programme of five sonatas. Olin Downes questioned (in the New York Times) whether the taste of a modern audience is best served that way, but added: 'Mr. Schnabel, by the quality of his thought, the poetry and the deep conviction of his performances, proved his right to make his programme as he pleases, and the more exceptional right to present himself as a sovereign interpreter of Beethoven.' Even Mr. Downes's doubts might have been dispelled when only a fortnight later Schnabel returned with another all-Beethoven programme (including both opus 110 and 111) and found Carnegie Hall completely sold out. The response was even greater than before. 'It was an exemplary audience,' reported Schnabel, 'even better than the first, and as usual the greatest participation came from the upper balconies, filled with the "lower" classes.'

Touring the United States was very different from ten years before. There were receptive and understanding audiences everywhere, and a new and different breed of critics seemed to have sprung up. He made a deep impression in western cities previously regarded as difficult. In fact, his only enemy this time was the climate. The wind in New York was 'arctic', and the heat in Texas 'African'. Even the famous Indian summer was not good for his throat, nor were the overheated hotels in winter. For one solid month he suffered from bronchitis. The demand to hear him was such that sometimes he had to play two concertos at orchestral concerts—Beethoven and Schumann in Chicago, and Beethoven and Mozart in Boston, where once again he had one of his most wonderful experiences under the aegis of Koussevitzky. The climax of the tour, to him, was the Mozart A major concerto (K. 488), which he was just then 'beginning to understand, to experience, and to realize'. 'What a joy!' he exclaimed in his next letter home.

All the letters from America this time breathe satisfaction and even happiness, despite his avowed longing for 'home'. He was at last fully reconciled to New York. The city which he had once called a railway station surrounded by a million windows now reminded him of ancient Venice and Athens in its power and arrogance, its audacious absurdity and creativeness—a place for greatness yet to come. Domestic difficulties and concern over the future of his family in a strange country preoccupied him, naturally, but the fact of his success in America was now beyond doubt, and made him see things in a brighter light.

For the first time his American managers now really began to 'promote' him—with circulars quoting the critics' praise, with pictures and the usual publicity chit-chat, although his co-operation in these endeavours was virtually nil.

When Schnabel sailed back to England on the *Ile de France* he was going straight to a family Christmas—the Schnabels' first outside Germany—an English Christmas complete with turkey and plum pudding, holly and mistletoe. The most significant Christmas present was the complete set of his own gramophone recordings to date, plus those he had made with Therese, sent surreptitiously by H.M.V. The holidays were followed, after a brief visit to Vienna, by a number of concerts in London and Manchester, at one of which

(Courtauld–Sargent) he played no less than three concertos by Mozart
—the composer who was rapidly becoming his supreme favourite.
But he also played the Brahms D minor with Boult and the B-flat
major with Beecham, whose talents he greatly admired but whose
vagaries he not always applauded.

★   ★   ★

From this point forward it may be said that most of Schnabel's
activities took place between two poles—London and New York—
with seasonal deviations to Tremezzo and meteoric flights to out-
lying points such as Vienna, Zürich or Florence, Warsaw or even
Moscow and Leningrad.   The spring of 1934 was remarkable for one
more long-delayed conquest and a far-flung adventure, both of
which had their comic aspects.   The conquest was Paris, the only
western capital which had virtually ignored him throughout his
career, and the adventure was Palestine.

Although he had played what he then called his best performance
of the *Emperor* concerto in the French capital five years ago, virtually
no one seemed even to know his name—until his Beethoven records
were being made in England and exported to France.   So it happened
that a manager actually engaged him to give a Beethoven recital in
the Salle Gaveau.   The programme was an all-sonata one culminating
in opus 111.   To everyone's surprise the hall was filled by an eager
and enthusiastic audience of record fans and students, many of them
holding copies of Schnabel's Beethoven edition on their laps; for this,
too, had at long last made its way into the Paris music shops.

Next day some newspapers wrote about Schnabel as if he were a
strange apparition, a phenomenon come to light in a world hitherto
too busy to notice it.   The critic of the *Action française* invoked the
spirits of Flaubert and Léon Daudet in his effort to convey an adequate
impression of this weird character who 'wears his white cravat like a
country doctor' and whose looks suggest 'a slightly mad and rather
comical pensioner'.

A still more fanciful writer described him as a kind of fanatical
amateur who had somehow 'mysteriously hit upon the real truth'.
'He plays as though he were a disciple of Beethoven himself. . . .   He
shows us how Beethoven, the most maltreated of all the masters, has
been abused, and used as a springboard for virtuosi who wish to
impose their personalities. . . .   Monsieur Schnabel's sensitive piety
restores to these sonatas a melodic and rhythmic continuity the like of
which we do not hear anywhere else.'   In short: ' . . . if there were

more Schnabels the pianists (*sic*) would be in danger of becoming
superfluous!' This perspicacious criticism, for all its charmingly
mistaken premises, had the virtue of its faults. Schnabel became overnight not just another great pianist but a 'discovery' which quickly
led to a stampede. From this time on the artist who had been in and
out of Paris for years without having enticed anyone to listen to him,
played only to crowded halls in the City of Light. In fact he was
back the following May, playing Schubert, Mozart and Beethoven
to a devoted audience of connoisseurs.

Between these two delightful encounters with the sophisticated
Parisian public Schnabel undertook—by way of contrast—a so-called
concert tour of Palestine, which in retrospect appears even more
Quixotic than his memorable mission to preach the gospel of
Beethoven in provincial Spain. Since he considered it a sort of
pleasure trip, he took Therese along to see the sights with him.

The state of Israel had not as yet been constituted, and at any rate
Schnabel was not a Zionist, being opposed to nationalism of any
kind. But he was always thirsty for knowledge and full of curiosity
about the country. As was his wont, he immediately began to play
all-Beethoven—four sonatas in one programme, but to almost empty
halls. Advised to change his programme, he compromised by playing
Beethoven, Mozart and Schubert sonatas, but still there was only a
meagre response. On one occasion the hall attendant, embarrassed
by the smallness of the audience, explained that after all the piano
'is not a Jewish instrument'. The real *yiddish* instrument, he said, is
the fiddle. But a more recent—and rather sophisticated—immigrant
came to thank him for bringing Beethoven to Palestine. 'Two
thousand years we have waited for him!' he murmured ecstatically,
but with a faint twinkle in his eye.

*   *   *

Back in Europe after this exotic spree, Schnabel was quickly
caught up in a whirl of activity which made the spring of 1934 one
of the most hectic of recent years—with two gruelling recording
sessions in Abbey Road, recitals in London, Paris and the south of
England, and a noteworthy orchestral concert in Vienna, conducted
by George Széll, at which he played three Mozart concertos, including
the C major (K. 503), which according to available records had not
been played there since Mozart's lifetime. This was closely followed
by his summer class at Tremezzo. In the restful atmosphere of the
Villa Ginetta there was no hint of fatigue, nor worry about the

rapidly worsening international situation in Schnabel's behaviour.
He seemed as well and as youthfully vigorous as his young pupils;
he conducted classes all morning, played tennis, swam, and delivered
his peripatetic homilies to the end of July; then after a brief family
respite in the Dolomites and at Forte dei Marmi, was back for another
round of teaching and the preparation of his still expanding repertoire
for one of the busiest inter-continental seasons of his career.

Politically passive as ever, Schnabel appeared to be completely
unconcerned by the threatening rumbles in the European arena—the
threat of civil war in France, Italian aggression in Ethiopia, the break-
up of the Disarmament Conference at Geneva, and the menacing
antics of the dictators in Germany and Italy. Less than a month
after his last concert in Vienna the Nazis murdered Chancellor Dollfuss
in an abortive *coup* which foreshadowed the end of his native country
and the coming of war. Writing to an American friend, Schnabel
commented rather airily on these 'lunatic political events'.

★   ★   ★

By October 1st he was back in England for some ten weeks of
recitals, the centre-piece of which was an entirely new series of seven
Queen's Hall recitals, as impressive in content as his Beethoven series
of two years before. They comprised nine Mozart and nine Schubert
sonatas, and eight complete cycles of Schumann pieces ranging from
the *Scenes of Childhood* to the *Davidsbündler Dances* and the G minor
sonata. None of these programmes was repeated in the dozen or so
provincial concerts he gave during this period; and in addition to
the piano cycle he and Therese performed Schubert's *Winterreise* in
London by special request. Commenting on his Schumann, the
critic of the *Observer* remarked aptly that his playing of it was 'more
picturesque' than anyone else's, which meant that as always Schnabel
found the particular style that is inherent in the music itself.

By Christmas of 1934 he was again on his way to America, where
he was to travel over much of the ground he had covered the year
before, with notable additions—some twenty concerts in all. This
time he played three times with the Philadelphia Orchestra and came
to know its phenomenal qualities. The conductor was his friend
Otto Klemperer, as guest. 'I had always thought that our European
orchestras were good, at least good enough,' he wrote home. 'However, those of New York, Philadelphia and Boston are much better,
indeed on an almost unbelievable level.' Yet in New York, where
he played the *Emperor* concerto the usual three times, he and Bruno

Walter struggled, through five repetitions of the work during rehearsal, against 'a certain insensitivity' of the musicians in order to achieve the desired result.

There were again two sold-out Carnegie Hall recitals, consisting of Mozart, Schubert and Beethoven, the second culminating in the *Diabelli Variations*; also one in a smaller hall 'filled with wealthy old ladies' to whom he played Schumann's *Scenes of Childhood*; and two joint recitals with Bronislaw Hubermann, at which Arturo Toscanini was present and took the trouble of telling Schnabel how moved he was by his playing. Another very welcome listener was the great scientist Albert Einstein, who had always loved Artur's playing but disputed his faith in the absolute power of music—never losing his sense of relativity. At his Boston recital Schnabel again received the same ecstatic reception as before, and a little later Koussevitzky made him come back to play the Schumann concerto with the Boston Symphony.

Everywhere he appeared—in the east and middle west—and especially in university towns like Ithaca, Oberlin and Ann Arbor, he created a kind of stir that was compounded of joyful experience, gratitude and respect, something not to be adequately described by the word success. To him the *least* enjoyable experience of this American visit was his playing of a Mozart concerto in a broadcasting studio for a commercially sponsored programme. 'My Mozart-by-air had to be launched from an indescribably coarse and unclean environment,' he reported. 'It took the greatest exertion on my part to keep it tolerably pure.' But on the whole he was happier with his performances than on previous American visits, partly because he now had the benefit of a new Steinway, with a differently adjusted action, more sensitive to his kind of touch and articulation.

Psychologically the most interesting fact about this particular tour is not that he was conquering America, but that America was conquering him. All the crudities and superficialities that once offended him, the harsh self-seeking of the careerists and the ruthless commercialism which invaded certain areas of professional life now seemed to blend with the natural vigour and expansiveness of a 'young' country. At first he had come into contact with the ubiquitous mediocrities; now he came to know the best and the worst, at any rate the exceptional. There was beauty, there was seriousness, passion, kindness and generosity—even reverence—in America, however much they might be overshadowed by the rank growth of indifference, vulgarity and greed. On previous visits he had been dependent on a small circle of acquaintances—former Europeans mostly—and had had only rare glimpses of a genuine American culture. This time he had leisure to see and hear, to go to the theatre, the opera and the museums, and get the feel of university life.

There were many of his old colleagues in America now, although the great exodus from Nazi Germany had not yet begun. Besides Walter and Klemperer, Hubermann and Feuermann, there was the cellist Joseph Schuster, who was married to his niece and pupil Poldi Lowbeer. There were other former pupils such as Rudolf Firkusny, Leonard Shure, Dalies Frantz, Martha Baird, Eunice Norton, Beveridge Webster and many more to make him feel at home in New York, and for the first time he wrote to Therese that 'year after next' he would like to play *only in America*. In saying this he was, of course, also thinking of his family and their future. Karl Ulrich was now enjoying a certain amount of success—in a Europe that was becoming less attractive and certainly less stable. As for Stefan, he was appearing in English drama, still as a student, and looking for a wider field abroad. Artur was determined to bring them both to America to become citizens of the New World. Therese, too, would find greater scope for her teaching in New York.

★   ★   ★

Schnabel's return to London in April 1935 was a distinct let-down after the stimulating American experience. The weather was cold and raw and he felt lonely, Therese having returned to Tremezzo to prepare the villa for his coming. By this time even Artur was distressed by the atmosphere of uncertainty and pessimism induced by political events, but he managed to concentrate on his immediate duties. These included a Beethoven recital in the London Museum, crowded to the doors with ardent enthusiasts, and the performance of Mozart's C minor concerto in the Queen's Hall. Two days later, he was in Paris to follow up his quaint triumph of the previous year, this time with Schubert, Mozart and Beethoven sonatas, including the hackneyed and much abused opus 57. The Press was now virtually unanimous in declaring him to be *the* great Beethoven interpreter of our time, with due appreciation of his other offerings. Guy de Pourtalès, a biographer of Liszt, writing in *La Presse* this time made a point of his great technical equipment but added:

'No matter how brilliant his technique, it is only the necessary and indispensable tool for the music. Uniting sensibility with power, he has given us an interpretation as perfect as it is personal, as expressive as it is moving.'

But in Paris, as elsewhere, the political skies were darkening. On March 16th, the date of Schnabel's last New York recital, Hitler had denounced the disarmament clauses of the Treaty of Versailles—a prelude to the remilitarization of the Rhineland and the first step toward war. In view of all the signs and portents, it may seem strange to find our artist preparing for another trip to Soviet Russia— his first in seven years. Was it his sense of adventure, or nostalgia for the primitive audiences who had shouted for Liszt's *Campanella* and applauded too soon after a Beethoven sonata? Or was it just curiosity?—for this was the peak year of the Soviets' new goodwill policy toward the West which encouraged so many foreigners to visit the country, including hundreds of badly needed technicians, scientists, and artists in search of gainful employment. In any case, the Russians were eager to have him, and he looked forward as eagerly to the trip. Schnabel left Tremezzo at the beginning of May and played both in Leningrad and Moscow, as in earlier years.

He was greatly surprised and impressed by the changes he observed: by the general atmosphere and the comparative freedom of move- ment and activity. Particularly memorable was the first Soviet- sponsored performance of Bach's Passion according to St. John, sung by the justly famous Russian choirs to the full Gospel text, all under the direction of his fellow-countryman Fritz Stiedry, then the regular conductor of the Leningrad Philharmonic Orchestra.

No sooner had Schnabel concluded his concerts than he was re-engaged for the next year but one. By that time, however, the notorious treason trials and political purges had begun and the formerly so useful foreigners were forced to leave in a general atmosphere of suspicion and hysteria. Nevertheless Schnabel, though he had can- celled his contract, was being importuned to return—pursued by letters, telegrams and long-distance phone calls to his little Italian village and tracked to various places where he was known to be engaged. But he never set foot in Russia again.

On the homeward journey, at the end of May 1935, he stopped for another of his periodic concerts in Vienna, where the home- grown Nazis were slowly but surely getting the upper hand, but where his aged mother still lived quietly and undisturbed; then he hastened home to his now beloved Tremezzo and his eager band of pupils. The annual summer classes were now at their peak, with fresh young blood arriving each year from America. Among the latest newcomers was Helen Fogel, who ten years earlier had made her debut in New York as a nine-year-old prodigy and who was

soon to become a Schnabel in her own right, as the wife of Karl
Ulrich. Almost without respite Artur plunged into another summer
of teaching and re-studying his repertoire, taking only a month's
holiday in the remote Swiss Alpine village of Saas-Fe, at an altitude
of more than 7,000 feet. In this literally rarefied atmosphere of
serenity, in full view of a vast panorama of snowy peaks, he was
prepared once again to return to his elevated 'sport' of composition—
for the first time in years.

★   ★   ★

Actually, Schnabel the composer had not set pen to paper for
nearly a decade, with the single exception of the summer of 1931.
Now, once again, his creative impulse was stimulated by having
played piano and violin sonatas with Bronislaw Hubermann. This
time, as always, the immediate inspiration came from close communion
with nature. The result was one of his most accomplished pieces of
workmanship: a sonata for piano and violin in four movements: the
first in classical sonata form, the second a unique interplay of different
rhythmic patterns, the third an almost mellifluous adagio, followed by
a rapid rondo, the whole thoroughly integrated and to reasonably
modern ears quite effective. The work was first performed in public
by his Viennese boyhood friend Bruno Eisner and the violinist
Alexander Schneider in New York in 1944, and has since become
one of the more frequently performed of Schnabel's works.

This successful return to musical creation gave him so much
satisfaction that he vowed to resume composition the following
summer, despite the constantly increasing pressure of playing and
teaching. That time, without the stimulus of Alpine altitude, he took
enough time off from teaching in Tremezzo to write his *Piano Piece in
Seven Movements*, for the benefit of any pupils who might have the
hardihood to try their prowess on the most advanced type of contemporary music. Following immediately after the sonata for piano
and violin, written the previous summer, this work represents
Schnabel's most mature style, using melodic, contrapuntal, chordal or
tone-cluster elements in rich profusion for the expression of musical
ideas in a highly idiomatic piano style. The whole work develops
thematically out of a short opening movement into ever more
expansive structures and returns in its last movement to the characteristic features of the first. In the thematic integration of the several
movements, the subtle differentiation of moods, and the elegance and

grace of its structure, this work displays Schnabel's mastery of composition technique at its best.

These two recent essays in composition in the sparse style of solo instruments had whetted his appetite for bigger things. Ideas were beginning to mature for a symphonic work of large proportions. From now on musical creation was again to become an absorbing though still periodic occupation, since his most intensive activity as a concert pianist was yet to come.

27. Floodtide of Success

THE years immediately preceding the second World War were certainly the most strenuous in Schnabel's pianistic career and probably also the most prosperous. In the course of these two seasons he achieved a degree of esteem bestowed on few musical artists in any generation, from the Atlantic seaboard to the borders of Soviet Russia, from Scotland and Scandinavia to Italy and Greece. But the most important addition to his sphere of influence in recent years was the United States. He had visited that country five previous times, but it was not till the winter and spring of 1936 that he was fully appreciated over so wide an area. During this comparatively short period he made his most successful American tour, reaching from coast to coast. He also made connexions and participated in plans which had far-reaching consequences in the country's musical life. During this time, also, his Beethoven sonata edition was re-issued in New York, and his English-made recordings were beginning to be distributed through R.C.A.–Victor, as agents of H.M.V.

The high point of his American season was undoubtedly the Beethoven series which almost completely filled Carnegie Hall seven times in January and February 1936. Despite some mechanical disturbances of which only he was conscious, the event was a colossal success. The critics lauded him in a variety of ways: one praised his depth of thought, his eloquence and tenderness, another his perfect logic and sense of proportion, still another his power and intensity. The *New York Times* man gave up the task, saying that 'those who were in the audience understood; for those who were not there, words would be futile'. With few exceptions the Press agreed with the *Herald Tribune* writer who called his 'complete disclosure of Beethoven's spiritual cosmos' the most important event of the season. He was equally happy in California, playing concertos with Otto Klemperer, now installed as conductor of the Los Angeles Philharmonic, and with Pierre Monteux in San Francisco. Here he also gave what he called his best piano recital of the year. On his return east he again played the Brahms B-flat concerto twice with Koussevitzky, but only because 'there wasn't enough rehearsal time for Mozart!'

This time Schnabel's success with the American public was indisputably great wherever he appeared. He had good reason to feel that there was a great future for his kind of music in the vast country which he had always regarded as a cultural extension of Europe to the west. His personal experience this time was much like his experience in England eight years before: after an even slower start than there he found himself suddenly a favourite—a kind of hero—and once again chiefly as the result of his faithful and deeply felt realization of Beethoven's works. Still severely critical of himself, he was by no means always satisfied, for personal success meant little when he felt, as he confessed, that only half of his performances met his own artistic demands.

Needless to say he maintained his well-known standards throughout this—and all—his American tours, regardless of place and audience: the same selection of large works and homogeneous groups; the same concentration and high spiritual tension; no 'playing down' to the audience, and no encores. Only once did he break this last and long-cherished rule—at a recital in Washington, D.C., and for a uniquely characteristic reason. What happened was that during the first of five Beethoven sonatas he felt himself gradually sliding away from the keyboard until he no longer reached the pedals, with deleterious results to the music. When the piece was finished it was discovered that the legs of his chair had brass knobs that slithered on the smooth floor. The error was soon rectified, but the damage, Schnabel felt, had been done. After the fifth sonata the audience was wild with enthusiasm and would not stop applauding. Suddenly he found himself walking toward the piano as in a trance and quite unconsciously sitting down, to play a sixth sonata: not (as he was careful to explain) as a reward for extra-persistent applause but because he owed an indemnity to Beethoven for the 'ruined' piece.

The sheer physical and mental effort demanded by this coast-to-coast tour may be gauged from the fact that he performed no less than 'four dozen different large works', by which he meant whole sonatas, concertos and cyclical works like those of Schumann, or whole groups such as the Schubert *Impromptus* and the twenty-four *Preludes* of Chopin. In one of his letters he admitted that he had 'frighteningly much to do'. Moreover, he had been giving recitals before he came to America—ever since the beginning of September, when he played three Mozart concertos in Vienna, two of them new to him and virtually unknown to the public. At fifty-four Schnabel was a fairly robust man, with no serious physical complaints except his occasional neuritis. But at the beginning of this American tour he had felt ill and was obliged to consult a New York physician. His gall-bladder was giving him trouble, and there was a disturbing diagnosis revealing a somewhat distended heart. He was ordered to give up all strenuous exercise including tennis and swimming and, worst of all, his favourite recreation of mountain-climbing.

Consequently he and the Schnabel family forsook their Swiss mountains that summer and like good American tourists went motoring along the Loire, 'doing' the famous chateaux and sunning themselves on the sands of Biarritz while the guns of the Spanish civil war were booming across the frontier. After this much-needed respite Artur was back in Tremezzo, teaching a large class as usual. But such was the demand for him in Europe that by the beginning of October he was playing in Switzerland, the Low Countries, France, Scandinavia and Great Britain—a solidly booked three months of concerts with a brief respite for Christmas, which he spent with Therese in Tremezzo (the plan of settling in London having been abandoned or postponed). It is clear that even at the peak of his success in America he still played more often in Europe—until the outbreak of war.

★   ★   ★

His next American tour, in this winter of 1937, was rather less than he had a right to expect after the great success of the past season. What America wants, or is supposed to want, is big names and novelties. Schnabel was now a big name in the biggest cities and the great cultured communities. But his managers frankly regarded him as a 'musicians' musician', not expecting him to have the mass appeal of the virtuosos whose repertoire is geared to 'audience demand'. Hence it was not surprising that his engagements for the current season were limited to some twenty cities of the east and mid-west and in the following season to even fewer, although that time they included the Pacific Coast.

He was frankly disappointed, but his discontent was not so much with his own treatment as with the conditions of musical life in which success depends on so-called popularity and the workings of the star system, of which he himself had been in danger of becoming an unwilling instrument. Democrat though he was, he firmly believed in an aristocracy of art. It was his conviction that only a minority in every generation is equipped by nature to appreciate certain values and to feel the spiritual elevation which comes with true musical experience; and that it is the obligation of the artist to satisfy this minority.

'The first stages in the public cultivation of musical art have always been initiated by such minorities, on an idealistic and rather exclusive basis. With growing success the appetite also grew, and this stimulated the wish to supply, reach and attract more consumers and eventually the masses. [He did not, of course, mean this in the current sense of social or economic distinction, for both rich and poor, high or low may be among the elect.] This appeal to the masses and the mixed audience inevitably led to the rule of mixed pro- grammes. In the long run the more superficial, ephemeral and cheaper types of music prevail, because the majority lives in that region. That is why, for the sake of the minority, a remedy becomes imperative from time to time.'

And evidently he felt that this time had come in America.

All this and more he argued with eloquence and persistence, for as always in his life the moralist and the reformer was at work inside the performing artist. And as in England a few years earlier, he now felt that the remedy had to be found; that a new start had to be made.

★   ★   ★

Certain young friends in New York and elsewhere caught fire from the glow of his agitation, and plans were made on the basis of his past experience with building new audiences—first in Berlin and later in London. Among the enthusiasts were Ira A. Hirschmann, a young New York businessman with a genuine love of music, and his future wife Hortense Monath, a former pupil of Schnabel. Together they developed the idea of a new concert society which should appeal to music-lovers interested in the cultivation of music on a broader basis, with programmes drawing on the entire literature of the masters instead of constantly repeating well-worn works of proven popularity. Disregarding current custom this society would give a subscription series of chamber music (in the broadest sense) in the moderate-sized Town Hall, at the presumably unpopular hour of late Sunday afternoon. The artists would be selected on the basis of their qualification for the works to be performed, and not because of the drawing-power of their names. Subscription prices would be as low as possible (at an average of less than a dollar) and the artists' fees commensurate. There would be no exploitation of personalities, no encores and no opening of doors for latecomers.

While the organization was left entirely to Mr. Hirschmann and the programming to Miss Monath, the fine hand of Artur Schnabel could be detected in the choice of composers—mainly Beethoven, Mozart and Schubert, Bach and Handel, Schumann and Brahms— mostly in integrated cycles, and including many neglected and rarely heard works. The name of the society, New Friends of Music, was reminiscent of the earlier Friends of Music founded by Schnabel's late friend Harriet Lanier, which had ceased to function after her death.

Needless to say, Schnabel offered his artistic collaboration, along with many eminent colleagues, both in ensemble and as soloist. When he left New York in the spring, to fill European engagements and teach his class in Tremezzo, the new society was still only a dream. When he returned in February 1937 it already had the first half of a highly successful season to its credit. Among the artists of that first season were virtually all the first-rate string quartets then in America, and among the large number of young pianists were several of Schnabel's best pupils and his own son Karl Ulrich. He himself participated in the final concert of the season, playing the piano part in unforgettable performances of Mozart's G minor quartet, Schumann's E-flat and Schubert's A major (*Trout*) quintets with the members of the Pro Arte String Quartet. Through the years Schnabel played for the New Friends of Music many times—often enough to cause some wags to nickname them the Old Friends of Schnabel. Sometimes he appeared in solo recitals, sometimes in chamber ensembles and some-times as soloist with its excellent but short-lived Chamber Orchestra.

During the second season Artur and Karl Ulrich Schnabel con-tributed two concerts comprising a considerable part of Schubert's music for piano four-hands—old favourites of Artur's which did not receive all the respect from New York's critics that he thought they deserved. This and other criticisms—not of himself but of the music he played—set him off on his habitual warpath. He became rather needlessly excited by such purely personal and ephemeral judgments, because he overestimated the influence of journalistic opinion on the general public. It was his private war against 'journalism' which he liked to consider the antithesis to 'eternalism'—the eternal values which the true artist cherished in his art.

★   ★   ★

As in England so now in America, Schnabel had reached a stage at which he felt he belonged, and was therefore entitled to be critical in his turn. He now knew and liked America much more than he did at first. The naïve simplicity of many Americans in matters of art he felt had something refreshing about it, and he was completely disarmed by the precious lady who came into the artists' room after a concert and inquired what kind of music he composed—was it 'emotion, colour, or perfume?' But the bald commercialism and the high-pressure advertising of the mass-production era he attacked with unmitigated frankness. His own second experience with commercially sponsored radio—a microphone interview which was followed by a song in praise of soap—occasioned a characteristic outburst:

' It is depressing to see how these splendid American people are maltreated and exploited, and how they are deliberately isolated from many of the noble things of which they are capable. But . . . the dawn will come!'

His experience with American audiences had been unexceptionable, although the majority regarded music as entertainment. 'They like the nobler music best,' he found, 'but they are happy with all kinds. It is the professionals and the so-called experts who try to persuade them that the approach to higher levels is possible only after thorough technical and material preparation.' This thesis—that the reputedly low taste of the public is due to bad or venal leadership— was a conviction of Schnabel's that would be difficult to disprove.

As on previous visits to America, Schnabel was surrounded by a growing circle of friends now being augmented by some notable voluntary exiles from Hitler Germany and Austria. Ernst Křenek, the most kindred spirit among contemporary composers, arrived in the hope of lecturing or teaching in the country which years ago had performed his best-known opera. The ever-successful Paul Hindemith came with the well-founded expectation of increasing his already international fame. There was also a considerable influx of Jewish and other liberal émigrés, whose arrival stimulated the mounting wave of anti-German propaganda based on the news of Nazi atrocities. Much as he deplored these tragic events, Schnabel kept aloof from all politics and was cool to the advocacy of racially inspired counter-measures which he felt were not the business of artists.

The worst, however, was yet to come, and even the stubborn aloofness of a Schnabel was going to be difficult to maintain. That very spring and summer, when he returned to Europe on the luxurious new *Normandie*, the two fascist dictators were reaffirming their Axis, and the outlook in Austria was becoming more threatening day by day. Schnabel thus far had not even contemplated a change of nationality, and the idea that his peaceful Tremezzo should ever become untenable never entered his mind. His class continued to assemble there every July and disperse for a holiday break in August.

This August Artur was perhaps more eager than ever for the cool pure air of Saas-Fe, for he was ready to begin a project he had nursed for years—the composition of a full-length symphony. He made excellent progress with it, and by mid-September the first movement was completed though not scored. Then, after brushing up his repertoire he was ready for another bi-continental season of concerts and for another round of recordings. The Beethoven sonatas having been completed and successfully marketed, Schnabel was now working on the Beethoven variations, Bach toccatas and the Brahms concertos, also on Schubert's *Moments Musicaux* and other works. It is only fair to add that by this time he was largely reconciled to the once so painful process of 'diskification', and that the swelling sales of his records contributed very largely not only to his income but to his increasing fame, so that the demand for his concerts was greater than ever, especially in Europe. He was, indeed, at the floodtide of his material success.

28. Citizen of the Universe

THE geographical pattern of Schnabel's new life—America, Europe, Tremezzo and the Alps—might have continued for years and years, so long as it satisfied his need of a useful and creative existence. At fifty-five he was the model of a man-in-his-best-years: vigorous, successful, indefatigable and irresistible. His fame and influence were now, in western terms, almost world-wide, and his interest in the artistic climate in the various countries on his annual round was as lively as though he belonged to all of them. He was at home wherever he went, lustily fighting his battle—against the mercenary 'sorry-go-round' and for artistic integrity—supported by his ubiquitous little bands of adoring friends.

It might have gone on indefinitely, had it not been for the dynamics of world events. But this was the autumn of 1937 and the clouds were slowly gathering for one of the great cataclysms of world history. Europe was in the final stages of an uneasy peace: civil war was raging in Spain; fascism was firmly entrenched in Central Europe, and the sinister Berlin-Rome Axis was about to divide the Continent into implacably hostile groups. Schnabel, a fugitive from one despotism, was living in the shadow of another, with an equanimity that appears fantastic from the viewpoint of today. Anyone gifted with political foresight might have realized that the time for peaceful international activity was running out.

Yet in September 1937 Schnabel was calmly preparing for a West European tour comprising no less than thirty concerts from Glasgow and Edinburgh in the north to Monte Carlo and Naples in the south, to be followed by the now customary tour of America; and he was expecting to repeat this programme in the following season, with the addition of an Australian tour and a return journey via the Far East. Here, at last, was the chance to see the world, and the idea appealed to his inquiring mind.

His energy was certainly at its peak as he began the season with a solid month of gramophone sessions in London, during which he perpetuated a dozen or more of his favourite Schubert pieces and recorded his monumental performance of the *Diabelli Variations* in a single day. The subsequent European tour was highly successful, for he was now at the height of his Continental popularity, and he promised to repeat the whole tour, with additions, in 1938. By contrast with this, the American tour, though coast-to-coast, was a disappointment to him, for his managers had secured fewer engagements than promised. Had the magic of his previous triumph worn off? Or had the smaller town audiences been frightened away by the Beethoven label and the reputed austerity of his programmes? Or was America just fickle? 'Here I am,' he wrote aboard the *Berengaria*, 'once again on the great annual journey. It has gradually lost the meaning which I imagined it had at first. . . . I myself am probably the principal cause, or rather my nature, which does not favour con-solidation but prefers marching on. . . .' All he hoped, as he reviewed in his mind the prospects of the coming weeks, was that he might 'succeed in making music which has meaning for me'. If so, even *this* journey would be justified. What really mattered to him at this point was that he—a man in love with music—was loved in return. 'I do not have to woo it so persistently any more,' he wrote to Therese. 'I have been heard (*erhört*)—what a beautiful word!'

In this spirit he was able to look forward to the mere dozen concerts or so between New York and San Francisco with something less than despair. What he found this time was that while his out-ward success was moderate, the inner participation was remarkable. 'Society' in the east was conspicuous by its absence, and the audiences included many young and rather poor people—predominantly male. The response was better and better as he went westward, and he finished his tour in a blaze of glory playing concertos under Pierre Monteux in San Francisco and Otto Klemperer in Los Angeles. Here his success was, in his own words, 'the greatest imaginable: no crooner or *Wunderkind* or musical trash-merchant could have more', either with public or Press. In San Francisco, he reported, he played for an audience of ten thousand 'on a lovely Easter afternoon—and on my own birthday'.

★   ★   ★

But it was a birthday he would have cause to remember for a far less happy reason than his San Francisco success. Just a month before, in March 1938, Hitler had invaded Austria, and the annexation of his native country was now a fact. Schnabel was playing in a little town in Texas when the news first reached him, but it was not until later that its full meaning came home to him: it meant that he was now a man without a country, a fact with very serious implications—especially for one like him. The lightning had played around him ever since his departure from Germany five years before; now for the first time it had struck home. Philosophical as always he wrote to Therese:

'It is a singular experience for a grown man to learn from the daily paper that he has lost his fatherland. Suddenly—even if one has often imagined such a fate—one has become just a human being, an earthly creature unconnected with any established order or constituted authority. But Life and the Universe as such don't maintain offices for issuing cards of identity and for the protection of the citizen! Such a predicament happily does not cut too deeply with the butcher, the baker and candlestick maker; but those who are endowed exclusively by Nature now have nothing left but their talent and its source. . . . Talent forbids one to be impersonal, or to become a hermit. Nor can it be bartered for something else. And yet one must be grateful for one's appointed task. . . . It is not easy.'

Now while Schnabel had never been what might be called a patriotic Austrian, he had nevertheless been conscious of his nationality and, since the advent of Hitler, rather glad of it. In recent years he had become convinced that his sons should acquire American citizenship, although he had never even considered this possibility for himself. Now obviously something had to be done. He was sure of one thing: he would resist becoming a German by annexation— the unwitting fate of millions of his countrymen. The two alternatives were British or American naturalization. He would have preferred the former, but since his boys were to become Americans their parents might as well follow suit. Of the fall of Austria he took a fatalistic view. To him it was the logical sequence of its long-deplored decadence. But broadly speaking it was much more than the end of a body politic; it was the end of a form of society which belonged to the past—a whole human concept responsible not only for the State but for many of the things of the spirit which humanity loves and needs. He had long felt that humanity is sick; and there was 'no hope for a quick cure at a convenient seaside resort'.

Back in New York, he decided to take the first steps toward naturalization, even though this would delay his departure for Europe till May. According to the United States immigration laws he had to leave the country as a 'visitor' and come back as an 'immigrant'— a bit of bureaucratic ritual made necessary by the well-known quota system. He took the customary journey to Havana, only to find that he was not what his passport said, an Austrian, but—since his birthplace had been annexed by Poland—a Pole! Finally, the whole

matter was transferred to the American consulate in Italy and eventually to London, where the Schnabel family was expected to fore-
gather in the following year. 'Alas,' commented Schnabel, 'we cannot
choose the period of history we would like to be born in. But . . .
a holiday on some other planet *would* be a tempting idea.'

Perhaps the only consolation in these troublous times in America
was the presence of the two Schnabel boys in New York. Karl
Ulrich had developed both as an artist and as a man, and had had a
gratifying success with his second recital in New York. His brother
Stefan was playing his first important part on the American stage, in
Orson Welles' much-talked-of production of Shakespeare's *Julius
Cæsar.*

All through this rather gloomy and partly idle period, Therese,
at home in Italy, had been suffering from an internal complaint and
finally had been advised to go to Montecatini for a cure. However,
her gradual recovery, with an increase in weight, confidence and
elasticity for the first time in two years, set a more cheerful tone for
their reunion in Tremezzo, soon to be enhanced by the arrival of the
sons. Since only a small number of pupils were expected that summer,
Artur had a good deal of time for his family, for visitors, and for
thought.

★   ★   ★

This was the critical spring and summer of 1938, when the peace
of Europe hung by a thread, when crisis followed upon crisis, building
up to the false cadence of the fatal Munich Conference. But it was
not temporal matters that occupied Schnabel's thoughts. For some
time he had been absorbed by the great project of composing his
first symphony. Accordingly he and Therese spent the rest of the
summer in the elevated Alpine solitude of Saas-Fe. Completely
shut off from the alarums and conflicts threatening the world, he
finished the composition in August, leaving the orchestration for a
later day.

This first symphony is a four-movement work of about forty
minutes' duration. Like all of Schnabel's mature works it is very free
in form and intricate in harmonic texture, and in a very general sense
adapts the style of the later string quartets to the symphonic form.
While frankly in the so-called atonal idiom (a misnomer, according
to Schnabel), it does not make use of the conventional twelve-tone
technique, but builds up very freely from definitely melodic themes
and many shorter motivic elements. The first movement is an
allegro, distinguished by a broad cantabile theme, the second an

amusing, scherzo-like vivace, the third a solemn largo and the last a powerfully expressive allegro of great motoric vitality. Needless to say, the work bears no trace of the fact that it matured in Schnabel s mind during one of the most troubled periods of modern history, leading inevitably to the second World War.

★ ★ ★

Indeed, like many people in continental Europe, he seemed oblivious to the danger that threatened; for during the very month of Munich he was planning the details of a concert tour around the world, which would mean a full year's absence from home. During the fateful Conference he was actually playing a recital in the Swiss city of Winterthur, when suddenly the lights went out and the hall remained dark. Schnabel was so deeply engrossed in the music that he played on through the rest of the programme without interruption, and not a person in the audience stirred. It was a silent commentary on the quality of his own concentration and his ability to communicate it to his listeners. But it was also symbolic of what was happening at that moment in history: for once again 'the lights went out all over Europe.'

The likelihood that the march of events in 1939 might interfere with the globe-encircling journey seems not to have been considered, and the possibility that what he called the 'common nonsense' of world politics might deprive the Schnabels of their adopted Italian home hardly entered his mind. The plan was for Therese to accompany him, and to leave the Villa Ginetta to the care of a small and faithful group of retainers and friends.

The Schnabels left Italy in October. The European part of the tour began in the south of France and ended up in England and Scotland, to which for the first time was added Ireland, North and South. After reading about the great Schnabel during the dozen years of his rising British fame, Irish music-lovers were all agog to hear him. And they were not disappointed, to judge from the charming account that Mr. Austin Brown has left us of his visits to Belfast and Dublin. But his sponsors might as well not have heard about him at all, so little did they know of what were considered his 'foibles'. In Belfast he played the *Emperor* concerto at a so-called celebrity concert, and was put down for two Schubert *Impromptus* after the intermission—in spite of his demurrer, for he insisted on playing the entire group. In Dublin he was booked to play twice on the same day—a barbarous custom which could not be changed, he was told, simply because there had always been two concerts on the same day. 'Ah,' said Schnabel, 'I see you are conservative. Now I shall be conservative, too. This piano is not level, and since I never play uphill I shall refuse to do so now.' To end the argument a spirit level was brought and the piano was actually shown to slope. The 'fault' was rectified, of course, and Schnabel played Beethoven, Schubert and Mozart at the evening concert 'as if inspired'.

By the end of his Irish visit Schnabel seemed fully aware, at last, of the seriousness of the world situation. 'The last time I saw you,' he said to his friend Brown, 'I knew we would meet again. Now I know that we shall *not* meet again, because war will come.' Yet nothing was changed in his plans, and early in February 1939 the Schnabels sailed for New York, where they went through the routine prescribed for legal immigration with a view to naturalization after the statutory five years. Artur filled such professional engagements as he had, from New York to San Francisco, saying farewell in both places with all-Beethoven recitals. On the way west across the continent, he made the valuable acquaintance of Robert M. Hutchins, president of the University of Chicago, who had proposed the idea of a series of lectures by Schnabel at the university. In mid-April the Schnabels sailed for Australia, and duly arrived at Sydney early in May.

★   ★   ★

Schnabel's Australian tour comprised all the principal cities of the continent—Sydney, Melbourne, Brisbane, Adelaide, Canberra, also far-off Perth and Hobart, the capital of Tasmania. He appeared nine times with orchestra, in every case conducted by George Széll, a musically congenial friend of long standing in Europe, playing twelve different concertos, of which only one, Beethoven's in E-flat, was repeated. He also played sixteen recitals with five totally different programmes, comprising twenty different cyclical works and complete groups such as the Schubert *Impromptus*. In addition he appeared with the Sydney String Quartet in a programme of piano quartets and quintets by Mozart, Brahms and Dvořák—all this in less than three months. The public's appreciation and the praise bestowed by the critics were commensurate with the quality and quantity of the performances—altogether a unique experience in the musical annals of the country. The reviewer of the Sydney *Sun*, summing up the impression of the ten concerts given in his city, said that Schnabel had 'given us new horizons in the interpretation of the classics', that he had been 'an inspiring, vitalizing presence in our musical culture', and hoped that a second visit would not be long delayed—a wish that was destined not to be fulfilled.

For his part Schnabel found Australia to be a stimulating and cheering experience. Musical life, still in its formative stages, had the freshness and receptivity of youth, and had not been complicated by the hypertrophic commercialism of America. He found that the people, though fed and overfed with the usual mixture of familiar favourites and bravura display, were willing and eager to accept his most exacting classical programmes. He in turn made all appropriate allowances and was genuinely moved by the efforts of amateur musicians and the uninhibited receptivity of the listeners. In Perth, a 'well-bred, clean and beautifully situated city', he played with an orchestra consisting of office employees, workers and artisans of both sexes. In general, he admired the youthfulness and simplicity of Australia, which he regarded as the 'third Europe' (America being the second in the course of cultural expansion) and he liked the friendliness of the people and their unmistakably English traits. He loved its wide open spaces and was fascinated by the rich variety and uniqueness of its flora and fauna. And—naturally—he took a special interest in one species, the platypus (*Schnabeltier* in German) as his namesake in the animal kingdom!

Altogether the tour was a pleasant change from the highly sophisticated European and the highly competitive American concert routine and also a relatively happy respite from the increasing worries engendered by the world crisis and its implications for the future of the Schnabel family. (Incidentally, while in Australia Artur and Therese received the news of Stefan's marriage to an American girl, to which they had cabled their hearty consent.) As the summer wore on the war clouds thickened, and it became obvious that the projected homeward journey via the Suez Canal might be too hazardous. While waiting for a decision Artur began the work of orchestrating his symphony.

By the middle of August the die was cast: instead of sailing westward to Europe the Schnabels boarded the *Monterey* for the United States, expecting to continue their journey via New York and the *Queen Mary* to England, where Artur was still expecting to play. Breaking his journey in California, he visited his friend Otto Klemperer who had undergone a dangerous operation and was hovering between life and death—a sad foreboding of a time which promised little but tragedy to the world. When they arrived in New York they learned that the *Queen Mary* would not sail, and that this was the end of the road. England—and Europe—would not see them again for the duration. 'Our thoughts and feelings are with you,' he wrote to John Tillett, his London agent. 'Who knows when we shall see you again? Evil has great endurance, and in the fight against it much of the noblest might be destroyed.'

When they would return again to their home in Tremezzo no one could guess. It was left to the care of the faithful Lorenzo and his wife, kindly Italian *contadini*, who had been their helpers and neighbours, to Peter Diamand the secretary, and Herta Kröhling, pupil of Therese and a devoted friend. Upon these good people now devolved the care of their property and personal effects, music, manuscripts and books and, in the violent days to come the difficult and dangerous task of saving what could be saved from the hands of the enemy. Schnabel and Therese, being 'provided with an unexpected vacation', settled down in a New York hotel, where Artur became completely immersed in his absorbing task of orchestrating his first symphony.

They had come full circle in their affairs. They had lost their German home, then their Austrian nationality; they were now forced to abandon their second home in Italy—for an indefinite time. And willy-nilly they were now in their future adopted country, the United States.

29. 'Marooned' in the New World

THE war not only meant banishment from one continent to another, but also a radical change in a long-established pattern of life. Schnabel was born an Austrian, had lived and thought as a German and a European in the fullest sense of the word—a man who believed passionately in the civilizing mission and colonizing energy of the old Continent. Living in Europe, he had been happy in the thought that every year he brought a little more of its spirit to America, where European culture lived on, rejuvenated and revitalized, to be radiated to the regions beyond. Now for the first time he was obliged to remain stationary in the New World, and this at a time when his personal honeymoon with America was over —after the first impact of his conquest had been spent.

'We are marooned,' he wrote to Walter Turner from New York. 'Grateful as I am to be here, I am not happy. . . . I feel great apprehension for the U.S.A., which in a sense I seem to love more and appreciate more highly than the majority of the people who "keep smiling".' The basis of his apprehension was the deterioration of society under the pressure of materialism, and its exploitation as an ever-expanding market for mass-produced articles.

'Here we have the strongest and purest expression of our loveless plutocratic-proletarian age. As for music, there is no understanding of the prerequisites of its appreciation. Its mystical origin and its transcendental essence is not admitted. . . . Obviously there is no place for me here.'

Much of this was a reflection of his general *malaise*—the pessimism of a man who feels out of step with his period and sees the traditional values being demolished by an insensitive generation in its mad rush for physical comforts. To some extent his feelings may have been exacerbated by the exigencies of war. Instead of giving recitals in Europe he was obliged to sit in America, where no appearances had been planned for him that year.

But by no means did he remain idle. Almost from the moment of his arrival he had been absorbed by the task of orchestrating his symphony—a 'fascinating, occasionally exacting and sometimes boring job', to quote his own words. But he managed to make the best

possible bargain with fate. Pretty soon he did not mind the lack of
the habitual platform activity. Had he not promised himself to
make an end of it at sixty, in any case? Next April he would be
fifty-eight. Here was an excellent chance to restore the balance with
the other two occupations of the professional musician—writing and
teaching. He was engaged in completing a symphony, and there
were bound to be quite a few talented pupils and young artists who
required his help and counsel. Therese in her turn acquired a few
singing pupils, for teaching was as indispensable to her sense of duty
as to her need for self-expression.

After ten days' search they found a pleasant but decidedly modest
apartment in the Peter Stuyvesant Hotel on Central Park West, the
windows of which overlooked the Park, with the glistening surface
of the old reservoir in the foreground. In the farther distance were
the opulent residences and luxurious apartment buildings of upper
Fifth Avenue which reflected the rays of the setting sun from a
thousand windows, and looking southward one could distinguish the
stark silhouette of midtown skyscrapers, lighted up by man-made
magic in the early winter evenings. The Schnabels chose this, their
semi-permanent abode, partly for its unpretentious friendliness and
convenience, but also for its proximity to the footpaths of the Park
along which Artur could take his daily strolls, undisturbed by urban
traffic and noise. There were two living-rooms, each with its piano—
small when compared to the vastness of their one-time Berlin studio
but nevertheless adequate. Both Artur and Therese intended to make
music and teach independently, and in due time the rooms reflected
the character of their occupants, thanks to rearrangements of furniture,
the gradual accumulation of books and paintings, presented—and in
some cases painted—by artist friends. A novelty to the Schnabels
was the tiny kitchenette, also the virtual lack of any but the most
rudimentary hotel service. 'Therese is cooking meals for the first
time in her life,' wrote Artur to a friend, 'and I like what she
cooks!'

There even developed a semblance of family life in the new home,
what with the presence of the Schnabel sons in New York. Both
were now married—to the complete satisfaction of the parents. Karl
Ulrich's wife was the very gifted young pianist Helen Fogel who
had spent several summers in the Schnabel class at Tremezzo, and
Stefan had preceded his brother into the blessed state, as already
recorded. Artur's grandson Christopher had come to New York to
study at Columbia University and already showed evidence of literary

talent. In the spring of 1940 a baby girl named Susan was born to Stefan and his wife. Incidentally, both of Artur's sisters and their husbands had recently arrived from Nazi-ridden Vienna to try and build a new existence in the New World.

Soon the rooms at the Peter Stuyvesant were a veritable beehive of friends, relatives and colleagues, and Therese had difficulty in rationing the visits so as not to overburden her too-much-sought-after spouse. Among his intimates at this time were Fritz Stiedry, who had just become the conductor of the New Friends of Music Chamber Orchestra on Schnabel's recommendation; also George Széll; the composers Ernst Křenek, who held a teaching post at Vassar College, and Roger Sessions, who had recently become professor of music at Princeton University. An increasing number of new arrivals from Europe came to see him, for the stream of refugees from Nazidom was now rising to a flood, and many of them were admirers whose hospitality he had enjoyed in the cities he had so often visited on his European tours. His correspondence with people whom he had come to know and like in America also increased. Indeed, he felt a growing urge to communicate with kindred souls and to pontificate on the problems—artistic, social and political—which now engaged his mind.

★　★　★

In the course of his rather frequent visits to Chicago in the middle 'thirties Schnabel had become acquainted with a group of people in academic circles who admired him greatly, both as a musician and an original thinker. Among them was Dr. Eric Oldberg, a famous surgeon and neurologist, the son of the American composer Arne Oldberg, who like Schnabel had been a pupil of Leschetizky in Vienna. Dr. Oldberg and his wife Hilda, an excellent amateur pianist, became Artur's hosts in Chicago on so many occasions that he nick-named their lovely home the 'Hotel Oldberg'. Then there was John U. Nef, professor of economic history at the University of Chicago and prime mover of its Committee on Social Thought, who had introduced Artur to Robert M. Hutchins, then the University's president. Nef was at that time planning a major work, *The United States and Civilization*, a subject which was bound to arouse more than common interest in Schnabel. A lively correspondence between the two led to a firm friendship, and it may be that Schnabel's ideas on a variety of subjects were not without influence on the younger man.

Hutchins' expressed desire to have Schnabel give some lectures at the University, encouraged by Nef, naturally intrigued him; but he had many misgivings, since tones were his proper medium of communication and he considered himself a 'dilettante' with words. He had always been a 'direct' musician, he wrote, not an 'indirect' one like the musicologist, the critic and the historian. The direct musician, he said, is a gardener, the indirect musician a botanist. Correspondence with Nef—and occasionally Hutchins—continued and skirted such subjects as the philosophical and moral aspects of art, the conflict of idealism and materialism, the 'total utilitarianism' of modern society, and the debased function of the human being to that of a compulsory consumer rather than a producer and creator of cultural values. By the end of 1939 the matter of the lectures had been settled in the affirmative. There were to be three, designated simply as 'Some Aspects of Music', to be given before a mixed audience of students and others during the following April.[1]

Unlike Schnabel's doctoral address at the University of Manchester, they were written in English, for by this time he had acquired an almost terrifyingly large English vocabulary, although his syntax still had strong traces of German. In substance the lectures were a random collection of thoughts aiming to define the nature of music and the various functions of the professional musician, all somehow brought into a plausible continuity. The effect was that of a dialectical *tour de force* in highly condensed thinking and vivid epigrammatic composition, ranging from classified definition through historical survey to speculative and sometimes indignant argument. His own opinion of them was that they 'seem to express clearly that art is high up, higher than anyone can hope to get; that it is more exacting and more rewarding to be a humble creature *vis-à-vis* the inexhaustible than a king among nonentities'. Commenting on his new rôle, he thought there was a certain element of the comic in it. Lectures on music seemed to him superfluous, uncreative and barren; in short, they were not part of his assignment. 'But,' he mused, 'it was good practice in English, and I even got paid for it!' He received many compliments on his resonant and effortless delivery which, he said, he had 'inherited from my actor son'. Despite this gently cynical reaction he seemed to enjoy the experience, surrounded as he was by some of his most admiring friends, who showered him with their solicitude and were already plotting a sequel to the experiment.

[1] Later these lectures were published in book form under the curiously Schnabelian title *Music and the Line of Most Resistance* by the Princeton University Press (1942).

A portrait taken in 1945

Schnabel with Carl Ebert, artistic director of Glyndebourne Opera, and Bruno Walter, the conductor, at the Edinburgh Festival of 1947

'I don't play in public this season,' Schnabel wrote to Walter Turner at the end of 1940, 'and am quite content with my abstinence.' Earlier that year, however, he had accepted two engagements: one at Vassar College, not far from New York, where his friend Křenek taught musical theory; the other at the Ann Arbor Festival (University of Michigan), where a former pupil, Joseph Brinkman, was now a professor. At Vassar it intrigued him to administer a 'heavy' dose of Bach, Mozart and Schubert to an audience of college girls, thus once again confounding the 'pessimists'. The Ann Arbor appearance (with the Philadelphia Orchestra under Eugene Ormandy) was to have an important consequence for his immediate future.

That future—the war years in America—certainly posed a serious problem to an artist whose income depended on his international activity and who now found himself cut off from all his 'markets' but one; and that one now seemed to be in the process of attrition. By a combination of circumstances the effective demand for his services, which had reached its peak in 1936–7, seemed to have tapered off. It could hardly be explained by the presence of so many artists now stranded in the United States, nor by the rather exclusive and exacting nature of his offerings, for on the highest audience level he was as much a favourite as ever. No doubt he was a difficult man for the commercial managers to handle, since he would not adapt himself to the prevailing fashion, and refused to co-operate in efforts to have himself 'built up' as a popular idol. 'It has not yet come to an open clash,' he wrote to a friend in England, 'or a definite isolation from my new environment, but I seem organically incapable of establishing genuine contact.'

Schnabel drew the obvious conclusion: he would have to return to the predestined tri-partite pattern of his career, and would now have to concentrate on the more sedentary of his occupations, composing and teaching. It was therefore a happy thought that prompted his friend Joseph Brinkman to suggest a substitute for the famous summer class of Tremezzo on American soil. While Artur was filling his engagement at the Ann Arbor Festival in May, Brinkman proposed that an experimental four-week teaching session be organized for the late summer, during the academic recess, when building and materials would be available. Arrangements were made accordingly and the announcements published for the opening at the end of August. There was no dearth of applications from talented young pianists in various parts of the country, all of whom were auditioned in advance, either by Schnabel in New York or Brinkman in Ann

Arbor.   The administrative duties were left to Brinkman and his very competent wife.

The experiment was a great success.   Classes were held daily, with eleven artist pupils and a much larger number of student-auditors.   As a result another class was announced for the following summer, and subsequently for every following summer until the end of the war.   Altogether, it was a satisfying though transitory reincarnation of the spirit of Tremezzo—that unique mélange of artistic experience and recreation, work and play, in the company of eager young people—now a happy memory of many English and American artists of the rising generation.

For the other customary summer activity—composing at high altitude—Schnabel's Chicago friends, the Oldbergs, found what seemed the ideal setting: a cottage at Bear Lake in the Rocky Mountains of Colorado.   Here, at 7,500 feet, Artur felt something of the bracing atmosphere which he had found ideal for musical creation in the Alps.   Artur and Therese went there in June and stayed until the beginning of the Ann Arbor class.   At the end of a month's work, interspersed with the usual walks with congenial friends, he had finished two movements of another string quartet, his fifth.

This quartet, finished in due time, remained his last work in the species.   It is in four movements of moderate length, with more concise melodic material, clearer design, and a more transparent texture than that in the earlier quartets.   It is uncompromisingly chromatic (*alias* atonal) and often sharply dissonant, but rich in its variety of thematic elements, and almost aggressively personal.   It was to be the first of Schnabel's works to be performed in the United States. Although it may not have any bearing on the contents of the work it is worth noting that it was composed at a time of great emotional stress felt by Schnabel, his associates and indeed by the American people in general, for it coincided with Hitler's massive aerial attacks, remembered as the Battle of Britain.   With all his apparent stolidity Schnabel was deeply distressed, and personally concerned about the fate of his English friends.   In his correspondence, however, he stressed only their fortitude and calm resistance.   'You are part of a great performance,' he wrote to one of them, 'in which everybody is justified in feeling proud—a perfect ensemble, all acting under their own impulses and their own control.'

*   *   *

Almost the only public appearance of Schnabel during the season of 1940–1—and certainly the most important—were two all-Mozart concerts of the New Friends of Music, conducted by Fritz Stiedry in Carnegie Hall, New York.   Schnabel contributed four concertos.[1] The performances were remarkable for the very close communion between soloist and conductor; and their outspoken success with the audience proved once and for all that all-Mozart programmes were as acceptable in New York as they had been in Vienna and London. In Schnabel's career they were symptomatic of an even more intensive preoccupation with Mozart, which was to become the great passion of his final years.

While there was little concert activity for Schnabel the pianist, there was a great deal for the teacher and composer.   Throughout the autumn months he sat in his Parkside abode, where younger pianists came to be instructed, and to play to him the works they were to perform in public while he, the master, might well have been pondering on the ironies of life, if his mind had not been creatively engaged.   It also happened that some attention was being paid to Schnabel the composer for the first time since his coming to America. His friend and colleague Bruno Eisner had begun playing his *Piece in Seven Movements* in public, and the Galimir Quartet gave the first performance of his fifth string quartet in New York, where it had what is euphemistically described as a mixed reception, and aroused the usual controversy in the Press.   Schnabel himself was absent on account of illness, confined to bed with a severe attack of bronchial pneumonia.   About the same time (in March) Therese suffered a rather serious accident, which laid her low for weeks.   Not till the end of April were both Schnabels well again, and Artur emerged in time to be an interested listener at the first International Festival of Contemporary Music of the I.S.C.M. to be held in America.   He found it not only stimulating but the quality of the output 'quite decent', which was high praise, indeed.

This interesting event, coming so soon after he had finished his first symphonic score, was an additional stimulus to further composition.   Schnabel felt an irresistible urge to continue in the orchestral medium, and the outlines of another symphony were already beginning to take shape in his mind.

[1] D minor (K. 466), C major (K. 467), A major (K. 488) and E-flat major (K. 482).

30. Composition at High Altitude

SCHNABEL had always preferred the mountains, both for creation and recreation. He loved the mountains for their manifold beauty and for the unique solitude they afforded for meditation. Most of his composing, beginning with his second string quartet in the early 1920's, had been done in some Alpine resort or other, where inspiration came on long walks and slow, plodding climbs. Hitherto he had missed his favourite Alpine scenery in America: even the pleasant Colorado holiday of the previous summer had not been an adequate substitute.

By a lucky chance he heard, in the spring of 1942, of an ideal spot in the mountains of New Mexico—a vast estate called Gascon Ranch, at an altitude of more than 8,000 feet. It was owned by a physician and inhabited by a small number of friends as paying guests, who spent much of their time on horseback, roaming on endless mountain trails to still greater heights. Here the Schnabels, intrepid pedestrians as always, believed themselves to be the first contemporary humans to travel on their own feet. In this 'indescribably beautiful spot' they spent the summer months preceding Artur's Ann Arbor class, living in luxurious primitivity in a large cabin all to themselves. Here he began his second symphony, making good progress with it in 1942, and here he was to finish the composition during the following summer.

Schnabel's second symphony is his largest and most elaborate work in that form; though it contains only twenty bars more than its predecessor, it is more vast in conception, and its contrasts are more daring. It consists of four movements: an energetic allegro, preceded by a slow introduction which is later integrated into the main body of the movement; a lively vivacissimo; an exceedingly slow and sombre-hued largo; and a final allegretto energetico, the most complex and most difficult of the movements.

So far as can be judged—as unfortunately one is thus far obliged to judge—from the manuscript score alone, the texture is clearer, more transparent, and the instrumental economy more striking both in the unity and balance, in the resultant clarity, and in the vividness of the colouristic profile, than in the earlier work. The large design, as well as the individual ideas, stand out in bolder relief. Needless to say, Schnabel's orchestra, for all of its bold and often startlingly original colouring, is an integral part of his musical personality, and would be inconceivable as a vehicle for any other music. It serves, as indeed all good instrumentation serves, to sharpen the essential musical outline, and is inseparable from the latter.

Schnabel was now so deeply preoccupied with composition that his pianistic career took a decidedly secondary place in his life. The few engagements that had been procured for the 1941-2 season he accepted without joy, as 'items in one and the same variety show'. Yet, whether he was playing Beethoven's C major concerto with Bruno Walter in New York or Brahms' B-flat major with a youthful conductor in Houston, Texas ('a vigorously growing and musically unspoiled community'), he always gave of his best, simply because music compelled him to do so. He looked forward with 'somewhat friendlier expectations' to a group of five New York concerts (under the ægis of the New Friends of Music) comprising the greater part of Schubert's piano works; and he was elated over the success of a monumental series of five concerts in Mexico City (three with orchestra) consisting of major works by Beethoven, Mozart and Schubert. But surely the most grotesque experience of the year (1942) took place in Chicago's popular annual summer festival at Ravinia Park, where he played four concertos in as many outdoor concerts to an audience of 20,000 'in defiance of bugs and beetles'. This he vowed never to repeat, being 'neither hardy nor philanthropic enough' for that kind of activity.[1]

The truth is that he was really getting tired of this eternal 'nomad life', and becoming more and more testy as it continued. Only once again during his remaining years did he undertake anything resembling the usual nation-wide concert tour, which has long been the routine of celebrated artists in America. In the winter months of 1942-3 he played recitals in the larger American cities from coast to coast, and, probably for the first time, he repeated the same programme in all of them. It was the beginning of the end, so far as his New York managers were concerned.

The following summer he and Therese once again spent on that wonderful Gascon Ranch, and here, having finished the orchestration

[1] It is worth noting that shortly after this he made his only gramophone records in America, Beethoven's G major and *Emperor* concertos with the Chicago Symphony Orchestra conducted by Frederick Stock, and issued by R.C.A.–Victor, the American affiliate of H.M.V.

of his second symphony, he embarked on a singularly novel project, two large movements for chorus and orchestra. The first, entitled *Dance and Secret,* is based on lines of Robert Frost which read as follows: 'We dance round in a ring, and suppose; But the secret sits in the middle, and knows.' The choral portions of this very lively work (in which the text is treated very freely and with much repetition) alternate with orchestral passages of some length, and the whole concludes with a long orchestral epilogue.

The second of these choral movements, entitled *Joy and Peace,* is a setting of large excerpts from Chapter 55 of Isaiah, slightly altered by Schnabel for his own purposes, together with the two opening lines of Chapter 60. Thus the text is much longer, as its content is more weighty and elaborate, than that of *Dance and Secret,* which bears somewhat the relationship of a scherzo to the broad and majestic slow movement (*largamente e con sublimita*).

Schnabel's choral writing, needless to say, makes the utmost demands on the performers. Despite their undeniable difficulties these movements seem, along with the orchestral *Rhapsody,* to be among the most immediately accessible of Schnabel's later works.

★   ★   ★

In 1943 Schnabel severed all connexion with the New York management concern which had represented him for nearly a decade in America. He had been progressively dissatisfied with their alleged lack of sympathy with his personal attitude to his 'only employer', his particular obligation to the art of music. American managers, he maintained, adhered to the curiously inverse ratio between quality and price: i.e. the greater the music, the lower the fee. Since they persisted in labelling him a 'musicians' musician' and since audiences are not made up of musicians, he decided that they had better stop trying to book him altogether. So he and they parted company, and he was at liberty to deal directly with such local sponsors as desired his services on his own terms.

He soon found that this was not difficult at all, and that the people who wanted him had no trouble finding his address. He now dealt with local organizations, managers or conductors directly, who wrote him at his eyrie in Central Park West. In effect, he became his own secretary and he rather fancied this old-fashioned and dignified manner of conducting his affairs. He wrote all his letters by hand, slowly and deliberately, in his precise and fastidious style, with the natural and expected result. In due time a small but satisfying number of appearances were arranged for the latter part of the 1943-4 and for the following season as well. He continued to appear as soloist with several of the most important orchestras of the country, particularly in New York, Chicago, San Francisco and Los Angeles, and with organizations such as the New Friends of Music and others, which were more than willing to take him at his worth. Thus he was able to give another Beethoven cycle, comprising the most exacting of the great sonatas and the *Diabelli Variations,* and fill Carnegie Hall to capacity three times. In Chicago the Orchestra gave a Mozart Festival, in which he contributed five different Mozart concertos in as many concerts, and which he called 'one of the happiest events' of his concert career.[1]

Schnabel admirers in Pittsburgh and Los Angeles had organized societies on the model of the New Friends of Music to cultivate the kind of homogeneous programmes he advocated, and now invited him to grace their series. All along the Pacific Coast, from San Diego in the south to Portland, Oregon, in the north, he was engaged to give recitals for groups of music-lovers predisposed to his kind of musical fare. This became the first of several small Pacific tours, with full or overcrowded houses everywhere—one of the most genuine conquests of his life. 'To exploit it,' he wrote to Therese, 'would be a desecration.'

As always, and now especially, he was eager to encourage unconventional or tentative groups of patrons without the usual machinery of management and the trappings of publicity, be it the Beethoven enthusiasts of Chicago University or the Needle Trades Union of New York, and following his past experience with the London Museum he gave a very choice annual recital among the masterpieces of the Frick Collection on New York's Fifth Avenue.

In the spring of 1945 a tiny group of young music-lovers in Toronto who had heard his records ventured to ask his terms for a single recital, which would mean a special trip from New York. They called themselves the 'Friends of Great Music', and wrote to the great man, with nothing to recommend themselves but some printed notepaper and their own enthusiasm. Schnabel replied to say he would be glad to come on May 1st, quoted his regular fee but asked for no contract or guarantee. The young men were amazed and duly delighted to see him arrive with his wife on the appointed day, turn up at the hall to try the piano, travelling by tram and carrying

---

[1] Mozart concertos in E-flat major (K. 482), C major (K. 467), G major (K. 453), B-flat major (K. 595) and D minor (K. 466).

his usual rolled-up umbrella. Not only was the concert a great success, but the little group flourished on the impetus given by Schnabel's appearance, plus their own idealism, for some years.

This informal way of doing things, without business intermediaries, suited his style of life, and for a while at least he prospered in his own quiet way. Economically he was certainly no worse off than before: he played still fewer concerts but mostly for higher fees, without having to pay commissions or the cost of press books and the usual printed puffs. He simply declined to furnish publicity or advertising matter about himself, on the quite reasonable presumption that for a man who had been before the public for fifty years there must come a time when the fact that he has 'rippling scales and a velvety tone' may be taken for granted. It was, indeed; and so it happened that Schnabel, the emancipated pianist, had enough engagements to fill his spare time—to the end of his war years in America.

31. Sage of Central Park West

WHEN Schnabel, at the age of sixty-one, emancipated himself from the 'tyranny' of management, he not only wanted to make an end of his 'nomadic existence' but devote himself more intensively to composition, which was to become the chief concern of his remaining years. Now that he had begun to write symphonic works, the sheer physical side of the activity consumed a greater proportion of his time, for aside from the arduous task of orchestration there was the supervision of the copyists and the correcting of score and parts. In the process his improvised hotel-room studio took on the semblance of a workshop, with piles of manuscripts and writing tools where there was only a piano before. But the piano was none the less busy, for teaching was still a major obligation as long as there were gifted young artists to be taught.

Teaching—and preaching—were still an intellectual necessity, for this was his way of thinking aloud, of settling problems in his own mind as well as the pupils', and relieving his over-active brain. In the course of years his teaching had become more and more advanced, more and more esoteric and philosophical. He had never been greatly interested in the physical side of piano playing, though he was never above 'showing a pupil how' by actual example. But Schnabel could accomplish more with a word, a verbal image, an æsthetic or poetic allusion than most teachers could with detailed directions or textbook remedies. At this stage of his journey he expected his pupils to be musically as well as technically proficient, and capable of forming an artistic concept of their own. He gave them the greatest latitude for individuality, and what he gave them was intended to be no more than guidance to the aspiring climber toward the heights. But there were always summits beyond those which the student had glimpsed—or imagined. 'Greater happiness,' he used to say, 'can only be achieved if more is expected of us.'

Apart from the few weeks of summer classes in Ann Arbor, the pupils were now limited to a very few chosen professionals, and young artists already before the public. They came to him whenever they needed his help and whenever he had time. As always these

consultations were of indeterminate duration, and they were likely
to expand into lectures on the moral and ethical significance of art,
commentaries on the problems of the artist and his duty to art, and
on the deplorable conditions of contemporary life. Nor were these
homilies confined to students. Friends and colleagues who came to
him for comfort or sociability, or to bask in the warmth of his personality, were given the benefit of his opinions on current events, his
cogitations on the meaning and the state of the world.

Sitting in his austere yet cheery living-room, high above the trees
of Central Park, with a haphazard collection of pictures, ancient and
modern, looking down from the walls, the white-haired Schnabel
held forth in the polished phraseology of a man of letters and the
deliberate measures of an elder statesman. His voice was soft and
pleasant, never agitated or emphatic, but his *obiter dicta* had a sound
of finality that discouraged contradiction. His movements were
getting slower, his walk more leisurely, but the calm, kindly gaze of
his grey eyes was as friendly as ever, even though his words increasingly reflected the seriousness of the times and his trend toward a
pessimistic outlook in view of what he considered to be the soulless
and self-destructive materialism of modern man. While not professing any formal religion, Schnabel was essentially a religious man
in the broad sense of the word. Spirituality was the predominant
side of his character as an artist, and idealism his guiding philosophy.

He had a near-mystical faith in what he called Nature, and in the
autonomous power of the Goethean trinity—the good, the true and
the beautiful. He spoke of Nature as of a deity—the source of man's
most precious gifts and the provider of its greatest joys. It was
responsible, too, for the essential inequality of human beings, which
determines our positions and our duties in life. 'It has singled out
the few as a nobility of the spirit; but this nobility is not a class but
an obligation—not only to receive and use but to develop and improve,
to strive upwards toward fulfilment.' The fate of the artist, therefore is 'a constant insecurity and dissatisfaction which is man's armour
against indifference, and expresses his faith in humanity and its high
destiny'.

Music he believed to be one of Nature's divine gifts to man, 'a
perpetual and inexhaustible mandate to our spirit'. 'The efforts to fulfil
this mandate,' he wrote, 'belong to the most exacting, most satisfying, and therefore supreme functions of man. . . .'

'Music has a permanent and immutable value for all: its essence and profundity are communicated to all who are equipped with an adequate receiver.

He who has this equipment knows what is there; though there is no way by which he can prove it.'

★   ★   ★

There was in these Central Park West days a faint and rather nostalgic reflection of the happy inter-war years in Berlin, when the young composers of the time dropped in to display their latest works, and examined his in return. The personnel had changed, though not completely; Ernst Křenek, now in his mature years, was still a leading favourite. Both he and his American colleague Roger Sessions were now among the accepted composers of their generation, and Schnabel never failed to attend a first performance of their works in New York. As regards contemporary music in general, times had radically changed. There was a greater demand for novelties, and especially for orchestral works, provided they had never been performed before. Indeed it was more often the newness rather than the greatness of a composition that caused it to be heard—with the likely result that it would not be heard again. (Schnabel's comment on this was that many works were born and buried at the same time—'from the cradle to the grave in one concert'.)

Discussion ran to other contemporaries, of course, and Schnabel rarely missed the press comments on the latest première. Schönberg was still the acknowledged 'old master' of his school, and Paul Hindemith was still the most successful of the younger (now middle-aged) group. Within this range Schnabel had a wide knowledge of the works of his contemporaries, genuine respect for some and admiration for a few. He accepted Stravinsky but had many reservations about his latest productions. He had no liking for Prokofief, nor for Shostakovich, whose wartime popularity he accepted for what it was. He found little affinity with the brittle music of the personally so gentle Béla Bartók, but had considerably more respect for Arthur Honegger and Darius Milhaud. Strangely enough he had little knowledge of English composers; but he evinced genuine interest in the works he had a chance to hear, notably those of William Walton. And he had an affectionate regard for Donald Francis Tovey as a man and a musician.

His chief object of castigation in these years was the decadence of society—in the western world and America in particular—just as it had been the decadence of Austrian society in the days of his youth. This, and the consequent decline of spiritual values he identified with the mechanization of life in the mass-production age, which had reached its rankest florescence in the United States. Willingly, if not enthusiastically, he had become an American. America, he thought, had the greatest opportunity for continuing and refining Europe's civilization. But owing to its encouragement of 'total utilitarianism' which made the consumption of goods the most important function of the citizen, it failed in its true mission—the creation of new cultural values. In this modern society of 'mass-produced bread and mechanized circuses' the demand (real or artificially induced) controls the supply, while in the world of art the supply (or inspiration) precedes the demand. Schnabel believed in an ideal democracy in which everyone's occupations and duties are preordained by Nature, i.e. through man's talents and abilities. But in the America of today, he felt, democracy was often interpreted as 'an obligation to spread confusion'. As a fugitive from one hateful despotism, he was fearful of a new kind of despotism arising out of a frantic struggle for economic power.

Nevertheless he looked to the United States and its British allies as the great liberators in the struggle for human freedom. 'Whatever the future of civilization,' he wrote, 'I believe that all idealists everywhere must now band together to end this war with success on our side. That this side is not quite the peak of civilization is our fate, not our fault, which notwithstanding we have to deplore.' He followed the news of the war with the dreadful fascination which gripped all sensitive people, and he scanned the daily newspapers with a canny and highly selective eye. He was as uncompromising in his hatred of the enemy as he was gentle and conciliatory after the victory.

But even in these trying times there were moments when the warming rays of his good nature broke through the war-time gloom, when the visits of the one-time cronies of Vienna and Berlin days conjured up memories of what now seemed like a Golden Age between the two wars. There was Fritz Stiedry, once the conductor and stormy petrel of the Berlin Opera, now trying to rejuvenate the crusty formalism of New York's 'Met' with quasi-Mahlerian revivals of Mozart and Verdi operas. There was Eugen Spiro, the veteran ex-German impressionist who had first painted Schnabel in his twenties, and now did it again in his sixties. There was Bruno Walter, now nearing seventy, who had conducted concertos for Schnabel for three decades and in four countries, Otto Klemperer, who after years of crippling illness still fought the good fight against the callous aloofness of a too-forgetful world, and George Széll, the brilliant conductor of the Cleveland Orchestra—an old friend since the Berlin days.

These and other good companions occasionally forgathered around the hospitable board of a friend of Artur's youth, now a neighbour on Central Park West—a hostess in the best Viennese traditions, who managed to produce the culinary miracles and the cultivated social atmosphere of a distant day amid the slowly fading gentility of New York's upper West Side. In this heart-warming environment the ageing Schnabel was often the centre of attention, solemnly listened to when eloquently espousing the old ideals, or deploring their neglect in this 'godless and loveless age', and eagerly applauded when he dispensed his favourite witticisms and verbal tricks. For Schnabel had long been famous for his humorous use of words, his picturesque similes and especially his *Schüttelreime* which, almost always in German, are as funny as they are untranslatable. If his puns and formulations in English seem somewhat contrived, it may be put down to artistic licence or the pardonable self-indulgence of a great and much-applauded idol.

But certainly his comparison of the typical virtuoso programme to a conducted tour of Paris ('from cathedral to night-club') was as apt as his classification of dance-interpretations of great music as 'pedi-festations of art'. When someone described a certain type of music as 'fireworks' he protested, for music, he said, always goes up, but fireworks inevitably come down. Even a purist in English may approve of his calling a somewhat too-clever conductor a 'one-and-a-half-wit', though his referring to a famous and notoriously eloquent one as Sir Thomas Speecham is probably out of bounds. But many will sympathize with his estimate of mediocrity: 'a very exalted grade, when you consider how much is below it and how little above'.

*   *   *

As the war wore on the Schnabels, like most American families, became involved not only emotionally but physically. Stefan, the younger son, as a German-speaking actor broadcast propaganda for the Voice of America, and then went overseas as a private in the O.S.S.; Christopher, Artur's grandson, joined the Army Intelligence Corps. Karl Ulrich, whose special mechanical gifts made it possible, engaged in war work in a radio factory in New England. Artur Schnabel himself, ineligible for any kind of direct war duty, made recordings of piano pieces and spoken messages to be broadcast over the Armed Services network abroad.

The last days of the war in Europe found Artur back in his Parkside lair, exhausted after an unwonted six weeks of 'platform-storming', suffering from violent coughing fits, and shocked by the death of President Roosevelt, whom he admired as a great liberal leader. 'I feel somehow more lonely,' he wrote to a friend, and his depression increased with the events that followed: Potsdam, the dropping of the first atom bombs, the mass-deportations of innocent people, and deeds of vengeance without a foreseeable end. In the final days of the struggle, tragedy deepened into personal bereavement: during a concert in St. Louis he learned that his aged mother in Vienna had become a victim of Nazi atrocity. . . . More passionately than ever he was convinced that there must never be another war.

Embittered as he was, he remained a steadfast pacifist at heart. From the early 1940's onwards he had carried on a lively correspondence with his friend John U. Nef, who had been so largely instrumental in getting him to lecture at the University of Chicago. He was keenly interested in Nef's study of war as a human problem and had often talked with him about the prospects of world peace after the war. He greatly admired Nef's forthcoming work, *War and Human Progress*, and its publication stimulated Schnabel's interest in the current pacifistic ideas and schemes for federal union, world federation and world government. When Nef sent Schnabel the text of a Manifesto on World Unity which he and a number of his academic friends were about to issue, Schnabel not only agreed to sign it but promised to propagate the idea among his influential friends, first in the United States and later in Europe.

Nef in his turn spread Schnabel's artistic gospel among his colleagues and friends in Chicago and its great university. Early in 1944 President Hutchins had invited Schnabel to repeat his successful experiment in lecturing to the students—this time as temporary incumbent of the Alexander White professorship. Schnabel had hesitated for some months, but finally agreed to conduct twelve seminar sessions in October 1945.

The summer preceding his seminar was to have been spent partly in Ann Arbor, teaching, and partly in New Mexico, composing; but circumstances connected with the ending of the war and the uncertainty of the future caused a complete change in plans. Artur and Therese spent June at home and July at a pleasant resort on the shores of Moosehead Lake in Maine, where they were easily reached by some members of the family, particularly Karl Ulrich and Helen, who were still in their wartime billet in Massachusetts. Here Artur composed one of his most successful and most accessible chamber music works, the piano trio. This may be called the most 'progressive' score he had produced thus far, being written in completely linear counterpoint and making use of the conventional twelve-tone row of the confirmed atonalists. Its texture is more than usually transparent and the dynamics less erratic than in his previous works, but the music is none the less expressive for that. (The work was first performed by the Albeneri Trio at the Berkshire Music Festival in Lenox, Massachussets, in 1947.)

★   ★   ★

In keeping with the general feeling of uncertainty at the end of the war, Schnabel seemed somewhat at loose ends. 'I have much and diverse work in hand, at least till next summer,' he wrote to Nef in September; 'I feel the "privilege" of being a freelance musician these days, with hope in most respects fading and patience short.' As a matter of fact, he had no reason to complain on the score of employment. He was at this time a very busy man with a variety of interests. In October he delivered his Alexander White Lectures in Chicago, and from the tone of these chatty and largely autobiographical talks and reminiscences he must have enjoyed himself hugely over a period of two weeks. Ranging over a complex of subjects from music to philosophy and from history to sociology and economics he carried on a free-wheeling argument which was always informative, lively, full of humour and amusing intellectual somersaults. The lectures were attended by an intelligent group of students and amateurs, who peppered him with questions and elicited a sparkling, informative and witty stream of repartee.

Apart from music, he took an increasingly gloomy view of the world. The news of current events was disturbing, what with the new flare-up of east-west antagonism since the signing of the Potsdam Agreement and the first signs of the Cold War. Despite the German débâcle he felt that Hitlerism and the worship of coercion were still rampant in the world—with changed *locale*.

His thoughts were increasingly on Europe and his anxiety to see the old Continent again increased from day to day. In February 1946, while giving a recital in the west, he wrote to Therese, asking her to apply for passports. In March he himself was home in New York, deep in travel plans and reserving passage for England. On March 27th he concluded his American season with an orchestral concert in Carnegie Hall conducted by F. Charles Adler, at which he played Beethoven's concerto in C major, Mozart's in B-flat (K. 450) and between them Bach's C major double concerto with Karl Ulrich—a very happy occasion. By the end of the month the Schnabels had in their possession the tickets for a passage on the *Queen Mary*—in the very stateroom which they had originally booked in September 1939 when the sailing was cancelled because of the outbreak of war.

Some time before this the news reached him that his first symphony would be performed in December by the Minneapolis Orchestra under Dimitri Mitropoulos, an intrepid pioneer in musical modernism. He was naturally elated, for it would be his first mature orchestral score to be heard—even by himself. 'Keep the date free!' he wrote to Nef with something like boyish glee.

An equally cheerful piece of intelligence had pierced the murky horizon of the previous months: he heard from Italy that most of his belongings except the motor-car, but including his manuscripts and books, were miraculously saved, having been secreted in the vicinity of Tremezzo and kept from the Nazis' clutches by a *tour de force* on the part of his brave custodians. He had already written to Peter Diamand, his former secretary, now living in Amsterdam, of his intention to go to Europe in the spring. And this in turn had released a string of requests for concert appearances in England, France, Belgium, Holland, Switzerland and Italy.

It was not long before the sage of Central Park West, the man who had renounced the 'nomad life', was packing his trunks for another round of far-flung concerts—in the battered cities of the old world.

32. Europe Revisited

ON April 24th, 1946—hardly a year after the fighting had stopped —Artur and Therese Schnabel set out, with the impatience of home-sick children, on the last lap of the global journey which had begun seven years ago. Real peace was still but a hope; but England was beginning to dig itself out of its ruins, and London—scene of Schnabel's greatest triumphs—was preparing a wonderful welcome, with no less than six concerts in the huge Albert Hall. Altogether he was looking forward to a heavy two months' schedule, with concerts in England and five countries on the Continent. But besides this immediate concern he was most eager to take stock of post-war conditions in Europe, report back to his friend Nef and his group of pacifist signers, and sound out the prospects for the cause of peace through unity. He had promised to 'work hard for world government' and for the first time in his life he hoped to take an active part in world affairs.

To understand this new preoccupation with matters beyond his artistic mission, it is necessary to recall the impact of the war on the lives of unpolitical but imaginative people rooted in the culture of Europe and tossed by the upheaval of war and revolution into strange environments and circumstances which seemed to negate the values they had laboured to create, and threaten to rob life itself of its meaning. Those seven incredible, world-shaking years had not only wrought tremendous material changes in the lives and fortunes of the Schnabel family; they had for a time destroyed the climate and atmosphere in which their life's work had been projected. Artur had always thought of America as the second Europe; but it was now the largest and most powerful area of civilization in the world, without which the first Europe itself could no longer exist. He himself had accepted citizenship in the light of this knowledge, and with the hope of doing service in the salvage of European civilization. This now became a part of the greater task of saving the world through the establishment of permanent peace. He had not been too discriminating in the political implications of this quest for peace; and he was ready to welcome anyone who sincerely professed the same exalted aim.

He was deeply affected by the sight of familiar landmarks now ruined, of whole quarters of his beloved London laid waste and, later on, by the areas of devastation in the other countries of the west. At the same time he was disturbed, from day to day, by the ominous news coming out of international conferences, by the Cold War propaganda, and the meetings of the United Nations illuminating the contest of power between the communist and non-communist worlds. He gave voice to his pessimism to such of his old friends as were still in London: Samuel Courtauld, the industrialist; Walter Turner, who was now the literary editor of the *Spectator*; Edward Crankshaw, an ex-intelligence officer in the British Army and now a foreign correspondent for the *Observer*; and others. Luckily all of them had come through the war unscathed, and so had his conductor friends, Malcolm Sargent and Sir Adrian Boult, and his former pupils, such as Clifford Curzon, Maria Donska, Betty Humby (Lady Beecham), Rita Macintyre, John Hunt and William Glock.

Altogether he was more deeply than ever impressed by the steadfastness, fortitude and tolerance of the British people, with whom he had felt a deep spiritual kinship and whose wartime ordeal he would have shared but for the exigencies of transport at the outbreak of war. Writing to Nef, he reported that on the whole he found the British cheerful and healthy, deservedly enjoying their respite after living through years in imminent danger of their lives. They showed, he said, 'great readiness to grapple with urgent necessities, and seemed prepared to make a frontal attack on what they thought to be doomed to perish in any case.' In other words, there was a willingness to go forward towards reform and a better life for all.

It was a pleasant experience to find his favourite stopping-place, the Hyde Park Hotel, intact, and many old acquaintances gathering around to greet him. His staunch and excellent managers, Messrs. Ibbs & Tillett, were—miraculously—still doing business at the same old offices, having missed total destruction by a hair, while houses were bombed out of existence just across the street. The Queen's Hall, scene of so many of his concerts, was now a ruin, and the only possible alternative was the Albert Hall, holding 7,000, for the six concerts—three of them recitals and three of them orchestral—all within eighteen days. Here, in the very hall he had once spurned because of its acoustic vagaries, he was cheered to its multiple echoes by an enormous crowd; but with the charming inconsistency of genius he reacted rather violently against a writer who permitted himself to remark jokingly that he could barely distinguish Bach's toccata in D from Mozart's rondo in A. By contrast, the critic of the *Daily Express* vowed that 'the last *pianissimo* notes [of Beethoven's opus 111] came clearly—one by one—to the balcony's highest bench'.

To recreate convincingly Beethoven's last three sonatas plus the *Diabelli Variations* in the circular vastnesses of the Albert Hall was indeed an undertaking he would not have attempted in his earlier years, not to mention the delicate works of Mozart and Schubert which made up a considerable portion of his recitals. The three orchestral concerts, comprising all five of Beethoven's piano concertos plus the triple concerto (with Arthur Grumiaux and Pierre Fournier) presented an only slightly less hazardous task.

After the comparatively thin American seasons of the past few years the almost overwhelming reception he received in London (and in several provincial cities) must have come as a terrific bracer to his spirits. The criticisms were predominantly in a lyrical vein. The *Daily Mail* spoke of his 'unfaltering grasp of the fullest meaning of great musical utterance', and concluded that his tonal quality, his beautiful *legato* and phrasing could be appreciated even in the Albert Hall, 'which is at present the only place able to hold the audience wishing to hear this still unexampled pianist'. Through all the years of his absence the British audience had remained as faithful as they were discriminating in bestowing their favours. But, as the *Musical Times* pointed out, thousands of music-lovers and young pianists were now hearing him for the first time, and it was this comparatively youthful public which helped to fill the largest halls for him during the remaining years of his career.

★   ★   ★

As in England so on the Continent: he was welcomed back in a dozen cities from Holland to Italy. Only the Paris concert had to be cancelled because of a strike. Everywhere he went he talked with acquaintances, old and new, to learn their opinions and attitudes in the sobering atmosphere of Liberation, and often within sight of the terrible scars of war. From the calm remoteness of Sils-Maria in the Swiss Alps he wrote to John Nef his first impressions—in anything but encouraging terms. 'Even for an absentee like myself,' he began, 'it is impossible not to be shaken by the reports of survivors and the sight of destruction, as were those who were present at the dance of death.' Yet, unlike the British, who seemed ready for change, the Dutch and the Belgians seemed 'past-bound', ready to start again with the same old mechanism for creating wealth and happiness, and nationalistic to a degree. As for the Swiss, having once again escaped actual war on their own soil, they were convinced they had solved all social and administrative problems, and were a model for the rest of the world. No one had many illusions about the future, and everywhere people seemed prepared to accept the possibility of a new war—this time with the United States and its friends on one side and Soviet Russia with its satellites on the other.

In this atmosphere of cynical defeatism his ideas on world government were, he admitted, not a welcome topic of conversation. Though everyone seemed to admit that world government would be the ideal form of society, no one believed that those who were now the masters in no-matter-how-small a unit, would want to become junior partners in another unit, no matter how large. Moreover, even after the narrowest escape from total annihilation by outside forces, they stuck to their conviction that Europe was still *the* decisive factor in whatever may happen on the terrestrial globe! 'Therefore,' Schnabel concluded, 'we should devote our greatest efforts to organizing an absolutely united, comprehensive and unambiguous vanguard in the United States.'

A little later, amid the sylvan glades of Sils-Maria, the dreamer sat down to sort out his thoughts on the future of mankind. He had never been politically minded in a practical sense. He had always been an idealist, and a critic of what is, rather than a designer of what should be. But he was now in his sixty-fourth year, a decidedly elderly man, with totally white hair and slowly dimming hopes. Intelligently sceptical of all reformers and world-improvers, he was nevertheless pathetically attached to the one great panacea of his choice—world government as the door to peace. All his life he had preached the power of love, order and unity through the medium of his art. Now, aroused to the dreadful danger implicit in atomic warfare, he was determined to do what he considered practical in a probably hopeless attempt to stave off the worst.

★   ★   ★

Artur Schnabel had grown very fond of the Waldhaus in Sils-Maria, a comfortable, roomy hotel tucked away in one of the folds of the Engadin valley, some 6,200 feet above sea level, surrounded by enormous woods and endless walks along gently rising slopes, with sudden vistas of a gleaming glacier or a snowy peak. It was decidedly less strenuous than some of his previous Alpine retreats, though probably still too high for a man of his years and build. But

it was very particularly rewarding to the leisurely climber in a contemplative mood.   And his room with its magnificent view was the
ideal ivory tower for the creation of music for an age beyond his
own.   Here, when not too preoccupied with the fate of the world,
he composed his *Seven Piano Pieces*—a companion to the *Piece in
Seven Movements* which he had written ten years before.

Compared with his protean labours of the recent summers, which
produced his three symphonies, this was almost in the nature of a
recreation.   Similar in form to their predecessor for the piano, the
Seven Pieces are more economical in their sonorities and more transparent in their harmonic texture.   They travel through a variety of
moods from tender lyricism to dramatic excitement, but in general
they are graceful and clear rather than massive and complex—
approaching the ultimate refinement in Schnabel's style.

Before leaving Switzerland, Schnabel stopped at Zürich, now
more than ever the cross-roads of western culture, and there had two
brief but surprisingly pleasant encounters.   On the broad terrace of
the Hotel Baur-au-Lac overlooking the Lake of Zürich sat no less a
person than Richard Strauss, now eighty-two.   Here, too, was the
wraith-like figure of Wilhelm Furtwängler, whom fourteen years
earlier he had rebuffed so sharply when the staunchly German
conductor tried to entice him back to Berlin under the Nazi régime.
White-haired and nostalgic about the joys of the happy times
between the wars, both men exchanged affectionate greetings and
mellow reflections with the once-militant refugee.   Strauss, the
Nestor of German music, then near the end of his days, still preserved
some of the sardonic humour for which he was renowned.   Furtwängler, solemn and of almost saintly demeanour, at long last showed
interest in Schnabel's compositions, and Schnabel had the score of
his *Rhapsody* sent to him in due course.   *Tempora mutantur.*

In September the Schnabels sailed back to New York and returned
to their hotel on Central Park West.   Looking back on his first post-
war visit to the continent which for half a century had been his home,
he must have been heartened to realize how much he had been
missed and how deeply he was appreciated now.   And he certainly
realized how much Europe still meant to him.   America had now
become his home, the place where he and his family were settled.
Instead of the old routine of living in Europe and touring in America,
he decided that henceforth he would make the best of both worlds—
live in America and annually offer his wares to the Continent of
which he was still a part and always would be:

'I recognize only now how much and how deeply I enjoyed the four and a half months in Europe, its timeless beauty, its ancient dignity and its still surviving *Gemütlichkeit*. Even the ever-present sadness, as at the parting of old friends, touches one as something genuinely human, and therefore true and even hopeful.'

The sadness, alas! was bound to deepen as time went by. Even now, in November, he heard of the death of one of his most constant and most valued friends—Walter J. Turner.[1] And it was not long before he learned that Samuel Courtauld, too, had passed away.[2]

*   *   *

Professionally he was now busy preparing and correcting the orchestral material of his first symphony for its approaching performance—an increasingly trying occupation because of his diminishing eyesight. Young pianists and pupils again came to him for advice and help with their repertoires, and as usual there were the friends who came for periodic walks and talks in the Park. In December he travelled to Minneapolis to hear his symphony, and several of his friends came from east and west to be present. He himself was more than satisfied with the result. The orchestra had done a magnificent job under the astonishing Dimitri Mitropoulos, conducting the vast and intricate score from memory. The press reviews ranged from respectful tolerance to friendly appreciation.[3]

The season's concert engagements in America included a three weeks' tour of California, fulfilling a promise he had given the year before, which brought him the usual enthusiastic reward. All this had left him considerable time to occupy himself with the cause of world peace, which had now become an obsession with him. He returned east in time to attend another World Peoples' Congress in March, but came away with grave doubts as to its efficacy and perhaps also as to the political objectivity of its sponsorship. In any case he was by this time already impatient for his next expedition to Europe, hoping once again to promote the Manifesto for World Unity, concerning which he had been corresponding with Nef for months.

As in the previous spring a number of important engagements again awaited him, both in England and on the Continent, and in

[1] November 18th, 1946.
[2] December 1st, 1947.
[3] The full score of the first symphony was published by subscription (Edition Adler) in 1945.

addition he was scheduled to resume his recordings for His Master's Voice, interrupted for the duration of the war. Now, for the 1948 recordings, he proposed to Walter Legge, its artistic director, a series of concertos by Mozart, Schumann and Brahms, also Brahms' rhapsodies, intermezzi and capriccios, Schumann's *Kinderszenen*, Bach's *Chromatic Fantasy* and Weber's *Invitation to the Dance*. Strange as it may seem, the process of making 'musical preserves'—once so abhorrent to Schnabel—had now, after years of forced abstention, become a pleasant and stimulating prospect!

In April 1947 he and Therese sailed for England to fill his various commitments, including another orchestral series in the Albert Hall, a number of recitals in London and the provinces, and the projected series of recording sessions in the old His Master's Voice studios (untouched by the blitz) in Abbey Road. On the Continent he once again filled a dozen or more engagements in Holland, Belgium and Switzerland, but was once more frustrated by the apparently customary strike in France. (What he regretted most was his hoped-for chance of seeing Paris again—a perennial joy of pre-war memory.) And as in the previous year he spent most of July and August in peaceful Sils-Maria—with the anticipated creative result: this time he composed what turned out to be his most successful though not his most extensive symphonic work, the *Rhapsody for Orchestra*. This virtually unique piece, probably the first in its category, is a one-movement work for full symphony orchestra—using the ingredients and essential characteristics of a symphony in less than symphonic dimensions. Like all of Schnabel's compositions it is a tapestry of closely woven and closely related ideas, all motivic material being derived from the opening eight bars. The composer himself described the piece as an 'independent, capricious, passionate, fantastic tribute to freedom and coherence'.

An extraordinary event brought him back to Britain that autumn before he went home. For the first time the now famous International Festival of Music and Drama was to take place in Edinburgh, and Schnabel was asked to appear not only as soloist (in Beethoven's G major concerto) but in a unique series of chamber music concerts to celebrate the various anniversaries of Schubert, Mendelssohn and Brahms. His collaborators in this memorable series included Joseph Szigeti, William Primrose and Pierre Fournier, and the programmes consisted of the trios and piano quartets of the three masters. This was the sort of task that Schnabel enjoyed to the full, and such was its success that a little later the series, extended to five concerts by the addition of other chamber works with piano by the same masters, was given again in London and broadcast to the nation. This was followed by a further set of chamber concerts with the same combination of artists at Geneva. Altogether he had prepared and performed seventeen different works ('none of them in the trifle category') during his so-called holiday, which also produced a major composition. He completed this terrific spurt of activity with a concert in Brussels and three days later sailed for America, where he still had a few autumn engagements to fill.

Reporting to Nef on his impressions of Europe this time, he was even less optimistic than before, and the outlook for 'mutuality' among the nations seemed definitely poor. 'The continued application of the intimidation machine had driven people into a new defeatism' and some of them into believing in the imminence of still another war. Thus his concern with the cause of peace and world government took an ever greater hold on his imagination and became the steady undercurrent of his thoughts.

In this mood he was not very receptive to new artistic ventures, such as the attempt of his Chicago friends to organize a series of five to seven Beethoven recitals, supplemented by lectures to the students of the University. 'Ten years ago,' he wrote, 'I would have responded with satisfaction if not with enthusiasm to this flattering suggestion. Today I am an old man, though I hope not yet inert for a while.' The truth is that he was frankly bored with the preparation of recitals, and he suggested that 'a somewhat wider attention to my function as a composer' would be more welcome.

This dispensation so devoutly wished was destined to be consummated in the year about to begin. The immediate future, however, held only another spate of concerts in the places where he was now most appreciated in America—on the Pacific Coast. For the most part they were not the 'strenuous' recitals he now tried to avoid, but orchestral concerts, three of them with a conductor he came to appreciate more and more—the seventy-two-year-old Pierre Monteux, who conducted Mozart concertos so beautifully.

This pleasant assignment was made even more agreeable by a 'lovely, peaceful, productive week' with the Nefs at Carmel, overlooking the Pacific Ocean—mentally remaking the world in the image of peace.

33. The Crisis

SCHNABEL'S Pacific Coast tour of the spring of 1948 was all but over: the last lap but one—seven concerts in ten days plus rehearsals and travelling. 'I regarded this as a test of my resilience [*Spannkraft*],' he wrote to Therese; 'it is, thank God, satisfactorily passed. At every stage I accomplished just about what I was capable of, and *almost* what I would have liked.'

Written in March, this revealing passage is the only hint that could be read as a warning, and only by someone whose receptive organs were sensitive to his moods. The last great effort was the group of Mozart concertos under Monteux, who after the rehearsals were over asked Schnabel's permission to conduct them all from memory—thus removing the last safety belt of less hardy swimmers. Then there was a long-sold-out recital in Portland, Oregon, at which the listeners were 'beside themselves—held in suspense by the *music*'. Nine days more and he would be home in New York, where on a Sunday afternoon he was to play Mozart and Beethoven sonatas with Joseph Szigeti—his last New York appearance of the season. Neither in his letters nor in his conversation was there another disquieting word; to the outside world he was still at the peak of his powers. Only Therese and possibly one or two other persons knew that something had imperceptibly changed, that henceforth Schnabel the pianist had to think of something else besides the music: he had—or should have—to think of his physical self.

But it was not in the nature of this man to spare himself, and especially not now. For some years he had silently hoped for what he had now begun to wish for openly—a little wider attention to 'my function as a composer'. Indeed, the wish was about to be fulfilled. In this very month of April, George Széll and the Cleveland Symphony performed the *Orchestral Rhapsody* he had written in Sils-Maria during the summer of the preceding year. His sonata for piano and violin had already been heard in Minneapolis and New York; and his piano trio had been performed by the Albeneri Trio at the Berkshire Music Festival of 1947. Now, to top all this, he received word that the first symphony, played first in Minneapolis under Dimitri Mitropoulos, was scheduled for a further performance in London that very spring. These prospects were cheering enough to help him forget the physical infirmities of the recent past.

Only once during the spring months did he feel a pain in his heart region, ominous enough to cause him to telephone his doctor; but the doctor was out, and next morning the pain was gone. On the other hand he had already arranged for another heavy summer schedule of recordings in London—'probably too much for a man of my age', as he wrote to Szigeti. He had probably never mentioned his age in this context before.

The season's playing done, Schnabel went to Cleveland to hear his *Rhapsody* conducted by Széll, a friend and colleague of many years' standing and a keenly intelligent admirer of Schnabel the pianist, though frankly not a partisan of Schnabel the composer. Nevertheless he gave the work a highly competent and letter-perfect reading, but possibly lacking the enthusiasm radiated by a true believer. Schnabel found it 'very instructive' but reported that the audience sat through it in 'arrogant lethargy'. The experience probably did not improve his humour, which in any case was not of the best and not likely to be improved by the notices of a rather provincial Press. In a letter to Nef after his return to New York he made no mention of the performance but dwelt on 'the lovely peaceful week' he and the Nefs had spent together at Carmel. 'I'll never forget this island of human affinity; to have it in my memory, alive, is very important in these days which tend to drag one into despondency'—a mood which had nothing to do with his present state but a great deal with the state of the world, now rapidly approaching a new international crisis which held the danger of armed conflict with Soviet Russia over the control of Berlin. It threw a deep shadow over the prospect of four months in Europe, and he found the preparations for the journey both irksome and fatiguing. Exhausted, he looked forward to his five days' rest while crossing the ocean. 'The anticipation of two months in Sils-Maria must give me strength,' he wrote—an altogether unaccustomed note for this usually serene and self-possessed man.

Two weeks after the Cleveland performance he was in London, looking forward with expectant curiosity to Sir Malcolm Sargent's performance of his symphony, a work which had required numerous rehearsals at its Minneapolis première. Sargent had the temerity to perform it at the Albert Hall after only three—a *Husarenstück* [1] Schnabel called it—but achieving astonishingly good results. British

---

[1] Roughly the equivalent of a 'dashing cavalry exploit'.

conductors, never spoiled in the matter of rehearsals, have learned to work fast and make the most of their time. According to the composer, the audience's reaction was 'not bad', and the work set off a lively controversy in the Press—most of the critics indulging in the indignant astonishment which had become the rule at Schnabel's premières. This was the first time a work of his was broadcast in England—by the courageous directors of the Third Programme. Whether by coincidence or design the piano soloist at this concert was Myra Hess, who played the Beethoven G major concerto, a work that had long been a favourite of hers as well as Schnabel's. A feeling of sadness clouded this otherwise happy occasion, caused by the illness and subsequent death of John Tillett, the concert manager who had served both these artists for so many years.

Schnabel's own health was causing serious concern to his friends, and he did not appear as a pianist in London that summer. The cataracts in both his eyes were troubling him increasingly. He was told that an operation was not advisable in his case, and he made the best of a lamentable situation by saying that he rather liked the strangely veiled and mysterious glow in which the visible world now appeared to him. Nevertheless—and unfortunately—he accepted a layman's advice and underwent some unconventional treatment which, in his own words, 'made things worse—at one time to an almost dangerous degree'. It seems that he was given thyroid injections which had a deleterious effect on his no longer rugged heart.

Despite all this, he put in two strenuous weeks of recording, which included Bach's *Chromatic Fantasy and Fugue*, some Mozart sonatas and Beethoven's cello sonatas with Pierre Fournier. He left London, visibly tired, and troubled in his mind about the thinking of Europeans in the light of recent political developments. This was the critical summer when the East-West tension was approaching its climax with the Soviet blockade of Berlin.

*   *   *

Regardless of political crises as of internal danger signals, Schnabel, always accompanied by the solicitous and now definitely worried Therese, left for his favourite Alpine resort to enjoy the invigorating air at 6,200 feet altitude. On the flight to Zürich he felt a pain in his chest but refused to see a doctor till they reached their hotel in Sils-Maria, where they knew of a famous physician, only to find him absent. A young substitute examined Artur but found no evidence of heart trouble. Thus reassured, the Schnabels settled down to the usual routine of work and walks—even occasional climbs—and soon he was deep in the composition of another symphony, his third, which he finished, save the orchestration, in the incredibly short period of four weeks. Hardly at the end of this task, he began to 'ramble over the keys', as he called it, trying over the six concertos he was expected to play in the course of the following month. And still he found time for companionship: Fournier, Backhaus and their wives were at his hotel, and George Széll came twice to visit him— concerned no doubt about his health.

Soon the anticipated summer repose was interrupted by a music festival in Lucerne, to which Schnabel contributed a performance of the Schumann concerto with the orchestra conducted by his Swiss friend Volkmar Andreæ; no sooner was this over than he was off to London and the Edinburgh Festival to play five Mozart concertos in three days with as many different conductors. And quite gratuitously he made a side trip from London to the south of England to lend his presence and prestige to a new venture inaugurated by one of his English pupils—a summer music school at Bryanston. Perceptibly slower in his movements, following out the dietary régime prescribed for him, and otherwise presenting the aspect of a convalescent, Schnabel persisted in carrying out the programme of one of the most strenuous summers of his career, almost as though he felt the need of continuous movement to keep the machine from running down. His Edinburgh duties over, he and Therese undertook the long journey back to Switzerland and on to Lake Como, to rest and attend to the shipment of his manuscripts to America.

Actually this purely incidental and somewhat nostalgic errand was just the kind of relaxation he needed. 'We are well,' he wrote Mrs. Tillett from Menaggio in late September, 'are having a kind of vacation here, and the weather is glorious.' But only five days later they were again in London before embarking for America, after Artur had gaily approved arrangements for two Albert Hall recitals in the spring of 1949!

Back in his Park-side home in New York, he wrote Nef a detailed account of his European summer, with only a casual reference to his health: 'I wasn't too well during the first few weeks. . . .

What worried him more than his own health, it seems, was the change in the post-war mentality of Europe under the impact of American power-political dominance.

'England, France and Italy seem materially, physically improved but morally deteriorated. Their one remaining distinction, a sense of nuance, is

apparently lost or discarded. Counter-colonization is marching on rapidly.
Primitivity is so convenient, thoughtlessness so promising, escape so attractive! The attitude of educated people was a great shock to me.'

With his fondness for verbal precision he used to say that disillusionment should be regarded as a good thing, since it meant getting rid
of illusions. But the process was none the less painful when he
experienced it himself. Paradoxically he may therefore have been
glad to return to his adopted country—the unwitting cause of his
European disappointment.

★   ★   ★

No sooner had he settled down in New York than Schnabel went
about his usual routine of work: teaching, playing, and thinking about
the orchestration of his new symphony, and the performance of his
Rhapsody for Orchestra by the New York Philharmonic-Symphony
under Mitropoulos in November. His first public appearance—an
echo of his recent chamber music activities in Edinburgh—was a
recital with Joseph Szigeti which drew a capacity audience to the
large Hunter College Auditorium, and which was to have notable
sequels on the Pacific coast the following spring of 1948. It was
another sign of Schnabel's renewed interest in ensemble playing—his
favourite occupation since the dawn of his career. But it also pointed
up the increasing difficulties imposed by his failing eyesight. Otherwise, however, his physical condition seemed to give him no cause
for worry, and even his eyes seemed a little better after some injections
with a cataract-absorbing fluid.

Alas! it was but the proverbial calm before a storm; but when the
lightning struck it first struck obliquely. At the age of seventy-two
the hardy and certainly mature Therese incredibly contracted a
severe case of mumps. Sad as it was in itself, the most fateful part of
this misfortune was that Schnabel was left to himself, deprived of the
loving vigilance of his patient wife, for in this very month of October
he had a recurrence of his chest pains and a severe warning from the
very doctor he should have consulted many months before. At long
last a strict régime was prescribed for him, but apart from this he
continued to live normally in all conceivable respects.

Therese was soon out of danger but remained in the care of a
nurse for the better part of six weeks, while Artur went about his
usual concerns. In November he attended all the four rehearsals of
his *Rhapsody*, and both he and Therese were present at the performance in Carnegie Hall. It was a truly great occasion. The work

received what Schnabel called an absolutely satisfying interpretation. Whatever doubts he may have had about its worth were gone, and he was gratified to recognize it as 'a good piece, of a type of which there is hardly another example'. Its public success this time was just about what he had expected: Schnabel himself was given a moving ovation, though much of it doubtless was a tribute to him as the great pianist and an almost universally loved artistic personality. In any case it was one of his most gratifying triumphs and surely one of the high points of his great career. Even the Press reviews could not dim its brilliance.

A little over three weeks after the great event, fate struck its bitterest blow. Schnabel's weakened heart, strained by the strenuous summer and the prodigal expenditure of energy following his return, was unequal to the excitements of recent weeks. On December 11th he suffered an almost fatal attack of coronary thrombosis, and for more than three weeks lay within the shadow of death under an oxygen tent. Luckily Therese had completely regained her health and was able to devote all her strength to his care, which became more and more arduous as the weeks of vigil wore on.

On Christmas Eve the crisis had been passed and the slow road to recovery—a partial one at best—began. The news of the near-catastrophe was kept from public knowledge, thanks to the fact that his American engagements did not begin till late in the season. But even those had to be cancelled and in mid-January Therese wrote to London that all his European concerts must be postponed for a year. By February he was considered out of danger, and was permitted to see friends—singly and sparingly—through the month of March. Not till late in April did he begin to play on his piano, and to make short and very slow walks in the Park—under the watchful eyes of a stern, dragooning nurse. His spirit was pathetically low, and he took none too kindly to the comforting words of solicitous friends.

To his great relief the doctors held out hope that he might be able to keep an engagement to play two Mozart concertos at the San Francisco Festival that spring, and thus redeem a promise made in gratitude to the courageous Mitropoulos, one of the first conductors to recognize Schnabel's creative genius. A wave of hope swept through the circle of followers and admirers who had learned of his plight through the grapevine of friends. He, however, seemed a broken man—not wholly without hope but coldly realistic in his self-analysis. Something, he felt, had irrevocably gone out of him. He would continue to compose, to say what he had to say. He would even play, for he still considered it an economic necessity. He certainly hoped to make more records, for that was an investment for his family's future. His sense of responsibility toward his dependents was unimpaired, but the time was running out.

★   ★

By the middle of April Schnabel was writing letters again, complaining to Walter Legge in London about the irksome 'medical regimentation' imposed by the doctors, and assuring him that he was much better: 'the grass is gradually beginning to grow on the ruin.' He was even talking about next year's London concerts, deciding what Mozart concertos to play, what Beethoven trios (with Szigeti and Fournier), and where. As for the present, all arrangements had been made for the San Francisco appearances in May, and he and Therese set out for the Coast on the 10th. Three and four days later he played his two Mozart concertos [1] in the Memorial Opera House, with Mitropoulos conducting, in the presence of an enormous, cheering crowd. It was a great and comforting occasion for all concerned and, according to him, 'neither strenuous nor harmful'.

But convalescence was slow, and contrary to expectations he had to spend more than a month at a San Francisco hotel. A minor operation was necessary in order to 'remove some bad matter' that had plagued him; but by July he was 'looking forward to better days'. After a long and futile search for a salubrious place in which to rebuild his health, he and Therese settled for a house at Los Gatos in Santa Cruz county, not far from San Francisco, belonging to a distant relative who accommodatingly spent the summer in Europe. Here, between the mountains and the sea, he led what he called a leisurely life but soon was 'back to his music paper'. In other words, he was orchestrating his third symphony. 'I am attracted by the "fun" of orchestrating—an almost entirely arbitrary process if one doesn't follow prescriptions,' he wrote to Szigeti. Only a few weeks earlier he had written that he was still 'a useless mass—a helpless worm'.

The third symphony is the shortest of Schnabel's symphonies, and consists of three movements, of which the first two are entitled Fantasia and Dance. The Finale consists of an Introduzione, followed by a Tema, given out by the solo piano, which is a quotation from one of his youthful works, and a series of free variations on the latter. It is cast in a more flexible mould than its two predecessors,

[1] G major (K. 453), B-flat major (K. 595).

and contains many evidences that his musical language has become·
more supple, more mature, and perhaps even more personal than in
the earlier works. The texture is, once again, clearer if not simpler
than in his preceding works; the Fantasia especially seems in a certain
sense the quintessence of Schnabel's music, in its far-flung lines and
its rhapsodic sweep. The daring entrance of the Tema in the third
movement, in the purest D major, is enchanting, as is also the gradual
transition from its close to the complex harmonies and tonal relationships which form the stuff of Schnabel's mature style, and consequently
of the movement as a whole.

During the weeks of his convalescence he had resumed reading—
not books of fiction to distract his mind but T. S. Eliot's *Idea of a
Christian Society,* which he thought tedious, and Somervell's con-
densation of Toynbee's *History of Civilization* which he found instructive and even fascinating. It is characteristic that one of the first
things he reached for was the latest issue of the weekly *Common
Cause* and very soon he was fulminating about 'academic' contributors
who felt it necessary to compromise with the current political trends.
'What I miss entirely is the *cantus firmus* "Peace is life; war is death!"
There is no way out of this truism.' Writing to Nef, he vented
his impatience with the 'slow' organizers of the United World
Federalists, then only 45,000 strong, which should be 'four and a half
million by now'.

However, the climate of the Santa Cruz region was just right for
him and by mid-September he was well enough to travel to Chicago
to spend some time with his friends the Oldbergs, then on to New
York and back to the unending quest.

Schnabel, toward the end of his career, _c._ 1948

Artur Schnabel in 1950

34. The Last Battle

WHEN the sixty-seven-year-old Schnabel returned home after his four months' sojourn in California his convalescence seemed to be complete. He had aged visibly as the result of his illness but showed no outward signs of infirmity. His hair and moustache had been white for some years; his movements, always deliberate, were slower and his step a trifle less firm, due perhaps to his steadily failing sight. His mood was reasonably cheerful though subdued, and there was still the same friendly smile and the occasional twinkle in his eyes.

'I am now fairly presentable again,' he wrote to Walter Legge in October 1949, 'but still a bit short of energy and out of the habit of being active.' Indeed, he had not touched the piano for ten months, with the single exception of the two Mozart concertos he had played at San Francisco in May. He had decided not to try the keyboard again till December and to let the result determine whether to give concerts again or not. But he was by no means idle in the interim He was working on some articles for a new magazine being launched by an academic group in Chicago, which turned out to be 'too low for the highbrow and too high for lowbrow' (the middlebrow having 'died out'), and he was preparing two lectures he had to deliver at Harvard University late in November. By this time he reported himself to be very busy again and continuously improving in health.

His projected encounter with the keyboard turned out to his satisfaction. As a result he confirmed a long-postponed engagement in Havana for March and a promise to play the Beethoven G major concerto with George Széll in a pair of Chicago symphony concerts the following month. Thus, after the longest hiatus in his half-century of concert performances, he decided to continue the career he had wanted to end at various times since he entered middle age. If ever there was a valid reason for stopping, it was now. He had passed through the first serious illness of his life, and he had been warned. But there were still things to do, and the urge to do them was irresistible. Those Mozart concertos were still revealing new and subtle beauties at every fresh performance. Some of the Beethoven sonatas he had recorded *in toto* had still to be re-recorded if he was to fulfil his obligation to their creator. 'These works become more and more amazing and mysterious,' he wrote to Nef some months later, 'while the preparation of their execution with ten fingers on a hundred keys may seem boring and often ridiculous'. It was clear that whatever he did, play or not play the piano, the quest—his assignment—would continue while he lived. The career had been imposed from above and would not be ended by him.

The concerts went well—better than anyone had a right to expect. He treated his first Havana audience to a Beethoven–Mozart–Schubert programme ending with Beethoven's opus 109, and it stood the test. The Chicago concerts, after the removal of an unsatisfactory piano and the arrival of a substitute, ended in a tremendous ovation. He had passed his sixty-eighth birthday as usual—in harness. On April 27th Therese wrote jubilantly to Mrs. Tillett in London that Artur had played five successful concerts, that he 'felt marvellous and was happy that he could do it without any strain'. That very evening Londoners heard the first European performance of Schnabel's *Rhapsody for Orchestra*, played by the Philharmonia Orchestra under Paul Kletzki, and a few days later the work was recorded by the Columbia Graphophone Company of Great Britain in a famous series of recordings sponsored by His Highness the Maharaja of Mysore.

A month later Artur and Therese sailed once again for England. Artur was scheduled to make some new recordings (Schubert's posthumous sonatas and all the Schubert *Impromptus*), but the concerts originally planned for London were postponed to 1951—the Festival of Britain year. The recordings, however, turned out to everyone's satisfaction and with much less strain than he had expected. He was delighted to be back in London again, in his 'cosy' Hyde Park Hotel, to be welcomed by his old and admiring friends whose ranks, alas! were slowly thinning out. . . . The weather was unusually fine and the light-blue skies of the English spring as luminous as he remembered them from his happiest years. But he was anxious now to get back to his beloved Swiss mountains and to composition, for something that would satisfy him was 'already prepared from within'.

The high altitudes were now forbidden to him because of his heart. Someone had selected a less elevated but exceptionally beautiful spot—the hotel at Axenstein, above the shores of Lake Lucerne, and not far from the spot where he and his son Stefan had stopped on their northward journey over a quarter-century before. In this idyllic place—'beautiful beyond description'—he sat down to write a piece in twelve-part counterpoint called simply *Duodecimet*—a short four-movement work which came as near to abstract music as anything he had ever written, yet obviously meant for performance, since indications for instrumentation are sketched in at isolated spots. Unhampered by material considerations, he came nearest to achieving what he had striven for in all his later works: the utmost freedom in melodic, rhythmic and polyphonic design and expression. The sheer intellectual concentration and the spiritual serenity required for this work suggests a remarkable faculty of withdrawal from the world into that realm of ideal creation which he characterized as 'transcendental' and which to him was the ultimate refuge of man on this earth.

★   ★   ★

It is all the more remarkable that in his sober and realistic moods he was still as turbulent and explosive as ever. He had kept abreast of world affairs throughout his convalescence, had seen his friends—one by one—and indulged in protracted arguments, though at a greatly reduced tempo, on the benches as well as the paths of Central Park, and now in his summer retreat. He had kept up intermittent correspondence with Nef and other friends, and could not rid himself of preoccupation with the cause of peace. The outbreak of the Korean War cast a shadow over a summer which promised to bring the resumption of the happy vacations that symbolized his reunion with the old continent without abandoning his allegiance to the new. 'We have a war,' he wrote Nef from Axenstein, 'a very shabby and shameful war . . . yet one with real mutual killing. How long and with what aim? For the first time I feel myself in danger of wanting to become indifferent, and I don't like it.' But there was no sign of indifference in his brooding on the future of civilization and what he considered the progressive brutalization of man; and he eagerly seized the opportunity of arguing about the state of the world during a visit from John Nef and his wife Elinor, for Nef had just completed his book, *War and Human Progress*.

About the middle of August the Schnabels moved to Menaggio on Lake Como, the residence of their friend Dr. Fritz Fischer, where they were in close touch with a younger generation of Schnabels, Karl Ulrich and Helen, now permanently installed in a house at Tremezzo and not far from the Villa Ginetta of precious memory. Altogether it may be said that with this prolonged and refreshing sojourn in one of the most salubrious parts of Europe the old pattern and tempo, if not the old vigour, of Schnabel's activity had been partially re-established. His confidence in his own capacities restored, he wrote to Mrs. Tillett—now sole head of the London management firm—asking her to settle the details of his projected return to English concert life in the spring of next year.

★   ★   ★

Late in September Artur and Therese sailed from Le Havre in anticipation of a fairly active season in America, with a little teaching and some playing, along with the happiest of all employments— preparing his recent compositions for performance. The third symphony was to have its first hearing under Mitropoulos and the New York Philharmonic Symphony either that season or the next.

The autumn months passed in rather leisurely uneventful fashion. Schnabel was again immersed in the re-study of Beethoven sonatas, with a view to recitals in New York and Chicago and, possibly, in anticipation of the re-recording of several of them for His Master's Voice. Friends came one by one; pupils more rarely than before, since he had to husband his strength. Reading and correspondence were becoming more difficult, as he was now nearly blind. His thinking and his conversation were still largely concerned with secular matters, since 'the troubles of human society in our rather unfortunate age', as he remarked to the young American painter Armand Merizon, 'hardly permit one to have an undisturbed mind'.

This recently acquired admirer was one of the first people to whom in an unguarded moment he confessed the wretched state of his health. The young middle-westerner had journeyed to Cleveland to hear Schnabel play Beethoven's C minor concerto with the orchestra conducted by George Széll—his first public appearance of the season. In answer to a frank question put to him before the concert he gave a frank answer: he was not feeling well, being 'incapacitated' by the terrible condition of his eyes and confused by the glare of the bright lights on the keys. What he did not say—or know—was that these were only the symptoms of a much deeper disturbance. Indeed he now felt doubtful whether he could go through with these concerts, and asked himself whether he should not give up playing altogether. He looked weak and downcast, and his young friend was deeply disturbed. But to Merizon's utter amazement Schnabel appeared on the platform that evening almost like his old self—serene and self-possessed—to play with the same expressive power, with all the apparent ease and the majesty of former years: a miraculous example of the spirit conquering the flesh.

The public's response was tremendous as always, without a hint of knowledge or suspicion that anything was amiss. The same experience was repeated at the second concert. It had been the most critical test of his powers, thus far. His own judgment of the performance was expressed dispassionately as 'pretty good'.

A little more than a week after he returned to New York Therese missed a step and fell, seriously hurting her back. For days she lay motionless and in severe pain; and her recovery required almost ten weeks—a misfortune as cruel as it was undeserved. Capably nursed though she was, it was Artur's task to keep her spirits high. Yet in the midst of all his troubles he still corresponded and planned the work-schedule of his British tour the following year. More immediate was the preparation of his Beethoven recital in New York, scheduled to take place at the Hunter College Auditorium in January. For some time after the Cleveland experience he had seriously considered cancelling it. But spurred on by a chimerical sense of pride or duty, he decided to go through with it and make it the crucial test of his career. Four Beethoven sonatas, including the *Pathétique*, the A major opus 101, the E minor opus 90, and the C major (*Waldstein*) opus 53. Here again were the same difficulties: failing stability and the still unexplained trouble with his eyes. But again the miracle occurred: his will-power and his complete identification with the spirit of the master raised him above the infirmities of the hour. He played as though in a trance, avoiding the terrible glare of the keys by looking sideways and upwards toward imaginary heights, but drawing from within himself the most profound revelation of the spirit of these works he had ever achieved, expressed with the most delicately precise articulation of every phrase. The climax came with the C major sonata (the *Waldstein*), when all earthly woe seemed to dissolve in the ethereal trills of the finale, evaporate in the luminous veils of iridescent sound. Never had even he, so it seemed, succeeded in conjuring up so magical a vision of the infinite.

One remembers certain concerts simply because they are unforgettable; this last recital of Schnabel in New York will continue to be one of the most precious shared reminiscences of kindred souls. The great auditorium of Hunter College was filled to capacity with one of the most representative musical audiences that New York's population could produce. Rumours about Schnabel's condition had spread through the profession and to a part of the public, so that many came with a sense of foreboding, to hear him once again. Surely Beethoven had never been listened to with more rapt attention, more devotion and a greater community of feeling.

To Schnabel the important fact was that once again it had taken less effort than he had feared. Yet there was a difference between this second test and the first; something unexpressed and indefinable; and it was this that made him—several weeks later—cancel the Chicago and the second New York recitals that were to have taken place in March and April. Still in ignorance of his real condition he wrote to Nef, that he was 'fortunately' not really ill, yet increasingly passive and increasingly 'bored with the amount of attention being spent on my body'. His body, in fact, was beyond human solicitude: the Hunter College recital was fated to be his last. His immediate and obvious trouble was his failing eyesight, which made writing more and more of an effort. But most disquieting was the remark that he had 'actually nothing to say'.

The months which followed the concert were not happy ones. Artur was struggling to regain his health—half-heartedly as it were, for he was not clear about the nature of his affliction. He had already foregone most of the little joys of life: his diet was the most stringent —no salt, no sugar, no stimulants of any kind. Years before he had given up smoking, once the uninterrupted accompaniment of all his informal working and leisure hours. Reading was becoming more and more difficult, and possible only with strong optical aids. His one indispensable recreation was still walking and talking with friends. But the pace of the once intrepid mountaineer had been slowed to a saunter, and the visits of friends had more and more to be doled out, lest they fatigue him unduly.

With all this he remained mildly good-humoured and friendly, though sombre and more than ever pessimistic about the future of civilization. 'The two-fold activity of feverishly trying to improve the way of life and at the same time to improve the way of death is a gruesome spectacle,' he wrote to Nef. He was profoundly and seriously discouraged by the failure of statesmen and leaders to control the use of the new forces unleashed by atomic science; and frankly alarmed at the prospect of a war of annihilation—unless reason and idealism could be rallied to the defence of what he called the 'higher values' of life. These morose speculations, further stimulated by the increasingly disquieting news from Korea, were not conducive to the restoration of health.

March and April were very difficult months. Artur had another attack of bronchial pneumonia, and not till the worst was over did the hard-tried Therese admit how ill he had been. On April 30th she reported that he was 'recovering nicely', that he looked much better and was no longer so depressed. He himself had written to Mrs. Tillett in London that one must not complain, but in comparison with former days he had to be content with the life of 'a sort of idler'. At the same time, however, he was able to comment jokingly on the new Festival Hall in which he was to play in June, hoping that it would be free from the 'artificial winds' as well as the echoes and reverberations of its predecessor. On April 21, however, he had written Walter Legge that he felt very doubtful about being able to make the promised re-recordings of Beethoven in June, adding that he was now often frustrated by a 'disturbance of equilibrium—certainly not the right condition for musical performance on a piano'. By early May he was feeling better than he had been for many months, and was looking forward with particular pleasure to the two Beethoven concertos he was to play with his old and greatly admired friend Otto Klemperer, who despite the tragic illness which had partly paralysed him was reputed to be at the very peak of his interpretive powers.

On May 25th the Schnabels sailed in what was now their favourite ship, the *Caronia*, and were soon settled in their favourite London hotel, the Hyde Park. They planned to fly to Axenstein after the concerts were over and repeat the pleasant routine of the summer before. In the meantime they would live quietly, accepting no invitations, and eating in their special little Kensington café where the French proprietor knew them well and served the dishes required by their very strict diets—'deliciously prepared'. Here very close friends came to eat with them and cheer them on.

* * *

By the middle of June Artur was ill again. The concerts had to be cancelled. Either as the result of medical advice, or because of an irresistible inner urge to see his beloved mountains again, or because of an almost child-like faith in the mysterious curative powers of nature, Artur himself decided on an immediate departure for Axenstein, going as far as Zürich by air. That this trip would entail the most frightful suffering of his life no one could foresee. The immediate cause was an acute attack of uræmia, the result of previously unexplained troubles resulting in a gradual deterioration of his kidneys. Through three abominable hours of noise and vibration, as

Therese described it, his pains were so terrible with no possible relief for the duration of the flight, that he was close to delirium before the landing of the plane. Speedily taken to the hotel in Axenstein he had immediate and competent medical care, and soon the acute symptoms were partly relieved. But his suffering went on almost without interruption with increasing strain on his greatly weakened heart.

The strain on Therese, whose vigilance and devotion provided all the conceivable succour and comfort in a desperate situation, may be left to the imagination. She provided the physical and emotional force which made the situation humanly bearable through many interminable weeks, while keeping the nearest friends informed. During the final week of July she reported a tragic improvement: the patient had for the first time ceased to beg for the merciful relief of death. About a week later he slept through several consecutive hours—for the first time since the crisis began.

A competent male nurse had been procured, whose intelligence and natural kindness did much to allay suffering and ease the burden. Under his care the Schnabels were to move to a small and charmingly situated sanatorium known as the Sonnenberg. Therese looked confidently forward to a slow convalescence in this lovely spot. However, a fresh crisis interrupted the plan, and they never reached the 'sunny hill' of their hopes. During a lull in the period of renewed suffering he made all necessary disposition for the future of his family, for Therese's residence in Tremezzo, and for the proper distribution of his earthly goods. Then Artur passed peacefully away, on August 15th.

He was buried, in the presence of a small group of friends and neighbours from the immediate vicinity, from Italy and from England, in the little cemetery of Schwyz, that idyllic spot in the verdant plain guarded by the two stark granite sentinels long familiar to him and designated in the guidebooks as The Myths. It was the landscape he had loved so well, the spot of which he had once remarked that he would not mind being buried there.

Despite his terrible sufferings he was able to look steadfastly on death, conscious of the great and unforgettable part to which he had been assigned. 'I have had a rich and wonderfully beautiful life,' he said to his wife, 'but now it is enough. You must not be sad: you must rejoice at my merciful release.'

35. Conclusion

IT was indeed 'a rich and wonderful life' that Artur Schnabel could look back upon in the final hours of his almost three-score-and-ten. Richly gifted from early childhood, favoured by nearly uninterrupted good health and a rare genius for friendship, he was privileged to labour at his appointed task unceasingly from youth to age, without ever swerving from his avowed dedication to his art or making the usual concessions to material success. He played, taught, wrote and thought music from his 'teens to his last days, and accepted the inevitable as he had envisioned it. 'Life's most revealing experience,' he said, 'is that as you get near the horizon your vision expands . . . toward infinity.'

He followed his vision, serving his only 'employer'—the art of music—with complete humility and a kind of proprietary solicitude which was often mistaken for stubbornness. 'My vocation was determined for me when I was a child,' he used to say; 'I have followed it ever since.'

His vocation was to be an all-round musician in the traditional eighteenth-century sense. This helped him to resist the blandishments of a premature fame as a 'virtuoso'—a word which he called 'self-contradictory'. Genuine virtue to him lay in a complete devotion to music, including not only playing and teaching but composing. He held fast to this idea even through the fallow periods of his expanding career as a pianist, and through the almost constant public neglect of his works. He accepted this stoically, and did little to encourage acceptance of his compositions, which became longer, more difficult and less accessible with the years. If he felt any disappointment or bitterness in this respect he never expressed it; but counted the rare and much belated performances of some of his quartets and symphonic works among the happiest moments of his life. He was seemingly so convinced of the authenticity of his futuristic visions that he was content to labour for a problematical posterity. Whether his faith will prove to be justified remains to be seen; but we know that it was the faith of a highly intelligent, self-critical man, capable of measuring his abilities by the most 'advanced' standards of his time.

As a teacher, Schnabel occupied a position of eminence through-out his professional life of more than five decades. His influence on his own and succeeding generations of pianists was probably the greatest since Liszt, however different in its orientation. He was the great advocate of inwardness in musical thinking, of truthfulness and clarity in musical expression. Faithfulness to the masters' will was to him the basic law of all piano playing, and the realization of their will was his sole and ultimate aim. Beauty of tone, power and speed were all factors subservient to that aim: the personality of the player was secondary; his business was not to arouse the admiration of an audience but to secure its participation in the musical experience. Hence his chief desire as a teacher was to achieve a deeper and wider understanding of the meaning and content of music, rather than keyboard proficiency. In this sense, his influence will continue, thanks partly to his own editions of the piano sonatas of Beethoven and Mozart (the latter only partially completed), and to his recordings of works by Beethoven, Mozart, Bach, Schubert, Schumann and Brahms, for an indefinite time.

*   *   *

So far as the present generation is concerned, it is Schnabel the pianist who occupies the most compelling position in the public's mind. In an age of pianistic giants such as d'Albert, Busoni, Paderewski and Rachmaninof, he is recognized as unique and inimitable in his way—not by virtue of any prodigious physical powers or technical brilliance (which he possessed abundantly), but by a self-effacing penetration to the spirit and meaning of the music itself. It was this utmost concentration on the composer's meaning, its profundity and nobility, its poetry and exaltation, its humour and wit, that gave his playing its unique quality, though yet always meticulously faithful to the text. Much has been written about the beauty of his tone, his perfect *legato*, his vivid rhythms, his finely graded dynamic range, his expressive modelling of the phrase, and his command of the musical structure—the *Gestaltung* of a piece. His was, as Walter J. Turner put it, 'the most virile, tender, passionate and intellectual playing' one had ever heard. It compelled attention, not by any external means, but as a crystal-clear, sustained and lucid argument from beginning to end. 'Music,' he used to say, 'must be experienced, not consumed.' It was this insistence on *experiencing* the music which accounted for the unfailing spontaneity of his playing—as though each performance were the first.

To him the core of this experience was love. 'Absolute music,' he wrote, 'exists in a region of personal experience which is closely identified with the eternal concept of love. Man discovered in music its peculiar fitness to be the carrier of this emotion.' To him a true musician was not only a man in love with music but one who was *loved by music*—whose mind and being was possessed by music'. And when it came to the music of the great masters his love was without reserve. 'We must love it as we find it,' he told his pupils, 'and love even what we believe to be its faults, for these are as intrinsic a part of the composer's make-up as his greatest achievements'.

Next to the quality of his playing the most distinctive factor in Schnabel's career was his choice of works. His programmes were models of good taste, almost from the days of his youth to the end of his career. All through the days of his ensemble playing he covered virtually the entire literature of chamber music, including a great many contemporary composers, not to mention the prodigious number of vocal works he performed with his wife. As he grew older his repertoire became more restricted in quality while still increasing in quantity, until he arrived at his well-known resolve to play only music that is 'better than it can be played'. This meant that he conceived it to be his duty to play those works of the great masters which presented perennial problems of interpretation, or re-creation. Thus in the course of time he arrived at the most exacting works of that select company of immortals—the masters of what we call the German school. Yet within that prescribed orbit was comprised an enormous number of works which were seldom played and still more seldom adequately performed. Thus his repertoire, though limited in the end to a mere handful of composers, has rarely been equalled in the quantity of works and never surpassed in the specific gravity of its worth. However, he never considered his reputed austerity a particular virtue, since he was actually pleasing himself. 'Some are many-sided,' he said, 'and some are one-sided. I am quite content to be one-sided. . . . I love those works which never cease to present new problems and are therefore an ever-fresh experience.'

Future generations will be indebted to Schnabel for his pioneer work in revitalizing the pianist's repertoire by restoring to it the neglected and lesser known works of the great classic and romantic composers. It was he who revived many of the forgotten piano works of Schubert, mainly the sonatas, which he was probably the first of his generation to play in public. Today they are recognized for the inspired creations they are, not only by the fact of his re-discovery but through his understanding of their spirit and originality. Even the popular *Impromptus*, which in his youth were 'the favourite occupation of governesses', had a rebirth at his very masculine hands.

There is little doubt that Schnabel will be remembered chiefly as the greatest Beethoven player of his time. The study of Beethoven was a natural step in his development, and it is significant that it came relatively late in his career. It was also appropriate to the generation in which he lived, and in which he had been preceded by the fiery and 'titanic' d'Albert, who in turn succeeded Hans von Bülow—the pugnacious pioneer who made up in courage what he lacked in piety.

By a curious but convincing logic, Schnabel's long preoccupation with Beethoven led him back to Mozart as the source and origin of this inexhaustible treasure. One by one, Schnabel revived the Mozart concertos and the piano sonatas, and this became the last great accomplishment of his career. 'Mozart's music is universal,' he wrote in his early sixties. 'It is transcendental and representative, above time and locality. It is the symbol of man's position in the universe and his reaction to the universe. It is the best that man can spiritually accomplish.' He had reopened a path which the new generation of pianists, many of them his own pupils, are following today.

*   *   *

Beyond his purely artistic endowment and accomplishment the most characteristic trait in Schnabel's personality was his essentially ethical attitude to music—a factor which informed not only his work but his daily life, and which was often misinterpreted as a kind of personal pride. Speaking for his colleagues, a well-known conductor said after Schnabel's death that he had been 'our conscience'. Music to him was truly sacred; and this fact gave a certain touch of solemnity and even severity to his manner.

He refused to admit that art is ever the response to a demand. On the contrary, he believed that all artistic creation—and re-creation —precedes the demand. 'A call must precede the echo,' he wrote. 'A caller who hears no echo will change his place,' though 'perhaps by intuition he will call only in the place where an echo awaits its awakening.' It is a propensity of dedicated people to speak in parables, to utter *obiter dicta* which are likely to be misunderstood. It was Schnabel's fate to be misunderstood by many people during much of his life; but by the same token he gathered around him everywhere small groups of disciples, who did understand him and who followed him with a singular loyalty and a sense of privilege. This little band of the faithful were never put off by his rigid adherence to principle nor by his stern judgment of those who fell from grace.

In matters of music Schnabel remained an inflexible purist to the end of his days. When he said that he served only music, he not only meant it, but he wanted all similarly endowed musicians to do the same. When successful artists played inferior music in order to please the public he maintained that they were really pleasing themselves. 'If they liked only the best,' he would say, 'they would be incapable of succeeding with the worst.' Everyone, he professed to believe, plays the music he likes. It was this critical attitude—not about how others played but *what* they played—that made him almost a lone wolf in his profession.

His judgment of other interpreters was generally fair, and even lenient—though not always free from gentle sarcasm. 'It could not have been better,' he said after the concert of an eminent colleague, 'but it should have been more beautiful.' When a new pianist was described to him as 'mediocre' he pointed out that mediocrity is 'a very exalted grade, when you consider how much is below it and how little above'. He was intolerant of bad or unworthy programmes, of unnecessary transcriptions or arrangements and all other forms of malfeasance against the composer. And there is no record of his ever having been guilty of any such himself.

*   *   *

From the moment Schnabel entered a hall, his concern was solely with the music. He walked toward the piano as though he were about to open a door; and when the door was opened the result was so compelling that the corporeal Schnabel almost ceased to exist. There was no attempt at contact with the audience except through the music, no outward appeal for their favour. While he played he wanted nothing but reciprocity for what he gave—full participation in the music. The most impassioned *fortissimo*, the most delicate delivery of a phrase or a bravura passage were produced by the same almost motionless and apparently effortless process. Once in a while there might be an involuntary turning of the head away from the audience—an unconscious gesture in the effort toward still deeper concentration. Sometimes, during an especially blissful phrase of Mozart, a beatific smile towards the upward regions would break unwittingly over his countenance, but even this was rare.

At symphony concerts his deportment was always correct and

cordial, within the bounds of dignity, with short, quick bows and a courteous acknowledgment to the conductor, and a handshake with the leader of the orchestra. Few artists could establish so warm a relationship with an orchestra, though there were times—at rehearsal— when the contact with the orchestra was too direct for the conductor's taste. What he could not tolerate was lack of attention, slipshod playing and inadequate rehearsal. Once, in London, the orchestra had too little time to rehearse a Mozart concerto adequately. After only forty minutes' work Schnabel protested and threatened not to play at the concert. Persuaded to relent, he sent a letter to *The Times* explaining the performer's duty to the composer. Since Mozart isn't here to defend his work, he said in effect, I must do it in his place.

Next to inadequately rehearsed orchestras, he hated inattentive or disturbing listeners. Asked about the relative merit of audiences, he liked to say that there were only two kinds: those that cough and those that don't. He was intolerant to the degree of petulance in his judgment of listeners who were insensitive or lacking in respect to the masters. Exasperated by a fashionable but cold-infected audience in springtime London, he once broke off in the middle of a Schubert posthumous sonata. Recalled by persistent applause, he inquired whether the listeners wished him to play the whole sonata again from the beginning. They did, and there wasn't a cough in the house for the duration of the four long movements.

The interruption of a work was anathema to him, whatever the cause. At an Edinburgh Festival, playing a Brahms piano quartet with three famous colleagues, first one then another broke a string. The damage repaired, the string players signalled that they were ready to proceed. Schnabel, however, suggested asking the audience whether it might not prefer having the work repeated from the beginning, and got enthusiastic assent. He could not bear the thought of 'damaged' performances: the composer had a right to be properly heard. It was this complete absorption by the music, and his sense of its importance to human life and happiness, that accounted for his inflexible insistence on the proper physical conditions for musical performance—a part of his never-ending fight against indifference, the arch-enemy of artistic accomplishment. Lecturing at Harvard University on 'The Limitations of Music', he said that the most serious limitation of music is its complete defencelessness.

'Music cannot of itself provide the intimacy and the privacy without which it cannot be given or taken. These conditions have to be the consequence of a spiritual or cultural conscience within the community as a whole.'

Raised in a generation and an environment in which music was held in reverence and enjoyed with discrimination, he became more and more conscious in his later years of a change in the general attitude toward art and its place in society. He felt that musical performance had lost much of its adequacy, dignity and purity. He regretted this as a deterioration of our culture, similar to that which affected other human creations in this age. 'Spiritual life,' he said, 'is not adapted to mass production—at least not yet.'

★   ★   ★

Any attempt at a characterization of Schnabel apart from his music is bound to fail, for the man without his music is incomplete. Yet he was a commanding and fascinating personality, a man of prodigious will-power who was certain to succeed in anything he undertook, with a personal charm which captivated people in various walks of life. Above all he was the possessor of a powerful mentality, an unabashed 'intellectual' with a vigorous curiosity and very keen powers of observation. His philosophy was a broadly human idealism, combined with a deep spirituality and benevolence which came close to Christianity, but without any sectarian ties. 'If we have the Sermon on the Mount,' he once said, 'we need little else.' The essential quality in his moral arsenal was a sense of duty— duty not only to one's social environment but to the spiritual universe which was reflected in the arts of man. Essentially he was what might be called a mystical agnostic.

He spoke of Nature as of a deity, the source of man's most precious gifts, the provider of his greatest joys:

> 'Nature is responsible for our endowments, which are unequal; it has singled out the few to be an aristocracy of the spirit, an aristocracy which is not a class but an obligation—not only to receive but to develop and improve and continue striving upwards toward fulfilment. . . . This implies a constant insecurity and dissatisfaction which is man's armour against indifference, and expresses his faith in humanity and its high destiny.'

To him, man's earthly destiny, symbolically speaking, was the writing of Beethoven string quartets or their equivalent. In other words, his true religion was music, which to him was the highest expression of man's aspiration.

Away from the subject of music, Schnabel was a gay companion, kind, good-humoured and—until the shadows of illness and world tragedy darkened his life—a sociable though hardly a gregarious person. In the choice conclave of friends he was always the centre of attraction and attention. All through his life he was fond of telling an amusing story or airing his feelings about the passing scene, and he had a decided weakness for his own jokes, *bon mots*, puns, and sundry linguistic tricks. 'I may be praised for my playing,' he said, speaking of his after-life, 'but I'll be punished for my puns.'

★   ★   ★

Summing up Schnabel's position in the culture of his time, one might say that he was above all an artist gifted with almost unique insight, with powers of interpretation and communication unsurpassed in his generation, and a creative genius of undoubted originality but of still undetermined calibre. Although a legitimate carrier of the great Germanic tradition in his complete identification with the masters of the classical and romantic past, he was a convinced modernist and a bold pioneer glimpsing with sharp clairvoyance the still untrodden paths of the future of musical art. In his own generation, covering the first half of the present century, he exercised a powerful moral influence in upholding the æsthetic ideals of the pre-Wagnerian era in an age of noisy materialism, mass-production, confusion and dilution of values. He would have been a towering figure in the music of any period; in his own he was indispensable and almost unique.

Apart from his artistic accomplishment, Schnabel was certainly one of the most articulate musicians of his generation and, as Lawrence Gilman said, a musical philosopher of real distinction: a man who not only inspired a small army of pupils and followers by precept and example, but who pondered and wrote widely on the origins and ultimate destiny of his art. He conceived music to be the outgrowth of 'an idealistic faith in an esoteric glory, and an indestructible power that is identical with humility, a power within the grasp of everyone if only he be guided by love, kindliness, abstinence and the willingness to suffer'.[1] Music to Schnabel was an experience which resulted from man's communion with his soul: it was not only the purest and most spiritual of the arts, but the sublimation of all that is great and noble in human experience—a 'mysterious, inevitable, tangible and producible reality, cosmically related and individually fashioned'. He experienced it both as the result and the source of inspiration. 'I hope,' he once said, 'never to see the day when I sit at a piano uninspired.' So far as we know, he never did.

[1] *Reflections on Music* (University of Manchester, 1933).

Supplement

ON ARTUR SCHNABEL'S COMPOSITIONS

BY ERNST KŘENEK

DURING Artur Schnabel's lifetime there were not many people who knew much about his activity as a composer. Those who did were mostly inclined to regard it as a hobby in which the master pianist indulged off and on when no more entertaining pastime seemed to be on hand. The fact, however, is that to Artur Schnabel composing music was just as important and permanent a vehicle of self-expression as piano playing. In the last two decades of his life the creation of music subjectively even took precedence over its interpretation. His earliest composition extant was written at the age of fourteen, and he never stopped writing music to the last year of his life. He has left an *œuvre* that would be impressive by its quantity if by nothing else.

If this comes to many as a surprise, the question arises as to how it happened that during the life of its creator this important body of music found so little recognition that even its existence has remained practically unknown. Here was a man who for many years stood in the limelight as an interpreter of music, commanding the respect, admiration and love of vast audiences all over the world. And yet only a few of his compositions were played occasionally without gaining a clearly defined place in the musical topography of the century. A comparison with other 'virtuosi' who were also composers insinuates itself. Both Franz Liszt and Serge Rachmaninof, the latter an older contemporary of Schnabel's, held dominating positions in the field of interpretation, but both were equally recognized as composers in their own right. An external difference of attitude may serve as an easy explanation. Unlike his great fellow-pianists, Schnabel never promoted his music as his own interpreter. For reasons of his own he never played any contemporary music as a soloist, and that included his own music as well.

However, this is not the whole story. To say that Schnabel's music did not find recognition because it lacked public appeal would be inconclusive. We could say this only if we at the same time realize that this music, in spite of its obvious lack of popular appeal, is of

317

remarkable and unusual significance. To some extent its very significance is a cause of its limited external success. In fact, Schnabel's
early compositions have all the conventional characteristics of pleasant,
effective piano music. But the author would have been the first to
protest vividly if anybody had ascribed to those works profound
significance. As soon as significance accrued, general appeal decreased
proportionately.

This, of course, is a well-known process which nearly every substantial composer has experienced since time immemorial. But for
most creators of new, untried artistic forms of expression the transition from relative popularity to relative loneliness somehow registers
with the public at large. Schönberg's loneliness, for instance, no
matter how real and harrowing it was, has always been a well-
advertised matter of public concern and a source of world-wide
recognition which was denied to him in the shape of plentiful performances because of the nature of his mature works. A man like
Schönberg created a new mainstream when he resolutely pitted
himself against the prevailing currents. If the river-bed which he
dug out with formidable energy at first carried only a few trickles,
it was bound to attract potent sources later on. Schnabel, as a composer, was much less interested in stopping the accustomed course of
the waters and in turning the tide. He opened up new channels
apart from the mainstream, fascinating to those who would follow
him on his inspirational wanderings. His work became as unconventional as any revolutionary spirit could wish, but it lacked
the sensational aspects of iconoclasm and zealous search for new
systematization.

By evoking the image of Schönberg rather than that of any other
contemporary composer, we meant to hint at the general atmosphere
of Schnabel's creative work. Both composers had grown up at
about the same time in the same environment and were exposed to
very similar influences. Although as human beings they were as
different as if they had come from different planets, their musical
evolution progressed along similar lines—up to a certain point. To
say that Schnabel developed differently because he was an interpreter
of music and a pianist in the first place, looks to us like substituting a
relation of cause and effect for a more deeply rooted distinction of
traits of personality.

Schnabel was as alert as could be to the demands imposed by the
historical evolution of the musical idiom upon anyone who wanted
to write music of any consequence. But he did not have the single-

track mind which it takes to focus and fight issues through to the bitter end. While he eventually wrote music which faced the issues as courageously as the best of his contemporaries among composers had done, he always retained, as a performer, a privileged access to a realm of music in which controversy was objectified, a thing of the past, resulting in sheer beauty. It is this pull toward the perfection, so obvious in the fulfilment of historically completed fact, which made it difficult for Schnabel to embrace wholeheartedly the controversial phenomena of a problematical present, to which he after all belonged. Hence came his aversion for any kind of musical 'theory'. It is our thesis that while Schnabel was blessed with uncommon imagination and inventiveness he had to struggle hard for the element of concentration which would impart to his work the significance potentially residing in it from the outset.

It is this absence of concentration that lends to some of Schnabel's compositions a touch which prompted less favourably disposed observers to call them amateurish, considering that those works were seemingly the casual product of the leisure hours of a man highly successful in a different field. It is interesting to notice that the most professionally turned-out compositions of Schnabel's are his early works. The amateurish touch—if a certain unconcern with generally accepted compositional procedures, a sovereign disregard for commonsensical 'practicality' may be so characterized—comes to the fore when Schnabel veers away from convention and begins to develop his own personal style.

In a purely sociological sense Schnabel became indeed an amateur composer, since in the same measure as in his creative work he moved into territories off the beaten track he achieved economic independence as a performer. He could afford to write music not only unpopular but also impractical according to current standards of performance, for while composing remained his central interest throughout his life, he did not depend on its results for his livelihood. His is not the only case of a composer who has had to pay for such enviable independence by being pushed further into unwarranted solitude.

Schnabel's Symphonies

SCHNABEL'S symphonies, like all of his music, offer formidable
difficulties to the performers, both individually and collectively.
Not only does he demand the utmost from them in a purely technical
sense; but the intelligible reading and performance of these scores
demands the utmost in musicianship and in musical understanding.
That some of these demands derive from an inherently problematical,
possibly even paradoxical aspect of Schnabel's music, can scarcely be
denied. For years of his life, composing seems to have represented
for him what may be described as a vital avocation, one into which,
to be sure, he was able to pour all the resources of his tremendous
gift of expression, his unsurpassed musicality, his inexhaustibly live
imagination. There is no music more personal than his, none which
more truly or more completely embodies a *man*, a musical person,
and one of the great ones of our time; and no music is more replete
with what can only be described as 'strokes of genius'.

It is therefore not on this level that the problematical aspect of
Schnabel's music lies. It lies rather in what may be called the realm
of artistic realism, that sense of actual possibilities which is probably
overvalued in our time, but which is nevertheless so essential and
almost instinctive an ingredient in the make-up of the composer
whose whole life and main preoccupation is with the exigencies of
his art. Such a composer learns to think, in every sense of the word,
in terms of his medium, and to find an inner harmony with it, by
virtue of which the so-called 'limitations' of the medium become
resources which he learns to utilize in the service of his expression,
and to transcend when the occasion demands. Awareness of these
limitations never represents for him a compromise; he has made
them his own and learned to think in their terms. When he makes—
as the greatest composers have constantly done—extraordinary
demands, he does so in the sense of the medium, with a clear feeling
for the results actually attainable; and however much he may demand
of the performer and the listener, he remains sufficiently aware of the
actual possibilities to reduce these difficulties to the greatest extent
consistent with the full realization of his ideas.

In Schnabel's music such difficulties are constant and formidable, especially in his orchestral music. It is not that he is lacking in respect for the performers or their instruments—to suggest such a thing would be absurd indeed. The difficulties reside wholly in the music itself; to make clear their nature would require pages of highly technical discussion, concerning such matters as musical articulation, balance, texture, metrical relationships, and, last but not least, the precise fluctuations of tempo demanded in his scores. It is difficult, even for the most devoted admirer of Schnabel's music, to answer the question whether equally or more satisfying results—in terms of actual realization—could not have been attained with less lavish expenditure of formidable demand; nor is it easy fully to answer the criticism that seeks to dismiss Schnabel's compositions as the work of an intensely gifted and extraordinarily resourceful musician who remained deliberately a non-professional as far as composition was concerned. What is undeniable and constantly challenging is the power of imagination, the abundant *Einfälle* of the most authentic kind. It is this which has made it impossible for the contemporary musical world wholly to ignore Schnabel's music, and which makes the enthusiasm of its devotees something decidedly more than a mere by-product of the attraction of one of the genuinely great musical personalities of our time. The more one studies these scores, the more indisputable one finds their evidences of authentic genius, and the more captivated one remains.

Appendices

I

COMPOSITIONS BY ARTUR SCHNABEL

COMPOSITION	FIRST PERFORMANCE	PUBLISHED
1. Three Piano Pieces (1896)	Berlin, 1899	N. Simrock, Berlin, 1900
2. Concerto for Piano and Orchestra (1901)	Berlin, 1901	
3. Ten Songs, Opus 11 (1899–1902)	Königsberg, 1900	Drei-Lilien Verlag, Berlin, 1903
4. Seven Songs, Opus 14 (1902–3)	Germany (date unknown)	Drei-Lilien Verlag, Berlin, 1904
5. 'Aussöhnung' for Voice and Piano (1902)	Berlin, 1903	
6. Three Piano Pieces (1906)	Berlin, 1918	Drei-Lilien Verlag, Berlin
7. Notturno for Voice and Piano (1914)	Amsterdam, 1920	
8. Quintet for Piano and Strings (1916)	Berlin, 1918	
9. String Quartet I (1918)	Berlin, 1919	Universal Edition, Vienna, 1922
10. Sonata for Violin Solo (1919)	Berlin, 1920	
11. Dance Suite for Piano (1921)	Berlin, 1922	
12. String Quartet II (1921)	Berlin, 1924	
13. Sonata for Piano (1922)	Venice, 1925	
14. String Quartet III (1923–4)	Berlin, 1931	
15. String Quartet IV (1924)		
16. String Trio (1925)	Vienna, 1936	
17. Sonata for Cello Solo (1931)	Los Angeles, 1950	
18. Sonata for Piano and Violin (1935)	New York, 1944	
19. Piano Piece in Seven Movements (1936)	New York, 1950	
20. Symphony I (1937–8)	Minneapolis, 1947	Edition Adler, New York

COMPOSITION	FIRST PERFORMANCE	PUBLISHED
21. String Quartet V (1940)	New York, 1942	
22. Symphony II (1941–2)		
23. Two Pieces for Orchestra and Chorus (1943)		
24. Trio for Piano and Strings (1945)	Lenox, Mass., U.S.A., 1947	
25. Seven Pieces for Piano (1946)	New York, 1952	
26. Rhapsody for Orchestra (1947)	Cleveland, 1948	
27. Symphony III (1948)		
28. Duodecimet (1950)	New York, 1956	

II

EXAMPLES OF CYCLICAL PROGRAMMES

THE CYCLE OF BEETHOVEN SONATAS

Played by Artur Schnabel in Berlin, London and New York,
1927, 1932 and 1936

Programme I

1. Sonata in D major, Op. 28
2. Sonata in A-flat major, Op. 110

---

3. Sonata in F minor, Op. 2, No. 1
4. Sonata in G major, Op. 31, No. 1

Programme II

1. Sonata in E-flat major, Op. 31, No. 3
2. Sonata in A major, Op. 101

---

3. Sonata in F major, Op. 54
4. Sonata in C minor, Op. 13
5. Sonata in C major, Op. 2, No. 3

Programme III

1. Sonata in A major, Op. 2, No. 2
2. Sonata in F minor, Op. 57

---

3. Sonata in G minor, Op. 49, No. 1
4. Sonata in E minor, Op. 90
5. Sonata in B-flat major, Op. 22

Programme IV

1. Sonata in A-flat major, Op. 26
2. Sonata in D minor, Op. 31, No. 2

---

3. Sonata in C minor, Op. 10, No. 1
4. Sonata in F major, Op. 10, No. 2
5. Sonata in E-flat major, Op. 81a

327

Programme V

1. Sonata in E-flat major, Op. 7
2. Sonata in C-sharp minor, Op. 27, No. 2
   (*Sonata quasi una Fantasia*)
   ———
3. Sonata in G major, Op. 14, No. 2
4. Sonata in B-flat major, Op. 106

Programme VI

1. Sonata in E-flat major, Op. 27, No. 1
2. Sonata in C major, Op. 53
   ———
3. Sonata in G major, Op. 49, No. 2
4. Sonata in E major, Op. 109

Programme VII

1. Sonata in E major, Op. 14, No. 1
2. Sonata in D major, Op. 10, No. 3
   ———
3. Sonata in G major, Op. 79
4. Sonata in F-sharp major, Op. 78
5. Sonata in C minor, Op. 111

★   ★   ★

SCHUBERT CYCLE OF SONGS AND PIANO COMPOSITIONS

Performed by Artur and Therese Schnabel in Berlin, 1928

Programme I

1. Sonata in G major, Op. 78
2. Lieder:
   An meiner Wiege
   Rastlose Liebe
   Auflösung
   An die Laute
   Die junge Nonne
   ———

3. Sonata in A minor, Op. 143
4. Lieder:
   Fahrt zum Hades
   - Sehnsucht
   Im Abendrot
   An die Musik
   Der Erlkönig

Programme II

1. Sonata in C minor, Op. posth.

———

2. *Die schöne Müllerin* (cycle)

Programme III

1. Sonata in A major, Op. 120
2. Lieder:
   Suleika
   Fischerweise
   Der Wanderer
   Heidenröslein

———

3. Lieder:
   Gruppe aus dem Tartarus
   Im Frühling
   Am Grabe Anselmos
   Der Jüngling an der Quelle
   Der Zwerg
4. Fantasia in C major, Op. 15

Programme IV

1. Sonata in B-flat major, Op. posth.

———

2. *Die Winterreise* (cycle)

Programme V

1. Sonata in A minor, Op. 42
2. Lieder:
   Der Kreuzzug
   Der Tod und das Mädchen
   Die Forelle

———

3. Lieder:
   Du liebst mich nicht
   Auf dem Wasser zu singen
   Ave Maria
   An die Leyer
   Der Musensohn
   Gretchen am Spinnrade
4. Sonata in D major, Op. 53

Programme VI

1. *Moments Musicaux*, Op. 94
2. *Schwanengesang* (cycle)

3. Sonata in A major, Op. posth.

SEVEN PROGRAMMES OF WORKS BY MOZART, SCHUBERT AND SCHUMANN

Played by Artur Schnabel in London, 1934

Programme I

1. Sonata in G major, Op. 78 . . . . . Schubert
2. Sonata in A minor (K. 310) . . . . . Mozart

3. Sonata in B-flat major (K. 570) . . . . Mozart
4. *Kreisleriana, Phantasien für das Pianoforte*, Op. 16 . Schumann

Programme II

1. Sonata in C minor, Op. posth. . . . . Schubert
2. *Kinderszenen, leichte Stücke für das Pianoforte*, Op. 15 . Schumann

3. Sonata in A major (K. 331) . . . . . Mozart
4. Four *Impromptus*, Op. 142 . . . . . Schubert

Programme III

1. Four *Impromptus*, Op. 90 . . . . . Schubert
2. Sonata in D major (K. 576) . . . . . Mozart

3. Sonata in B major, Op. 147 . . . . . Schubert
4. *Davidsbündler*, Op. 6 . . . . . . Schumann

Programme IV

1. Fantasia, Op. 17 . . . . Schumann
2. Sonata in F major (K. 332) . . . . . Mozart

3. Sonata No. 2, Op. 22 . . . . . . Schumann
4. Sonata in A major, Op. posth. . . . . Schubert

Programme V

1. Sonata in A minor, Op. 143 . . . . Schubert
2. Sonata in C major (K. 330) . . . . . Mozart
3. Sonata in A major, Op. 120 . . . . . Schubert

4. Sonata in C minor (K. 457) . . . . . Mozart
5. Fantasiestücke, Op. 12 . . . . . . Schumann

Programme VI

1. Moments Musicaux, Op. 94 . . . . . Schubert
2. Sonata in B-flat major, Op. posth. . . . Schubert

3. Sonata in C major (K. 309) . . . . . Mozart
4. Carnaval, Op. 9 . . . . Schumann

Programme VII

1. Sonata in A minor, Op. 42 . . . . . Schubert
2. Papillons, Op. 2 . . . . Schumann

3. Sonata in B-flat major (K. 333) . . . . Mozart
4. Sonata in D major, Op. 53 . . . . . Schubert

THE PIANO CONCERTOS OF MOZART

Played by Artur Schnabel with various orchestras in Europe,
Great Britain, United States and Australia

No. 9 in E-flat major (K. 271)
No. 12 in A major (K. 414)
No. 14 in E-flat major (K. 449)
No. 15 in B-flat major (K. 450)
No. 16 in D major (K. 451)

No. 17 in G major (K. 453)
No. 18 in B-flat major (K. 456)
No. 19 in F major (K. 459)
No. 20 in D minor (K. 466)
No. 21 in C major (K. 467)
No. 22 in E-flat major (K. 482)
No. 23 in A major (K. 488)
No. 24 in C minor (K. 491)
No. 25 in C major (K. 503)
No. 26 in D major (K. 537) *Coronation*
No. 27 in B-flat major (K. 595)
In E-flat major for two pianos (K. 365)

III

ARTUR SCHNABEL DISCOGRAPHY

(COMPILED BY BERNARDO COHN)

	His Master's Voice (England)	*R.C.A.–Victor* (U.S.A.)
BACH, JOHANN SEBASTIAN (1685–1750)		
Chromatic Fantasia and Fugue, D minor, and Prelude and Fugue, D major, from *The Well Tempered Clavier*, Book I, No. 5	DB 9511/2 DB 21150/1	
Concerto for Two Claviers and Orchestra, C major. Artur and Karl Ulrich Schnabel with London Symphony Orchestra, Boult	DB 3041/3 DB 8242/4 (Auto)	M 357 (14409/11) DM–357 (16819/21) LCT–1140
Italian Concerto, F major	DB 3732/3	M–806 (18103/4) DM–806 (18105/6)
Toccatas, C minor and F major	DA 1613/6	M–532 (1952/5) DM–532 (2080/3)

BEETHOVEN, LUDWIG VAN (1770–1827)

Piano Solo

Bagatelles:		
Seven, Op. 33	in Soc. Vol. XV	
Six, Op. 126	in Soc. Vol. XIV	
A minor, *Für Elise*	in Soc. Vol. XV	
idem (final side in album)	DB 1694 (A 156)	7673 (M–158)
idem (final side in album)	DB 7514 (Auto)	17176 (DM–158)
idem (with Rondo in C major, Op. 51, No. 1)	DB 2361	14322
idem (final side in album)		15500 (M–580)
idem (final side in album)		16068 (DM–580)
Fantasia, G minor, Op. 77	in Soc. Vol. XV	
Minuet, E-flat major	in Soc. Vol. XV	
Rondos:		
A major	in Soc. Vol. XIV	
idem (last side Sonata, Op. 111)	DB 21343/9677	
C major, Op. 51, No. 1 (final side in album)	DB 1944 (A 170)	7899 (M–194)
idem (final side in album)	DB 7377 (Auto)	16606 (DM–194)
idem (with *Für Elise*)		14322

BEETHOVEN (continued)

Piano Solo (continued)

G major, Op. 129 (Rondo in Soc. Vol. XIV
a capriccio, *Wut über
den verlor'nen Groschen*)
idem (final side Sonata, DB 9748
Op. 78)

Sonatas:

No. 1, F minor, Op. 2, No. 1	in Soc. Vol. VII	
No. 2, A major, Op. 2, No. 2	in Soc. Vol. IV	LCT–1155
No. 3, C major, Op. 2, No. 3	in Soc. Vol. VIII	
No. 4, E-flat major, Op. 7	in Soc. Vol. XI	
No. 5, C minor, Op. 10, No. 1	in Soc. Vol. XII	
No. 6, F major, Op. 10, No. 2	in Soc. Vol. VI	
No. 7, D major, Op. 10, No. 3	in Soc. Vol. XII	
No. 8, C minor, Op. 13 (*Pathétique*)	in Soc. Vol. VI	
No. 9, E major, Op. 14, No. 1	in Soc. Vol. II DB 21438/9 DB 9729/30 (Auto)	LCT–1110
No. 10, G major, Op. 14, No. 2	in Soc. Vol. VII	
No. 11, B-flat major, Op. 22	in Soc. Vol. V	
No. 12, A-flat major, Op. 26 (*Funeral March*)	in Soc. Vol. IX	
No. 13, E-flat major, Op. 27, No. 1	in Soc. Vol. II DB 21402/3 DB 9698/9 (Auto)	LCT–1110
No. 14, C-sharp minor, Op. 27, No. 2 (*Moonlight*)	in Soc. Vol. IV	LCT–1155
No. 15, D major, Op. 28 (*Pastoral*)	in Soc. Vol. III	LCT–1154
No. 16, G major, Op. 31, No. 1	in Soc. Vol. XI	
No. 17, D minor, Op. 31, No. 2	in Soc. Vol. VIII	
No. 18, E-flat major, Op. 31, No. 3	in Soc. Vol. VI	
No. 19, G minor, Op. 49, No. 1	in Soc. Vol. III	LCT–1154
No. 20, G major, Op. 49, No. 2	in Soc. Vol. V	
No. 21, C major, Op. 53 (*Waldstein*)	in Soc. Vol. IX	

Sonatas (continued)

No. 22, F major, Op. 54	in Soc. Vol. VIII	
No. 23, F minor, Op. 57 (*Appassionata*)	in Soc. Vol. V	
No. 24, F-sharp major, Op. 78	in Soc. Vol. I	LCT–1109
idem (with Rondo a capriccio, Op. 129)	DB 21476/7 DB 9748/9 (Auto)	
No. 25, G major, Op. 79	in Soc. Vol. XII	
No. 26, E-flat major, Op. 81a (*Les Adieux*)	in Soc. Vol. IV	LCT–1155
No. 27, E minor, Op. 90	in Soc. Vol. I DB 9713/4 DB 21404/5 (Auto)	LCT–1109
No. 28, A major, Op. 101	in Soc. Vol. VII	
No. 29, B-flat major, Op. 106 (*Hammerklavier*)	in Soc. Vol. X	M–403 (14598/603) DM–403 (16519/24)
No. 30, E major, Op. 109	in Soc. Vol. II DB 21337/9 DB 9674/6 (Auto)	LCT–1110
No. 31, A-flat major, Op. 110	in Soc. Vol. III	LCT–1154
No. 32, C minor, Op. 111	in Soc. Vol. I DB 21340/3	LCT–1109
idem (with Rondo in A major)	DB 9677/80 (Auto)	

Thirty-two Sonatas, complete in album.	LM–9500

Variations:

Six, F major, Op. 34	in Soc. Vol. XIV	
Fifteen, E-flat major, Op. 35 (*Eroica*)	in Soc. Vol. XV	
idem (with Concerti for Piano and Orch.)		LCT–6700
Thirty-three, on a waltz by Diabelli, Op. 120	in Soc. Vol. XIII	

BEETHOVEN SOCIETY: 15 volumes of Sonatas and various piano works (H.M.V.) (Separate listing from above).

His Master's Voice
(England)

Volume I:
No. 24, F-sharp major Op. 78   DB 1654/60
No. 27, E minor, Op. 90
No. 32, C minor, Op. 111

	His Master's Voice (England)	R.C.A.–Victor (U.S.A.)
Volume II:		
No. 9, E major, Op. 14, No. 1	DB 1818/24	
No. 13, E-flat major, Op. 27, No. 1		
No. 30, E major, Op. 109		
Volume III:		
No. 15, D major, Op. 28 (Pastoral)	DB 1953/9	
No. 19, G minor, Op. 49, No. 1	DB 7366/72 (Auto)	
No. 31, A-flat major, Op. 110		
Volume IV:		
No. 2, A major, Op. 2, No. 2	DB 2086/92	
No. 14, C-sharp minor, Op. 27, No. 2 (Moonlight)	DB 7575/81 (Auto)	
No. 26, E-flat major, Op. 81a (Les Adieux)		
Volume V:		
No. 11, B-flat major, Op. 22	DB 2211/7	
No. 20, G major, Op. 49, No. 2	DB 7680/6 (Auto)	
No. 23, F minor, Op. 57 (Appassionata)		
Volume VI:		
No. 6, F major, Op. 10, No. 2	DB 2354/60	
No. 8, C minor, Op. 13 (Pathétique)	DB 7777/83 (Auto)	
No. 18, E-flat major, Op. 31, No. 3		
Volume VII:		
No. 1, F minor, Op. 2, No. 1	DB 2463/9	
No. 10, G major, Op. 14, No. 2	DB 7850/6 (Auto)	
No. 28, A major, Op. 101		
Volume VIII:		
No. 3, C major, Op. 2, No. 3	DB 2646/52	
No. 17, D minor, Op. 31, No. 2	DB 7970/6 (Auto)	
No. 22, F major, Op. 54		
Volume IX:		
No. 12, A-flat major, Op. 26 (Funeral March)	DB 2850/5	
	DB 8078/83 (Auto)	
No. 21, C major, Op. 53 (Waldstein)		

His Master's Voice   R.C.A.–Victor
(England)   (U.S.A.)

Volume X:
No. 29, B-flat major, Op. 106 DB 2955/60
(*Hammerklavier*)
Volume XI:
No. 4, E-flat major, Op. 7   DB 3151/7
No. 16, G major, Op. 31, No. 1 DB 8266/72 (Auto)
Volume XII:
No. 5, C minor, Op. 10, No. 1 DB 3343/8
No. 7, D major, Op. 10, No. 3 DB 8379/84 (Auto)
No. 25, G major, Op. 79
Volume XIII:
Diabelli Variations, Op. 120 DB 3519/25
Volume XIV:
Six Variations, F major, Op. 34 DB 3623/9
Fantasia, G minor, Op. 77   DB 8679/85 (Auto)
Six Bagatelles, Op. 126
Rondo a capriccio, G major,
Op. 129 (*Rage over the lost penny*)
Rondo in A major
Volume XV:
Seven Bagatelles, Op. 33   DB 3783/9
Bagatelle, A minor (*Für Elise*) DB 8672/8 (Auto)
Variations in E-flat major,
Op. 35 (*Eroica*)
Minuet in E-flat major

(The six sonatas that were in the first two volumes, unavailable for many years, have been re-issued on L.P. discs in England by H.M.V. as 'Memorial Editions', and in the United States by R.C.A.–Victor as 'Treasury of Immortal Performances'.)

Cello and Piano

Sonatas:
No. 2, G minor, Op. 5,   DB 2391/3   M–281 (8807/9)
No. 2, w/Piatigorsky   DB 8181/3 (Auto) DM–281 (16973/5)
No. 3, A major, Op. 69,   DB 6464/6   M–1231 (12–0408/10)
w/Fournier   DB 9123/5 (Auto) DM–1231 (12–0411/13)
                                LCT–1124
No. 4, C major, Op. 102, DB 6500/1   WDM–1370 (45 r.p.m.)
No. 1, w/Fournier   DB 9555/6 (Auto) DM–1370
                                  LCT–1124
No. 5, D major, Op. 102, DB 6829/31   LCT–1124
No. 2, w/Fournier   DB 9438/40 (Auto)

Piano and Orchestra

Concertos: (Cadenzas by Beethoven)
Concerti for Piano and   LCT–6700
Orchestra, Complete,
Sargent, London Sym-
phony Orchestra (with
Variations and Fugue,
E-flat major, Op. 35,
Eroica)

No. 1, C major, Op. 15, Sargent, London Symphony Orchestra (with Bagatelle *Für Elise*)	A–156–DB 1690/4 DB 7514/8 (Auto)	M–158 (7669/73) DM–158 (17176/80)
No. 2, B-flat major, Op. 19, Dobrowen, Philharmonia Orchestra	A–403–DB 6323/6 DB 9099/102 (Auto)	
(2) with Sargent, London Philharmonic Orchestra	A–238–DB 2573/6 DB 7945/8 (Auto)	M–295 (8897/900) DM–295 (16948/51)
No. 3, C minor, Op. 37, Sargent, London Philharmonic Orchestra (with Rondo in C major, Op. 51, No. 1)	A–179–DB 1940/4 DB 7377/81 (Auto)	M–194 (7895/9) DM–194 (16606/10)
No. 4, G major, Op. 58, Dobrowen, Philharmonia Orchestra	A–393–DB 6303/6 DB 9032/5 (Auto)	LCT–1131
(2) with Stock, Chicago Symphony Orchestra		M–930 (11–8416/9) DM–930 (11–8290/3)
(3) with Sargent, London Philharmonic Orchestra	A–181–DB 1886/9 DB 7340/3 (Auto)	M–156 (7661/4) DM–156 (16586/9)
No. 5, E-flat major, Op. 73 ('Emperor'), Galliera, Philharmonia Orchestra	A–433–DB 6692/6 DB 9326/30 (Auto)	
(2) with Stock, Chicago Symphony Orchestra	DB 6184/8 DB 9011/5 (Auto)	M–939 (11–8430/4) DM–939 (11–8322/6) LCT–1015 WCT–19
(3) with Sargent, London Symphony Orchestra	A–146–DB 1685/9 DB 7509/13 (Auto)	M–155 (7639/43) DM–155 (16581/5)

BRAHMS, JOHANNES (1833–1897)
Concertos (piano and orchestra):

No. 1, D minor, Op. 15, Széll, London Philharmonic Orchestra	A–326–DB 3712/7 DB 8614/9 (Auto)	M–677 (16380/5) DM–677 (16392/7)
No. 2, B-flat major, Op. 83, Boult, B.B.C. Symphony Orchestra	A–245–DB 2696/701 DB 7997/802 (Auto)	M–305 (8981/6) DM–305 (16717/22)
Intermezzi: A minor, Op. 116, No. 2 and E-flat major, Op. 117, No. 1	DB 6505	
Rhapsodie: G minor, Op. 79, No. 2	DB 6504	
Lieder: Liebestreu (with Schubert Lieder)	DB 1836	
Nicht mehr zu dir zu gehen	DA 1294	

DVOŘÁK, ANTONIN (1841–1904)

Piano Quintet, A major, Op. 81, with Pro Arte Quartet	A–214–DB 2177/80 DB 7676/9 (Auto)	M–219 (8305/8)

MOZART, WOLFGANG AMADEUS (1756–1791)

Piano Solo

Rondo in A minor, K. 511	DB 6298
Sonatas: No. 8, A minor, K. 310	DB 3778/80 DB 8764/6 (Auto)
No. 12, F major, K. 332	DB 6336/7
No. 16, B-flat major, K. 570	DB 6839/40

Chamber Music

Piano Quartet No. 1, G minor, K. 478, with Arte Quartet members	A–213–DB 2155/8 DB 7665/8 (Auto)	M–251 (8562/5) DM–251 (17031/4) LM–6130

Piano and Orchestra

Concertos: No. 19, F major, K. 459 (Cadenzas by Mozart) with Sargent, London Symphony Orchestra	A–282–DB 3095/8S DBS–8298 (Auto) DB–8299/301	M 389 (14538/41S) DM–389 (16548S/51)

Mozart (continued)

Piano and Orchestra (continued)

No. 20, D minor, K. 466   L-HMV-1012
(Cadenzas by Beet-
hoven), with Süsskind,
Philharmonia Orchestra

No. 21, C major, K. 467   A-291-DB 3099/102   M-486 (15084/7)
(Cadenzas by Schna-   DB 8355/8 (Auto)   DM-486 (16279/82)
bel), with Sargent,
London Symphony
Orchestra

No. 24, C minor, K. 491   L-HMV-1012
(Cadenzas by Schna-
bel), with Süsskind,
Philharmonia Orchestra

No. 27, B-flat major,   A-221-DB 2249/52   M-240 (8475/8)
K. 595 (Cadenzas by   DB 7733/6 (Auto)   DM-240 (17053/6)
Mozart), Barbirolli,
London Symphony
Orchestra

Two Pianos and Orchestra

Concerto in E-flat major,   DB 3033/5   M-484 (15072/4)
K. 365 (Cadenzas by   DB 8216/8 (Auto)   DM-484 (16286/8)
Mozart), with Karl   LCT-1140
Ulrich Schnabel, Boult,
London Symphony
Orchestra

SCHUBERT, FRANZ PETER (1797-1828)

Piano Solo

Allegretto, C minor (with   A-350-DB 3755
Sonata, B-flat major,
op. posth.)

Impromptus:

C minor, Op. 90, No. 1   DB 21320   L-HMV-1027
                              BLP-1007

E-flat major, Op. 90,   DB 21335   L-HMV-1027
No. 2   BLP-1007

G major, Op. 90, No. 3   DB 21335   L-HMV-1027
                              BLP-1007

A-flat major, Op. 90,   DB 21351   L-HMV-1027
No. 4   BLP-1007

F minor, Op. 142, No. 1   DB 21382   L-HMV-1027
                              BLP-1030

A-flat major, Op. 142,   DB 21500   L-HMV-1027
No. 2   BLP-1030

SCHUBERT (continued)

Piano Solo (continued)

B-flat major, Op. 142,	DB 21500	L-HMV-1027
No. 3	BLP-1030	
F minor, Op. 142, No. 4	DB 21500	L-HMV-1027
	BLP-1030	
March in E major (with	DB 3760	M-888 (18540/1)
Sonata No. 17, D major)		DM-888 (18541/3)
Moments Musicaux, C major,	DB 3358/60	MO-684 (17021/3)
A-flat major, F minor,	DB 8392/4 (Auto)	
C-sharp minor, F minor		
and A-flat major, Op.		
94, Nos. 1–6		

Sonatas:

No. 17, D major, Op. 53	DB 3756/60	M-888 (18536/40)
(with March in E major)		DM-888 (18541/5)
No. 20, A major, op.	A-286-DB 3103/7S	M-580 (15496/500)
posth. (HMV last side	DBS 8322 (Auto)	DM-580 (16068/72)
blank; Victor with	DB 8323/6	
Für Elise)		
No. 21, B-flat major,	A-350-DB 3751/5	
op. posth. (with Alle-	DB 8826/30 (Auto)	
gretto in C minor)		

The following sonatas have been re-issued on L.P. discs as ' Memorial Editions'; they were deleted from the catalogues some years ago:

No. 20, A major, op.	DB 21418/21
posth. (last side blank)	DBS 21422
	DBS 9733 (Auto)
	DB 9734/7 (Auto)
No. 21, B-flat major, op.	DB 21353/7
posth. (last side Alle-	DB 9700/4 (Auto)
gretto in C minor)	

Piano Works for Four Hands
With Karl Ulrich Schnabel

Andantino Varié, B minor,	DB 3518	M-436 (14829)
Op. 84, No. 1		AM-436 (14833/40)
Divertissement à la hongroise,	A-346-DB 3529/32	M-436 (14825/8)
Op. 54	DB 8812/5 (Auto)	AM-436 (14833/40)

Marches:

G minor, Op. 40, No. 2	DB 3527	M-436 (14831)
B minor, Op. 40, No. 3	DB 3527	M-436 (14830)
		AM-436 (14833/40)
Marches Militaires, Op. 51,	DB 3527/8	M-436 (14831/2)
No. 1 in D major, No.		AM-436 (14833/40)
2 in G major, No. 3 in		
E-flat major		

SCHUBERT (continued)

Piano Works for Four Hands (continued)

Lebensstürme, A minor, Op. 144 (Allegro caracteristical)	DA 1646/7	M-437 (1872/3) AM-437 (1874/7)
Rondo, A major, Op. 107	DA 1644/5	M-437 (1870/1) AM-437 (1874/7)

Chamber Music

Piano Quintet, A major, Op. 114 (*The Trout*), with Pro Arte Quartet and C. Hobday (cbs.)	A-259-DB 2714/8 DB 8095/9	M-312 (14032/6) DM-312 (16923/7)

Songs (Lieder)
Therese Schnabel-Behr with Artur Schnabel at the piano

Der Doppelgänger (Heine), *Schwanengesang* No. 13	DB 1833
Die Stadt (Heine), *Schwanengesang* No. 11 (with Schumann lieder)	
Gruppe aus dem Tartarus, Op. 24, No. 1 (Schiller)	DB 1834
Der Kreuzzug (Leitner)	DB 1835
An die Laute, Op. 81, No. 2 (Rochlitz)	
Der Musensohn, Op. 92, No. 1 (Goethe)	
Der Erlkönig, Op. 1 (Goethe) (with Brahms lieder)	DB 1836

SCHUMANN, ROBERT (1810–1856)

Kinderszenen, Op. 15	DB 6502/3	
Piano Quintet, E-flat major, Op. 44, with Pro Arte Quartet	A-215-DB 2387/90 DB 7922/5 (Auto)	M-267 (8685/8) DM-267 (17003/6)

Songs (Lieder)
Therese Schnabel-Behr with Artur Schnabel at the piano

Der Soldat *Frühlingsnacht* (with Schubert lieder)	DB 1833
Der Schatzgräber (with Schubert lieder)	DB 1834

WEBER, CARL MARIA VON (1786–1826)

Aufforderung zum Tanz, Op. 65 (Rondo brilliant, D major)	DB 6491

RECORDINGS OF COMPOSITIONS BY ARTUR SCHNABEL

	England	U.S.A.
Concerto for Piano and Orchestra		
Helen Schnabel, Adler, Vienna Phil-	LPA 1068	SPA 55
harmonia Orchestra		
Piano Pieces (Seven)		SPA 13
Helen Schnabel, pianist		
Piece in Seven Movements		SPA 13
Dika Newlin, pianist		
Rhapsody for Orchestra	LX 8843/4	
Walter Süsskind, Philharmonia	(Columbia)	
Orchestra		
Songs		
Erika Francoulon, Helen Schnabel	LPA 1068	SPA 55
Youth Piece (Reverie)		SPA 13
Helen Schnabel, pianist		

Note.—R.C.A.-Victor recordings with prefix LCT, LM, or L–HMV, and His Master's Voice with prefix BLP are 33⅓ r.p.m. discs.

R.C.A.-VICTOR (U.S.A.) RELEASES OF THE BEETHOVEN SONATAS

No. 1, F minor, Op. 2, No. 1	LM–2158	No. 9, E major, Op. 14, No. 1	LCT–1110
No. 10, G major, Op. 14, No. 2	"	No. 13, E-flat major, Op. 27, No. 1	"
No. 28, A major, Op. 101	"	No. 30, E major, Op. 109	"
No. 2, A major, Op. 2, No. 2	LCT–1155	No. 11, B-flat major, Op. 22	LM–2153
No. 14, C-sharp minor, Op. 27, No. 2 (Moonlight)	"	No. 20, G major, Op. 49 No. 2	"
No. 26, E-flat major, Op. 81a (Les Adieux)	"	No. 23, F minor, Op. 57 (Appassionata)	"
No. 3, C major, Op. 2, No. 3	LM–2154	No. 12, A-flat major, Op. 26	LM–2157
No. 17, D minor, Op. 31, No. 2	"	No. 21, C major, Op. 53 (Waldstein)	"
No. 4, E-flat major, Op. 7	LM–2156		
No. 16, G major, Op. 31, No. 1	"	No. 15, D major, Op. 28	LCT–1154
		No. 19, G minor, Op. 49, No. 1	"
No. 5, C minor, Op. 10, No. 1	LM–2152	No. 31, A-flat major, Op. 110	"
No. 7, D major, Op. 10, No. 3	"		
No. 25, G major, Op. 79	"	No. 22, F major, Op. 54	LM–2155
		No. 29, B-flat major, Op. 106 (Hammerklavier)	"
No. 6, F major, Op. 10, No. 2	LM–2152		
No. 8, C minor, Op. 13 (Pathétique)	"	No. 24, F-sharp major, Op. 78	LCT–1109
No. 18, E-flat major, Op. 31, No. 3	"	No. 27, E minor, Op. 90	"
		No. 32, C minor, Op. 111	"

INDEX

344